The Birth of Nations

The Birth of Nations

Philip C. Jessup

Columbia University Press
New York and London 1974

The author gratefully acknowledges the following permissions to quote from published material: Dean Acheson, *Present at the Creation: My Years in the State Department,* by permission of W. W. Norton & Company, copyright © 1969 by Dean Acheson; Robert Shaplen, *The Lost Revolution: The U.S. in Vietnam, 1946–1966,* by permission of Harper & Row, copyright © 1966 by Harper & Row; Henry W. Levy and Bernard Postal, *And the Hills Shouted for Joy,* by permission of the David McKay Company, Inc., copyright © 1973 by Henry W. Levy and Bernard Postal.

Library of Congress Cataloging in Publication Data

Jessup, Philip Caryl, 1897–
   The birth of nations.

  Includes bibliographical references.
  1. States, New. 2. United Nations. I. Title.
JX1977.2.A1 J48   341.26   73-15515
ISBN 0-231-03721-X

In Memory of
RALPH BUNCHE
to whom
So Much is Owed
by
THE UNITED NATIONS
and
therefore by
All of Us.

Acknowledgments

This book incorporates and extensively amplifies the Barnette Miller Lectures which I was privileged to deliver at Wellesley College in November 1971. Much of chapters 3 and 4 and some other fragments, are based on work done at the Council on Foreign Relations when I was Whitney Shepardson Senior Visiting Research Fellow, 1970–1971. At the Council I had the benefit of the assistance of an invited Study Group of experts who met from time to time with Joseph E. Johnson as chairman and Charles Yost as vice-chairman. Susan Vine, who was my invaluable research assistant at the Council, acted as rapporteur of those meetings, which dealt with many additional subjects not included in this book. Portions of the manuscript written while at the Council have had the benefit of the skillful editing of Robert Valkenier.

I cannot list all, and it would be invidious to mention less than the whole roster of the changing personnel of the Study Group at the Council, who took the trouble to read advance copies of drafts of parts of the manuscript utilized here and who made valuable critical suggestions. Numerous others, by correspondence or by making available to me unpublished

manuscripts, have also put me in their debt and I have mentioned many of them in the footnotes.

Under the established rules of the Department of State, I
have been able to refresh my recollection by consulting files
covering matters with which I was officially concerned when
serving under Ambassador Warren Austin at the United States
Mission to the United Nations between 1947 and 1949, and as
United States Ambassador-at-Large from 1949 to 1953. Fortunately, my files were largely still intact as they had been ex-
pertly arranged during my service in the Department of State
by my extraordinarily skillful administrative assistants, Ver-
nice Anderson and Teresa Beach. The facilities for research in
the Department were all that the most exacting might have
desired and for them I extend my warmest thanks to Dr. William M. Franklin, Director of the Historical Office; Dr. Arthur C. Kogan, Special Assistant to the Director; Dr. S. Everett
Gleason, former Chief of the Foreign Relations Division, Historical Office; Mr. William P. Sparrow, Records Services Division; and many of their colleagues and assistants. At the
United States Mission to the United Nations in New York, Mrs.
Anne Gustav, Chief of the Files Section, and all the members
of her staff, cheerfully and quickly provided from their very
efficient system, any item which I was able to identify in even
the most general way.

I welcomed this fourth opportunity to deal with the Columbia University Press as my publisher, and am grateful to an
old friend, Robert J. Tilley, Assistant Director and Editor in
Chief, for making this possible. At the Press I have had the
kindly and expert help of Joan McQuary, Chief Manuscript Editor, and am indebted to Laiying Chong and Susan Bishop for design and lay-out.

Although only my name appears on the title page, the writing of this book was a joint venture with my wife. We were
together on our travels in Asia and at the United Nations; her
letters and scrapbooks are among the prime sources we used

to recreate situations. From other sources, we jointly copied extracts and took notes. She read and corrected manuscript and proofs. Finally, the index has been principally her burden. We both express our thanks to the Rockefeller Foundation for affording us the opportunity to utilize the unique qualities of the Villa Serbelloni in putting finishing touches on our work.

July 1, 1973   Philip C. Jessup

Contents

	ABBREVIATIONS	xiii
1	Introductory	1
2	Midwife to Korea	19
3	Indonesia Is Born	43
4	Prenatal Pains of Morocco and Tunisia	93
5	The Abortive Empire of Bao Dai	153
	Postscript:—Pushtoonistan	207
6	The United Nations Delivers Libya and Somalia	211
	Eritrea Is Stillborn	
7	The Birth of Israel	255
8	"Manchukuo"—an Illegitimate Child	305
	EPILOGUE	335
	NOTES	337
	INDEX	349

Illustrations: on various ambassadorial assignments, after page 152

Abbreviations

ANZUS	Australia–New Zealand–United States Security Treaty
CFM	Council of Foreign Ministers
CIA	Central Intelligence Agency
ECA	Economic Cooperation Administration
ERP	European Recovery Program
EUR	Bureau of European Affairs, Department of State
FAO	Food and Agriculture Organization
FE	Bureau of Far Eastern Affairs, Department of State
FEA	Foreign Economic Administration
GOC	Good Offices Commission of the United Nations
JA	Jewish Agency
LA	Bureau of Inter-American Affairs, Department of State
NATO	North Atlantic Treaty Organization
NEA	Bureau of Near Eastern, South Asian, and African Affairs, Department of State
NSC	National Security Council
OAS	Organization of American States

OFRRO   Office of Foreign Relief and Rehabilitation Operations, Department of State

OSS   Office of Strategic Services

SA   Ambassador-at-Large, Department of State

SEA   Office of Southeast Asian Affairs, Department of State

UNA   Bureau of United Nations Affairs, Department of State

UNRRA   United Nations Relief and Rehabilitation Administration

UNSCOP   United Nations Special Committee on Palestine

USUN   United States Mission to the United Nations

The Birth of Nations

1

Introductory

New and miniscule nations are now baptised into full membership in the United Nations with frightening frequency. It is a nationhood explosion. The UN membership has swollen from 50 in 1945 to 132 in 1972. At least eight more countries are pregnant with the likelihood of early admission. With simulated virgin innocence, Portugal indignantly rejects, as assaults upon her honor and integrity, the repeated demands in the General Assembly and in the Security Council that independence be granted to Angola, Mozambique, and Guinea (Bissau). Fragmentation of existing states may add to the roster but the prospects of consolidation, whether peaceful or violent, are dim. In the Treaty of Paris of 1783, England recognized that the erstwhile thirteen colonies had each and all become "free sovereign and Independent States;" they soon merged into a single United States of America. Since 1945 the emergence of former dependencies into nationhood has progressed in a variety of ways. Some, like our American ancestors, have fought their way to freedom. Some have been set free voluntarily and, to a generally unrecognized degree, others owe their present existence to pressures and actions in the United Nations.

As a representative of the United States between 1948 and 1953, I took some part in the natal stages of a number of countries. I venture gratefully to accept the accolade of "diplomatist" which Dean Acheson generously conferred on me in one of the last essays he wrote before his death.[1] I was indeed an *amateur* diplomatist and my official ambassadorial duties were performed largely in the United Nations or in connection with the Organization.

The cases which I am recalling here illustrate various types of national birth pangs. In describing "The Abortive Empire of Bao Dai" it is fair to say that there was a political abortion before there was a more or less normal birth into nationhood followed, alas, by what one may call a childhood of terror and anguish. In the one chapter in which I have digressed into a situation with which I had no personal contact, it seemed interesting to present an example of national bastardy—the case of Manchukuo.

The ordering of the chapters is admittedly arbitrary and, to an extent, subjective. Thus the Korean story is put first partly because it was the first case with which I dealt officially and partly because it offers vivid verbal support to the metaphorical use of the notion of the "birth" of nations. Indonesia, Morocco, and Tunisia are the clearest examples of the dilemma which faced the United States in deciding whether to support emerging nationalist ambitions even at the cost of friction with old friends and allies in what was considered during the Truman administration to be the key area of American interest, namely Western Europe, where the NATO alliance was being forged. Vietnam, from the viewpoint of U.S. foreign policy, had many of the same facets. The birth into nationhood of the former Italian colonies of Libya and Somalia involved a unique role for the United Nations. The emergence of the State of Israel from the old League of Nations mandate over Palestine was *sui generis* in that although it followed upon, it did not result from, fighting the previous semicolonial ruler or from any voluntary donation of independence. The historical case of Manchukuo is in a separate category and comes at the end.

An arrangement more strictly chronological or topical or ideological might, to be sure, present a more orderly progression. In a book of this kind I do not feel the need for such stylistic symmetry. Perhaps the literary style of this book (if indeed it has any style) is baroque, which the dictionary says is marked in literature by "complexity of form and bizarre, ingenious, and often ambiguous imagery." I must agree that the attempt to cling to the imagery of the obstetrical metaphor suggested by the book's title does, at times, create some ambiguity.

This book is not an autobiography nor does it attempt to be a history of U.S. foreign policy during the Truman administration; nor is it a history of the various countries whose birth-pangs are described. I am interested in what Lawrence Stone has called "the roots of political action: the uncovering of the deeper interests that are thought to lie beneath the rhetoric of politics," but I do not aspire to follow him into the field of prosopography. Having been accorded, under established rules of procedure, access to unpublished official records of events with which I was officially concerned, I am content to make available to subsequent writers some of the details of which history is made, as I recall them, not as a documentary record. I take my text perhaps from what Flavius Josephus wrote nearly two thousand years ago: "To place on record events never previously related and to make contemporary history accessible to later generations, is an activity deserving of notice and commendation." [2]

Since 1945 the United States has had to train officials in the expertise needed for conducting what has come to be known as "parliamentary diplomacy," that is, diplomatic negotiation within the framework of an international organization like the

United Nations whose committees, councils, and assembly operate under rules of parliamentary law. The more traditional
procedures still provide the essential preparation for organizational action and for the broader ranges of foreign policy. The
practice of parliamentary diplomacy has its cumbersome aspects. Delegates to the UN General Assembly, or a representative on the Security Council or on some other council or committee, operate under instructions but often have to meet
sudden parliamentary maneuvers not anticipated in the instructions, which have been forged in the complicated structure of the Department of State.[3] If there is time, instructions
may be changed, but when Senators Hickenlooper and Mansfield reported on their experiences as members of the U.S. delegation to the UN General Assembly in 1959, they pointed to
some of the difficulties:

These changes almost invariably require prior clearance from Washington. The requirement would not be so burdensome, perhaps, if
only one bureau of the Department of State were involved in sanctioning them. Not infrequently, however, even a slight change in
the phrase of a statement of an official position at the UN may call
for clearance by any number of bureaus and offices scattered
throughout various executive agencies and departments.[4]

I can remember the octogenarian Senator Green as a delegate to a General Assembly, exploding with irritation on being
shown a telegram from the State Department marked with the
favorite most-restrictive classification, "Eyes Only." "Eyes
only!" he shouted at me, "What did they think we would do
with it?"

The ensuing accounts will give a picture of some of the bu-
reaucratic intricacies which are perhaps unavoidable. Having
served in the State Department in 1924, 1930, 1943, and during
several years after 1945, I am struck by the dominating influence of the size of the bureaucracy: the larger it gets, the slower
and more complicated the process of reaching a decision.
There would be ups and downs in the ascending line plotted

on a graph, but the generalization is sound. Today, in the search for a departmental decision, one may pass from a specialized desk officer to a director of a division or bureau to an assistant secretary for a region—all on the same geographical plane, quite apart from the necessity to coordinate with officers responsible for other substantive considerations. This is a far cry from the days when the system of geographical organization was elaborated under Secretary of State Knox. Actually, the first State Department order setting up a geographical division is dated March 20, 1908, and reads as follows:

Mr. William Phillips, a clerk of the $900 class, is hereby designated Chief of the Division of Far Eastern Affairs (correspondence, diplomatic and consular, on matters other than those of an administrative character, in relation to China, Japan, Korea, Siam, Straits Settlements, Borneo, East Indies, India, and in general the Far East.)

It is only human that a desk officer (now known as a "Country Director") should tend to take his assigned country as a client, the advancement of whose interests is to be his primary concern. Will an officer charged with the direction of a division or bureau dealing with the affairs of international organizations tend to overemphasize the value of the United Nations, the OAS, or some other organization in the fear that it may otherwise be neglected or ignored?

On the basis of long and distinguished service in the Department of State and with the Senate Foreign Relations Committee, Francis Wilcox suggests that these questions are to be answered in the affirmative:

Specialists tend to fall into two traps from which they must be rescued from time to time. In the first place, they tend to lose their perspective. They become so engrossed with their own special areas that they attach more importance to them than they deserve, or they fail to relate them to other important problems that beset us. When I served in the Department of State, for example, the Assistant Secretary in charge of European Affairs vigorously defended the interests of his clients in Western Europe, often presenting their

views with greater clarity and conviction than the Europeans
themselves. In retrospect, reflecting on my own responsibilities for
UN affairs at that time, I probably attached more significance to
the role of the UN in American foreign policy than it merited.[5]

Further, will a legal adviser be too legalistic to appraise broad
issues of policy? Is there an overall planner who makes it his
business to blend all interests and all points of view? Are some
officers preoccupied with day-to-day issues? The most recent official analysis of the organization and functioning of the Department of State concludes:

> If decisions are to be made in greater awareness of the policy goals
> established through the process of interest identification, the task
> forces concluded that the Department's planning function and its
> decision-making process must be greatly strengthened and linked to
> each other. They believed that a stronger planning function was es-
> sential if the Department's decision-makers were to succeed in look-
> ing beyond their present preoccupation with day-to-day issues.[6]

I do not wish to obscure my conviction that the foreign policy of the United States should, as through most of our history,
be directed by the Department of State under a Secretary of
State who is not only the titular ranking Cabinet officer but
who is actually in charge of the formulation and execution of
foreign policy. The practice under the Nixon administration of
eroding the roles of the Secretary of State, the Department of
State, and the Foreign Service, by centering the control of foreign policy in the White House, may produce some dramatic
tours de force but demonstrably cannot adequately care for all
the multiple facets of our international interests on a permanent basis. It is tragic error to relegate the State Department
and the Foreign Service to a status in which they would be no
more important in foreign policy than the dinosaur is of current ecological significance.

In 1889 James (later Lord) Bryce described in *The American Commonwealth* the position of the Secretary of State as it
used to exist:

The most dignified place in the cabinet is that of the Secretary of State. . . . In early days, it was regarded as the steppingstone to the presidency. Jefferson, Madison, Monroe, and J. Q. Adams had all served as secretaries to preceding presidents. The conduct of foreign affairs is the chief duty of the State department; its head has therefore a larger stage to play on than any other minister, and more chances of fame. His personal importance is all the greater because the President is usually so much absorbed by questions of patronage as to be forced to leave the secretary to his own devices. Hence the foreign policy of the administration is practically that of the secretary, except so far as the latter is controlled by the Senate and especially by the chairman of its committee on Foreign Relations. . . . It is often said of the President that he is ruled, or as the Americans express it, "run" by his secretary.

O tempora, o mores!

It may be true that a centralized autocratic White House bureaucracy can be well equipped to handle the constant conflicts and rivalries among the various bureaus and departments of the United States government, although experience does not convince one that this is true. It is certain that the White House monopoly is ineffective in handling the multifaceted dimensions of our international relations. Richard Neustadt brought out the problem effectively in testifying before a Senate subcommittee in 1965:

. . . relationships between allies are something like relationships between two great American departments. These are relationships of vast machines with different histories, routines, preoccupations, prospects. Each machine is worked by men with different personalities, skills, drives, responsibilities. Each set of men, quite naturally, would rather do his work in independence of the other set. If one government would influence the actions of another, it must find means to convince enough men and the right men on the other side that what it wants is what they need for their own purposes, in their own jobs, comporting with their own internally inspired hopes and fears, so that they will pursue it for themselves in their own bargaining arena.[7]

In the first years after the establishment of the United Nations in 1945, the ablest of the American career diplomats found the procedures of "parliamentary diplomacy" somewhat strange and unwieldy, as I have already intimated. Dean Acheson, when Secretary of State, found the United Nations quite a bore; so did George Kennan.

In 1951, George Kennan modestly acknowledged in the foreword to his Walgreen lectures at Chicago, published under the title *American Diplomacy, 1900–1950,* that he was "a novice in the field of diplomatic history." He is now an eminent authority in that field. In 1951 he delivered a scathing attack upon what he saw as the American "legalistic-moralistic approach to international problems." I suggested to him at the time that parts of his lectures had apparently been written in some haste, with which he modestly agreed. I confess that as a lawyer I bristled at some of his notions of the rather stupid rigidity of law and of the legal mind which created the international institutions. I like to think his mature considered view is reflected in a letter published in the New York *Times* on September 25, 1966, when he urged a policy of moderation in the Vietnam war:

. . . a number of weighty considerations deserve our scrupulous respect, among them:
The temper of world opinion generally;
The deeply pondered and earnest views of the Secretary-General of the United Nations;
The similar views of Pope Paul VI, and the great anxiety shown on this score by the world community and other religious communities generally;
The effect the Vietnam conflict may have on the future of the United Nations as an institution. . . .

Although, as I shall explain in chapter 6, President Truman did not always keep in mind the way in which matters have to be handled in the United Nations, I had two personal experiences with him which reveal the quality of the man. During one of the interminable attempts to settle some minor aspect of the problems in Palestine, the United Nations set up a small committee on which the United States was to be represented. As Deputy Chief of the U.S. Mission to the United Nations, I was then in charge of the Palestinian items and was informed that President Truman had appointed Mr. X as our representative on this committee. We did not know Mr. X but learned that he had been a faithful Democrat and he seemed an agreeable person when he arrived in New York to take up his duties.

At the time, the U.S. Mission was located in offices at 2 Park Avenue and we customarily used the Vanderbilt Hotel next door as quarters for persons temporarily in town on UN business. Mr. X was assigned a room and told that his committee was to meet at 4 P.M. and that he would be called for at 2:30 to drive out to Lake Success, which was then the UN headquarters.

At the appointed hour one of our staff phoned his room; there being no answer he went up and knocked at the door— no answer except sounds of snoring. The hotel was asked to open the door and Mr. X was found stretched on the bed with an empty quart bottle on the floor. He missed the meeting, and the performance was repeated the next day.

I telephoned Bob Lovett, then Acting Secretary of State, and explained the situation. He told me to take the first plane to Washington and he would arrange for me to see the President. We went to the White House together and I told Mr. Truman the story and its impact on our image in the United Nations.

With the vigorous pungency of epithets which were in his vocabulary, he said "they" had told him X was on the wagon and when he was sober he was a good operator. Turning to Lovett, the President said: "Pick out a good man for that committee; I'll have X's resignation within an hour." And so it was.

The more striking example of President Truman's attitude toward the United Nations I recall vividly from the meeting in Blair House on June 25, 1950, when he flew back to Washington and assembled the principal officials concerned to decide how to meet the North Korean invasion of South Korea. The chief Cabinet officers were there, the Chiefs of Staff, and various others from the State and Defense departments. The actual debate and decisions were made at and after dinner, but as we were gathered in the outer room before dinner and the President had heard the latest news from Dean Acheson and General Bradley, he sat on the window seat and I heard him repeating, half to himself, "We can't let the UN down! We can't let the UN down!"

It is impossible to imagine President Nixon uttering or harboring any such sentiment—in a crisis, or in the run-of-the-mill activities of the United Nations.

In his biography of Dean Acheson, Gaddis Smith gives another illustration. The President had summoned the congressional leaders to the White House on June 27, 1950, to hear Dean Acheson's grim description of the Korean crisis. Truman picked him up: "But Dean, you didn't even mention the UN!" The President then laid heavy emphasis on the fact that the United States was working through the United Nations.[8]

Stressing the glacial mobility of the large foreign policy bureaucracy, or the aberrations induced by the stresses of war or of belated efforts to extricate the United States from the Vietnamese quagmire, cannot be allowed to minimize the impact of individuals upon the system. For example, Henry L. Stimson and Dean G. Acheson were both trained lawyers, but the former needed to concentrate on one problem at a time, while the latter's brilliant mind could shift its focus from one subject to another with the rapidity that the variety and complexity of his responsibilities required when he was "present at the creation."

When General Marshall, as Secretary of State, presided over meetings of the U.S. delegation to the third session of the United Nations General Assembly in Paris, the question often was whether the United States should support or oppose some particular draft resolution or an amendment thereto. One pre-designated member of the staff would briefly lay the problem before us. The Secretary would then go around the table asking each one of some fifteen persons to express his or her view. He would begin with the senior member, Ambassador Warren Austin, then ask Mrs. Eleanor Roosevelt, and so on down to junior advisers. When the last one had spoken, General Marshall would say, with scarcely a pause: "The position of the delegation will be as follows . . ." He could (and did) similarly dispose of problems before the Joint Chiefs of Staff when he was Secretary of Defense.

There is, of course, no one uniform procedure by which decisions on foreign policy are reached. Within one country, the United States for example, the procedures change with time and with personalities. If Khrushchev's memory is reliable, or if he records accurately what he remembers (and I do not rely on one or the other hypothesis), such procedures, even in a monolithic state, range the whole gamut from "King Stalin's" impetuous impressionistic fiats to the later detailed deliberations in the Presidium of the Central Committee. Khrushchev boasts that in the Cuban missile crisis his "side's policy was, from the outset, worked out in the collective leadership. . . . Every step we had taken had been carefully considered by the collective." [9]

In the United States, fortunately, we can have a strong-willed President with a tendency to monopolize foreign policy, like Franklin D. Roosevelt, without the Soviet pattern of purges. Or a Harry S. Truman can rely on the judgment of a brilliant Secretary of State, albeit one who never ignored or minimized the fact that the ultimate responsibility was the President's. At one stage or another in our history, the Cabinet or the National Security Council has played a part.

Not all decisions on foreign policy are made by the Secretary of State or in the State Department. Roosevelt in wartime is a prime example. In more recent times, a disarmament agency, an establishment dealing with foreign aid, or another in charge of propaganda (labeled "public information"), or a CIA or a Pentagon may run with the ball and think it has scored a touchdown, although it may actually be a touchback. The cases I analyze are often ones in which the Secretary of State is harassed and ambushed, but not ones in which he is routed. A really vertebrate Secretary of State may imitate Secretary Charles Evans Hughes, who was asked by a correspondent what he thought of the report that Secretary of Commerce Herbert Hoover had urged the President to transfer the entire consular establishment to his care. Mr. Hughes replied: "Mr. Hoover would make an excellent Secretary of State."

Although foreign policy decisions should be constructed in the Department of State, after originating there they may be vetted in a National Security Council or elsewhere and may, in the end, be made not alone by the Secretary of State, but by the President. If made by the President, he may act on the advice of a Colonel House or a Harry Hopkins or a McGeorge Bundy or a Henry Kissinger; but if the fair-haired boy of the White House is also architect and building constructor, the system is widely askew. One could write another book to supplement those already published in order to justify or demolish this emphasis on the optimum role of the Department of State. I merely express my own point of view without attempting justification, although I am glad to draw attention to recent statements by two masters of diplomacy, Dean Acheson and Charles Yost, in support of this view.[10]

In the conduct of World War II, it was the President, without the help or often the knowledge of the Secretary of State, who made the great political decisions as at Yalta, Teheran, Cairo, and Casablanca. Nevertheless, according to the most authoritative witness, Charles Bohlen, Roosevelt, at Yalta anyway, "seemed to be guided very heavily by his advisers," who included Bohlen, Harry Hopkins, and H. Freeman Mathews.[11]

When it came to planning for the postwar world, the grand design of the United Nations was produced in the State Department with Leo Pasvolsky as manager and James T. Shotwell as the inspiring coach of the intellectual team. However, before the United Nations Organization was born at San Francisco in 1945 and laid a clutch of specialized agencies, as they are called in the Charter, four separate international organizations were produced. The first was FAO (Food and Agriculture Organization), with which I had no connection and which was still in swadling clothes when in 1943 UNRRA was born. This United Nations Relief and Rehabilitation Administration was conceived to meet the immediate need for relief in the war areas and UNRRA was to be the organizational instrument. The preparatory work was to be done by the United States.

President Roosevelt asked former Governor Herbert Lehman to take charge of OFRRO (Office of Foreign Relief and Rehabilitation Operations), which for administrative convenience would be set up in the State Department but would not be subject to the Secretary of State. Anything the Governor wanted to help him in his task—just ask the President, Roosevelt assured him.

Governor Lehman, who had been an admirable governor of the Empire State, did not know the magic of the machinations by which one wartime bureau or bureaucrat prevailed over another. One had to be more than an able administrator to pilot a new boat through those reefs and shoals. Necessary foreign communications had to go through the State Department, which meant collecting as many as fourteen "career" initials on an OFRRO draft. OFRRO was not established until 1942 when recruiting manpower meant generally robbing other government agencies or scraping the bottom of the barrel. Frustration piled on frustration as clever officials with the current political know-how maneuvered out of the White House orders nullifying in practice what had just been given to Governor Lehman.

In September 1943, OFRRO was merged with Lend-Lease and
the Board of Economic Warfare to form FEA, the Foreign Economic Administration.

The UNRRA Agreement was signed in the East Room of
the White House on November 9, 1943. The first Council session of the new organization met the next day at Atlantic City.
This was an international conference launching an international organization. It was natural enough for the State Department to take charge, with the understanding that the climax of
the meeting would be the election of Herbert Lehman as the
first Director-General of UNRRA. Accordingly, the Division of
International Conferences of the Department of State, under
Dr. Warren Kelchner, secured for the meeting an Atlantic City
hotel and as Secretary-General minded the housekeeping. Assistant Secretary of State Dean Acheson was chairman of the session. It was left to me as Director of Personnel and Training in
OFRRO to recruit and as Assistant Secretary-General to direct
the first really international secretariat of the post-League of
Nations world. The personnel were American, but they were
loyal to their international functions and left raging the former
executive officer of OFRRO whose nationalistic orders I refused to follow. Actually I was impervious to his threats since I
was not a governmental careerist and was about to return to my
work as a professor at Columbia University as soon as the
UNRRA meeting ended.

My next task was similar, although the titles were different.
In 1944, at the invitation of the Treasury Department (not the
State Department), I was Assistant Secretary-General of the
Bretton Woods Conference where the governments planned
the next step after Relief and Rehabilitation, namely, Recon-
struction and Development for which the International Bank
was created, along with the International Monetary Fund.
They later became specialized agencies of the United Nations.

In contrast to Governor Lehman's difficulties in setting up
UNRRA, in this instance, Roosevelt supported Secretary of the

Treasury Morgenthau, who relied on Harry Dexter White, a positive, sometimes arrogant, figure who had little use for the State Department or even for John Maynard Keynes. The Protocol Division of the State Department was allowed to hire, reopen, and rehabilitate—as far as possible—a New Hampshire resort hotel which had been closed during the war. Boy Scouts were still unloading truckloads of desks and chairs as the delegates' limousines were rolling up to the door. The hotel was inadequate, but we made do. A cot in a former servant's room sufficed for an Assistant Secretary-General, who had little time to spend on it.

As Assistant Secretary of State, Dean Acheson, who deals generously with both Morgenthau and Harry White, had to play his important substantive role in designing the International Bank, in a curtained-off corner of the ballroom which formerly contained the bar.[12] There, too, he helped a bewildered journalist write his daily dispatches on the conference—reports for which the correspondent subsequently was awarded a distinguished prize in journalism.

Probably my own most important contribution to the success of the conference consisted in winking at a flagrant violation of Dr. Kelchner's ruling that, due to the limited accommodations, no wives could be included. When a Belgian delegate told me that his wife, whom he had not seen in four years, had escaped from Germany and had made her way to New Hampshire, I explained to the delegate that there was a postern gate which led from the garden into the hotel and which was not locked or watched after dark.

In the years since 1945, when statements have constantly been made to the effect that the United Nations is the cornerstone of our foreign policy, it has been quite impossible to reconcile that very broad and vague concept with the demands of particular regional policies. We saw this very strikingly illustrated in 1956 when the policy of support for the United Nations and the principles of the Charter led the United States to

take a stand against other members of the grand alliance of
NATO and to oppose in the General Assembly France's and
Great Britain's action in Egypt.

Thus, broad labels such as "a United Nations policy" or a
"peace policy" are no more helpful than the labels cast in terms
of geographic regions. Labels mislead and generations of
schoolchildren supposed that President Monroe originated the
Monroe Doctrine, although he merely approved what Adams
had written. Former Prime Minister Harold Macmillan, recording in his diary a meeting with Secretary of State John Foster Dulles in December 1956, wrote that Dulles said he "wrote
most of the Presidential statements himself. When they had to
be tough, they were made by the Secretary of State. . . . When
they were idealistic, they were made by the President but written by the Secretary of State." [13] The Truman Doctrine originated with Dean Acheson as Under Secretary of State. A Franklin D. Roosevelt may make a speech notable by a magical
phrase—"We have nothing to fear but fear itself'—[14] but no
one in high office in Washington in recent decades has had
time to write all his own speeches. The speechwriters may or
may not be given a theme; Dean Acheson used to say, "Don't
give me a Christmas-tree speech"—one on which each official
would hang a comment on his pet problem or project.

Gaddis Smith, in his biography of Acheson, writes: "He intended that his speeches should be carefully studied and believed. The historian, like the contemporary diplomatist, must
heed the speeches, for they are no ghost-written collection of
clichés turned out by a band of tired underlings, but immediate expressions of Acheson's ideas." [15] That is largely true, but
the pace at which one had to work under Acheson was often as
exhausting as it was exhilarating and the "underlings" often
did make contributions which Acheson welcomed even though
he polished them in his own superb style.

Of course not all policy decisions are put in speeches, nor do all speeches declare policy, although they may state formal conclusions.

George Kennan has said that speeches are "not an inconsiderable means of influencing what goes on in the world." Bill Moyers, President Johnson's Press Secretary, testified that "Policy in major speeches is very important as a means to start things going." John Leacacos gives examples of cases where the speaker's name is attached to the policy enunciated in the speech:

Not that major speeches can always be successfully organized in advance, or even come out as planned. The famous Marshall Plan speech was preorganized in 1947. The historic reference to Point IV (for technical assistance to underdeveloped countries) in the inaugural speech of President Truman in 1949 was not. Under Secretary of State Robert Lovett was horrified at the idea of Point IV and instructed the Department's Counselor, Charles E. Bohlen, to cut it out. President Truman reinserted the proposal when the draft came back to the White House. Another speech that was a major instrument of United States foreign policy was that of President Eisenhower before the United Nations in September 1958. Therein he proposed a UN force as a permanent body in the Middle East, an Arab Development Bank, and arms control for the Middle East, prescient proposals in light of the 1967 Arab-Israeli war.[16]

Just to illustrate further the gap which may exist between the mind of the speaker and the text of the speech given to him to read, I recall that it used to be the practice to prepare a scenario for a high official who had to preside over a formal session of a conference. Different size or color of type, plus a generous sprinkling of parentheses, were supposed to signal to the reader the lines he was to read and those which alerted him to the role of another actor. At the closing session of the Bretton Woods Conference in 1944, we had such a scenario for Secretary of the Treasury Morgenthau, who had practically nothing to do with the substantive work of the Conference in establishing the International Bank for Reconstruction and Development and the International Monetary Fund. At one point the scenario looked like this:

SECRETARY MORGENTHAU: I CALL UPON THE REPRESENTATIVE OF AUSTRALIA.
    (The Representative of Australia will arise and move
    a vote of thanks to the United States.)

The Secretary was nearsighted and read aloud the parenthetical sentence as well as his own. The official verbatim record of this session naturally omits this item.

As following chapters will illustrate, the representatives of the United States (or of most other governments), when making formal statements in the General Assembly or the Security Council of the United Nations, are broadcasting to the world the policy of their governments and their words must be measured; usually they will be tailored but the names of those who cut and sew the pattern and the cloth remain anonymous. Perhaps this is why it seems to me that the names and detailed accounts of the roles played by many an individual in the dramas which make up the record of the United Nations belong in the pages of history.

2

Midwife to Korea

I have used the title *The Birth of "Nations"* but the international lawyers would say that I am really talking about the birth of "states"—and they would be correct. Perhaps one merely recalls the first of D. W. Griffith's gigantic screen epics entitled *The Birth of a Nation*—it was a good title for a good picture and it suits the theme of this book. Whatever they should be called, political groups need to be "born" into the international society. Hyderabad, Assam, and the Iroquois Indians, for example, all have sought to have their grievances redressed by the International Court of Justice, but the Court had to refuse them a hearing because the Court can hear only "states" and they were not states. I shall start here with the birth of the Republic of Korea.

The Korean case, as it came up in the United Nations in 1947, was not quite typical of the cold war situations which subsequently divided the United States and the Soviet Union on so many issues with almost automatic regularity. In November 1947, although the two delegations in the UN General Assembly were at odds on proposals to deal with Korea, they voted together on the basic resolution to provide partition with economic union for Palestine—a story to which we return in chapter 7. The lines had been drawn, however, in Iran in 1946 and the Truman Doctrine, warning the Soviet Union away from Greece and Turkey, was also in 1947. It was of course in Korea that the cold war burst into flame in 1950, and in retrospect the Koreans emphasized Soviet opposition in 1948 to the UN moves which established the independence of the Republic of Korea.

Since the cold war was a dominant force in most United States foreign policies during the Truman administration, it is appropriate to indicate here the ways in which it influenced American attitudes toward certain developments in the Far East. It would take us too far off course to go into the complex story of the "China tangle," but the following background gives the setting for policies followed toward the independence of Korea, Indonesia, and Vietnam as well as of the French protectorates in Tunisia and Morocco described in chapter 4.

The upsurge of nationalism at the close of World War II appealed to American public opinion. This search for self-development and independence by the peoples themselves had for us more reality than Woodrow Wilson's somewhat disembodied principle of "self-determination" after World War I, although that slogan has now been recaptured by the Third World. President Franklin D. Roosevelt anticipated the Third World in his eagerness to end or curtail colonialism. It is a pity he was dissuaded from his purpose to prevent the French from returning to Indochina. De Gaulle and indeed France itself could be scorned and humiliated in 1945 but Churchill was as steadfast as Gibraltar against a policy of the dissolution of colonial empires. The Labour government's reversal of the Churchillian doctrine by the emancipation of India and other dominions and colonies spared us some but not all troubles with our English cousins. Indonesia presented the first of a series of competing European and Asian claims to U.S. support that involved us in policies which at times were schizophrenic. The

controversies with France, especially concerning French possessions in North Africa, kept boiling on the front of the diplomatic stove for years. In the end, and with the help of the
United States, four former dependencies were born into separate statehood and later baptised into UN membership.

There were three interrelated forces or impulses which certainly influenced and to an extent controlled the policies followed by the Truman administration from 1948 to 1952 in
dealing with the situations which unrolled in Asia and in
North Africa. One was the anxiety about the intentions and
capabilities of Soviet Russia. The second was the tendency to
identify Russia with communism. The third had to do with the
means and measures by which the first two dangers might be
met or averted; in Europe this meant the Marshall Plan and
NATO while elsewhere it meant securing the good will and
confidence of the peoples in the colonial areas of Asia, the Middle East, and North Africa.

It was indeed the era of the cold war and American opinion
accepted the view that world communism was monolithic, aggressive, and controlled by Moscow. Some of the Republican
opposition—and with growing intensity after 1949, the China
Lobby—seized upon the fear of communism and magnified it
for their own ends. In the 1950s Senator Joseph McCarthy ap-
propriated to himself the role of defender of the American
faith against the "traitors" and a wave of persecution swept
over the country. But the McCarthy era was subsequent to the
events which I treat in the Korean and Indonesian stories, and
the whole movement with which he was associated had its impact on foreign policy principally in regard to China, to which
I refer only in passing. It is difficult two decades later to recap-
ture the intensity of that prevalent fear of communism after
World War II, just as I could not now convey an appreciation
of the widespread American conviction during World War I
that every German was a bloody-handed monster—a conviction
I shared as a junior in college who, before enlisting, protested

against the time spent in the classroom when we might have had more military drilling even with our wooden guns.

But the bugaboo of a Communist under every bed and at every desk in the State Department did have its relation to the genuine conviction in the government that Russia might pose a military threat. The expansion of Soviet influence was seen as a direct menace to American security. Although George Kennan has explained how he was misunderstood and his views misrepresented after he wrote the famous "X" article in *Foreign Affairs* in the summer of 1947, "containment" of Russian Communist expansion became U.S. government policy. Kennan, to his dismay, found that his identity was soon exposed and his article overwhelmed in a "veritable whirlpool of publicity" which soon attributed to him a "doctrine of containment" that was thought to be an exposition of the foreign policy of the administration. He particularly regrets the wholly inaccurate interpretation which Walter Lippmann and others gave to his views as described (too carelessly and inadequately, he admits) in the *Foreign Affairs* article, namely that he advocated the use of U.S. military force to "contain" the Russians. In his *Memoirs* Kennan explains that while he would not have denied that the Russians might use violence to advance their ends, his analysis was that it would be domestic rather than international violence. Kennan's policy of containment "related to the effort to encourage other peoples to resist this type of violence and to defend the *internal* integrity of their countries." [1]

As far as I can reconstruct the thinking in the State Department in those years after 1947, I believe it correctly interpreted and generally accepted Kennan's real policy of containment as he has since explained it. It was in this frame of reference that on August 9, 1950, during the Korean war, I wrote a memorandum addressed to Dean Rusk, then Assistant Secretary of State for Far Eastern Affairs. The memorandum recommended that the Policy Planning Staff study the possible development of indigenous Asian manpower capable of self-defense against aggression by local guerrilla forces trained by the Communists. This, I believe, was in accord with Kennan's concept of "containment"; there was no suggestion of the use of American military forces.

It was the stupidly contemptuous attitude of the American military for the fighting spirit and skill of the Asians that led to the rejection of this concept, with the resulting slaughter of thousands of Americans. In connection with the cases which I am discussing in this and in the succeeding chapter, I have found no documentary evidence in the archives and have no personal recollection of any plan—aside from the defensive strategy of NATO—to use military force against the Soviet Union except perhaps in case the Russians had sent their own armies into action in Korea. It is in the light of this analysis that I think the reader must understand the various statements of policy I refer to in the following pages.

The Truman Doctrine on Greece and Turkey was enunciated in 1947; the Marshall Plan was proposed in the same year and launched in 1948; the NATO treaty was signed in Washington on April 4, 1949. Inevitably, Europe was the focus of United States concern. There was strong bipartisan support for the European policy. On the other hand, as Dean Acheson graphically describes, when the utter incompetence of the Chinese Nationalist government delivered the mainland of China to the Communists, the Republican opposition gleefully proclaimed that the Communist victory must have been due either to the incompetence of the State Department or to the treason of its personnel. Muck was thrown on the Department —the muck of McCarthy and McCarran. Most dastardly and of enduring damage to the national interest was the smearing of an exceptionally able and totally dedicated group of persons, the Foreign Service officers and scholars who were specialists in Far Eastern affairs. Our subsequent failure to understand Asian psychology in the Vietnam war can be traced in part at least to that disastrous "purge."

Secretary Acheson decided to lay the facts about China before the American people and the world. The decision was sound in principle and a counter to the tactics of the political opposition, but it was not an easy one since many officers of the Department counseled against it; Walton Butterworth, the Chief of the Office of Far Eastern Affairs, and I were in favor. President Truman agreed. Butterworth directed a skilled group who began the collection of the documentary record, which came to be known as the China White Paper of 1949. Later, the Secretary designated me to act as editor in chief, perhaps on the theory that my university background might be an earnest of academic objectivity in the production of a political document. Impartial objectivity in presenting an honest record was our goal and guide. In 1971 Acheson wrote: "In spite of the storm of abuse directed at this document by the ideological and partisan political foes of the policy it reported, it has stood up admirably for thirty years as the definitive factual history of the period. This is due to Jessup's editing and supervision." [2]

Meanwhile, we had been giving consideration to other steps which might be useful in helping to determine the general lines of our future policy in the Far East. The area was one in which I had developed a strong academic interest but my familiarity with Asian problems had been acquired only by eye and ear—I had never been there.

The Policy Planning Staff was responsible for focusing attention in the Department on the need for a vigorous Asian policy. In that group the lead was taken by one of the ablest of our Far Eastern experts, John Paton Davies. His intellectual leadership on these matters was probably reported by the spies who, I am convinced, were in the Department working for the China Lobby crowd, and it led to the amputation of his distinguished diplomatic career. In any event, on July 8, 1949, George Kennan, then Director of the Policy Planning Staff, sent to Under Secretary James E. Webb, Deputy Under Secretary Dean Rusk, Counselor Charles Bohlen, and me as Ambassador-at-Large, a memorandum which Davies had drafted. Kennan stated that this memorandum was not a final Staff recommendation but was designed to suggest a program which might create a new and hopeful atmosphere in our East Asia and South Asia policy. It was in line with the containment policy as described above.[3]

The memorandum began by noting that our policy toward Asia was, in American public opinion, suffering from an acute case of negativism; it seemed to be a "do-nothing" policy. It was not generally understood that the actual situation in Asia made a wide range of solid action impossible. The White Paper, which was then being compiled, might provide a rational explanation of our policy—and there was much in the record of which we should be proud—but it would also provide fuel for our critics. Public opinion might agree that we had justified inaction in the past but it would ask where do we go from here? We needed a change of climate in both American and Asian opinion. East and South Asia were becoming surcharged with nervous apprehension of invasion or subversion. We had to act with a real sense of theater to catch people's imagination. An illustrative timetable was proposed. In that very month of July, we should start discussions with congressional leaders and have frank talks with the British and Canadians.

The Philippines was seen to be capable of playing a strategic role. President Elpidio Quirino should be invited, with considerable fanfare, to Washington to discuss mutual interests. We should give him assurances of aid against any external attack and should agree on a combined defense board and the establishment of a U.S. base in the Philippines. Political considerations should prevail over any technical objections of our military establishment. There should be more economic support and announcement of plans to establish a regional university in Manila where the independent governments of East and South Asia could send technicians for training in the development of their own countries in a spirit of mutual cooperation. This would be our counter to Moscow's "University of the Toilers of the East." If congressional leaders and the National Security Council approved, we should sound out the Philippines and Australia on the desirability of a three-power defense treaty along the lines of NATO; eventually Canada, Japan and possibly New Zealand might be brought in.* In anticipation of successful outcome of the talks between the Indonesians and the Dutch, we should intensify our preparations for military and economic assistance to Indonesia. A variety of measures for strengthening the Thai government were proposed. There was detailed discussion of the steps to be taken toward the conclusion of a peace treaty with Japan and of the provisions of such a treaty. Davies suggested that I should tour the Far East and South Asia (as indeed I did in 1950), talking with government leaders in all the capitals on issues of mutual interest. Special emphasis was placed on India and talks with Nehru. Chiefs of mission in Delhi and Karachi should follow up topics raised in my conversations. Before the White Paper was published, the Davies memorandum continued, the President should make a speech pointing up the principal conclusions and setting forth in affirmative, confident tones the future course of our policy not only toward China but toward all of East and Southeast Asia. Although his suggested calendar of events was too rapid for action by the Department, much of Davies' program was eventually followed.

Secretary Acheson agreed with a suggestion I made that we invite two outsiders to join the Department for a time as advisers. In the prevailing political atmosphere in Washington it would have been impossible to select persons already prominently identified with Asian affairs since they too would have been denounced as partisans of this or that faction. The decision was to select two men of high public standing with a

---

* In the event, there was the ANZUS treaty of 1951—Australia, New Zealand and the United States.

broad international viewpoint, who had some knowledge of Asian affairs but who were not specialists. On the day the White Paper was released (July 29, 1949), the Secretary announced the appointment of Raymond Fosdick, former President of the Rockefeller Foundation, and Everett Case, President of Colgate University. They were valiant and valuable counselors.

The Consultants, as Fosdick and Case were called, submitted a memorandum to the Secretary on August 29, 1949, suggesting that he discuss with Ernest Bevin and Robert Schuman, the British and French foreign ministers who were to arrive in the United States in September, a statement which would register a sympathetic appreciation of the nationalistic aspirations of the peoples of Southeast Asia. There was a full realization in the Department that Moscow was quick to embrace nationalist groups in colonial areas, perhaps hoping that the colonial powers would be sufficiently inelastic to provoke so-called "wars of liberation."

One week later John Davies drafted a statement which might serve the suggested purpose; a paragraph from his draft gives the tone:

Although we have always held that governments long established should not be changed for light and transient causes, with equal conviction we maintain that the passionate and insistent demands of colonial peoples for their independence must be satisfied.

George Kennan objected to the clause beginning "with equal conviction . . ." I tried my hand at two alternative —rather sonorous—paragraphs:

As a product of our history and of a conviction which the experience of generations has confirmed and which the Charter of the United Nations records, we maintain that peoples are entitled to satisfy their political aspirations to develop self-government. We have therefore welcomed Burma to its place in the United Nations. . . .

We appreciate the advantages flowing from a transfer which is based upon mutual accommodation. We recognize the foresighted statesmanship of those who transfer authority and the sense of deep responsibility with which those who take authority assume the burdens of government.

I inquired of the chiefs of the offices concerned with Western Europe, the Near East and Africa, and the Far East, respectively George Perkins, George McGhee, and Walton Butterworth, whether they agreed that such a statement should be discussed by the Secretary with Schuman and Bevin. I also wondered whether we could extend the geographical scope beyond Southeast Asia to include, for example, Korea and China. I admitted that too broad a generalization should be avoided because of the delicacy of France's problems in North Africa. The idea of dealing with the matter on a tripartite basis was abandoned but the possibility of some such pronouncement was still retained. Assistant Secretary for Near East and African Affairs, George McGhee, wrote me on September 21 that although they would like to change the drafting and discuss the timing of such a statement, his office was generally interested in the idea.

Charles Yost, already well advanced along his brilliant diplomatic career, was then attached to my office in the State Department. Early in September 1949 he prepared a memorandum which we sent to Rusk, Kennan, McGhee, Butterworth, and Charles S. Reed, Director of the Office of Philippine and Southeast Asian Affairs. It picked up a suggestion made in the memorandum of the Consultants, as a variation of or supplement to the point in the first Davies memorandum, which contemplated that our interest in the Asian area would be dramatized by an extensive trip of the Ambassador-at-Large. The new proposal was for a "Permanent Ambassador to the Far East," a role somewhat like that of Malcolm McDonald, who had established headquarters at Singapore as British High Commissioner with wide geographical responsibilities. The Consultants originally used the designation "High Commissioner" and suggested that Ralph Bunche be appointed to the post. The whole idea was disapproved by Reed in the Southeast Asia office and by McGhee. I shared this view since such a roving officer, if he played a significant role, would have been a constant irritant to the regular ambassadors—the British situation with their numerous dependencies in the Far Eastern area provided no analogy. We suffered enough in those and later days by the existence in capitals like Paris of a bevy of persons with ambassadorial rank charged with military, economic, or other special functions. As Ambassador-at-Large I was always conscious of this problem and tried to avoid bypassing our regular diplomatic staffs. Mr. Kissinger apparently has had a different policy.

In response to my request, Secretary Acheson sent me a top-secret memorandum dated July 18, 1949, which read as follows:

You will please take as your assumption that it is a fundamental decision of American policy that the United States does not intend to permit further extension of Communist domination on the continent of Asia or in the southeast Asia area. Will you please draw up for me possible programs of action relating to various specific areas not now under Communist control in Asia under which the United States would have the best chance of achieving this purpose? These programs should contain proposed courses of action, steps to be taken in implementing such programs, estimate of cost to the United States, and the extent to which United States forces would or would not be involved. I fully realize that when these proposals are received it may be obvious that certain parts thereof would not be within our capabilities to put into effect, but what I desire is the examination of the problem on the general assumptions indicated above in order to make absolutely certain that we are neglecting no opportunity that would be within our capabilities to achieve the purpose of halting the spread of totalitarian communism in Asia.[4]

The memorandum did not specify what was "within our capabilities" but the expression is to be read in the light of the "containment" policy as already described. I find no indication in the record that there was any thought of embroiling Ameri-

can manpower in war on the Asian continent; the whole theme
of the China White Paper was contrary to such commitment.

The same conclusion is indicated on the basis of the documents for the period which are included in the Pentagon Papers.[5]

Secretary Acheson's directive was in line with a Department
of State policy statement on Indochina, dated September 27,
1948, and the National Security Council studies on "The Position of the United States with Respect to Asia," NSC 48/1,
which were discussed with the President at a meeting on December 30, 1949; the conclusions of the study were approved
subject to some amendments. The objectives were to reduce
and eventually to eliminate "the preponderant power and influence of the USSR in Asia" and to develop military power in
selected non-Communist nations of Asia "to maintain internal
security and to prevent further encroachment by communism."
The Soviet Union and communism are used alternatively without much differentiation.

Although I have evaded the bonds of exact chronology, the
foregoing gives the backdrop against which the Korean drama
unfolded.

I may be challenged for dealing with Korea under the head-
ing of the *birth* of nations, since Korea was an ancient state
with a long historical background. But Korea needed a rebirth
since it had been conquered by Japan and was under Japanese
rule from 1910 to 1945. At the end of World War II Korea was
virtually cut in half at the 38th parallel by a wartime agreement which the United States made with the Soviet Union.

During the war, at the Cairo Conference in December 1943,
the leaders of the United States, Great Britain, and China declared that they, "mindful of the enslavement of the people of
Korea, are determined that in due course Korea shall become
free and independent." This pledge was reaffirmed at the Potsdam Conference of 1945, and when the Soviet Union declared

war on Japan on August 8, 1945, it committed itself to support this declaration for the independence of Korea.

At the time of the Japanese surrender, Russian troops were well into Manchuria and near the Korean border. Some of their forces moved into Korea on August 12, 1945, when the nearest American forces available for movement into Korea were in Okinawa, 600 miles away, and in the Philippines, some 1,500 miles away. Somebody had to take the surrender of the sizable Japanese force in Korea and the U.S. military and State Department authorities agreed to let the Russians take the surrender north of the 38th parallel, while south of that line the Japanese would surrender to the Americans. If this agreement had not been reached, Russian forces would have occupied the whole of Korea before American troops arrived. It was not even contemplated at the time that this line would be a long-term division of the country because the Russians would consistently refuse to agree to a unified independent Korea. It was thought that an agreement had been reached at the Council of Foreign Ministers in Moscow in December 1945 but, after two years of fruitless negotiation, the United States in September 1947 referred the Korean question to the General Assembly of the United Nations and introduced a resolution calling for the creation of an all-Korean government elected throughout the whole country under United Nations observation.

The General Assembly on November 14, 1947, over the opposition of the Soviet bloc, established the United Nations Temporary Commission on Korea, composed of representatives of Australia, Canada, China, El Salvador, France, India, the Philippines, Syria, and the Ukraine. The Ukraine refused to serve on the Commission. The Commission was to go to Korea and consult with people throughout the whole country. They were to prepare for elections to be held in March 1948. Since the General Assembly would normally not be in session from December 1947 to September 1948, the Commission was authorized to consult the Interim Committee of the General Assem-

bly which, on U.S. initiative, was created at that same Assembly
session.

The Commission went to Korea and was given every assistance by the American forces and authorities south of the 38th
parallel, but the Russians refused to let its members enter the
territory north of that line. The Commission then decided on
February 6, 1948, to consult the Interim Committee (also
known as the "Little Assembly") on the question whether, in
light of the Soviet action, it should carry out its task only in
the part of Korea occupied by American forces.

The story of the debates in the Little Assembly is worth
mentioning because it is so generally ignored in books on the
United Nations.[6] For Korea, those debates were vital and play
a prominent part in the history of the Republic. In January
1948, as a deputy to our Ambassador to the United Nations,
Senator Warren Austin, I was representing the United States in
the Little Assembly, which had begun its work by studying
general problems of peaceful settlement, including limitations
on the use of the veto in the Security Council. The Little Assembly was boycotted by the Soviet bloc, which asserted that it
was an attempt to evade the procedures specified in the Charter
with a view to imposing the will of the U.S. controlled majority on the Socialist minority. Toward the end of January, I was
assigned the task of assisting in the Korean case, and I began
the usual round of consultations with other delegations and
with Andrew Cordier, the extraordinarily able *chef de cabinet*
to all the Secretaries-General of the United Nations until his
retirement in 1962. With his powerful, stocky frame, unruffled
demeanor, and fantastic memory, he was a tower of strength
and the dominant parliamentarian at all meetings of the General Assembly. To me, he was a constant source of information
and wise advice, and his qualities stood him in good stead
when he later became president of Columbia University in a
time of student unrest.

On February 3, 1948, Cordier told me that the Korean Commission intended to report to the Interim Committee that it was impossible to meet the deadline set by the Assembly resolution for elections in Korea and that the Commission questioned the expediency of holding any elections at all. I recommended, in accordance with the position which the United States had decided to take, that the Commission should proceed with the elections, with or without consulting the Interim Committee; it was up to the Commission to decide in the first place. Two days later Cordier told me that the Canadians (Canada had a representative on the Korean Commission) opposed holding elections only in the South since this would jeopardize ultimate unity with the North. In their view, it would be better to have no elections. But the Commission decided to consult the Interim Committee and sent word that the chairman, Parakat Menon of India, and Victor Hoo, the Chinese member of the UN Secretariat who acted as secretary to the Commission, would come to Lake Success. Cordier informed me that Padilla Nervo, the permanent representative of Mexico to the United Nations and Chairman of the Interim Committee, was prepared to convene a meeting to hear the views of the Korean Commission, and he was willing to meet the desire of Victor Hoo that the date should be February 19.

There was a general feeling, shared by Cordier, that it would not be wise to call a special session of the General Assembly to discuss Korea since this would merely emphasize the opposition of the Soviet bloc. Padilla Nervo told me he thought it undesirable to invite Gromyko, the Soviet representative at the United Nations, to attend the Interim Committee meeting, since it might merely stimulate him to propose instead calling a special session of the General Assembly.

In my conversations, I found that Dr. José Arce of the Argentine, and Joseph Nisot of Belgium, shared the American view of the situation, but that the United Kingdom was reluctant. The British representative at the United Nations, Sir Alexander Cadogan, who was one of the ablest and most experienced diplomats, was recommending to London, however, that they should support us. Nasrollah Entezam of Iran, who would later be President of the General Assembly, also thought the Commission should get on with its task, planning for elections in all of Korea, and carrying them out as far as possible.

I discussed the strategy of the meetings of the Interim Committee with Padilla Nervo and we were agreed that the two principal questions were:

1. Should the Commission proceed as far as possible?

2. Was the March 31 date set by the General Assembly an absolute deadline?

On February 12, Pierre Ordonneau of the French delegation told me that they agreed with our views. George Ignatieff of Canada, however, told Gordon Knox of the U.S. delegation that the reason Canada opposed elections just in the South, was that it put the United Nations on record as sanctioning a division of Korea which would be overrun by the Russians as soon as American troops were withdrawn—and the United States was determined to withdraw its forces. Canada did not want the United Nations to take sides in what they saw as a dispute between the United States and the USSR. On the basis of further information, I reported to Durward Sandifer in the UN Bureau of the State Department (UNA), that Australia would also oppose holding elections in the South and that Canada would probably withdraw from the Korean Commission if their position were voted down. On February 18, the Department telegraphed the U.S. Mission in New York that the Australian delegate on the Korean Commission seemed to have gone to Korea bent on proving that U.S. administration in South Korea was that of a police state. American representatives in Seoul reported that the Australian was definitely anti-American and was leading the opposition.

When the Interim Committee met at Lake Success on February 19, Menon, as chairman of the Korean Commission, made an opening statement, summarizing the situation and asking the Interim Committee to advise them how they should carry out the General Assembly's resolution. We had already sent to the State Department the draft of the speech I was to make in the Committee, but we revised it after hearing Menon; the drafting was done largely by the group of advisers with whom I worked. There were various suggestions for a brief adjournment to enable delegates to confer and the Department agreed, provided the adjournment was to a date not later than February 24, but it was emphasized that there was no change in the U.S. position in favor of the Commission's getting on with its job.

As soon as Menon finished speaking, one of our staunch friends, Ambassador Muñiz of Brazil, as had previously been arranged to meet the British request, moved an adjournment until February 24. I stated that we reluctantly agreed in view of the possibility of further support for our conviction that the Commission should proceed with its task. It was thought that this brief but firm indication would help to curb a feeling of disappointment in Seoul.

It was encouraging to find how helpful many of the delegates were. Lester ("Mike") Pearson of Canada, who was to be later President of the General Assembly and winner of the Nobel Peace Prize, said to me that he personally favored the United States position although his government was opposed; he hoped to be authorized to confine his own remarks to certain legal points, and regarding possible Canadian withdrawal from the Commission, he assured me there would be no dramatics harmful to Canadian-American relations. Later, he told me he might be instructed to argue more widely, but that his own view was unchanged. Sir Alexander Cadogan told me that he disagreed with the instructions he had from London and had asked to be allowed to support the United States. On one occasion, and I think it was this one, when I went to see him in his office, which was then in the Empire State building, he pushed a telegram across the table to me and said, "Look what those

stupid people in London want me to do!" Dr. T. F. Tsiang, the
head of the Chinese delegation, offered his help to persuade
the Arab and Indian delegations to support us. But Ambassador Selim Sarper of Turkey told me that the Arab states and
Pakistan would oppose us because of the U.S. stand on Palestine; they would be waiting to hear what the United States
would say in the Security Council on that subject. I was able
to tell him that we understood Pakistan would join Iran in
supporting us.

When the Interim Committee reconvened on February 24, I
delivered the speech we had prepared and the Department had
cleared. In the committees of the General Assembly, as in the
Security Council, one speaks from one's seat and other delegates, if so minded, listen with their earphones to the original
language or to one of the translations.

The speech rehearsed the history of the Korean question
since the Cairo Declaration of 1943. There was emphasis on
the desire of the United States to see an independent Korea,
representing the will of all its people. The United States did
not wish to dictate to the Koreans or to obtain any special privilege. It was our view that the Korean Commission should proceed with its task, and we made some detailed suggestions of
methods and procedures they might find useful. Stress was laid
on the point that the elections should be for a *national* assembly. As the Commission observed the elections:

[it] might be hoped that it would not be obstructed in its work
when it reached the 38th parallel, but even if that should prove to
be the case, two-thirds of the Korean people would have elected
their proportional share of the National Assembly. One-third of the
people would have been denied the opportunity of electing their
own representatives to the Assembly, and the Korean people and
the whole world would know who had denied them that opportunity. Nevertheless, a Korean National Assembly would exist, would
be in a position to consult with the Commission on the establishment of a National Government of Korea, as envisaged in the General Assembly Resolution, and might be able to negotiate with Ko-

reans in the North regarding their participation in the National Government.

We introduced a draft resolution which affirmed that it was "incumbent upon the United Nations Temporary Commission in Korea" under the terms of the General Assembly resolution of November 14, 1947, and in the light of subsequent developments, "to implement the program. . . . in such parts of Korea as are accessible to the Commission."

I joined in the debate again on February 25. The psychological moment for such an intervention is a matter of nice appraisal of the attitude of other delegations and the way in which the discussion is going. Such an appraisal requires experience in UN meetings, and this was my first participation in a meeting of this type. I therefore relied on my "coach," just like a member of a football squad who awaits the moment when the coach tells him to dash out on the field to substitute for one of the players. My coach was David Wainhouse of UNA in the State Department, and he had all the qualifications for the role. He was skilled not only in parliamentary diplomacy but also as a cellist.*

The main point I stressed in my intervention was that under the General Assembly's resolution, the Commission was to supervise elections to a Korean *national* assembly and it was then for that assembly to establish a *national* government for Korea. In the view of the U.S. delegation, the national government so established would remain open to future participation by "other elements of the population of all Korea." This argument was designed to influence other delegates who feared that they might be voting for the perpetual division of Korea. Menon, the chairman of the Commission, told me that the statement I made for the United States had persuaded him to

* When we landed at Cherbourg en route to the 1948 session of the General Assembly in Paris, we were impressed to see David greeted on the dock by a Frenchman delivering to him a new bow for his cello which he had ordered from Washington.

change his position and come over to our side. My statement continued with a proposal which the Committee approved—I do not recall whose idea it was. The proposal was that the resolution to be adopted should be short and concise, but that the Commission should annex to the resolution a report containing an explanation of the reasons which had led the Committee to adopt the resolution. Such a report, I suggested, might contain the following points:

That it should give an affirmative reply to the first question raised by the Temporary Commission with a view to ensuring full application of the General Assembly's Resolutions; recognize that these Resolutions provided for the election of representatives of the Korean people and the constitution, by these representatives, of a national assembly, even in the present circumstances; stress the need for ensuring the holding of free elections in an atmosphere of order and justice; that the Interim Committee should take note of the United States undertaking to co-operate fully, to this end, with the United Nations Temporary Commission on Korea; that the national assembly, when elected, as provided for, should not constitute the final or complete form of Korean government since it was for the Korean people themselves to decide on the final form of their national government. Lastly, that when the members of the national assembly were elected, they should be encouraged by the very terms of the General Assembly's Resolutions to consult the Temporary Commission as to further measures for achieving their independence, and that then as now they should endeavour in complete freedom to consult also with Koreans in other parts of the country or other political groups which had not taken part in the elections, in order to determine the form of government which the Korean people wished to establish.

After a short debate, the Interim Committee decided to request the U.S. representative to prepare a note containing the suggestions he had submitted, in order that they might be considered at the Committee's next meeting to be held on Thursday, February 26.

Accordingly, on the following day I read the statement which we had elaborated, and the U.S. resolution was then carried by a vote of 31 to 2 with 11 abstentions. The negative votes were those of Australia and Canada, but New Zealand gave the United States strong support. The abstainers included three Latin American delegates, five from the Middle East, and three Scandinavians. But Lebanon spoke effectively in favor of the U.S. resolution and we learned that other members of the Committee were favorably impressed by the fact that our relations with the Canadians and Australians were excellent despite the difference of opinion on the merits.

The Temporary Commission on Korea was split when it came to vote on the question whether it should accept the conclusion of the Interim Committee, but it decided by a majority vote to do so and the elections were duly held on May 10, 1948. Professor Goodrich summarizes the results:

The election appears to have gone off more smoothly than most members of the Commission had anticipated. Out of a total population of about 20 million, 7,036,750 voted; those voting constituted about 72 per cent of the qualified voters. A substantial number no doubt abstained in protest, as the leftist groups had organized a boycott of the elections. Nevertheless, the number of abstentions was considerably smaller than had been anticipated by members of the Commission. . . . While there were claims of irregularities, the evidence submitted was not such as to cause the Commission to believe that the outcome of the election had been materially affected.[7]

It was nearly two years after the decision of the Interim Committee, when my wife and I, having embarked on the trip which John Davies had suggested in the preceding July, arrived in Tokyo on January 5, 1950. There we were guests of General Douglas MacArthur who, one might say, then reigned in Japan in place of the emperor. He very kindly loaned his own beautifully fitted plane, *The Bataan,* to fly us to Seoul for our Korean visit, the first of the independent states on our itinerary.[8]

In Seoul there were the usual festivities. I was then U.S. Ambassador-at-Large, and we stayed with our Ambassador to

Korea, John Muccio, one of the ablest and most outspoken of our career diplomats. He was probably the only person who could talk back to the octogenarian Korean President, Syngman Rhee, and be listened to. We were taken up to the 38th parallel, where we walked through trenches and looked through field glasses to see the emplacements of the North Koreans not far away. The Koreans were anxious and worried about an invasion from the North, which actually came five months later. They clamored for more arms, and our military advisers urged that they be furnished anti-aircraft and anti-tank guns and other weapons. In a personal letter to Dean Rusk on January 15, 1950, I recommended such supplying and the State Department tried to get action from Congress but did not succeed. Actually President Truman had urgently requested substantial economic aid for Korea, but this legislation was defeated in the House on January 19. Truman and Dean Acheson, as Secretary of State, strongly pressed for a reversal of the vote and finally an aid bill was passed on February 10. But adequate military supplies were not furnished and when the attack of the Communists came on June 25, 1950, the South Koreans could not stop them. But this is not an account of the Korean war.

At the risk of being convicted of egotism, I am bound, in order to justify the title of this book, to quote some passages from the speech of the Korean Foreign Minister, Ben Limb, at a ceremony at the Seoul National University when on January 13, 1950, they conferred on me an honorary degree. One is well aware on such an occasion that it is not an individual person who is being honored, but the representative of the United States; it was one of the ways in which the Koreans showed their appreciation of the support they had received from the United States. The picturesque imagery of Ben Limb was intended to be flattering, although as one reads it today it is amusing.

Foreign Minister Limb described the progress which the Republic of Korea had made and said:

But this Republic could not have done all this if it were not born first. . . . It is a far cry from those bleak days of 1947 when the birth of our nation was a matter of grave question. Anxiety was in the air. The labour of birth was intense. Our nerves were shredded by the pains induced by Soviet poison. The world stood aghast, fearful that this Red poison might produce a stillborn child.

But God was with us. He gave us a skillful midwife, named Jessup! There, in the birth chamber at Lake Success, in the cold November of 1947, the battle raged between the Soviet poison and American blood transfusion. The skill with which the stream of pure blood of American Democracy was transfused by Midwife Jessup finally saved the life of the baby Republic of Korea. I know because I was there!

In those sensitive days, in the great halls of the United Nations, when the cold, cruel barkings of the Soviet Russians and their satellites were as biting as the icy blasts out on the open meadows of Flushing, Dr. Jessup in his great dignity showed the listening world how unworthy were the Soviet attempts of sly aggression. Day in and day out, I sat in those UN halls, my eyes glued on Dr. Jessup's lips, praying to the Almighty to give increased strength and wisdom to this great international lawyer. Those were dramatic days!

First a few nations stood up for Korea and Dr. Jessup. Then some more. When Dr. Jessup put in his final rebuttal, a veritable stampede of nations occurred for Korea and Jessup. There the famous UN Resolution of November 14, 1947 became a reality. Midwife Jessup triumphed, for there the birth of the Korean Republic was assured. The UN Commission on Korea then began to act. The May 10th election was held. The Government of the Republic of Korea was established on August 15, 1948.

Regardless of the literal inapplicability of the Foreign Minister's metaphor, one can note in the *Random House Dictionary* that an alternative definition of a midwife is "a person or thing that assists in a creative process." One may say that the United Nations was the "thing" and I happened to be one of the "persons" who did assist in the UN's creation of the Republic of

Korea. As Professor Goodrich says, the adoption of the resolution by the Interim Committee in 1948 "was an act of the greatest importance for all concerned." [9] It was a victory for a United Nations solution of the problem of establishing a Korean government. It was a victory for the United States since it was only in this way that the American occupation forces could be withdrawn. It was a victory for a great majority of the Korean people who wanted independence and who could not have obtained it in any other way.

In the light of subsequent events, when the North Koreans attacked across the 38th parallel, the role of the United Nations in helping to establish the Republic of Korea added a particular reason for invoking the United Nations and contributed to the stand of many governments in support of resistance to the aggression. In contrast, the United Nations played no role in the evolution of the independent states of Indochina and there was no comparable inclination to have the Security Council play a part in trying to make peace in Southeast Asia.

It has taken twenty-four years to prove unfounded the fears of those governments who opposed the Korean elections in 1948 on the ground that the country would be permanently divided. On July 4, 1972, a joint (North and South) Korean communiqué announced agreed principles for "reunification of the fatherland," including the declaration that "as a homogeneous people, a great national unity shall be sought above all, transcending differences in ideas, ideologies and systems."

Who can say that without elections there would have been no bloodshed? As for the stretch of twenty-four years, in Elihu Root's famous apothegm, that is "Long as measured by our lives, perhaps, but not long as measured by the lives of nations."

3

Indonesia Is Born

The story of the birth of Indonesia as an independent state after centuries of Dutch colonial rule is intimately connected with the united Nations from that Organization's earliest days. The period of gestation proved to be a long one. The first session of the UN General Assembly met on January 10, 1946, and it was in the next month that there was a Ukrainian proposal for a United Nations commission of inquiry into what Russia's Andrei Vyshinsky described as the attempt of British and Japanese troops to suppress the Indonesian nationalist movement. This proposal received the votes of only the Ukraine, the USSR, and Poland. It was generally, and plausibly, thought that this Soviet move was designed as a riposte to the backing by the United States and Great Britain of Iran's appeal on January 19, 1946, to the Security Council against Soviet support of an insurgent movement in Iran.*

* The United States favored the action which the Security Council then took, which was merely to encourage the continuance of the negotiations between Iran and the USSR. Iran reintroduced the issue in March 1946 after Acting Secretary of State Dean Acheson told the Iranian ambassador that we could not act for, but only in support of, the Iranian government. Ensuing discussions in the Security Council led to Soviet Ambassador Gromyko's absenting himself from

Briefly, the essential factual background of the Indonesian situation as it engaged the attention of the United Nations from 1946 on was as follows. During the war, Indonesia had been occupied by the Japanese who, in pursuance of their effective propaganda of "Asia for the Asians," had permitted the formation of an Indonesian independence preparatory committee to prepare for ultimate independence. Two Indonesians taking a leading part in these steps were Sukarno and Mohammed Hatta, who proclaimed the independence of the Indonesian Republic as early as August 1945.

When the war ended, the Allies nonetheless transferred the military control of Indonesia from General MacArthur to the British, pending the reestablishment of Dutch civil administration. The British thus had the responsibility for disarming the Japanese, but in dealing with Sukarno and Hatta found themselves embroiled with their Dutch allies, who considered the Republic a Japanese puppet state created by collaborators with whom they would not negotiate. A frail bridge was built when Sukarno asked Soetan Sjahrir, who had refused to deal with the Japanese, to form a cabinet largely composed of those who had resisted Japan. But negotiations between the Dutch and Sjahrir broke down until patched up under British auspices.

Finally, on November 15, 1946, there was signed what is known as the Linggadjati Agreement in which both sides made concessions. The Indonesian Republic agreed to a federal type of government of which it would form part, and the Netherlands recognized the existence of the Republic. What kind of "recognition" this was, continued to be disputed, especially when the Republic attempted to establish its own foreign relations with the United Kingdom, the United States, Australia, China, India, and several Arab states, all of which recognized the Republic *de facto*.

---

the Council meetings—a precedent which the Russians followed in 1950, thus unintentionally enabling the Security Council to act on the invasion of Korea.

In July 1947, following a period of disorders, the Dutch announced that they no longer considered themselves bound by the Linggadjati Agreement and resorted to what they called a "police action." India and Australia called upon the Security Council to act. India invoked Chapter VI of the Charter of the United Nations while Australia called for stronger action under Chapter VII to end the threat to the peace. As they had argued against the Ukrainian item in the preceding year, the Dutch alleged that this was a question within their domestic jurisdiction, since Indonesia was not a sovereign state. This argument was based on Article 2(7) of the Charter which provides that the United Nations is not authorized "to intervene in matters which are essentially within the domestic jurisdiction of any state . . ."

The United States was ready to support a move by Belgium (which throughout acted as best friend to the Netherlands) to ask the International Court of Justice for an advisory opinion on the issue of domestic jurisdiction. The Permanent Court of International Justice in 1923 had rendered a famous advisory opinion on the domestic jurisdiction clause of Article 15(8) of the Covenant of the League of Nations and the United States was not reluctant to allow the successor Court to deal with the similar problem under Article 2(7) of the UN Charter. (The old Court's opinion had been rendered in connection with French nationality decrees in Tunisia and Morocco and it was in connection with those two protectorates that the issue was frequently raised after the establishment of the United Nations.) In the Indonesian case, the Council was prepared to and did move quickly, but did not favor reference to the Court. On August 1, 1947, it called for a cease-fire and a settlement of the dispute by arbitration or other peaceful means. The question of domestic jurisdiction was sidestepped, the United States view being that the adoption of a cease-fire resolution was in any event within the Council's competence. Since fighting continued, the Soviet Union proposed the appointment of a commission composed of all members of the Council to supervise the cease-fire. On that proposal China and the United Kingdom abstained, the United States voted in favor, and France vetoed.

The Western powers then resorted to a device which insured the nonparticipation of the Soviet Union in the supervisory body. It was a little less obvious than saying that the commission should be composed of the representatives of those members of the Security Council whose names, in French, did not begin with "U," but the result was achieved by having the commission composed of those members of the Security Council who had career consuls in Batavia (as Jakarta was called then) —the Soviet Union had no consul there. Similar descriptive devices were considered in subsequent years in connection with the troubles in Palestine.

The Indonesians had wanted the appointment of an actual organ of the Security Council, but that was not technically the status of the Consular Commission in Batavia since the resolution merely called on the states with consuls there—Australia, Belgium, China, France, the United Kingdom, and the United States—to ask those officers to observe the operation of the cease-fire and to keep the Council informed. This technical difference was designed to meet the Dutch objection to actual UN participation in what they claimed was a domestic question. The Dutch representative in the Security Council announced his government's willingness to have the consuls function in this way.

On August 25 and 26, 1947, the Security Council again called on the parties to respect its earlier resolution and appointed a Good Offices Commission (GOC)* to be composed of one member designated by the Netherlands, one by the Repub-

---

* "Good Offices" is a technical term which describes the role of an intermediary who acts merely as a channel of communication between the parties to a dispute. The Good Officer is thus differentiated from a "mediator" who may himself initiate proposals which he submits to the parties.

lic of Indonesia, and a third to be chosen by the first two. The proposal for this solution originated in the State Department. The stipulated procedure resulted in the naming of Belgium and Australia, with the United States as the third member. Thereafter for three years the United States remained not in the eye of the hurricane, which is a spot of relative calm, but in the center of the vortex toward which the swirling elements were constantly drawn.

The United States was represented in Indonesia during the efforts to solve the problem by three men of very different types. President Truman appointed as our first representative on the GOC, the president of the University of North Carolina, Frank P. Graham, a kindly gentleman devoted to the cause of peace through the United Nations, who subsequently had the frustrating task of serving as UN representative with the India-Pakistan Commission concerned with the question of Kashmir. The second man was Coert du Bois, a Foreign Service officer who served during what one may call "the middle period" until his health broke down. The third was Merle Cochran, a top-ranking officer in the Foreign Service, who supplied the toughness and strength needed finally to bring about a settlement. Each of the three had able assistants.

Before the United Nations established the GOC, the United States itself tendered its good offices, but then cooperated fully with the UN Commission. In the President's annual report to Congress on the United Nations for 1947, it is said that the purpose of the GOC was "both to insure the cessation of hostilities in Indonesia and to make easier the coming together of the parties to iron out their difficulties. . . . This is the first time that this procedure of pacific settlement of a dispute has been undertaken by the United Nations."

The U.S. government frequently invoked its "neutrality" as a member of the Commission but actually played the dominant role as a mediator while Australia (in large part) and Belgium acted as advocates of the parties who designated them. Graham

would have welcomed a strictly neutral role but could not tolerate the lack of progress and, at a later stage, joined his Australian colleague in submitting informally to the two parties a
plan for an overall political settlement. Joseph Scott, one of the
able deputies to the U.S. member of the GOC, has told me how
it came about that this proposal was broached and finally accepted aboard a United States warship, the naval transport
U.S.S. *Renville*.

Scott had talked with Dean Rusk, who was in charge of UN
matters, in October 1947 before leaving the State Department
to take up his duties in Indonesia. If any unforeseen trouble
developed which might call for an American public ship, Scott
was told he should telephone Rusk. The GOC held its first
meeting in Australia and was confronted by the fact that the
Dutch insisted on meeting in Indonesia, while the Indonesians
demanded that they meet elsewhere. Scott telephoned as arranged, and was told to go to Singapore to talk with the U.S.
Commander in Chief of the Western Pacific about the avail-
ability of a suitable ship. The *Renville* was made available and
gave its name to the agreement reached on board on January
17, 1948. Captain David Tyree, who commanded the *Renville*,
is credited with a share in the successful result.

The basis for the agreement was worked out by Scott and his
colleague Charlton Ogburn and broached privately by Graham
to the Dutch Governor General van Mook and his deputy van
Vredenburgh, saying that he wished to show them what was
merely a "delegation working paper." Van Mook did not read
the paper but handed it to van Vredenburgh. About a week
later, Scott recalls, van Vredenburgh, late one night asked Ogburn and Scott to come to see him at the palace. It seemed
strange that Graham had not been asked, but after consulting
him, the two men went to the palace. Van Vredenburgh was
standing in the hallway to greet the two Americans; he had a
glass of champagne in his hand and a servant stood by with two
other glasses for Ogburn and Scott. Van Vredenburgh said he

wanted to congratulate "les enfants terrible"; their "informal working paper" had been adopted by the U.S. State Department which had convinced the Dutch government that it must be accepted. Accordingly, he said, they were prepared to meet with the Indonesians on the *Renville*.

Essentially, as finally embodied in the Renville Agreement, the plan provided for the later recognition by the Netherlands of a United States of Indonesia of which the Republic of Indonesia would be a component part. In the meantime sovereignty was to remain in the Netherlands, thus postponing the birth of an independent state. It seems that the Dutch and the Indonesians signed with conflicting understandings of what had been agreed to, but at the time it was considered an achievement of the GOC and applauded by both the Dutch and the United States governments.

Secretary of State George Marshall signed a telegram, approved by Dean Rusk and others representing the UNA and Southeast Asian divisions of the State Department, congratulating Graham on bringing the parties together and paying tribute to his patient efforts "in making the Good Offices Commission an effective instrument of the United Nations." In March, Dutch Ambassador Eelco van Kleffens sent an official letter to the Department expressing the thanks of his government to Graham.

The attempt to carry out the agreement revealed the wide differences in interpretation. The Australian and U.S. representatives proposed a compromise plan which the Republic accepted but the Netherlands rejected. This plan provided for elections in Java, Sumatra, and Madura, to a constituent assembly charged with the duties of selecting an interim government to operate prior to the transfer of sovereignty, and of drafting a constitution for the United States of Indonesia.

The story is a long one and I try to give just the highlights. However, it is only by following the drama act by act that one can bring out to the full the conflicting pulls of American in-

terests in building up the Western European community, so
ravaged by the war, and at the same time in establishing
friendly relations with the emerging countries of Asia, the Middle East, and northern Africa. At this stage, the term "third
world" had not yet been coined and the delivery of the independent African states south of the Sahara was still distant. As
will be noted, the interest of the United States in European affairs, usually predominant as it was with the French in Indochina, took second place in the Indonesian case—not, I think,
because the Netherlands is a smaller country than France, but
because the struggle of the Indonesians for their independence
was perhaps more widely known in the United States, aroused
greater sympathy in those years closer to the time when we had
broken up Japan's co-prosperity sphere, and gained substantial
support in the Congress. Moreover, in Indonesia, no native opponents of the able leaders of the Republic had the standing or
prominence with which in Indochina Ho Chi Minh opposed
the rather ineffectual Bao Dai. We thought the Dutch were
stubborn and uncooperative; the Dutch considered us ignorant
and interfering. Throughout, the cold war was a dominant factor, and one of the principal motivations was the felt need to
"contain" communism.

It is only for developments in and after 1948 that I have the
documents which enable me to explore the details of this case.
As noted in chapter 2, I had served as Ambassador Warren
Austin's deputy in the Interim Committee of the General Assembly (commonly known as the "Little Assembly") from January to June 1948, but there I dealt with the early stages of the
Korean case and with general plans for the organization of procedures for pacific settlement. I was one of the three United
States representatives to the second special session of the General Assembly from April 16 to May 14, 1948, but in that session I represented the United States in the debates on Palestine. I became Deputy Chief of the U.S. Mission to the United
Nations (USUN) and deputy representative on the Security

Council on June 3, 1948. I find it necessary to mention these biographical details to explain why I do not try to give a full history of the Indonesian case in the United Nations but concentrate instead on a limited part of the entire period.

Although the usual conflict between the views of those officers in the Department in charge of West European Affairs and those concerned with Asian and UN matters was evident during most of the Indonesian case, congressional attitudes and public opinion, generally, favored the Indonesians. Secretary of State George Marshall, with his experience in guerrilla warfare in the Philippines, was convinced that the Dutch could not obtain a military victory and therefore supported plans favoring Indonesian independence, while Robert Lovett, as Under and Acting Secretary of State, was more inclined to help the Dutch in their effort to find a solution by maintaining their position. Many of our Dutch friends were bitter. I found particularly disturbing letters from Dutch veterans who had fought with the liberating American army in Holland and who sent back their American decorations with strong language about our "treachery" to an ally.

The diversity of views in the State Department had already appeared from a draft memorandum dated January 5, 1948, and written by William Lacy, Assistant Chief of Southeast Asian Affairs (SEA), and by Frederick Nolting of the European Bureau (EUR). It was designed to go to the Secretary over the signatures of Jack Hickerson, Chief of EUR, and Walton Butterworth, Chief of the Far Eastern Bureau (FE), but they did not approve it. The memorandum commented on recent cables from Frank Graham in Batavia which suggested that the United States must now choose between supporting the Dutch and supporting the Republic; Lacy and Nolting recommended we support the Dutch.

A telegram had been sent to Graham on January 7, confirming a telephone message to him from Dean Rusk, who was then Director of the Bureau of United Nations Affairs (UNA), say-

ing that the Department would back up and support Graham.
However, Dutch acceptance of an agreement with the Republic
must not be exacted in Washington but achieved on the *Renville;* ten days later the Renville Agreement was signed.

The Security Council considered the First Interim Report of
the GOC on February 17, and was in general pleased with the
conclusion of the agreement, although the Soviet representative
accused the GOC of bringing improper pressure on the Republic to accept the Dutch "ultimatums." In the Department,
UNA, FE, and EUR all approved a memorandum for the Secretary of State to guide him in talking to the Dutch ambassador, in which there was much stress on the killings and reprisals by the Dutch military forces.[1] The Dutch, it was written,
had been reluctant to allow additional military observers from
Great Britain and Australia, had attacked the GOC, and had
sought to undermine the Republic's confidence in Graham. Instructions to the U.S. Mission to the United Nations by telephone and telegraph stressed strong support for the Renville
principles. On February 28, 1948, the Council adopted two resolutions, both supported by the United States. One asked the
GOC to report to the Council on the Indonesian complaint
that the Dutch were already violating the Renville Agreement
by constituting new states on conquered Republican territory,
and the other expressed general satisfaction that agreement had
been reached on the Renville principles.

As the months passed, the attitude in the State Department
changed. For example, although at the Mission in New York
we worked closely with the Republic's representative, L. N.
Palar, the Dutch informed the Department that they had intercepted telegrams from Hatta to Palar urging him to stir up the
Security Council. The Department agreed with the Dutch that
further action in the Security Council should be deferred while
they sought agreement in Batavia; Graham was accordingly instructed to ask Hatta to stop his instructions to Palar.

At this point in February 1948, Foreign Service Officer

Coert du Bois, replaced Graham in Batavia and warned the Department that if the Dutch used military force, with probable initial successes, the situation would soon deteriorate into one like that in Indochina. On May 28, the American embassy in The Hague reported that the prestige of the Security Council was at low ebb and that U.S. interference was resented. The embassy thought the Dutch army might have to be used. Its maintenance was a heavy economic burden and Dutch military circles believed their army could win a quick victory and then the troops could be brought home—their "bring-the-boys-home" problem was not very different from ours at the end of World War II. Quite naturally, our embassy at The Hague promoted the point of view of the government to which it was accredited; in the same telegram there were rather scornful references to "untried Indonesian democracy."

On May 28 also, the Department cabled our representatives in Batavia expressing doubts whether the Republic really wanted to carry out the Renville principles now that that agreement had immobilized the Dutch army. There were reports, fostered by the Dutch, that the Republic was leaning toward the Communist party, which had strength in the islands. Rumors and denials flew back and forth. The Netherlands embassy in Washington kept assuring the Department that the Dutch would not resort to military action, which Ambassador van Kleffens said early in June would be obvious foolishness, but the Department thought van Kleffens did not fully agree with his government's policies. The Department accepted these assurances and told du Bois to reassure the Republican delegation. But du Bois, at the outset considered by the Department to be pro-Dutch, was now the target of heavy Dutch criticism reported by our embassy in The Hague. Contrary to what van Kleffens was saying, the embassy reported that the Dutch government could not bind itself never to use its army.

It was at this stage that du Bois and Thomas Critchley, his Australian colleague on the GOC, presented their plan jointly,

but on a personal basis, to Hatta and Lieutenant Governor-
General van Mook; the proposal could not be made by the
GOC since the Belgian member would not agree; the Dutch
protested against the initiative of the two members. Du Bois
said their "working paper" was one gesture of United States belief and confidence in the ability of the Indonesians to govern
themselves. He told the Department that if their plan was not
supported, his usefulness would be ended, United States prestige in Southeast Asia would sink to a new low, and there
would be great damage to the United Nations. "This," he said,
"is all we can do. The rest is up to the Department." Ambassador van Kleffens said the du Bois-Critchley plan had been
leaked to the press and would be published in *Time* magazine.
The Department warned du Bois to keep the plan private, to
stick to his role as a "good officer" and not to try to arbitrate;
du Bois said it was the Dutch who leaked the story to the press.

When the Security Council took up the Indonesian case on
June 17, I was authorized to make a statement which led the
President of the Council to modify his intention to call on the
GOC for full background information. Since du Bois was asked
by the Department to be guided by that statement as to the
timing and substance of a GOC report to the Security Council,
the gist of it needs to be quoted:

It seems to me [I said] that the Security Council is, happily, still
operating in this matter in the general realm of agreement of the
parties. We are not dealing with a situation in which failure has resulted from the efforts of the Security Council and the Committee
of Good Offices. We are not sitting in judgment on a case in which
one or the other party has brought about a failure of negotiations. . . .

I am sure that the Security Council would not wish to transmit
any instructions or requests which, in the judgment of the Committee so closely in touch with the situation as it exists, might hamper
it in its work. I think that if it were true that the Security Council
had decided that it, at this distance from the scene, would itself undertake the actual mediation between the parties, and if the Com-

mittee of Good Offices were merely an agent for collecting information on the spot and transmitting it to the Security Council, which would then conduct the negotiations between the parties, we might very well ask at each point that they tell us all these facts, that they give us their judgment as to whether this party is correct in its assertion or whether that party is correct. But that, I take it, is not the situation. . . . The Security Council in this case is following, as I think it has wisely followed in other cases—notably at present on the case of Palestine—the practice of leaving a large measure of responsibility and discretion to those on the spot who are charged with the mediatory function. . . .

Nothing, it seems to me, could be more injurious to the continuing conduct of the mediatory function than to compel the person in the position of the mediator to make public declarations as to the justification of the position of this or that side at various stages of the proceedings. . . . I believe that we should leave it to the discretion of the Committee of Good Offices to furnish the Security Council with the information which is pertinent and necessary for the purposes of the Council. Those purposes, surely, are to continue to exercise good offices through the Committee and to further the progress of the negotiations between the parties.

Thus, in my opinion, we should not attempt to press the Committee of Good Offices to register judgment on the merits of the positions taken by the parties, and we should not attempt to elicit positions taken by the Committee on questions of the justification or non-justification of those positions. . . .

On June 23, I made another statement in the Security Council, which I had elaborated with Charles Noyes of the U.S. Mission, and Joseph Scott, who became the U.S. deputy representative on the GOC. The statement declared that while we did not back any one plan, we thought all GOC suggestions and the du Bois-Critchley plan should be considered. We in New York and the officers in the Department were at a disadvantage since we had not then received the full text of the plan.

On July 6, 1948, du Bois, his health impaired by the strenuous pressure of the task, left Batavia for the United States. The Department selected to succeed him one of the outstanding members of the Foreign Service, Merle Cochran, who even-

tually became the first U.S. ambassador to the independent
state of Indonesia.

By July 12, the Department had been able to study the text
of the du Bois-Critchley plan and to suggest amendments. Divisions of opinion were reconciled, as shown by a memorandum
prepared for Acting Secretary Lovett by Nolting, Acting Assistant Chief of the Division of Northern European Affairs, and
cleared by Samuel Reber as Deputy Director of EUR, Butterworth as Director of FE, and Rusk as Director of UNA. The
memorandum said that the evidence indicated that Dutch
thinking was crystallizing in a way which raised the question
whether the United States should continue to be a member of
the GOC.* It was believed that if the United States stood
firmly behind the redraft of the du Bois-Critchley paper, the
GOC as such and the two parties probably would accept it unless in the meantime the Dutch committed themselves to some
alternate course. It was realized that the recent Dutch elections
showed some shift to the right which made it harder for the
Dutch government to compromise. (This is an angle which
Dirk Stikker, the Dutch Foreign Minister, stresses in his memoirs and which was frequently pointed out by the U.S. embassy
in The Hague; the division of opinion in the Netherlands was
reflected in the Dutch parliament and in the press as well.
Other views were held by the Dutch officials and the military
in Indonesia. There were even differences between the Queen's
Court and the Foreign Office. As one former American Foreign
Service officer has expressed it to me, the problem of colonialism had become for many Dutch people, after the war, a problem of conscience.) A new U.S. team, Cochran and Scott, was
going to Batavia. Lovett was urged to talk to Ambassador van
Kleffens, stating that the Dutch seemed to think the GOC

---

* This point was raised repeatedly, the idea being that as a member of the
GOC we had to be neutral and not favor either side; if the Dutch actions forced
us to take sides against them, we would first have to abandon our neutral status
on the GOC.

should be merely an advocate of Dutch ideas but actually no plan had a chance of being adopted unless it originated in the GOC. The United States should give its advice to the Dutch government even though this involved even further responsibilities. Lovett acted upon the memorandum and was assured by van Kleffens that the Dutch parliament would not freeze the situation by enacting new legislation; any new law would be purely permissive.

The Security Council suddenly scheduled a meeting on Indonesia for July 27, 1948, after the Indonesians broke off the discussions under the GOC's auspices. The Department telegraphed our representatives in Batavia that it hoped the Indonesian delegation would be instructed to tell the Council that negotiations were not broken off and that the GOC had excellent prospects for success. The Department had adequate assurances from the Netherlands that negotiations would be resumed as soon as Cochran arrived on the scene. But the word from Ogburn of the U.S. delegation with the GOC in Batavia (in an "eyes only" for Charles Reed, Chief of SEA) was that the Republic was convinced the United States was supporting the Dutch and our reluctance to use the Security Council confirmed that view. The Republic believed that a solution could not come from the GOC but only from Washington. The U.S. representatives on the GOC complained that they had had no recent instructions from the Department and no comment on the du Bois-Critchley paper, which I had told the Security Council was not to be submitted to it.

On July 28 also, I sent from New York a memorandum to Dean Rusk containing the draft of a statement I planned to make in the Security Council regarding a GOC report on trade restrictions in Indonesia. I said that our purpose was to support the GOC but to avoid a Security Council resolution condemning the Dutch. We would support an expected Chinese resolution calling on both parties to resume negotiations. My draft was approved by telephone and I used it in the Security

Council on July 29 when a resolution was adopted urging the parties to comply with the Renville principles. This was a day after Cochran had stopped to see us in New York; I asked him to get us more information on aspects of the du Bois-Critchley plan which seemed to me to be anti-Republic.

On the following day Reed replied to the telegram from Og- burn, outlining the Department's policies at that time. He re- peated the Dutch assurances that they did not contemplate fur- ther police action but would transfer sovereignty in accordance with the Renville Agreement. The United States intended to maintain its neutrality as a friend of both parties. The Depart- ment was far from opposing Indonesian nationalist aspirations. It was impressed with the current Dutch attitude but Dutch predilections were not the reason for the Department's opposi- tion to having the negotiations carried on in the Security Council. (It is not clear to me what other reason there was.)

On August 2 the Dutch embassy in Washington sounded an- other note, presumably appealing to the anti-Communist posi- tion of the United States: the Netherlands might have to act against the Communists in Indonesia. The reaction in the De- partment is shown in a telegram to Cochran in Batavia on Au- gust 31. The Department was now worried by the Dutch atti- tude and feared the downfall of the respected Hatta government, which might be succeeded by one controlled by the Communists. Cochran and the Department were in agree- ment that the situation was rapidly deteriorating and a new Dutch proposal to the GOC was essential. But the draft agree- ment which the Dutch had proposed, Scott reported, was not suited to be submitted to the GOC.

James Barco, who had been in Indonesia until August 16, before returning to the UNA office in the Department and working closely with the U.S. Mission to the United Nations in New York, sent on September 3 a graphic description of the sit- uation to his chief, Dean Rusk. Barco said the two parties had almost reached the point where peaceful settlement would be impossible. The Republic believed the Dutch had no intention of transferring true sovereignty to an independent United States of Indonesia; large tracts of the Republic's territory had been lost to the Dutch military forces; the Republic's leaders feared a renewal of Dutch military action which would wipe them out. Barco agreed that Hatta was being overtaken by the Communists. Although Indonesian sentiment was pro-American, they were losing faith in the United States. If the Dutch used force again, the Security Council could not stop it without resort to sanctions and Indonesia would be lost to the West both politically and economically. Barco recommended that the United States submit its own plan to the Dutch with the warning that if they did not in good faith move toward Indonesian independence, the United States would state in the Security Council that the Dutch were not carrying out the Renville Agreement and that the United States would withdraw from the GOC, recognize the Republic, and establish direct trade relations with it.

Cochran and Scott in Batavia generally agreed with Barco's analysis and pleaded for Department support of a plan supplementary to Renville which they had drawn up. On September 8, the Department approved their plan and congratulated Cochran and Scott; the Dutch would be asked to hold up their own proposals.

The next day this stand was reinforced. Cochran could tell Hatta that the United States would support and help him. The American embassy in The Hague was urged to talk informally with officials at the Foreign Office stressing that support for Hatta was the key point. Like messages were sent to Brussels and to Canberra and to the Dutch embassy in Washington. On September 10, I arrived in The Hague with Jack Ross, chief assistant to Ambassador Austin at the United Nations. Ambassador Herman B. Baruch—who does not stand out as a distinguished diplomat—reported that we had talked with Dutch officials on all subjects on the coming General Assembly agenda, and also about Indonesia. Baruch unjustifiably thought we were completely satisfied. Actually we were making a tour of several European capitals in preparation for the General Assembly and our "satisfaction" was not focused on the Dutch policies toward Indonesia although Baruch, as usual, expressed his entire confidence in them. He later reiterated the point that it must be realized that the Dutch government might not command a parliamentary majority for any plan not acceptable to Dutch opinion.

Acting on the Department's authorization, Cochran and Scott presented their plan to both parties, to the dismay of the Dutch, who thought they should have been consulted separately first. As usual, the Indonesians welcomed the plan and the Dutch had objections. It was at this stage that Dutch Foreign Minister Dirk Stikker suggested coming to Washington.

Stikker, who later became a close friend of Dean Acheson's, and I may say of mine, took over the portfolio of Foreign Minister of the Netherlands on August 7, 1948, facing an uneasy domestic political situation and the possibility of renewed Dutch military action in Indonesia. He recognized that the attitude of the United States was crucial and decided to go to Washington. In his memoirs he records with some bitterness that Secretary of State Marshall, after trying to dissuade him from coming to Washington, spared him less than an hour and slight consideration on September 17, although Marshall spent three hours the same evening at a dinner given for him by United Artists where he made a long off-the-record speech in which he outlined the policies which the United States would follow at the coming meeting of the UN General Assembly in Paris. Stikker felt that he failed to impress the Secretary of State with his argument that the Dutch, with three centuries of experience in the Indies, could make wiser decisions than Merle Cochran and the few other American observers who had been there for three months. [2]

The State Department's memorandum of Stikker's conversation with Marshall is rather different. Lovett, Jack Hickerson of UNA, and Butterworth were with the Secretary of State, and Stikker was accompanied by Nico Blom, who came with him from Holland, and by Ambassador van Kleffens. Stikker stressed the Communist menace and the Dutch willingness to help the United States fight communism; this was a usual ploy. Parts of the Cochran plan, he warned, could not rally a majority in the Dutch parliament. Marshall replied that he had followed Indonesian matters closely. He was impressed by the fact that for the first time all elements of the American government concerned with the problem were now unanimous in regarding the Cochran proposals as fair and on the need to act quickly. He referred to his own experience as a mediator * and said that the United States was as opposed to communism as were the Dutch. He cited the experience of the Philippines as illustrative of the importance of supporting nationalism. Matching Stikker's parliamentary difficulties was his trouble with Congress in regard to supporting the Dutch through the European Recovery Program (ERP).[3] In the ensuing talks, after Marshall withdrew, Lovett stressed the vital role of Hatta as the rallying point against Indonesian Communists. The United States position was firm and stern. The Dutch had to meet their own parliamentary problem, but the United States would back Cochran and would not negotiate in Washington any changes in his plan.

Cochran was reporting that the Dutch harassing tactics in Indonesia would make it impossible for Hatta to negotiate but feared this might be a situation which the Dutch were planning as an excuse for police measures. The Republic was simultaneously harassed by a Communist revolt, launched on September 18 and headed by a man named Muso who had just returned from a twelve-year stay in the Soviet Union. Cochran was told to inform Hatta we would give him further economic aid to help put down the Communist revolt but he must not

* He had returned from his China mission in January 1947.

be too rigid in negotiating with the Dutch. The people did not rise to Muso's call, the Republic's army suppressed the revolt by the end of October 1948 and Muso was killed in a skirmish. R. K. Nehru, the Indian Minister, had told Butterworth and other departmental officers that India was worried about the Communist situation in Indonesia which had been made more dangerous by the dilatory tactics of the Dutch. Charles Reed called in H. A. Helb of the Dutch embassy, urging a change of tactics; Helb was stiffly uncooperative.

On October 1, 1948, when the U.S. delegation to the General Assembly was in Paris, the Department sent word to Harding Bancroft and Dean Rusk (I was deeply involved in the case of the Berlin Blockade) that they could inform the Chinese President of the Security Council that if the Indonesian case was brought up anew in the Council, it would be more effective for the Council to try to induce a settlement than to increase the powers of the GOC. If the group in Paris and Cochran agreed, and if the Security Council resumed its consideration of Indonesia, the Department would tell the Dutch embassy that it supported Cochran's proposals, would support appropriate Security Council measures to give them effect, and would help the parties carry them out. If thereafter there was no prospect of settlement, the United States might withdraw from the GOC. On the same day, the Dutch embassy told the Department that they were complying with the U.S. desire for friendlier negotiations.

On October 4, Secretary Marshall, who had arrived in Paris for the General Assembly, accompanied by Ambassador Jefferson Caffery and Charles Bohlen, met with British Foreign Secretary Ernest Bevin and his aide, Frank Roberts. Bevin sought to intercede for the Dutch but Marshall replied with strong assertions of complete agreement between American representatives in Batavia and in Washington that the Dutch were stalling. Bevin said that the Dutch made the mistake of thinking that a few troops could clean up a jungle country; the British knew better but the Dutch troops were restive. (The United States, like the French, later made the same mistake in Vietnam.) Marshall with Harding Bancroft also met with Dr. Wang Shih-chieh, the Chinese Foreign Minister and head of their delegation at the General Assembly, repeating what Marshall had told Bevin. Wang feared for the lives of Chinese residents if hostilities were resumed and said that nationalism in Indonesia was so firmly rooted, there was no possibility that the Dutch could win by military measures.

Cochran had taken pains to keep his proposals secret but reported that they were disclosed in a Rotterdam paper, clearly due to an official leak. Such official leaks are no novelty. But Ambassador Baruch, faithful to the Dutch cause, kept reporting from The Hague what Stikker had told him of the chaos in Republican territory; a thousand natives had been murdered and the Republicans were infiltrating Dutch territory. Stikker said he had talked with Paul Henri Spaak, the Belgian Foreign Minister, and with Bevin and Robert Schuman and the Scandinavian Foreign Ministers and that all agreed that elections as proposed in the Cochran plan would be valueless since they would be held amid anarchy, murder, and terror. Stikker warned that the West's defense against communism would be weakened even in Holland as well as in the rest of Western Europe. Baruch reported evidence that the Dutch were planning military action; in Washington van Kleffens sought to introduce a soothing note, praising Cochran's judgment and equanimity. The Department thought he was combatting his Foreign Office and had a 50–50 chance to win. Lovett was taking a hard line in Washington, like Marshall's in Paris.

But on October 12, the Department tried to play both sides of the street. From Washington they asked Palar, the Republic's representative at the United Nations, not to act just yet on his instructions to make a report to the Security Council, and Rusk in Paris was told to delay any convening of the Council. Palar agreed to wait a week, and Dragon Protitch of the Secretariat agreed to hold up for the same time the GOC's telegram to the Council. But the American embassy in The Hague was being instructed that we were impatient with the Dutch delays and that the Indonesians had a right to go to the Security Council. In Paris, however, Jan Herman van Roijen, a very able and fair-minded member of the Dutch delegation to the General Assembly, told Hayden Raynor of the U.S. delegation that the Dutch were united in their opposition to the Cochran plan and did not think Hatta was anti-Communist. (This was just two weeks before the final defeat of the Communist rebels by the forces of the Republic.) Van Roijen added the Dutch were thinking of pulling out of Indonesia as the British had pulled out of Palestine, and asked Raynor to convey this message to Austin or Jessup, whichever one would sit on the Security Council.

The pattern of telegraphic communications on the Batavia-Washington-Paris-Hague circuit was unchanged. A rather pathetic dispatch from the American embassy in The Hague begged the Department not to criticize the Dutch publicly or to encourage the American press to be critical. Public opinion in Holland was inflamed and the role of the United States was questioned and misunderstood in the Dutch press. (The dispatch did not say whether the Dutch government was trying to keep its press from criticizing the Americans.[4]) Fear of another police action was widespread.

At this point, November 1, 1948, Stikker went to Indonesia and made sincere efforts to negotiate with the Indonesians. He risked, and received in the Dutch parliament, severe criticism for making a trip up-country to talk with the Indonesian leaders who were at Kaliurang, on the outskirts of Jogjakarta. In Paris, however, van Roijen warned me that it was violations of the truce by the Republic which made negotiations impossible. Unless such violations ceased, he foresaw limited military action to clear pockets or possibly a more general police action. He repeated his suggestion that the Dutch might withdraw, leaving Indonesia in the UN's lap. Cochran thought this suggestion was pure bluff. In Washington it was noted that the congressional doubts about continuing the aid program to the Netherlands were increasing; the Department was encouraged by Stikker's efforts but wondered if he would succeed in carrying his points at home. If the Dutch proved to be recalcitrant, van Roijen at the United Nations in Paris was to be warned that a Dutch resort to force would have a most unfavorable reaction on American and world opinion. This view was repeated by Cochran to Stikker on the latter's second visit to Batavia, although Cochran was trying to help Stikker and had been instructed to avoid anything like a threat of cutting off aid to an important member of Western Union in the current stage of European developments. Two of Cochran's aides, however, tried unsuccessfully to persuade him to warn the Department that, military action being probable, the Dutch should be held back by whatever sanctions were necessary.

In the first half of December 1948, all the American telegraphic traffic on the Indonesian situation was being repeated to the Paris embassy, much of it being marked "For Jessup only." Perhaps this was to prevent leaks, perhaps merely to indicate to the embassy and to the delegation at the General Assembly that they were not involved, since in Ambassador Austin's absence due to his illness, I was Acting U.S. Representative to the United Nations. A telegram of December 6, which went the circuit of Batavia-Hague-Paris, gave the line that the situation should be played down as much as possible to avoid prejudicing the representations which the United States was making to the Netherlands in an aide-mémoire. It gave our analysis of the Indonesian situation with the statement that we were trying to be helpful so that the Netherlands would not start on a course of action which, no matter how good the motives, could only weaken the newly emerging Western European structure to the lasting disadvantage of the nations composing it. The text of the aide-mémoire was toned down for Stikker's sake and he was grateful, but Lloyd Steere, the American chargé in The Hague, said the Dutch Foreign Office read it with pained surprise. On December 10, van Roijen told James Hyde that, in the light of the Dutch political situation, military action in Indonesia was impossible. Negotiations in Indonesia, he said, had not been broken off, and it would create a very bad situation in Holland if the Security Council met at that time. Palar agreed to a few days' delay. We never doubted van Roijen's sincerity, but on the same day we received the text of the long Dutch reply to the aide-mémoire. It contained an implied threat of police action if the Republic did not accept the Dutch position, which was to set up an interim government in Indonesia without the participation of the Republic. Cochran telegraphed there was now no alternative but resort to the Security Council. The Dutch had closed the door on further help by the GOC in negotiations. If the Dutch carried out their plan, the GOC could not safeguard the truce. Our cooperation with Palar in Paris is indicated by the authorization I received to show him—in case he had not already seen it—a copy of a conciliatory letter which Hatta wrote to Cochran. The letter seemed to open a way to negotiations and was thought to result from Cochran's skillful advocacy.

The solid front in the State Department is indicated by a memorandum sent to Acting Secretary Lovett on December 13 by Hickerson from EUR, Butterworth from FE, and William Sanders, Acting Chief of UNA. After summarizing the nature of the Dutch rejection of our aide-mémoire, the memorandum took as its assumption that if the United States, in the Security Council and separately, stood firm on its previous positions, the Dutch could be persuaded to change their stand. The United States might have to withdraw from the GOC and end at once financial aid, mainly in the form of the $30 million ECA (Economic Cooperation Administration) funds allotted but not yet committed for the first quarter of 1949. The ECA had already advised the Dutch that there was no commitment to further aid for Indonesia even when there was an allotment. The recommendation to Lovett further suggested telling the Dutch we considered it unwise to invest further in that area whose economic and political future was so uncertain; that we were considering recognizing the Republic in accordance with the statement in our aide-mémoire about recovering our freedom of action if the Dutch did not accept our views.

The memorandum warned that if we did not take a stand as strong as that, we might be forced by public opinion in the United States to resort to punitive sanctions which would not lead to a solution. If the Dutch resorted to military action, the reaction in the United States might be so strong as to jeopardize Dutch participation in the military assistance plans which the United States was offering to the governments of Western Europe. A military settlement in Indonesia would not be permanent and would aid the Communists. If we acted as strongly as the memorandum recommended, it was realized that it might force the resignation of the Dutch cabinet but the successor government might be more inclined to agree to a settlement. The United States should take that risk.

On December 17, Nolting and Benjamin Hulley, who were in charge of Northern European Affairs, reinforced those recommendations, stating that it would not endanger the European structure and would have an effective impact on the Dutch. Two days earlier, Hickerson had phoned the chargé in The Hague to convey the same position. He stressed the importance we attached to Hatta's conciliatory letter to Cochran, and said that while we valued our relations with the Netherlands, the Indonesian issue was an important factor not only in those relations but in our general policy.

The Belgians had been consistent supporters of the Dutch but on December 14 Ambassador Alan Kirk reported from Brussels that Spaak thought the Dutch were being obstinate and that military action would hurt everyone. Spaak suggested a top-level meeting of the GOC with the three countries represented by Spaak, Lovett, and probably Herbert Evatt from Australia; they could summon Hatta and the Dutch Foreign Minister to meet with them. The State Department gave serious consideration to this suggestion but thought that the letter from Hatta to Cochran opened the door for negotiations. Moreover, the Spaak plan might seem to the parties to be an attempt to impose a solution on them whereas we thought the solution should result from resumed negotiations. The Department hoped that Spaak could influence the Dutch.

On December 14, the day that Kirk reported Spaak's initiative, I telegraphed the Department that the Dutch representative on the Security Council told me that Hatta had sent a telegram to Stikker which contained important concessions; the Dutch accordingly hoped we could delay a meeting of the Security Council. The delegate of the Republic asked if we wanted to request a delay, but in accordance with the advice received by telephone from Robert McClintock, Rusk's assistant, to my associate in Paris, James Hyde, we said that we were not asking for a delay. The Indonesian representative sent a letter to the Chinese delegate who was then President of the Security Council, stressing the existence of a threat to the peace and asking for a meeting of the Council before it recessed. He wanted the assurance which a Security Council resolution would afford that the situation in his country would not worsen and that negotiations would be resumed under GOC or other auspices. The Council should call upon both sides to refrain from military action during the next three weeks and should ask the GOC to present the case to the Security Council in a full-dress debate in the second week of January. The immediate meeting would not be for the purpose of going into the merits but to draw attention to the seriousness of the situation. Palar and the Australian delegate were both putting pressure on the President of the Council to call a meeting for December 16. I asked for the Department's instructions.

The Department replied promptly. It preferred that there

should be no full-dress debate in the Security Council for several reasons, including the fact that I was in the hospital, that the Council wanted to recess over the holidays, that the Hatta letter gave promise of new productive negotiations, and that it hoped our representations to the Dutch would bear fruit. It suggested that the President of the Council might merely make a statement "taking note" of the situation. If a GOC report was tabled or if a resolution was proposed, I should say that the United States needed time to study the matter and that the Council should ask both governments to report on the progress of the negotiations. I do not know the reason for his action, but the President of the Security Council refused to inscribe the Indonesian item on the provisional agenda and the Council adjourned for a Christmas recess subject to call for an emergency session. Ambassador Jacob Malik of the Soviet Union asked that three days' notice be given of any emergency meeting, but the Council did not agree to his request. It was in the light of this development that my wife and I left for the Riviera on December 17; within twenty-four hours it was clear that I had chosen the wrong time to leave Paris.

December 1948 was for me a hectic month. The Berlin case in the Security Council, for which I was given responsibility, was not very active but on December 11, the last day of the session, the General Assembly established the Palestine Conciliation Commission composed of France, Turkey, and the United States. A little later there was severe fighting in the Negev, and Israeli forces crossed the Egyptian frontier. I represented the United States in the Assembly debates on Palestine, but John Foster Dulles substituted for me in making a speech on December 9 because on the previous day I had gone to the American Hospital in Neuilly with virus pneumonia.

On December 15 I left the hospital just long enough to attend a meeting of the Security Council, where I sat in my overcoat on the stage of the Palais de Chaillot. While the December winds blew through the wings and down my neck, I cast the vote of the United States for the admission of Ceylon to the United Nations, but the Soviets vetoed it. On December 17, my wife and I took the *wagon-lit* for Beaulieu on the Riviera for a period of convalescence. I wrote to my family in America on December 19 that the sun was shining: "The phone just rang—'Paris calling'; the Security Council meets in emergency session on Indonesia tomorrow. A military plane is flying down from Paris to pick me up at the Nice airport and take me back to Paris." The message was from James Hyde, of our delegation in Paris, an old friend of mine who carried the brunt of much of the Indonesian case both in New York and in Paris. Joe Scott was in the plane to brief me; we sat in the radio operator's cubicle in a rather vain attempt to keep warm before we reached Paris late that night. But I must go back and fill in the Indonesia details.

The Dutch government's reply to the Hatta letter sounded like an ultimatum. As the Department understated to the Counselor of the Dutch embassy in Washington, if their delegate read that reply to the Security Council, it would give a very unfavorable impression.

On December 18, Butterworth telephoned Chargé Steere at The Hague at 1 A.M. but did not get the call through for four hours. Steere was to give a sharp warning to the Dutch saying that we would act in the Security Council as we had warned and the Dutch must take the consequences. But Steere reported that Stikker said the Dutch cabinet had already acted and he could not receive Steere, who then spoke to A. H. J. Lovink, a lower official, and apparently watered down Butterworth's warning. Later that day, Stikker told Steere that military action would start in two hours, since many of their troops were due to return home and morale factors required action! From Batavia, Cochran reported the Dutch had lost their temper and would lose their cause. At 11:30 P.M. on December 18, 1948, Cochran was told that the Dutch were terminating the Renville truce. He was refused use of the telegraph to notify the other members of the GOC who were not in Batavia.

On the morning of December 19, Dutch paratroopers captured the airfield at the Republican capital of Jogjakarta. By midafternoon, Sukarno, Hatta, and other cabinet officers of the Republic were captured and imprisoned. The Dutch forces quickly occupied the principal towns in the territory of the Republic. This "police action" unified the State Department in favor of the Indonesians.

McClintock drafted a telegram to Paris which was initialed by Butterworth and Hickerson and cleared in principle by Lovett. It said it was now evident that the Dutch had decided to set up an interim government without the Republic; in my absence, the embassy should at once consult the UN representatives of Belgium and Australia as members of the GOC and ask if they would agree to an emergency session of the Security Council. If they agreed, the request in the name of the three governments should be for a session "tomorrow." If they refused, the embassy in Jessup's name (since I was the only available American authorized to sit in the Security Council) should ask the President of the Council to call the emergency meeting, although the Department would prefer to avoid unilateral action. The main purpose of the meeting would be to warn the parties, expressing concern over the resumption of fighting in violation of the Council's cease-fire order. On a top-secret basis, I was authorized to ask other members of the Council what were the views of their governments about further action, including the sanctions which might be used under Chapter VII of the Charter. They should be told that the United States was making a top-level review of policy and of its Charter commitments, including action under Chapter VII. The GOC, it was clear, had not succeeded in its task and the members of the Council as well as the UN Secretariat should know that the United States would not continue to serve on an organ that was frustrated, if the Council did not support the GOC plan or if both parties rejected it. We would not withdraw, however, until the GOC had had time to report on the immediate situation.

The possibility of delay in the receipt of this telegram, filed in Washingtion at 3 P.M. (9 P.M. Paris time and a Saturday) was met by a telephone call from McClintock to James Hyde, who had just returned to his room at the Hotel Crillon, across the narrow rue Boissy-d'Anglas from the American embassy, which made it a preferred location for U.S. delegations. Hyde had had dinner with Joseph Scott, who was on his way back to the United States after six months' service with the GOC in Indonesia. Hyde was told to call an emergency meeting of the Security Council in my name for the next day, Sunday, and to keep Scott in Paris. He intercepted Scott just as he was about to get into a taxi for the airport. They decided they could not get the Council to meet on Sunday but called a meeting for Monday. Sunday, as already mentioned, Joe Scott flew down in the military attaché's plane to pick me up in Nice and brief me on the flight back to Paris.

In Washington, on December 18, Helb, the Counselor of the Dutch embassy, handed Butterworth a memorandum which sought to explain the basis for the Dutch action. Butterworth pointed out that the alleged bases were not established and that one, it had been admitted in The Hague, was an error. Butterworth recorded that since neither van Kleffens nor Helb was the architect of this Dutch policy he felt free to tell Helb that his government had done a grave disservice to itself and to the "christian nations" of the world. Helb seemed to agree but the next day, following instructions, he again called on the State Department to say that his government had heard that the United States proposed taking the initiative in calling for a session of the Security Council. Such an initiative would have a bad effect on Dutch opinion (again that old refrain!) and Helb hoped we would act only with others. He was told that Paris had been so instructed: Australia had agreed to join the United States but Belgium would not. That same day, December 19, there was another instruction to me on the same lines. The United States, I was told, did not want to assume a position of solitary leadership; so often in the past we had been out in front alone. We should therefore get as many sponsors as possible for Security Council action. (Actually this was standard operating procedure.) I was to call attention to the GOC report that hostilities had broken out and say that the first task of the Security Council was to call for a cease-fire. A resolution to that effect could be offered. The Council could also ask the GOC for a full report. I was informed that the United Kingdom wanted to support the United States in every way possible but was opposed to sanctions.

From Paris we had to report that we were not sure of getting a quorum for the Council meeting, which the Australians had joined us in requesting. The President of the Council that month was Ambassador van Langenhove of Belgium, which was not a helpful element, but he did call a meeting for Monday, December 20. Since the Soviet and Ukrainian delegates had not arrived, the other members of the Council had an informal discussion, agreeing to start the substantive discussion on December 22. But I called attention to our grave concern over the fact that the Belgian and Australian members of the GOC were being prevented from communicating with their U.S. colleagues and with the Australian deputy in Batavia. We then had the support of the Chinese, Syrian, and Colombian delegations for our anticipated resolutions.

In Washington, Acting Secretary Lovett on December 20 reviewed the situation with President Truman, who said that the United States should not hesitate to call the Dutch military action what it actually was, but we should not take a position in the Security Council which we could not maintain either due to the defection of allied nations or to the inadequacy of our own resources. Lovett told Australian Ambassador N. J. O. Makin that the United States as a member of the United Nations was prepared to associate itself wholeheartedly with the actions of that Organization, but we were awaiting detailed reports from Indonesia on the breach of the truce. He repudiated the charges made by an official of the Australian Ministry of External Affairs that the United States was to blame for the situation. In reply to a specific question from Makin, Lovett said that we were studying the problem of sanctions and would soon decide about holding up further aid to the Netherlands under the European Recovery Program. Lovett then received Indonesia's representative, Sumitro, and brought him up to date on the same points. Lovett expressed regret that the Soviets had delayed the Security Council meeting for two days, nor could he make a final statement about sanctions, but said I was discussing the issue in Paris. On that same day, the ECA suspended authorization for securing supplies for the Dutch in Indonesia.

Ambassador van Kleffens called on Lovett on December 21 to deliver a repetition of an old position of the Netherlands. Alluding to a report that I had already branded Dutch action in Indonesia as a breach of the peace, he presented the argument that the Indonesian matter was an internal one with which the United Nations was incompetent to deal. The Netherlands, as a loyal member of the United Nations, had voluntarily accepted the GOC, but a "breach of the peace" was excluded by definition. Lovett replied that he was familiar with the Dutch position on that point and did not propose to go into it then. The Ambassador said that someday the United States would be glad that the Dutch took this action to end chaos and to enable a real United States of Indonesia, including the Republic, to come into being. Twenty years later, a number of my Dutch friends in The Hague (but not including Dirk Stikker) were ready to admit that we had saved them from the tragic waste of lives and money which we failed to persuade the French to avoid, and which we inherited, in Indochina.

That we were saving an ally from catastrophe was indeed the gist of the message which the Department had sent to the American embassy in Moscow on December 17, 1948, in response to that embassy's analysis of the situation. The Department referred to the British military failures in Malaya and those of the French in Indochina where they had merely succeeded at great cost in consolidating Communist control over the Vietnamese nationalist movement. The French now had to reconstruct a nationalist movement making use of uncertain leaders, or fight a hopeless war, or abandon Indochina to the Communists. But to assume in advance that all nationalist movements were Communist would mean that we would have to support the colonial powers all along the line, even though we knew that they could not maintain their positions by force and that the American people were opposed to their attempting to do so. In short, the Department said, if the Dutch army tried to suppress the guerrilla movement in Indonesia, they would be bled. Tragically, the United States itself was to prove the truth of this diagnosis with its own dead and wounded in Vietnam, Laos, and Cambodia.

On December 21, after a breakdown of the telecon, Dean Rusk sent me a long telegram "eyes only" which he said would give me an authoritative background to help me interpret and apply specific instructions. His summary covered much that has already been written here, but as a full picture of departmental thinking just before I was authorized to denounce the Dutch in the Security Council, it deserves repetition.

The conflicting interests of the United States which were affected by the Dutch actions in Indonesia, Rusk stated, were on the one hand the need for solidarity and political and economic stability in Europe, and on the other hand our "long-established policy favoring the rapid development of non-self-governing people toward self-government and independence" and the setting up in colonial areas of governments based on the wishes of the people. The second objective was reinforced by our duty as a member of the United Nations to support the Security Council in maintaining peace. The Dutch action, which was lamentable from all points of view, encouraged the spread of communism, and was a serious blow to the establishment of self-government in the area. The United States did not want "to condone or wink at Dutch action in Indonesia." While the United States must act in good faith as a permanent member of the Security Council to support the United Nations in maintaining peace, we were not obliged to act alone if others were unable or unwilling to share in the task. The Soviet Union would not try to bring about a real settlement quickly; China was incapable of sharing the responsibility; the French and the British were not willing to move fast.

Then came a sentence expressing a doctrine of lasting validity: "The United States cannot accept the role of world policeman either in a military or in a political sense if other permanent members refuse to join in action by the Security Council" for maintaining peace. If the Security Council acted on the basis of the votes of seven members of which only the United States was really able to act, it would involve commitments we did not want and could not undertake.

The message continued by saying that we did not intend a general break with the Dutch; if we priced our association with others on the basis of their reaching the highest standards we would get into "not too splendid isolation." If we had proceeded on that basis, we would have broken with Russia on Berlin and Korea; with Albania, Yugoslavia, and Bulgaria on the Greek issue; with France on Indochina; with Britain and the Arab states on Palestine; with India on Hyderabad; and with Pakistan on Kashmir. Some others might have broken with us had they held us to the same standard.

We wanted peace and a real settlement in Indonesia, it went on, but the Dutch would not agree with us and the Security Council would not impose sanctions. Lacking strong assistance from Britain and France, we must seek full exposure of the facts to rouse world opinion, to bring public pressure on the Dutch, pressing others in the Security Council—especially the British and French—to use their influence. At the same time we must demonstrate to the Asian people the interest of the

United States in promoting self-government in that part of the world as revealed by our record. On the one hand we were to assign full responsibility to the Dutch, and sustain the interest in self-government in the Security Council; on the other hand we were not "(repeat not)" to propose or support sanctions against the Dutch in Europe. There might be some types of sanctions which could be applied to the Dutch in Indonesia but I would need special instructions to advocate them. A Security Council resolution condemning the Dutch if they defied a Security Council resolution was not excluded; but again action must be geared to factual reports from Indonesia and every effort must be made to act jointly with others, especially with the British and French if possible.

I do not have a complete catalogue of the hours at which various messages were received or sent, but the flood of telegraphic and telephonic messages left us in Paris somewhat uncertain about our next steps. I reflected this situation in a telegram to Rusk on December 22 at 5 P.M. (which probably crossed his long background message) saying that we were not sure what the Department wanted to get from action in the Security Council. I had assumed from all the messages received, that the United States was to take a vigorous line; but the telecon the previous night (before it suffered a mechanical breakdown) seemed to suggest that we were not to attempt to get any effective action by the Council. The United States, I thought, was fully committed to the position that the Dutch were at fault. This was the sound position which did have unfortunate consequences in Europe but strengthened the standing of the United States in the Far East and was a major contribution to a successful struggle against communism in the area. I quoted the Indian and Chinese delegates, Manilal Desai and Ching-lin Hsia, as considering this struggle vital. Desai was arguing that the Communists could not be beaten by resort to military measures but only by supporting moderate nationalist movements. Dening, the United Kingdom delegate, agreed. I thought we should capitalize on our support to the Republic, but this did not mean invoking sanctions against the Dutch under Chapter VII of the Charter. Although the Department was having top-level discussions about sanctions, I had not been told the outcome. I suggested that in the Security Council we should be forthright and not evasive; I could act more effectively if I knew exactly what the Department wanted to avoid.

Rusk replied promptly to my telegram of December 22. The Department fully agreed that the Dutch were at fault, but this conclusion did not indicate what we should do about it. They agreed with my appraisals of the Dutch and our action in the Far East and its connection with the struggle against communism. He warned that we did not "espouse" the Indonesian case as such, but the word was not vital. We pursued our own interests and policies; today we were critical of the Dutch, tomorrow perhaps of the Indonesians. He agreed I should be forthright in the Council and they liked my "excellent" opening statement there; but we did have to use caution in view of our great responsibilities or we would be involved in many armed actions all over the world in cases which had previously been before the United Nations. He urged me to come back with further questions if I was still in doubt since it was of the greatest importance that we keep together in that extremely complicated situation.

It should be remarked here that this was the first time the Security Council had met away from the New York area apart from the occasions when top officials of the Department were in Paris with the delegation to the General Assembly. At Lake Success, we had a little booth and our own wire to Washington so that the Department could coach the American representative at any moment, especially since the practice in the Security Council at that time of having every statement translated consecutively into French and Russian provided intervals for telephonic consultation. Communication with Paris in December

1948 was not quite so facile; we had no telephone of our own in the Palais de Chaillot.

Meanwhile we were drafting a resolution in Paris with China, Syria, and Colombia as co-sponsors and the Australians actively supporting. The essential parts called for the withdrawal of the Dutch troops and the release of the political prisoners. The Department wanted the text toned down, Bancroft told Scott on the telephone on December 21, to which Scott replied we had to include certain points to avoid the introduction by others of a stronger resolution.

As the Security Council debate began on December 22, I chided Malik for his two-day delay and he pleaded that it was a long way from Moscow: I suggested he should have flown the airlift from Berlin. I made an opening statement in the Council. Van Roijen spoke for the Netherlands, repeating the arguments that the Security Council was not competent in a domestic matter such as this, that Indonesia was not a sovereign state, and there was no threat to international peace and security. It was very much the same speech the Dutch had made in the same case in July 1947.

On December 23 at 10 p.m. I telegraphed that the French, Argentine, Belgian, Canadian, Syrian, and Australian representatives in the Security Council all were asking us what the United States would do if the Security Council adopted a resolution calling on the Dutch to stop or to take certain steps and the Dutch defied it. In a rare burst of speed, the Department replied at 7p.m. Washington time that same evening, saying we could not answer the other delegations; it depended on the reasons for the Dutch defiance and on the reactions of other Council members. But the passage of the Security Council resolution was not fruitless; it would only be the failure to pass any resolution that would be futile. The resolution we were backing would clarify responsibility and mobilize public opinion. I was told we could not buy votes on such a resolution by pledging

in advance certain U.S. action. Others must also meet their responsibilities. The Department had been talking with the British and French but the results so far were disappointing.

The British view was conveyed to the Department by Ambassador Sir Oliver Franks on Christmas Eve. Bevin said they
would vote for our resolution in the Security Council but made
no commitment beyond that; he was especially wary about
sanctions. Lovett told Franks that the Dutch were guilty of a
"deliberate affront to the United Nations" and that the United
States was "constitutionally obligated" to take the steps it was
taking in Paris. He hoped that the moderate measures we proposed would reduce the pressure on us to take more extreme
measures. We were still a member of the GOC and hampered
by the neutrality that status theoretically imposed; but we had
to balance our obligations to the United Nations, keeping in
mind also our great concern for the North Atlantic arrangements. Lovett hoped that the British would influence the Australians, whose attitude we had not found helpful in the cases
of Indonesia, Korea, or Greece. Franks admitted they also had
found the Australians no less irritating. The Department followed up this conversation with a telegram to London hoping
the British and French would bring pressure on the Dutch to
accept the Council's resolution in order to avoid serious effects
on Western solidarity and on U.S. public opinion.

Also on Christmas Eve, the Department sent me instructions
on what to do if the Dutch, in pressing their argument about
this being a domestic question from which the United Nations
was barred by Article 2(7) of the Charter, should suggest asking
the International Court of Justice for an advisory opinion on
the point. I was to say that we would support such a request to
the Court but it must not prevent or delay action by the Security Council and the question should be referred to the Court
only when hostilities had ceased, the *status quo ante* had been
restored, and the peaceful methods which the Charter enjoined
had been resumed. Dutch Counselor of Embassy Helb, in

Washington, had told McClintock of UNA that if the matter were referred to the Court and the Court's opinion were adverse to the Dutch contentions, they would bow before the Court, whose presence in Holland meant very much to them.

But a message from London sent on Christmas Day reported that the British had been informed that if the Security Council directed the Dutch to withdraw their forces, they would not comply. The British were urging them not to make a flat refusal but to suggest a complete peace plan of their own. The Foreign Office warned the State Department not to press too hard against typical obstinacy—not to "ram your head against a stone wall" but to be constructive. A clash with the Dutch was bad for Western Union and for the Western powers' relations with East Asia.

When the Council voted on December 24, the resolution which we had introduced jointly with China, Colombia, and Syria, reflected the Department's caution; it called on both parties to "cease hostilities forthwith" and to withdraw forces to the old Renville truce lines; the GOC was to report. Australia put in an amendment calling for the release of the prisoners. As amended, the resolution was then adopted 7 to 0 with Belgium, France, the Ukraine, and the USSR abstaining, although the provision for troop withdrawal failed in paragraph-by-paragraph voting.*

When the Council reconvened after Christmas on December 27, the situation was bleak. The Dutch statement was not satisfactory to us or to other members of the Council, especially since there was no mention of the release of Sukarno and the other political prisoners as called for in the Council's resolution. On tougher resolutions offered by the Ukraine and the Soviet Union, the United States abstained and the resolutions had no more than 5 votes in favor. Resolutions were drafted by

* A slight contretemps: on December 24, the New York *Times* printed a correction, explaining that four paragraphs of van Roijen's speech in the Council had inadvertently been ascribed to me!

this and that delegation, one after the other. On December 28, the Council adopted, 8 to 0, a Chinese resolution calling on both parties to cease hostilities and telling the Netherlands to release the political prisoners forthwith and to report to the Council within twenty-four hours; Great Britain joined Belgium and France in abstaining. The Council also reactivated the old Consular Commission and asked it to report. On December 29, van Roijen made a conciliatory speech saying that hostilities would cease in Java by December 31 and shortly thereafter in Sumatra. He did not mention the prisoners. The Indonesian representative said that since his government was imprisoned, he could not give its response to the resolution.

The Council adjourned to meet again in Lake Success in January. My wife and I sailed for home on the *America* on December 30, 1948, after I had taken part in the Security Council session of December 29 where a resolution was adopted calling on the Israeli and Arab governments to stop the severe fighting which had broken out as the Israeli forces moved into the Negev—but that is another story. My friends in the Department were most considerate in insisting that I get the relaxation of a boat trip and assured me they would make provision for representation in the Council if it met before I landed. It was hoped that Ambassador Austin would have recovered and would be available at that time.

Meanwhile Cochran continued to report and to urge stiff action by the United States; he was called home for consultation. Other governments were indicating their opposition to the Dutch actions; Sir Benegal Rama Rau, the Indian ambassador, conferred at the Department with Butterworth, Rusk, and others. Rusk, following the lines of the long background instruction he had sent to me in Paris, explained to the Ambassador the danger of our trying to force votes in the United Nations by unilateral, economic, or other pressure.

We landed in New York on Thursday, January 6, 1949, and I learned that the Security Council would meet on the Indonesian case at 2:30 the next day. Ambassador Austin wrote me that his recovery was progressing and he hoped to be back in New York on January 18.

The Department sent to me at the Mission in New York the text of the phrasing they would prefer for a Security Council resolution which I might introduce at the meeting on January 7, but Rusk then told me on the phone the reasons why they did not want me to introduce a resolution at the same Friday session. They also indicated the lines of a speech I might make if necessary, but warned that the points had not all been cleared in the Department and that I could follow the instructions I had received in Paris and my initial statement in the Security Council.

The points which were still subject to clearance included a declaration that the United States saw no "adequate justification" for the Dutch military action, which was contrary to the Renville Agreement and to the Security Council resolution. Their continued actions were in defiance of the Security Council and they had given no satisfactory report on the release of the prisoners. The United States could not associate itself with any aspect of the military action of the Dutch, who had not exhausted the available ways to a peaceful settlement but rather made it more difficult to reach an agreement in Indonesia. This was a matter of international concern with which the Security Council must deal. The United States would not regard any solution as valid unless it were the result of *bona fide* negotiations, free of all duress and in accord with the agreements of Linggadjati and Renville.

These points were generally along the lines which Butterworth recommended in a memorandum to Bohlen on January 7, although he urged that I introduce a resolution quickly to fend off others which might be less acceptable. Butterworth continued with the suggestion that the Acting Secretary of State should call in the Dutch ambassador to tell him that Dutch policies were helping the Soviets, creating a breach in the Western front, arousing opposition in American public opinion, and perhaps moving Congress to take punitive action by cutting aid to the Netherlands. The memorandum also recommended a step which was much discussed, namely that we should withdraw from the GOC as Cochran recommended, on the ground that the Dutch made its position impossible.

At the Council meeting on Friday, January 7, Ambassador van Roijen made a detailed statement for his government, asserting adherence to the Linggadjati and Renville agreements and stating that steps were being taken to comply with the Security Council resolutions, but his statement did not convince the Council. On January 11, I was able to speak vigorously within the limits of the Department's tentative instruction of January 6 and was not told to tone it down.

There ensued several weeks of intense activity. On January 12, after 8 P.M., I telegraphed to the Department from New York the text of a draft resolution I had discussed with Sir Alexander Cadogan, the United Kingdom delegate, and with my old friend General Andrew McNaughton of Canada, who was President of the Security Council for the month of January. Their reactions were favorable, as were those of J. D. L. Hood of Australia and Rau of India. After consultation with the Department, some changes were made and, as I had hoped, the draft resolution, designated at this stage as a "working paper," was introduced on January 14 by Cuba on behalf of the delegations also of China, Norway, and the United States. It was a strong resolution that included comprehensive proposals for settlement to be facilitated by the members of the GOC, which was to be transformed into a more active body called the United Nations Commission for Indonesia.

On January 17, the Dutch embassy in Washington told the Department they did not see how any amendment could make that "working paper" acceptable to the Dutch; the whole trouble was blamed on the Indonesian Republic and the old argument was repeated that this would be a gross interference in a domestic Dutch problem in violation of Article 2(7) of the Charter. But on the same day I had a friendly talk in New York with van Roijen, who called on me on instructions from Foreign Minister Stikker. The gist of the message was that both du Bois and Cochran were prejudiced, and that the adoption of this proposal would make any solution impossible. The same day I talked with Francois De Rose of the French delegation, who warned that France would veto any resolution which would give more extensive powers to any United Nations body in Indonesia. I told the Department I doubted this; but if the French did veto, it would be a question of UN competence and we should at once introduce a resolution requesting an advisory opinion from the International Court of Justice. Since the Council would meet again on Wednesday, two days later, I needed instructions before then.

Tuesday, January 18, Rusk met with Butterworth and Hickerson (the UNA-FE-EUR troika) and talked to me twice on the telephone. Caution was again in the saddle. I should not get too far "out in front"; I should act only if there were at least seven members of the Security Council ready to support; we must not solidify Dutch opposition to a solution in Indonesia; the position of the United Kingdom was crucial since they might be able to influence the Dutch. The Department was not pressing for an immediate resolution—it was a question of timing. I said that I would be talking during the day with the delegates of China, Norway, Cuba, Canada, the United Kingdom, and Egypt. If there were seven in favor of the resolution, was I authorized to have it introduced? Rusk consulted his two colleagues and telephoned back that they would reluctantly agree both to the content of the resolution and to the timing, but would I please remember that this was not our main objective. He said the French embassy had told Hickerson France would veto, as De Rose told me, and that there was a difference of opinion in the Department whether to proceed if this were true. I should talk with the French delegation to learn their

specific objections to the draft. Other members of the Mission
in New York, especially Scott and Charles Noyes, were also in
frequent telephone communication with the Department and
reported some changes in phrasing after we had talked with the
Norwegian and Chinese delegates. The Dutch planned to ask
McNaughton to postpone the Security Council meeting but the
Chinese were insisting it should be held no later than Thursday. At 11:27 P.M. on Tuesday, January 18, I was able to telegraph the Department that the Canadian and British delegates
agreed to our revised text and would urge their governments to
support the resolution. But McNaughton advised against having seven co-sponsors, which would appear as if we were "gang-
ing up" on the Council. Fawzi Bey of Egypt would vote for our
resolution but would not co-sponsor since he would speak in
favor of an even stronger draft.

The next afternoon I had an hour's talk with my old friend,
Alexandre Parodi, the legal adviser at the Quai D'Orsay with
whom I had worked most congenially at Paris when we dealt
with the Berlin Blockade case. I emphasized to him that we
could not acquiesce in the Dutch theory that the Indonesian
Republic, which was represented at the Security Council table,
had ceased to exist. The Dutch had not complied with the
Council's demand that they release the political prisoners, not
offering any legal argument but merely excusing their noncom-
pliance. The Security Council, I said, could not condone a resort to force, especially when it was in violation of the truce
agreement. I told Parodi that China, Cuba, and Norway were
co-sponsors of the resolution and that Canada, the United
Kingdom, and Egypt agreed to vote for it. I reminded him that
Nehru had convoked, in New Delhi, a conference of nineteen
Middle Eastern Asian and Australasian countries that was sure
to denounce the Dutch and might induce the Security Council
to take more vigorous action. Parodi thought the amended
draft was a great improvement, especially since it omitted the
demand for immediate withdrawal of the Dutch troops, and he

would now recommend to Paris that instead of a veto they should abstain on jurisdictional grounds. I urged that we seek to keep the tone of the Council meeting calm, and Parodi agreed to urge the Dutch to be moderate; I would try to persuade Palar of Indonesia and Rau of India to follow suit.

From abroad, our embassy in The Hague reported a talk with Stikker and A. H. J. Lovink, the Secretary-General of the Foreign Office, at the former's home. Stikker had secured a postponement of a meeting of the parliamentary chamber to avoid inflaming public opinion, since there was growing resentment of U.S. interference in Dutch internal affairs. In the eyes of Indonesians and Asians, the United States was on record as taking sides openly with the Republic. If the proposed resolution were adopted, Stikker warned, the Dutch would be finished in Indonesia, and all Western influence and prestige in that area would come to an end. Holland would be impoverished and communism would gather strength in the Netherlands as it already had in France and Italy. (It is gratifying to note in 1972 that Stikker's dire prophesies were not fulfilled either in Indonesia or in Holland.)

On January 21, 1949, Dean Acheson became Secretary of State. I am sure he was scarcely aware that I was speaking about Indonesia in the Security Council on the day he took the oath of office in Washington, but my speech was sent to New Delhi for possibly advantageous use at Nehru's conference there. Acheson did not have much enthusiasm either for the United Nations or for the cause of the Indonesian Republic and although he was "present at the creation" of the independent state of Indonesia, he does not devote much space to it in his account of his distinguished public service. He does say:

In both Indochina and Indonesia colonial rule was beyond the power of either France or the Netherlands. Both resisted our efforts to move them toward preparing for independence. The French fought to the end; the Dutch capitulated under pressure. In both cases independence was to bring results close to disaster.

I would say that due to our own mistakes the disaster actually overtook us in Indochina but in Indonesia that result
was averted. After the somewhat agonizing and lengthy postnatal throes of Sukarno's rule, Indonesia has been advancing
steadily and rapidly and the Dutch have returned there on
friendly and economically advantageous terms, despite the conflict over New Guinea, or West Irian. There was genuine
warmth in the greetings which Queen Juliana and President
Suharto exchanged when she and Prince Bernhard arrived in
Jakarta (the name was changed from Batavia in December
1949) on August 26, 1971. She was the first ruling sovereign of
the House of Orange to set foot on Indonesian soil.

On January 28, the resolution, which had undergone such
meticulous scrutiny and which Stikker prophesied would have
catastrophic consequences, was adopted by the Security Council
without a dissenting vote. It called upon the parties to cease all
military operations and guerrilla warfare; called upon the
Netherlands to release immediately and unconditionally the
political prisoners and to restore the officials of the government
of the Republic to their headquarters at Jogjakarta; and recommended that the parties with the help of the United Nations
Committee immediately enter into negotiations for the establishment of a federal, sovereign, and independent United States
of Indonesia.

As will be seen, the end was not yet. Spaak of Belgium was
trying to mediate between the Dutch and the United States. In
New York I was having friendly talks with van Roijen, who indicated that the Dutch would make a moderate statement in
the Council. On January 31, Stikker told our embassy they had
a new plan for settlement and hoped for two or three days'
delay. At the same moment the Department instructed our embassy that it would take an "extremely serious view" of a ru-
mored Dutch request that Cochran not return to Indonesia;
Cochran's intercession with Hatta and other Republican officials could be most helpful. But the Department did say it
would not push the Dutch too hard, a gesture which appar-

ently led to what was considered an inspired story in the New York *Times* that we were giving the wink to the Dutch on non-compliance with the Council's resolutions. I issued a denial at Lake Success but warned Rusk that if the Dutch did not show a more cooperative spirit, there would be pressure for stronger action by the Security Council. There was danger to the position of the United States and to the confidence of friendly delegations, especially Canada, if we now backed away from our support of the Security Council resolution. Perhaps in response to an indication of Secretary Acheson's preoccupation with NATO, I said I fully realized the importance of that aspect of our policy and therefore urged that we try to persuade the United Kingdom, France, Belgium, and Canada to make joint representations to The Hague.

Meanwhile the Dutch were being uncommunicative and uncooperative with the GOC staff in Batavia. Cochran got back there on February 15 after consultations in New York, Brussels, and The Hague. He spent an hour and a quarter with the Queen in The Hague and reported that she was well informed on events in Indonesia. He reexpressed his high opinion of Stikker, who faced a cabinet crisis on the very day Cochran reached Batavia, and he restrained his Australian colleague, Critchley, from sending a hot report to the Security Council.

The Department was also grappling with a congressional problem in Washington. Senator Brewster of Maine introduced a resolution on February 7 to stop all Marshall Plan aid to the Netherlands; the Department notified the chairman of the Senate Foreign Relations Committee on February 25, that such action was "untimely and inappropriate." But early in March, Averell Harriman, who was directing the Marshall Plan in Paris, told Stikker that, in view of its obligations under the Charter, the United States might find it necessary to refuse to furnish military equipment assistance to the Dutch until they had complied with the Security Council resolution for a settlement in Indonesia.

On March 1, 1949, I was confirmed by the Senate as Ambassador-at-Large and moved from New York to Washington; accordingly, on March 10 I resigned as Deputy Representative on the Security Council. Ambassador Austin had happily now recovered his health and returned to his duties at the United Nations. I did keep in touch with the Indonesian case, especially as one of the U.S. delegation to the second part of the General Assembly's third regular session, which met in New York from April 5 to May 18, 1949. Australia and India— much to the annoyance of the British, the Dutch, and the Americans—without advance warning put the Indonesian case on the agenda of the General Assembly. However, as the news from Indonesia became more favorable, the same two delegations proposed a postponement of the discussion of the item until the autumn session of the Assembly.

Since this account does not pretend to be a history of the Indonesian affair, but only seeks to describe the birth pangs of the new Republic and what may be called the role of the United States as a midwife, I can bring the story to a close.

The Dutch did yield to pressure and proposed a Round Table Conference at The Hague. After long debates, the Security Council gave the new UN Commission for Indonesia a free hand to help toward a settlement; in substance they achieved this early in May in setting up the Round Table Conference which met in The Hague from August to November 1949. It was a success and Cochran, who attended, again made his contribution to that result. The formal transfer of sovereignty to the United States of Indonesia took place on December 27, 1949. Indonesia was born, but its baptism as a member of the United Nations did not come until a year later. Just a month after the birthday, my wife and I made an official visit to Jakarta where, with the help of Ambassador Cochran, President Sukarno was getting off to a promising start. I was impressed by his ability to quote at length from the inaugurals of Abraham Lincoln, a hero whom, alas, he soon ceased to emulate.

In a sense, the United States and the Soviet Union were both

on the side of Indonesia, but the Soviets attacked every proposal as being in reality hidden attempts to help the Dutch.
The Soviet delegate vetoed, on December 13, 1949, a Security
Council resolution felicitating the parties on the results of the
Round Table Conference because, said the Russian delegate,
the agreement merely provided for reestablishing Dutch colonial rule in a disguised form. Up to this point, however, the Soviets had generally merely abstained to express their view that
every resolution was too mild.

Two letters I received, although they are unduly personal,
do indicate that in the long run the policy of the United States
contributed to a result which left three parties—the Netherlands, Indonesia, and the United States—good friends, each
with the other. One letter was from J. G. De Beus, one of the
Dutch representatives with whom I dealt at the United Nations and who, in August 1949, wrote from Batavia, where he
was head of the Far Eastern Office of the Dutch Foreign Ministry:

This week, when the cease-fire in Indonesia was at last signed and
promulgated, my thoughts could not help going back to you as the
main author of the Security Council resolution of January 28 which
has constituted the basis of the final result . . . in the end this resolution which at first was considered unworkable by some, has indeed led to its aim: a cease-fire in Indonesia, and has opened the
possibility of a final solution of the Indonesian problem at the
Round Table Conference in The Hague. It will, I am afraid, for-
ever remain a subject of debate whether the same result might have
been achieved along different paths, but at any rate there can be no
doubt that your work has borne fruit and I wish to congratulate
you on that score.

He paid his tribute to van Roijen, which I enthusiastically
echoed.

The other letter was from L. N. Palar, the representative of
the nascent Indonesian Republic with whom we dealt in New
York and in Paris. I wrote him on September 29, 1950, to con-

gratulate him on the admission of Indonesia to membership in the United Nations. He replied:

I want to thank you . . . and to tell you that I cannot but recall on this happy occasion, how you stood by us in our darkest hour nearly two years ago in Paris and sincerely worked in our behalf. It seems fitting to me, at this time, to express once more my deep personal appreciation for the immeasurable assistance you have given to our cause and for the steadfast part you have played in helping Indonesia achieve her goal.

Haec olim memenisse juvabit—along with the exuberant imagery of the Korean Foreign Minister in Seoul!

As already mentioned, the United Nations was brought into this picture in the Organization's infancy, that is in 1946, and the whole Indonesian question was debated in the United Nations during the first four years of its existence. The United Nations proved its value. It would have been inconceivable for the United States to have promoted the evolution of Indonesian independence through unilateral diplomacy. It was only with the aid of United Nations mechanisms that Indonesia was born in 1949.

4

Prenatal Pains of Morocco and Tunisia

Any discussion of birth, even if it be metaphorical, must have some reference to motherhood. Accordingly, when one is speaking of the "birth of nations," it is quite appropriate to consider the "mother country." Dictionary-wise, this is a term particularly applicable for colonies and it is colonies (or their first cousins, "protectorates") which will be dealt with in this chapter. Women's Lib would undoubtedly prefer "mother country" to the Germanic "fatherland" although it could tolerate the French *"mère patrie,"* which etymologically suggests both parents. In the political-metaphorical application, however, the father is generally not identifiable, unless one turns to the figurative meaning of "father" as "one who exercises protecting care like that of a father." In this sense, those who help a dependency to be born as an independent state have "fathered" that new member of the Family of Nations. By and large, the mother country would prefer to stand alone in a matriarchal relation, minimizing the role of any such father. Such was the attitude of France who, as *"mère patrie,"* resented the interest the United States took in the aspirations of the French protectorates of Morocco and Tunisia. France was in travail for a decade until she agreed to independence for both states in 1956.

It is not easy for great colonial powers meekly to watch their overseas dominions escape their grasp. Germany, Italy, and Japan perforce submitted to their imperial dismemberment by treaties of peace. Most of the victors in 1919 did not like Woodrow Wilson's insistence on the League of Nations mandate system as a device for depriving them of the traditional spoils. The UN Charter substituted the UN trusteeship system for the League mandate system. After World War II, the principal allied powers agreed to let the UN General Assembly decide upon the future of the Italian colonies in Africa.

As will be noted, Franklin D. Roosevelt was dissuaded from his desire to bar the French from returning to Indochina, and we have already followed the fate of the Dutch in Indonesia. As narrated in chapter 7, the British abandoned Palestine, cooperated from the outset in the UN trusteeship system, and then wisely secured the advantages of many friendly relinquishments. Out of the British Commonwealth, however, there emerged the critical cases of South Africa and Rhodesia. Spain had little left and gradually let most of it slip away, even attaining in Asian-African circles the cachet of being "anti-colonial" by demanding that Great Britain (after two centuries of possession) return to her the British Crown Colony of Gibraltar. Portugal, as if still living in the Age of Discovery, sought the shallow refuge of pretending that Angola and Mozambique were not colonies but simply departments of the motherland. The Russians were strong and harsh enough to maintain the fiction that their mélange of peoples formed a happy and contented Union of sovereign Socialist Soviet Republics, constitutionally free to separate but without any desire to do so.

France was almost bled white in its futile fight to hold on to Indochina. The United States supplied economic transfusions, committing us to a course which led us also down a disastrous path. Although Guinea in 1958 rejected membership in the new French community, the Saharan colonies in due course in the early 1960s took on the trappings of sovereignty and acquired membership in the United Nations. But Algeria, annexed in 1842, was heavily populated by French *colons* and was considered an integral part of France. After eight years of bloody conflict, Charles de Gaulle had the courage to recognize its independence in 1962. Morocco and Tunisia were French protectorates, and it was their efforts to be born into full independence which were championed by the Arab-Asian bloc in the United Nations, resulting in some four years of controversy between Paris and Washington. Our relations with the Arab states had been most severely strained in the first debates over Palestine and later over Israel, but our predilection for France, our "traditional friend and ally," in these North African cases, was an element in the distrust of the Arabs of our friendship for them.

French paternal assistance to the American colonists when they rebelled against their mother country was by no means disinterested. In 1776 the Comte de Vergennes, French Minister of Foreign Affairs, instructed his ambassador in Madrid to propose to the Spanish government plans for joint action against England. In 1777, when Lafayette sailed for America to tender his services to the Americans, he is said to have been "full of a vague and passionate animosity against *Albion perfide,* and of romantic enthusiasm for a regenerated world," but in later years he wrote: "The destiny of France was in the balance as well as that of England . . . if England could retain those Thirteen Colonies in her empire, there would be an end to our West Indies, to our possessions in Africa and Asia, to our maritime commerce, and consequently to our navy, in short to our political existence." The memory of the Seven Years' War (1756–1763) in which France lost Canada, and Lafayette's father lost his life, was still fresh and galling.[1]

After American independence, diplomatic relations between the United States and France were somewhat chaotic. During the wars growing out of the French Revolution, French privateers preyed on American commerce and there were naval "battles" as American armed ships recaptured some of the vessels the French had seized. In 1798 the hostilities at sea were of a magnitude which led the Supreme Court of the United States to characterize the situation as one of "limited war." In that year Congress declared that, due to the wrongful acts of France, the United States was no longer bound by the treaties it had concluded with France. Subsequently there were negotiations about recompensing American citizens for the losses incurred through the acts of the French, and a treaty of 1800 recognized that these so-called "French spoliation claims" should be settled. A further treaty of July 4, 1831, stipulated how the claims were to be paid; but the French parliament would not appropriate the funds, and there was warlike talk in the U.S. Congress in 1835; French payments began in the following year. Later generations of Americans forgot the quarrels and remembered Lafayette. I remember that when, full of idealism and inspired by the French stands on the Marne and at Verdun, we landed from our troop transports at Brest in the spring of 1918, it did not seem corny to repeat General Pershing's fabled declamation: "Lafayette, we are here!"

So in the 1940s and 1950s the United States was acting in its own self-interest in aiding the restoration in Europe of French economy and power, but publicly it seemed like paying an old debt. When our interests diverged, as they did on the North African colonial issues, the French tended to consider us ingrates and we tried to atone with flowery speeches about our "traditional friendship." (I frankly skip over the events of World War II and the story of Charles de Gaulle.)

The evolution of a general policy for handling this continuing conflict between our desire to support our Western European friends and allies and our eagerness to build confidence in the ranks of the Arab-Asian states and their emerging partners has already been adumbrated as an aspect of U.S. policy in Asia. The recurrent momentary crises provoked by particular cases such as Tunisia and Morocco had an inevitable impact on the long-range planning, but the search for the *via media* with the smoothest pavement and the fewest necessary detours, tunneled along and surfaced from time to time. This account will attempt to follow the tunnel before surfacing in Morocco and Tunisia.

On April 11, 1952, in accordance with a suggestion of David Bruce, who was transferred from the Paris embassy to become Under Secretary of State in February 1952, I talked with Secretary Acheson about a possible approach to smoothing our relations with our European friends when colonial issues came to the fore. I had earlier suggested that when the Secretary talked with the British and French about plans for a Middle East Command, he might take the opportunity to discuss more broadly the whole colonial problem. Bruce had remarked that when we discussed these matters with our European friends, they tended to think we were preaching to them and became defensive. He thought that if the British would take the initiative in calling in the French, the Dutch, and the Belgians, they might all together come up with some ideas which they would wish to raise with the United States. Perhaps, Bruce suggested, this thought might be passed on to Sir Oliver Franks, the British Ambassador. Consideration could be given to the use of our Point IV aid programs to help with projects in colonial areas which the administering powers could not afford. I reminded Dean Acheson that we had had group talks with the British and French about some of these problems in 1950 and 1951, but those were at a relatively low official level. Actually, Sir Gladwyn Jebb had led an English group of eight and Jack Hickerson had been chief of an American group of nineteen selected from UNA and the geographical divisions. Bruce had not attempted to list detailed points which the colonial powers might discuss among themselves, but we had spoken of the training of native personnel in administrative tasks and confiding to them a larger share in administration so as to prepare

them for at least local autonomy or self-government; such training was already included in some of our aid programs. Although the French had a training school of this kind in Tunis,
it was inadequate. It was Bruce's thought, with which I agreed,
that if the colonial powers could come forward with active con-
crete programs, adquately publicized, people might be convinced that they were really moving ahead in the development
of these countries or areas and the hostility of the Arab group
might be assuaged.

Acheson thought the idea was worth a trial. I could point
out to Sir Oliver that the United States had recently come a
long way to meet our European friends. A short time back we
had taken a stand popular among the American people, in
favor of complete independence. But in the Tunisian and Moroccan cases in the United Nations, we had abstained, thus
bringing down on our heads heavy attacks from the champions
of dependent peoples. One of the difficulties was that the
French and British did not inform us in advance of the steps
they were about to take. They forged ahead, creating a difficult
situation, and then demanded that we give them full support.
They did not recognize that we had a right to be interested in
these problems, although they did insist that we back them up
when they got in trouble. Acheson said that when Anthony
Eden was recently in Washington he had discussed with him
the problems in Iran, pointing out that all we asked was that
our suggestions receive some consideration, although at times
we had the impression that our suggestions were not even received politely and that the British even seemed irritated that
we had made them. I asked Acheson whether he thought the
personal relations between Sir Oliver and Eden as Foreign Secretary were such that Franks, if so inclined, could effectively
take this up with Eden. Acheson was doubtful and agreed to
my suggestion that Franks could identify some permanent official of the Foreign Office who would be sympathetic and might

steer the matter from inside and see it through. We recognized that the whole move would be futile unless one or more individuals who saw the problem as we did would be prepared to guide it. The Secretary noted that we should ascertain the facts about extending foreign aid to colonial areas, whether there were any legislative restrictions, and whether our plan, if carried out, would arouse antagonism on Capitol Hill.

I did have a half hour's talk with Franks at the embassy on April 21 but did not distribute my memorandum of the conversation; I merely reported to Acheson that I thought Franks was interested and would ponder the idea. I had told Franks that the problems of American relations with the colonial powers had interested me for a long time before I was in government service. I recalled that a British-American group in the preceding autumn had talked about how we could minimize the irritations which colonial problems infused into our relations with both England and France. I said it occurred to me that if someone inside the British government on his own volition talked with the French, Belgians, and Dutch about better coordination in the future, we might avoid the difficulty we faced in being asked to give 100 percent support when we were not kept informed before a crisis arose. Franks said he generally agreed. Talking as if he were back at Oxford and I at Columbia University, he said that the trouble was that in England, the Colonial Office had over a long period resented Foreign Office interest in colonial problems and, in turn, the Foreign Office had been slow to realize the foreign policy importance of the colonial issues. Progress had been made, but the difficulties still existed. British policy, especially in Africa, was to look forward to independence with a free choice about joining the commonwealth, whereas the French thought of incorporating their colonies as French departments, a situation, Franks said, somewhat comparable to Alaska and Hawaii in the American system.

THE MOROCCAN QUESTION

Dean Acheson has summarized the Moroccan question as a Franco-American issue in the autumn of 1951. It was a period when many problems were being discussed among the top leaders of France, England, and the United States, both in Washington and in Ottawa, where a NATO meeting was held. French Prime Minister Robert Schuman told Acheson the French cabinet was "gravely concerned" by our informing the French that if the Moroccan question were raised in the next UN General Assembly, we would not support them in opposing even the inscription of the item on the agenda. Schuman said France was granting us vital air bases in Morocco and was trying to make a modern democratic state in that country although opposed by "a reactionary Sultan and the medieval attitude of the Berbers." [2] Acheson gave Schuman to understand that we supported their efforts in Morocco but had different ideas about tactics in the United Nations; these points were developed later. It was at this same juncture that British Foreign Secretary Herbert Morrison, also in Washington, was complaining to Acheson about British troubles in Egypt, especially in regard to the Sudan. Like Schuman's plea regarding Morocco, Morrison argued that it would be impossible for his government to reach a solution if the Egyptians felt that the United States supported them against the British.

On September 25, 1951, I had a long conference with David Wainhouse and Howard Elting of UNA in the State Department. Wainhouse said that UNA was concerned over the French tactic of interpreting the talk which Acheson had had with Schuman as constituting an unqualified pledge of U.S. support for the French in Morocco. Since this issue was possibly coming up in the General Assembly, we might not be able to agree with the French; and if there was any misconception, it should be cleared up before the Assembly met. What, he asked me, was the Secretary's position? The Secretary, I replied, was aware that there were conflicting views in the Department; he had followed a cautious course and had not promised the French unqualified support. Wainhouse said there had been a telegram from the U.S. delegation in Ottawa dated September 19, stating that Schuman had asked for a written exchange of letters spelling out U.S. support for France and disclaiming any U.S. interest in Moroccan internal affairs. I checked with "Luke" Battle, the Secretary's assistant, and confirmed the fact that there had been no further exchange, written or oral, between Schuman and Acheson on this subject, but that there was considerable stirring in the Department on the subject of Morocco. I asked Battle to keep in mind that UNA had an interest in the subject equal to that of the European and Near Eastern geographical divisions. I suggested to Wainhouse that we needed to clear a departmental position as guidance for a pending call from French Ambassador Henri Bonnet; the drafting of such a paper was up to NEA, but UNA had to play the role of mediator. Wainhouse remarked that the French attitude and general policy were very like those of the Dutch in the Indonesian case.

On the day of that conference with Wainhouse, the U.S. embassy in Paris telegraphed the texts which the French had drafted for a desired exchange of notes dealing with French cooperation in NATO and U.S. support for France in North Africa. (Tunisia as well as Morocco was involved.)

On October 4, 1951, Egypt requested the inclusion on the General Assembly's agenda of an item entitled "Violation of the Principles of the Charter and of the Declaration of Human Rights by France in Morocco." On October 9, Ambassador Bonnet called on Secretary Acheson to state that he was instructed to say that France would fight the inclusion of this item on the agenda since it was an internal matter and not within the competence of the United Nations; France attached great importance to having U.S. support. The Secretary told Bonnet that we agreed the United Nations was not competent in the sense of adopting a resolution condemning France or sending a commission of investigation or other measures of that kind but, as a matter of tactics, it was better not to fight against the inclusion of the item on the agenda when the French were not sure they had enough votes to block inscription. If that vote were lost, then there would be a second debate on the same points. Acheson recalled that when the Communists put on the agenda a complaint against the position of the United States on Formosa, we welcomed the opportunity to state our views; tactically we managed to avoid any discussion of the item by placing it at the end of the agenda where, due to the pressure of other items, it was never reached.

Secretary Acheson could have anticipated another striking example of this same policy of the United States to welcome an opportunity to rebut charges. In the session of the General Assembly in Paris in December 1951, we agreed to having inscribed on the agenda the following item proposed by the Soviet delegation:

Complaint of aggressive acts of the United States of America and its interference in the domestic affairs of other countries, as instanced by the appropriation of 100 million dollars to finance the recruitment of persons and the organization of armed groups in the Soviet Union, Poland, Czechoslovakia, Hungary, Romania, Bulgaria, Albania and a number of other democratic countries, as well as outside the territory of those countries.

Speaking for the United States in Committee I (Political and Security) of the Assembly, I stated that we were eager to have this item brought up and debated soon, in order that the canard could be buried. It was duly interred. There were other instances of our same policy.

On the occasion of his conversation with Secretary Acheson in October 1951, Ambassador Bonnet doubted whether French opinion would tolerate their allowing the item to go on the agenda. Acheson then asked what Schuman proposed to do with the exchange of notes which he had suggested to emphasize Franco-American solidarity. Bonnet was not sure but thought that they might be published.

Acheson explains in his memoirs how he was caught up in the tradition founded on the slogan of Senator Arthur Vandenberg that the United Nations was "the town meeting of the world." This posture required the conclusion that anything could be discussed in the United Nations although action was limited by the terms of the Charter. Acheson did not favor this view, which he thought led to preposterous results since, in normal legal proceedings, a question of jurisdiction would be decided before the subject was discussed or debated. Although I think this full elaboration was not conveyed at the time to Bonnet (who was not as congenial to Acheson as his diplomatic colleague, British Ambassador Sir Oliver Franks),* when the matter came to be discussed at the Assembly in Paris, Acheson engineered an agreement that led to the postponement of a decision on the question of inscribing the item.

Meanwhile the battle raged inside the Department. Two days after Bonnet's call, George McGhee, head of NEA, wrote to James Bonbright, who was No. 2 in EUR. McGhee said the texts sent from Paris were quite unacceptable. They went far beyond what was agreed in the Acheson-Schuman talks by linking our policy toward Morocco, Tunisia, and Algeria with commitments under NATO, military arrangements with France, and the treaty base of our case in the International Court of Justice. (This case is described later in this chapter.) If we agreed to the French proposals, we would prejudice our argument in the Court and perhaps nullify any advantage we might get from the Court's decision. A flat pledge in advance to support France in North Africa would injure us in the Near East, the Far East, and the United Nations. Acceptance of the French position was "politically impossible." It would

* In commenting on a later stage when he talked to Bonnet about the Tunisian question, Acheson writes: "In him Gallic logic consisted in stubbornly asserting an erroneous conclusion deduced from an erroneous premise" (p. 638).

tie our hands in the United Nations and make us renounce our responsibilities under the Charter. McGhee suggested the text of a draft reply to the French government.

George Perkins, Assistant Secretary for EUR, replying to McGhee on October 12, 1951, could not agree to making a statement which would say that it was "politically impossible" to give unqualified support to France in the United Nations— it might be possible. He would tone down McGhee's draft. Since NEA would not accept independence "within the French Union" as a goal for Morocco, there could be a vaguer reference to the "political evolution" of Morocco. No French government, Perkins said, would agree to stating that France was responsible for bringing about self-rule in Morocco.

On the same day, Ambassador David Bruce in Paris telegraphed to the Secretary a summary of French thinking about the North African situation. The French asserted that they lost out in Syria in 1945 and the British lost in Iran earlier in 1951 largely because the great powers did not work together and were incapable of forming a united front to deal with the "passionate wave of nationalism in the Middle East." Schuman appreciated his talks with Acheson but needed something in writing to reassure the French cabinet of Franco-American solidarity regarding the situation in North Africa. It was important for him to have such a written statement for use in the forthcoming parliamentary debates. After all, Bruce thought, our interests must be similar to those of France in North Africa, and we should be able to agree on how to handle the Moroccan issue in the General Assembly.

In reply, Ambassador Bruce was told to try to persuade the French not to fight the inscription of the Moroccan item on the agenda, but to seize the opportunity to explain their position—this is what Acheson had told Ambassador Bonnet in Washington. The French should be reminded that in an old case the Permanent Court of International Justice had advised the Council of the League of Nations that the French nationality decrees in Tunisia and Morocco were not purely domestic questions since the interpretation of treaty rights was involved. In the United Nations, the Department cited the precedents of the treatment of Indians in South Africa, and of Russian-born wives of Chilean diplomats who were not allowed to leave the Soviet Union when their husbands returned home. As the Secretary had told Ambassador Bonnet, the United States would oppose any condemnatory resolution. The best solution would be for the French to persuade Egypt to withdraw the item!

The next messages came from Philip Bonsal, our Counselor of Embassy in Paris, who had been in The Hague during the Indonesian crises and understood the colonial conflicts. He telegraphed on October 15 that it would be hard for the French to accept our position; could we not help by making a general statement of our solidarity with the French in their handling of the Morocco situation? Two days later Bonsal reported the views of Roland de Margerie in the Quai d'Orsay, noting that he was such a good friend of the United States that his views were entitled to special consideration. De Margerie thought that if the item were inscribed on the agenda of the General Assembly, the French would refuse to participate in the debate and would consider void any action by the United Nations. At the same time, tripartite talks on issues coming before the Assembly elicited the views of France and Great Britain that they would continue their voluntary participation in the United Nations' appeal for the filing of information about dependent territories although the British feared this would lead to further UN interference in colonial administration. The State Department replied firmly to Paris on October 19 that we could not give the French a blank check for the future in North Africa. But on October 28, the embassy reported that Schuman still wanted a written statement of U.S. support.

As Bonbright from EUR explained to Deputy Under Secretary Freeman Mathews on October 29, 1951, the French government had to explain to its parliamentary opinion why it

would grant military facilities in Morocco to a state which did not support French policies there. Moreover, in Moroccan opinion, it was argued, military and political power were insep
arable, and if there was a divergence on policy there must equally be a split on military questions. The next day Ambas
sador Bruce telegraphed from Paris the text of a statement which the French wanted us to join in issuing. It read:

The relations between Morocco and Tunisia, on the one hand, and France, on the other, are the exclusive concern of these powers; in maintaining order and stability in those territories France acts in the common interests of the members of the North Atlantic Com
munity.

The argument about a joint statement continued.

After the General Assembly met in Paris on November 6, 1951, Dean Acheson's strategy succeeded. Our Canadian friends stated that the item needed more study and proposed that con
sideration be postponed for the time being. The French said the Assembly was not competent. Ambassador Warren Austin for the United States doubted if discussion at that time would really advance the cause of the Moroccan people. The Arab and Soviet delegations argued that the Canadian postponement motion was not in accord with the Assembly's rules of proce
dure. On November 9, the Canadian motion was put to a vote and was carried 6–4–4. All of this took place in the General Committee, which makes to the full body recommendations about items proposed for the agenda.

When the issue came up in a plenary session on November 13, the Egyptian representative argued again that the Commit
tee's decision was improper under the rules of procedure. The French delegate made an impassioned statement defending French policies and actions in Morocco and again asserting that this was a domestic question. The Egyptian delegate re
plied that this statement required careful consideration and moved that the debate be postponed for a few days. At a lunch-

eon on November 14, General Carlos Romulo of the Philippines told me that only twenty-four delegations favored including the item on the agenda; Secretary-General Trygve Lie remarked that the Arabs were always poor parliamentarians; Moshe Sharett, of Israel, said the Arabs got away with it because they were always treated like spoiled children. When the debate resumed on December 13 Ambassador Ernest Gross for the United States stated that his delegation would vote for the postponement on the ground that this was in the best interest of the parties. Finally, the American strategy scored a narrow victory in a vote of 28 to 23 with 7 abstentions. This was the end of 1951 but by no means the end of our differences with France over Morocco.

THE SITUATION IN TUNISIA

Meanwhile in Tunisia the situation was reaching crisis proportions. In January 1952, Habib Bourguiba, a very moderate and able Arab leader who later became the first president of independent Tunisia, announced that his negotiations with the French had broken down and that Tunisia would appeal to the Security Council. The French arrested Bourguiba and other leaders of his Neo-Destour political party; serious rioting broke out in Tunis. The U.S. delegation to the General Assembly was still in Paris in January and February 1952 and was in touch with Tunisian representatives who had come to the French capital. Our principal contact man was Edward Plitt, U.S. diplomatic agent at Tangier, who maintained cordial relations with all the Arab group but kept the French informed that he was doing so. Azzam Pasha, Secretary-General of the Arab League, was active in seeking support for consideration either in the General Assembly or in the Security Council. Plitt informed me that the U.S. help in December 1951 to defer consideration of the Moroccan case in the General Assem-

bly had solidified the Arab attitude against the West, and overnight the cordiality of the Arab delegates toward him had
changed. However, after Azzam Pasha had been invited to a re-
ception given by Mrs. Roosevelt and had had lunch with me,
he began to help arrange further talks with the Arabs and the
atmosphere improved.

On March 19, 1952, Secretary Acheson summoned Ambassador Bonnet to the State Department, suggesting the wisdom of
releasing the arrested leaders and of announcing a forward-
looking policy on which negotiations would continue. Bonnet's
response was the stubborn plea that this was a domestic French
question. On April 2, eleven Arab-Asian states asked that the
Tunisian question be put on the agenda of the Security Council; four other states of that group endorsed the request. On
April 5, Under Secretary Bruce told Ambassador Bonnet that
the United States would not vote to put the Tunisian item on
the agenda but would abstain in order to create a more auspi-
cious climate for Franco-Tunisian negotiations. Bruce said that
the French would have to create a representative cabinet in
Tunisia and that we would expect them to do this within a day
or two. Bonnet was also told that all extraordinary measures
like martial law, curfew, and censorship should be terminated
and the political leaders released. Finally, he was informed that
the U.S. decision to support the French position was temporary
and could only be maintained if progress were made with an
acceptable reform program.

As Jack Hickerson, in charge of UNA, reminded Bruce in a
long memorandum of April 25, our abstentions in the Security
Council on April 14, after two previous days of discussion in
the Council, resulted in the defeat of three resolutions designed to secure consideration of the Tunisian matter. Hickerson noted that the cabinet which the French set up in Tunis
was composed not of representative leaders but of relatively obscure career civil servants. The extraordinary measures had not
been repealed nor the political prisoners released. It was re-

ported that the Arab-Asian group was considering another meeting of the Security Council or a special session of the General Assembly; the Department had to review its policy and be prepared to take steps to deal with the situation before it was too late.

Furthermore, in Hickerson's view, if the Tunisian case was again raised in the Security Council, the United States could probably prevent its inclusion on the agenda, but the consequences would be serious. There would be an immediate outburst of violent criticism of the Department's policy both at home and abroad. Second, if the Arab-Asian states were blocked in the Security Council, they would probably seek a special session of the General Assembly, and even our most strenuous efforts might not prevent them from rallying the support of the 31 UN members required to convene such a session. If we tried to block them and failed, this would constitute the greatest defeat we had suffered in the UN and could not fail to jeopardize our future leadership in the Organization. Third, if there were a special session, we would find ourselves aligned with France and other "colonial" powers pitted against a group of 15 Arab-Asian states, 5 members of the Soviet bloc, Yugoslavia, some Latin American states, and the Scandinavian group. We might muster enough votes to prevent the opposition from securing the two-thirds vote required in plenary for a substantive resolution, but in committee we would be involved in a bitter debate and definitely could not prevent the simple majority needed in a committee to adopt a resolution which might condemn the French, express sympathy for the Tunisians, and decide to send a UN commission to Tunisia.

Even if there were no special session, Hickerson continued, the Tunisian question would certainly be discussed in the seventh regular session in the fall unless in the meantime the French had reached a satisfactory agreement with the Tunisians. Our difficulties in a regular session would be the same as those already described, and the net result would be that we

would lose our moral and political leadership in the UN, reinforce its trend toward radical measures or neutralist sentiment,
and thus drain off support from any measures of our own, such
as those dealing with major East-West issues.

As the officer responsible for United Nations Affairs, Hickerson naturally stressed the effect of these possible developments
on the Organization itself. Its general effectiveness, he wrote,
would be impaired. The continuation of our existing policy
would strengthen the belief that the United States was interested in the UN only to use it as a tool in the service of our
own narrow interest. On the contrary, the preservation of the
vitality of the United Nations was of fundamental importance
for the free world. It was being noted that consideration of the
Tunisian item in the Security Council had been blocked by the
votes of six NATO countries; it would not be to our advantage
to alienate future Arab-Asian support for NATO efforts to
strengthen Europe against aggression. Furthermore, if our efforts to deal with the Tunisian problem were frustrated, there
would be recourse to violence in more dependencies of France
and of other states and it would become impossible for us to
use international instrumentalities to encourage orderly progress of dependent peoples toward self-government, which was
always our objective. His conclusion was that we should avoid
telling the French we would abstain on the issue of putting
Tunisia on the Security Council agenda; it would be better to
discuss it there where we could influence the debate than to
have it come up in the General Assembly.

Such was the point of view of the Bureau of UNA. It was
emphasized also in a memorandum of the same date from two
of Hickerson's assistants to Robert McBride in EUR (Western
Europe), who was circulating a draft of a telegram to our embassy in Paris. I suggested to McBride that the telegram should
emphasize our need for precise information about the French
plans for Tunisia. The Secretary in a press conference, and
Ambassador Ernest Gross in the Security Council, had both

gone quite far in giving the impression that we were familiar with the French plan and found it promising. Actually, the Department had sent Gross on April 4 the text of a statement which read: "The French program of reforms, in our view, appears to constitute a basis for the resumption of negotiations looking toward the establishment of home rule in Tunisia."

I noted that if it should now become known that we did not really know what the French program was, we would be in a difficult position. The French should keep in mind the point which Acheson had stressed to me, that we could not continue to support the French unless we were fully informed. We should also stress the fact that our problem was not only one of meeting American public opinion but also a question of a larger common interest which we shared with the French, namely, our general relations with the Arab states.

From the Bureau of Near Eastern, South Asian, and African Affairs, Henry Byroade told Under Secretary Bruce that his Bureau agreed with the Western European Office that he should again call in Ambassador Bonnet and repeat what he had said on April 5, namely, that we would have to vote to put the Tunisian item on the agenda of the Security Council if the French made no progress toward settlement. Bruce should emphasize to Bonnet that since we abstained there had been growing dissatisfaction with our policy in Arab-Asian circles and also in the American press and in Congress. Byroade also stressed the point I made, that is, the common interest we and the French had in protecting our political and military positions vis-à-vis the Soviet bloc and the Arab-Asian group.

The telegram was sent to Paris on April 28, 1952, with instructions that it should be shown to a high-level officer at the French Foreign Office who should be given a paraphrase of it. The embassy was also informed that Under Secretary Bruce had discussed the Tunisian question along the lines of the telegram with Jean Monnet, the great Frenchman who was the architect of Schuman's Coal and Steel plan, the forerunner of the

European Economic Union. The telegram reflected the various points of view which had been suggested during its drafting, and its Department-wide importance is reflected in the fact that it was cleared by Bruce, his deputy, "Doc" Mathews, Counselor Charles Bohlen, the chiefs of EUR, NEA, and UNA (as well as several subordinate officers in each of those offices), and also by Paul Nitze, who headed the Policy Planning Staff, and by me as Ambassador-at-Large. This means that it was supported even by important officers who in general were staunch supporters of France. The message put particular stress upon the importance of our receiving a copy of the finished French plan. It was pointed out that pressure was building up at the United Nations for a special session of the General Assembly. The United States still felt that the French had committed a grave error in arresting the prominent nationalist leaders; the French would not receive Tunisian support for any commission or body they might establish unless some prominent nationalist leaders were included. Our position was under reconsideration.

While this telegram was being drafted, Ridgeway Knight, a Foreign Service officer of great ability who worked with me for a time but was then in EUR, wrote a detailed memorandum on "United States Policy Towards Colonial Areas and Colonial Powers." In praising the excellence of Knight's memorandum, I suggested to his chief, George Perkins, on April 30, that we had to keep in mind three different groups: the colonial powers, the dependent peoples themselves, and the champions of those peoples. The "champions" included chiefly the Arab-Asian and the Latin American groups, many of whom had themselves recently acquired independence and some of whom asserted an idealistic interest. Looking ahead we must realize that the hostility or even the neutrality of these dependent peoples and their champions might add a serious burden in case we became involved in war. However, we could not determine or control the timing of the attainment of independence by various dependent peoples.

Knight had pointed out that we had a difficult problem of "selling" our views to a variety of audiences and of making our position clearer to the American public. Although I thought the British and French were perhaps now more ready to recognize our interest in some of their problems, e.g., in the Sudan and in Tunisia, they were still suspicious of our motives, although our record in Indonesia should have proved that there was no basis for the suspicion that we were trying to supplant the Dutch economically in that region. We must continue, I thought, to stress to the colonial powers that we all have a common problem which we must meet together and that these questions are not solely their internal domestic concern.

In arguing with the champions of dependent peoples we could, without accusing them of being two-faced, point out that they had situations like those of the colonial powers as, for example, India's relations with Nepal and Tibet and Pakistan's conflicts with Afghanistan over the tribal demand for the establishment of an independent Pushtoonistan. If Pakistan applied to Pushtoonistan what its spokesman, Ahmed Bokhari, stated in the Security Council when discussing Tunisia, it would have to follow a very different policy. And India could be reminded of its attitude toward Hyderabad when that princely state sought the help of the Security Council; Egypt's attitude toward the Sudan would be called "imperialistic" if held by England.

On May 6, 1952, a memorandum prepared by NEA was sent to the Under Secretary in accordance with his request, which followed a suggestion of mine, for a joint reappraisal and recommendation by NEA and EUR about future U.S. policy regarding the Tunisian question. The memorandum was based on the hypothesis that the French would fail to carry out in Tunisia a reform policy of the kind which Bruce had suggested to Bonnet on April 5. In that event, Tunisia, it was assumed, would have been inscribed on the agenda of some forum in the United Nations. The memorandum took into account that

Tunisia must not be permitted to become an issue between the United States and France or continue to undermine our relations with the Moslem world. This was obviously a tall order to fill. Resting on these assumptions, the memorandum suggested five points to be approved for future policy:

1. An attempt to convince the French and the Tunisian nationalists that they needed to reach an agreed settlement of their basic differences.

2. To assist in attaining that objective, the United States should sponsor a resolution in the appropriate UN forum establishing a Good Offices Commission to review and make recommendations on the Tunisian question. The resolution would set forth the composition and terms of reference of the Commission.

3. In presenting such a resolution to the United Nations, the United States would lay the groundwork for our future policy if no settlement ensued. The United States would let it be known that in such event, we would support a review in the United Nations of the entire question of colonialism with a view to the development of a program for the more effective implementation of principles underlying Chapter XI of the Charter.*

4. In the absence of or pending consideration of the problem in the United Nations, the United States would continue to urge the French, as it had on April 5, to initiate an acceptable reform program. The next approach to the French should take place before the National Assembly reviewed the Tunisian matter, which it planned to do on May 20.

5. The same policy, *mutatis mutandis,* would be applicable in the case of Morocco.

The memorandum then gave reasons for the conclusions reached. The prime consideration was what would now be called the product of the cold war psychology. It was the same

---

* Chapter XI is entitled "Declaration Regarding Non-Self-Governing Territories."

point which I had indicated in my memorandum of April 30. The NEA-EUR memorandum stated that our strategic requirements in North Africa demanded political stability in that area. Political stability was currently threatened by the impasse between French colonial policy and the rise of Arab nationalism. As they stood at the moment, French intentions and the ambitions of the Arab nationalists were mutually exclusive. The continuing blandishments of the Communists left open the possibility that the nationalists in French North Africa, although basically non-Communist, might as a last resort risk collaboration with the Communists if they felt it was hopeless to fulfill their aspirations by other means. Like considerations held open the possibility that, in the event of war or its apparent imminence, the nationalists might withhold their collaboration or even oppose the West until their demands were met. Therefore, the memorandum concluded, the passage of time without settlement of the Franco-Tunisian (or Franco-Moroccan) issue, served Communist aims and was contrary to the national interest of the United States. This was clearly the adoption of a realistic rather than an idealistic or moralistic approach. Probably no approach which was not realistic would have received Department-wide approval; it would hardly have convinced Secretary Acheson, and certainly would not have persuaded the French.

Harold B. Hoskins of NEA had informed me that the memorandum would be discussed on the following day by the Board of Planning but I wrote him at once to say that I was leaving for New York and jotted down some thoughts on first reading. It seemed to me that the proposals met the stated criterion concerning our relations with the Moslem world, but not the other criterion of our relations with France. I suggested that we avoid using the term "colonialism" in connection with the possible overall UN review. The very term seemed to connote an acceptance of all the criticisms directed at the administering states. I hoped we could find a term which would carry the idea of a concern with all dependent peoples, thus (as I suggested in my earlier memorandum) hinting at the beams in the eyes of some of the Asians. Before the type of public statement in the UN contemplated in point 3, I thought we should make further efforts to consult with the British and French and possibly other states, and that we should emphasize the importance of continuing informal consultations with the Arab-Asian group also.

Although I do not have documentary evidence, I assume that the views of UNA were presented at the meeting of the Board of Planning; it would have been likely that Hickerson as Assistant Secretary for that bureau would have agreed with its recommendations. In any case, a week later he sent a memorandum to the Secretary stressing points he had made in his long memorandum to Under Secretary Bruce. Hickerson recommended that the Secretary tell Ambassador Bonnet that as he had been warned, we had to reconsider our position since the French had made no progress. Reports from Paris and Tunis indicated things were going from bad to worse, and there was every indication of special UN meetings in which France would be bitterly attacked.

On May 19, Paul Nitze, head of the Policy Planning Staff, sent his staff's views on the Tunisian question to Under Secretary Bruce, which generally coincided with those already stated. There was, naturally, emphasis on our military requirements and the strategic importance of the Middle East and South and Southeast Asia. The memorandum dealt in detail with the situation in the United Nations and agreed with the view that it would be better to have the matter raised in the Security Council than in the General Assembly. (A memorandum from NEA noted that a case first raised in the Council may later come up in the Assembly.) The Staff remarked that to many people an abstention seemed like a negative vote, and in my comment on the memorandum I stressed the need to explain to the public the significance of votes cast in the United

Nations. From UNA, Hickerson, in a paper drafted by David Popper, agreed generally but noted that the Policy Planning Staff had omitted an important angle, namely the risk of impairing the strength, integrity, and utility of the United Nations which, it was stated, plays a vital part in our leadership of the free world. So far, the United Nations had been the sacrificial victim of our Tunisian tactics.

On May 22, 1952, I left Washington with Secretary Acheson for the final stages of the negotiations for attainment of independent status by the Federal Republic of Germany. From Bonn we flew to Paris, where the official signing of the agreements took place in the Salon de l'Horloge at the Quai d'Orsay. Then followed talks on French problems in Indochina and in North Africa. It was on the afternoon of May 28 that Dean Acheson, as requested by the French, went to the Quai d'Orsay for what we expected would be a talk with Schuman and a few of his associates about the North African problems. Ambassador James Dunn, George Perkins, Ridgeway Knight from Perkins' office, Woodruff Wallner and John Utter, who were experts on Arab-African questions, and I went with the Secretary. We found ourselves confronting the Premier, Antoine Pinay, Schuman, and two other former premiers—Henri Queuille and René Pleven—as well as Jean Letourneau, Minister of France Overseas, and a battery of other personages. Acheson describes the scene, which remains fresh in my memory.

As he wrote, the French attacked the attitudes of the American administration, the Congress, and the press toward French policy and conduct in North Africa. He recounted:

. . . Pinay pronounced the indictment with passion and clarity. In a word, our failure as a government to stand firmly and staunchly beside France in denouncing United Nations discussion of her internal affairs encouraged its continuance, while the sympathetic attitude toward Arab complaints voiced in press and congressional discussion—all this despite everything France had done to grant us air bases in North Africa—inflamed them. Wishing to get the whole subject fully exposed before replying, I encouraged all our French friends to speak at length, holding nothing back. They fully enjoyed complying and disclosed—while also easing—a good deal of pent-up resentment in the process.

Although the chance was small that reason could reach the heart of this highly emotional problem, I was determined to have a try at it. To begin with, I said, we should raise frankly and dispose of an unspoken suspicion, which one did not need to dig deeply to find, that the United States did not wish to strengthen but on the contrary would like to replace French influence in Africa. This was totally untrue. I wished to make this unmistakably clear. We believed that France had contributed vastly to North Africa and had more to contribute. While many Americans criticized French policy, no one wished to supersede France in Africa or to eliminate her influence. I insisted upon this point fully and frankly and, whether or not my hearers were convinced, they accepted it.

Even such intelligent Frenchmen as my present hearers, I continued, seemed to believe that criticism of French policy in North Africa by American and congressional opinion was inspired and even guided by the American Government. This showed vast ignorance of our society. Even when the Government desperately wished to guide opinion, as in the case of the Marshall Plan and the North Atlantic Treaty, it required colossal effort and large privately organized participation to do so. On one subject, however, private American opinion needed no guidance and had been historically consistent and vigorous—its tradition of sympathy for any people who alleged that they were oppressed by any other people. This was the heart of our anticolonialism and it made little difference whether or not the allegedly oppressed were, in fact, oppressed. A prima facie case was made out if they were of a different race or color from those complained against.

My foreign friends protested that this was irresponsible opinion, to which I agreed, adding that most opinion was both irresponsible and ignorant, although on the whole, the American public was better informed by their press and radio than most. For instance, I asked, how many French ministers present knew that in Puerto Rico we had the problem of moving from a colonial relationship to something else and in what direction we were moving? No one knew.*

---

* Actually, the drama of the moment when Acheson challenged his distinguished audience to reveal their familiarity with Puerto Rico was epic.

Another attitude of Americans that entered into the problem we were discussing was that they believed nothing should be regarded as immune from discussion. They had no reticences and suspected that those who had were covering up something that would not bear examination. This included the private lives of public people. As a result, the prime defense of the French in the United Nations —that French North African problems were internal matters and could not be discussed—was to most Americans a confession of guilt. To them talk was not interference; everyone at home and abroad talked about our problems—divorce, crime waves, race relations.

Perhaps, I concluded, the Americans, as pictured, appeared as interfering, nosy people whom the French would do well to regard with distaste. However, before reaching this conclusion, we might examine another characteristic, which—aside from our usefulness in repeatedly coming to the rescue of our friends—might commend us. Almost as deep-seated as our sympathy for the underdog had been our sympathy for the constructive as opposed to a destructive approach to any problem. To be "constructive" was one of our highest accolades. I urged my hearers to ponder the implications of this attitude. The French policy of silence on the issues in North Africa, of negative acts like the arrest of the Tunisian leaders, could never bring a sympathetic response in America. But if the French side were the proposer of solutions and others assumed the negative role of objecting, picking flaws, dragging feet, the French would have seized the constructive position with its strong claim to sympathy.[3]

Dean Acheson explains that Pinay tried—unsuccessfully—to lure him into issuing immediately a written statement announcing American support for French policies in North Africa. As reported in the telegraphic account to the State Department, the Secretary said he could make no supporting statement until he had seen the French plan for Tunisia and had discussed it with President Truman and the Cabinet. But at a far corner of the Quai d'Orsay, the official spokesman for the Foreign Ministry was informing the press that Acheson had been forced to admit that the United States had been following a mistaken policy and actually fully supported the French program in Tunisia. But no propaganda in the press could dispel the impression which Acheson's persuasive advocacy made on his hearers. My own admiration for his performance was shared by former Premier René Pleven, who whispered to Acheson when the meeting closed that if he ever ran afoul of the law and was guilty as charged, he would want to retain Dean Acheson as his lawyer.

Back in Washington at the Secretary's usual morning staff meeting on June 3, I asked that work be commenced on drafting a public statement relating to our stand on the French position in North Africa, since the French would be pressing the Secretary to make a statement. The Secretary agreed and the Secretariat notified George Perkins in EUR that his office should take responsibility for the drafting in conjunction with NEA and UNA. When drafted, the statement should be submitted to the Secretary for approval. But Acheson told the staff meeting that we would have to oppose any special session of the General Assembly to consider Tunisia, although we could not keep the question off the agenda of the regular fall session and we would not try to do so. In the event, the Arab-Asian group mustered only 23 UN members in favor of a special session, which was 8 short of the majority required for such a call.

THE MOROCCAN CASE IN THE INTERNATIONAL COURT OF JUSTICE

At this point, I shall break the chronological sequence in order to recount another aspect of the Franco-American disputes over Morocco—an aspect which involved another organ of the United Nations, namely the International Court of Justice.[4]

The disputes with France over Morocco began as a bilateral controversy about the interpretation of the legal rights of American businessmen in Morocco. These rights, the United States asserted, flowed from treaty relations between the United States and Morocco beginning as early as 1787, and particularly a treaty of 1836. In 1906, the Sultan had convened a conference at Algeciras in the hope of getting international agreement to reforms needed to end the chaotic financial and economic condition of his country. The treaty signed at the conference, known as the Act of Algeciras, was ratified by fourteen states, including the United States and France. In 1912, France established a protectorate over Morocco and negotiated with various governments concerning the recognition of that status. It is unnecessary here to recite the details of the legal problems and their solutions, but the United States, while finally recognizing the protectorate in 1917, insisted on maintaining the old treaty rights of its nationals. Some of the American interpretations of those rights were very far-reaching indeed, and subject to controversy. The State Department, however, was under constant pressure from American business interests in Morocco who sought the broadest possible interpretations of U.S. treaty rights, giving them special advantages in the application of measures for the control of imports and foreign exchange which were put into effect by the French authorities in December 1948. As will be noted, the business interests were able to enlist the powerful support of the Congress. The protesters were led by Colonel Robert Emmet Rodes, an American businessman involved in Moroccan trade and president of the American Trade Association of Morocco, the membership of which represented most of the American business interests in that French protectorate.

The French decree of December 30, 1948, curtailed imports into Morocco, allegedly in the interest of reducing the pressures on the dollar resources of the franc zone, an objective with which the United States was in sympathy in line with its general program of stimulating European, and specifically French, economic recovery. As the protectorate government, France requested United States assent to the application of the import restrictions to American businesses. While the matter was being negotiated, the authorities in Morocco began applying the decree to Americans. Ernest Gross, who had been Legal

Adviser of the State Department and who had become Assistant
Secretary of State for Congressional Relations, in reply on June
1, 1949, to a letter from Senator Walter George, described the
situation and stated that this action of the authorities in Morocco was considered illegal in view of the treaty rights of
American citizens in Morocco. On June 10, the United States,
after further negotiations, gave its provisional assent to the application of the decree for a three-month period under certain
conditions.

Colonel Rodes objected in numerous letters to the State Department. In answering his letter of June 9, 1949, Under Secretary of State James E. Webb referred to seven other letters
which the Department had received from him, all dealing with
this subject. Webb enclosed a memorandum explaining the
French and American arguments, noting that all of this information had already been communicated to Colonel Rodes, and
to Senator Henry Cabot Lodge in a letter of February 17, 1949.
Negotiations with the French were to continue during the
three months and, if agreement was reached on the protection
of American interests, it was intended to renew the assent "for
an indefinite period of time." The letter then adds this interesting paragraph:

> Your letter also expresses concern over the question of jurisdic-
> tion within the Department. In this connection it should be
> pointed out that policy decisions of this nature are made only after
> the views of all interested Divisions of the Department, both geo-
> graphic and economic, have been taken into account. As such, they
> have the approval of high officers of the Department, and represent
> what may be called Department policy. It is also our policy, in such
> matters, to obtain the concurrence of other interested agencies of
> the Government.

On July 29, 1949, Assistant Secretary Gross replied to a letter
from Senator Leverett Saltonstall, who had received an appeal
from some of his constituents. Some of the facts were restated
and the letter continues:

Your constituent remarks that Morocco is an independent country. This is not correct, in that the major part of the country is a
French protectorate, and France is responsible for its foreign relations. He also states that the United States has well-defined treaty
rights in Morocco and that the State Department is relinquishing
two important rights of these treaties, namely, most-favored-nation
and "open door" treatment in assenting to the decree of December
30, 1948. As a matter of fact, the interpretation of United States
treaty rights in French Morocco has consistently presented a problem to this Government, and consequently these rights cannot be
termed well defined. Furthermore this Government did not relinquish the rights of most-favored-nation and "open door" treatment
in assenting to this decree. United States assent was given as a temporary expedient with full reservation of existing United States
treaty rights.

The businessmen resorted to the third branch of the government of the United States—the judiciary.[4] On September 6,
1949, Colonel Rodes and his Trade Association filed suit in the
U.S. District Court for the District of Columbia seeking a temporary restraining order, a preliminary injunction, and a permanent injunction to preclude the Secretary of State and his
subordinates "from acting under color of alleged authority and
purporting to give further assent of the United States to" the
decree of December 30, 1948. The complaint further sought to
restrain the Secretary "from any other action that would temporarily or permanently waive, relinquish, impair or extin-
guish the Treaty rights in Morocco of United States citizens
and commerce, without first obtaining the advice and consent
of the United States Senate as required by the Constitution of
the United States."

It is unnecessary to follow all the pleadings in the case. From
a legal and constitutional point of view, the government's arguments were impeccable. An affidavit by Willard L. Thorp, Assistant Secretary for Economic Affairs, gave a clear picture of
the necessities of our economic foreign policy, and another affidavit by George C. McGhee, Assistant Secretary of State for

Near Eastern, South Asian, and African Affairs, described the negotiations in Morocco and Paris, in which he played a leading part. The case was argued by Edward H. Hickey, Special Assitant to the Attorney General, who stated that if the plaintiffs were aggrieved, their recourse must be to the Congress for legislative action, not to the courts. April 19, 1950, Chief Judge Bolitha James Laws granted the government's motion for summary judgment in their favor, noting that the "present decision is confined to the point that this Court may not enjoin the Secretary of State in the matter of his giving or withholding his assent to proposed decrees which may or actually do consititute legal breaches of a treaty." Rodes *et al.* appealed and their appeal was dismissed November 20, 1952.

Meanwhile, although the State Department had temporarily assented to the application of certain of those French measures to Americans, it informed the French Foreign Office on December 2, 1949, that since there had been no satisfactory response to its representations, no extension of its temporary assent would be justified, unless an agreement were reached almost immediately.

On December 7, 1949, the French embassy communicated to the State Department the text of an application instituting proceedings which France proposed to file at that time with the International Court of Justice at The Hague in order to obtain an authoritative ruling on the controversy. The next day, the United States extended its assent to the application of the Moroccan control measures and urged France not to go to the Court; France complied temporarily.

Negotiations continued, but the American importers were dissatisfied. Congressional opinion accepted their view that the United States had treaty rights which were being violated by the French. In the Senate, Senator Burke Hickenlooper of Iowa was among those so convinced that he was sincerely indignant. He sponsored the "Hickenlooper Amendment," which directed that funds given by the United States to aid the economy of foreign countries should not be available to any country of which a dependent area failed, in the opinion of the President, to comply with the treaty rights of the United States. The State Department thereupon notified the French that the United States might have to withdraw its assent to the application of the import controls. When the case on a revived French application of October 28, 1950, reached The Hague Court in 1952, the United States did not claim the right to have the last word on the interpretation of its treaties with other states. As Adrian Fisher, the Legal Adviser of the Department, explained to the Court: the United States, when it was informed that the French government was going to refer the case to the International Court,

felt that it was inappropriate for it to attempt to make a unilateral decision as to what its treaty rights were, even from the point of view of enforcing its own law, and for that reason *no finding* was made by the President under the Hickenlooper Amendment and the assent to the Decree of December 30th, 1948, was never withdrawn. It is in effect up to this date. Moreover, it was felt inappropriate by the United States to have in its own legislation an amendment which might appear to have the effect of being a sanction on a matter which was before this honourable Court. As a result, when the next General Appropriation Act was considered by the Congress of the United States, the Hickenlooper Amendment was stricken out; it was not reinstated in the law, it is not law to-day.

Actually, it was striken out when the Senate-House conferees agreed to eliminate it while the case was before the International Court.

This account will not enter into all the byways which branched out from the main course of the international litigation. There was a flurry when Spain showed an interest, and the Paris embassy of the United States dreaded the possibility of a Spanish-American united front against France. There were long technical arguments, both domestic and international, about a move by the United States to make sure that France was acting both for itself and for Morocco, so that the latter would also be bound by any judgment of the Court. This move was objected to by the French Legal Adviser, André Gros, who thought it resulted from the pressure of the business group and was "inelegant." Assistant Secretary McGhee talked bluntly in Washington with French Ambassador Henri Bonnet about the bad impressions McGhee had gained on a recent visit to Morocco. McGhee told Under Secretary Bruce there would be real trouble if French General Alphonse Juin continued to quarrel with the Sultan. The French countered with a protest over the fact that Bourguiba, the Tunisian nationalist leader, had been received by officials in Washington; McGhee replied that Bourguiba came with a French passport, the State Department had given advance notice to the French embassy, and there had been no protest.

The United States wanted the pleadings in the Court case released to the public which, under the Rules of Court, could only be done by a Court order "with the consent of the parties." France did not consent. Gros said that the national practice in U.S. courts could not control the International Court. He swept aside the American argument that many individuals in the United States were interested in following the case, because, he pointed out, when a government takes up a claim, that claim is under international law a dispute between governments, and individuals play no part. The State Department said it also wished to distribute copies to Congress; the French agreed because the Congress was part of the government. The Department asked for 600 copies, but when the Registrar of the Court reminded it that the documents were not public, the request was reduced to 250 copies.

Now at common law, one who promotes litigation in the courts might be cited for champerty or maintenance, but at international law, the promotion of the litigation of an international dispute in the International Court of Justice may entitle the promoter to be nominated for the Nobel Peace Prize. It was the situation in the Moroccan case that submission of the issue to the Court at The Hague offered the State Department an escape from a dilemma; in the face of the clamoring business interests, it could scarcely repudiate a long history of claims to special American extraterritorial rights in Morocco by conceding the French arguments, nor could it, in the face of the prime policies of the Marshall Plan and of NATO, contemplate cutting off aid to France through the enforcement of the Hickenlooper Amendment. Fisher, the State Department's Legal Adviser, had given an opinion that the President did not have to make a finding while the case was before the Court, and the Economic Cooperation Administration (ECA) had concurred in that opinion. Domestic obstacles to friendly diplomatic negotiations may conveniently be overridden by the rather bland assertion that nothing can be done while the case is *sub judice*.

Fisher's hard-headed realistic reasons for willingly submitting the case to the Court at The Hague were happily endorsed on a more idealistic level. On March 30, 1951, a memorandum reported the results of a meeting of about a dozen officers of the State Department, mostly from the Legal Adviser's office, from NEA, and from EUR. The meeting agreed that the United States could escape the jurisdiction of the Court.

But the Department takes the position that, in view of its acceptance of the principle of compulsory jurisdiction and in view of its constant support of arbitration as the proper means of settling disputes, it would not be proper, nor desirable, to use those technicalities to challenge the jurisdiction of the Court in this case.

But Fisher, having escaped one set of horns, found himself threatened by a new impalement. Any trial lawyer may find that his adversary has set such a trap for him, but Fisher was confronted by a veritable legal Minotaur, rarely, if ever before encountered in the labyrinths of litigation. As a lawyer, it was his job to win a lawsuit. As only one of a group of top officials who were responsible for maintaining friendly relations with France and, particularly, to avoid exacerbating French irritation over the position which the United States was taking in the General Assembly, he was not free to disregard diplomatic considerations. At the same time, Fisher's principal assistant in dealing with the case, Joseph Sweeney, was being urged by the American business groups to object to the jurisdiction of the Court and to withdraw our recognition of the protectorate. They claimed some persons in the Department were trying to sabotage the position of the United States.

The skillful Legal Adviser of the French Foreign Office, André Gros, in the opening written pleading in the International Court (of which he is now a judge), attacked the Act of Algeciras on which the American claims rested, asserting that as times had changed so must the interpretation of its text. The United States reply, or counter-memorial, filed on December 20, 1951, met this argument by intimating that if this French contention was sound, then France was on shaky ground in relying on its Treaty of Protectorate, which was only a few years younger than the Act of Algeciras. When the French read this argument, to use the vernacular, all hell broke loose. The French ambassador in April 1952 hastened in to see Secretary Acheson and Under Secretary Bruce, complaining that the United States was trying to undermine the French position in Morocco by saying that their protectorate had no valid base. As my account goes back over the history of this issue in Franco-American relations during the preceding months, it will be apparent why Secretary Acheson felt it necessary to administer a mild reproof to his Legal Adviser and why Fisher from then on was overwhelmed by advice from the Department's officers concerned with France and European affairs generally, and from our embassy in Paris. He was caught in a web the strands of which had already been woven.

Fisher was being buffeted principally by political officers in the State Department and in our Paris embassy, whose business it was to watch over the relations between France and the United States. But we have also noted that George McGhee,

Assistant Secretary for NEA, in a memorandum of October 11, 1951, had protested to EUR that some of that division's proposals would prejudice our argument in the Court and perhaps nullify any advantage we might get from the Court's decision. The disagreement between NEA and EUR over our policy regarding Morocco was as wide and almost as impassioned as the difference between Rabat and Paris.

As already related, the French were annoyed by statements in the U.S. counter-memorial; they asked that we withdraw it. Since our brief had already been printed and distributed to the judges, it clearly could not be recalled. Bonnet's protest at the State Department was reinforced by Gros, the French Legal Adviser, to our embassy in Paris. He referred to one argument in the U.S. brief as a "useless dirty trick." Gros added that if Fisher developed such points in his oral argument in the Court, there would be an acrimonious debate that would delight the Polish and Soviet judges and feed the Communist propaganda.

The French reply was filed with the Court on February 13, 1952. The problems confronting Fisher in handling the case are further illustrated by the fact that his aide, Sweeney, distributed in Washington an English translation of the reply, inviting comments from three other legal officers in the Department, from the Commercial Policy Staff, from the Office of Economic Defense and Trade Policy, from the Monetary Affairs Staff, from the offices of NEA and of Western Europe, as well as the Mutual Security Agency, the International Monetary Fund, the Treasury Department, and eight private lawyers representing the various business interests in Morocco.

Then on April 18, 1952, the United States filed its final reply brief, called a rejoinder. The Department braced itself for a new attack by Ambassador Bonnet. James Bonbright, the Deputy Assistant Secretary of State for EUR, anticipating that he, instead of Under Secretary Bruce, might have to see Bonnet, on May 9 told McBride, one of his assistants, that he would like to be able to throw a few barbs in reply, since Bonnet could be at times rather offensive. Bonbright indicated that perhaps there was some justification for the French criticism of our first brief because it was an answer to the French memorial which was weak and ineffective, but the French reply was a strong and skillful paper which had to be countered vigorously by the United States. McBride prepared a paper pointing to some of the items in the French reply to which we objected.

On May 13, 1952, Bonnet, accompanied by his aide Gabriel van Laethem, called on Under Secretary Bruce, who had McBride with him. Bonnet said we could avoid unfortunate misunderstanding by making some changes in our rejoinder. We had interjected some political points in our legal argument, he asserted, and those points would be picked up by the Moroccan nationalists, some of whom were already claiming that our stand at The Hague proved our basic sympathy with their cause. Bonnet specified certain passages and said that Foreign Minister Robert Schuman wished to talk with Secretary Acheson about the whole situation in North Africa. Bruce made no commitment, but said he would tell Fisher what the Ambassador had said about the points in the brief. Fisher was then in Morocco en route to The Hague, although the Court had postponed the oral argument from May 26 to June 9 because the Court's docket was so crowded. (Eighteen years later the Court's docket was empty!)

On June 3, Secretary Acheson conferred with Bruce, Perkins, Fisher, and others. This was just a week after his brilliant performance at the Quai d'Orsay, and he was worried for fear that the calming effect of his persuasiveness there would be lost in a battle of pleadings in the International Court. Acheson agreed that the briefs already printed could not be recalled, but Fisher should make an oral statement which might contain some changes or corrections of points in the briefs. Since I had been with the Secretary and knew the positions he took in Paris, he said that all papers should come to me and that rapid action was essential.

On that same day, Bonnet and van Laethem again called on Bruce, who repeated the points made by Acheson at the staff meeting and gave Bonnet a copy of a draft of a statement which Fisher might make at The Hague. Bonnet conceded it was fairly satisfactory, but said their opponents in Morocco would not quote it but would quote the objectionable statements from our printed brief. Disclaiming any intention to discuss the legal aspects of the case, the ambassador at once plunged into one of the technical legal points which the French found objectionable; George Perkins cut him off by saying that we would not have thought of using the point in question had not the French themselves first introduced it in their brief, to which we were replying. Two days later van Laethem came back and talked with McBride. He said they were so worried about the statements in the U.S. rejoinder they were thinking of withdrawing the case altogether. He wanted to know what position the United States would take in that event. The Department sent a telegram to Paris on this issue. At the suggestion of my aide, Louis Pollak, I inserted in it a statement to the effect that they could not withdraw the case unless we consented, and we would not consent unless they agreed to our claims of our treaty rights, although their future exercise could be negotiated.[5]

As of June 6, I summed up the situation as follows: "We would like to avoid, so far as is consistent with the proper argument of the case, anything in the proceedings which would further injure French susceptibilities." The Department had telegraphed to the embassy in Paris the text of the statement Fisher planned to make. The gist of it was that the overall status of the French protectorate in Morocco was not in issue and the United States did not wish to question the present relationship between France and Morocco but looked forward to the evolutionary development of that relationship. On June 20, our Paris embassy vigorously urged certain deletions due to French sensitivity and their fear that the United States was supporting the Arab-Asian states' intervention in Tunisia and Morocco. Fisher countered strongly, and eventually the embassy cleared the proposed statement.

Then on July 15, 1952, Professor Gros made the opening oral argument in the Court for France. To the lawyers representing the United States it seemed that Gros' argument was not only highly political but contained misrepresentations, including the suggestion of fraud practiced by American consuls in Morocco, the imperialistic character of our economic aid program, and the allegation that the United States position on its treaty rights was harmful to the Moroccans themselves and was preventing the making of needed reforms. The American legal staff considered the argument was designed to stir the emotions and enlist the sympathies of the judges. Acting Legal Adviser Jack Tate informed Acheson that Fisher wished, in the light of Gros' remarks, to change the statement he had been instructed to make, going back to an earlier draft which would avoid the implication that we supported all aspects of their protectorate policy, a concession which Fisher thought would lose the case. Fisher had received some comfort by flying from The Hague to Vienna where Acheson arrived on June 29. I had some difficulty in persuading the Secretary of State that he really should squeeze into his jammed schedule an extra half hour for his badgered Legal Adviser, who needed top clearance for the type of argument he wanted to make about the French exchange controls in Morocco.

When Fisher addressed the Court on July 21, he carefully avoided charging the French with corruption or bias, but felt obliged to demonstrate that the exchange control orders did not actually protect the franc but were merely a device for excluding Americans from a market in which the United States claimed it had a treaty right to participate. The Secretary authorized him to make the argument as he planned it. The basic difficulty was that the United States, through Fisher, had to insist that Morocco still retained a separate identity from France and that the rules of the Act of Algeciras still applied—at least to Americans. The French could not deny that, unlike Algeria, Morocco was not a part of France, but they hated to make the admission. Nevertheless, in its judgment the Court was able to say: "It is not disputed by the French Government that Morocco, even under the Protectorate, has retained its personality as a State in international law." [6]

The Court handed down its judgment on August 27, 1952. It was unanimous in holding that the United States was entitled under its treaty with Morocco to exercise certain consular jurisdiction in that country. But on some aspects of those consular rights under the Act of Algeciras the Court held in favor of the United States by 10 votes to 1, and then by 6 votes to 5 rejected other similar claims which the United States asserted.

The Court was unanimous in holding that the United States was not entitled to claim that the application to American citizens of all laws and regulations in the French Zone of Morocco required the assent of the United States. The Court rejected also by 6 to 5 a claim of the United States about exemption from certain taxes. But the Court was unanimous also in holding that the French decree of December 1948, which discriminated against Americans in favor of Frenchmen, was contrary to the obligations of France under the Act of Algeciras. Accordingly, about a month later, a new French decree was issued in Morocco, repealing the decree to which the United States had objected, and recognizing the claimed rights under the Act of Algeciras. On three other lesser points the Court was split, 6–5, 7–4, and again 6–5. The judges from Egypt, Brazil, and India joined the American judge, Green Hackworth, in a dissenting opinion favoring some of the American contentions.

The judicial hurdle had been jumped, each side winning a little and losing a little. The net result of the litigation on

Franco-American relations was not politically very significant since both sides turned to concentrate on handling the North African problems as items on the agenda of the forthcoming session of the General Assembly.

THE UNITED NATIONS DISPOSES OF
THE FRENCH PROTECTORATES

In 1952, four of the principal organs of the United Nations were actively involved with Tunisia or Morocco or with both of them. The question of French administration in Tunisia came before the Security Council in April. Both Tunisia and Morocco were on the agenda of the General Assembly in the autumn. The International Court of Justice, having received the printed arguments and listened to the oral pleadings of both sides during the summer, rendered judgment on August 27 in the *Case Concerning Rights of Nationals of the United States of America in Morocco*. The fourth principal organ, the Secretariat, of course, could not escape involvement in the matters before the Security Council and the General Assembly, although in general it played its role behind the scenes.

For reasons explained in chapter 3, in my involvement as U.S. spokesman in the Indonesian case, I had a strong personal predilection for the aspirations of the peoples who were seeking an end of the foreign controls which had characterized the colonial period and who were clamoring for recognition of their independence. As described in chapter 6, I dealt in the General Assembly also with the question of the former Italian colonies in North Africa, a question which came to the United Nations because the principal powers agreed in the Italian Peace Treaty in 1947 that, since they were unable to settle the future of those colonies, they agreed in advance to accept any disposition decided upon by the General Assembly. With the aid of this United Nations midwifery, Somalia and Libya were born.

Throughout the summer of 1952, many of the officers of the State Department participated in discussions of a reappraisal of the problem confronting the United States in dealing with the "colonial issue." On Hickerson's initiative, supported by Perkins and John M. Allison, a working group was reactivated; the group included Ward Allen from EUR, Ruth Bacon acting for Allison, who was in charge of FE, Gerig and Cargo for UNA, and Louis Pollak from my office (SA). Among the reviewing officers were Deputy Under Secretary Mathews, Bohlen, Nitze, Byroade (then in charge of NEA), Allison, Hickerson for UNA, and Miller for the Bureau of Inter-American Affairs (LA).

Concurrently, the Policy Planning Staff was working out a plan for what was called a Middle East Command, which was designed to enlist the support of the states of that area in a common defense system that we hoped to build up with British help. I wrote Paul Nitze on June 9 that I hoped their studies could be pressed with a sense of urgency. We should try to discuss this matter with the Arab states before we had to make a declaration favoring the French program in Tunisia. The time was propitious since Anglo-Egyptian affairs were relatively quiescent, and it would be very helpful if we could develop a sense of partnership with the Arab states before the General Assembly opened. It would be hard to deal with them thus after the usual bitter arguments were delivered in the Assembly. So, too, any explosive incident in North Africa, in Arab-Israeli relations, in Egypt, or possibly in Iran, would make approaches to the Arab states more difficult.

In July the Department told the U.S. Mission in New York to talk with Sir Gladwyn Jebb, the British representative, in order to get his general views about handling the North African questions in the United Nations. On another day they were told to try, through contacts in New York, to dissuade the Neo-Destour party in Tunisia from their attempts to disrupt the talks then going on between the French and the Bey, since those talks seemed promising.

It was on July 30, 1952, that the thirteen Arab-Asian states, who had failed to muster the necessary number of votes to convoke a special session on Tunisia, proposed that item for inclusion on the agenda of the regular session. In September I drafted a telegram to Bruce and Perkins in London, telling them that the Department had almost reached a decision to tell the French that we would vote in favor of including that item on the agenda. One reason was that the Bey had rejected the propositions made to him by the French and negotiations were at a standstill.

It was also evident that the item would be inscribed, regardless of any opposition by France and the United States, and if we voted for inscription we would be in a better position to help the French in the debates. The French were aware that we considered the General Assembly competent to consider the issue, but the United States in voting for inscription was committing itself only on the procedural issue and not on substance. The Department understood that Schuman planned to reserve the French position on the issue of competence but to make a strong affirmative speech outlining their Tunisian program. This seemed to the Department an excellent plan, which would give us the opportunity to support the French. It was not then considered desirable to make an official advance statement of our position, but in response to questions from delegates or from the press we would state our point of view as outlined above. The Secretary cleared the telegram, which had been approved by Byroade for NEA and by Bonbright for EUR.

Bruce had already informed me that he agreed with UNA that we should not then make a public statement about our position, but as he was leaving for a meeting in London, he had told Byroade that the decision about favoring inscription could be made while he was away. The timing of any statement should be considered in relation to the convening of the French parliament; he would discuss this in London with

James Dunn, our ambassador to France. The French asked us not to disclose our position, at least not until after their cabinet meeting on October 7. Acheson and Bruce agreed and our Mission in New York was so informed on October 2, but they were still free to tell other delegations confidentially. I suggested it might be a good idea to merge the Tunisian and a Moroccan item on the agenda of the General Assembly. Bonbright agreed because, despite their differences, the two cases were alike in what we thought the General Assembly should do about them, namely to urge the parties to negotiate. However, Bonbright thought it would be a mistake for France or for the United States to propose the merger. We should explore the idea discretely with the French first and then mention the idea to some moderate friend like João Carlos Muñiz, the permanent representative of Brazil.

Meanwhile, Dean Acheson, who always wanted to get at the substance behind procedural decisions, told a meeting of his senior advisers on September 18, 1952, what he wanted as a basis for a decision on these Arab-Asian actions in the General Assembly. In preparation for this meeting he had asked Paul Nitze and me that morning to prepare an outline he could use with the other officers. One point we made was that our relations with our European partners could stand more strain than could our relations with the Arab-Asian group, but we should tell the former that we were not trying to choose between them and their anticolonial antagonists. On the other hand we could tell India, Indonesia, and Burma that we were not trying to persuade them to give up their vaunted position of political neutrality. They should understand that we believed there was real danger of war and we had to be prepared to win the war if it came and meanwhile had to develop the strength which would deter the outbreak of war; to effect such deterrence was to win the cold war.

At the afternoon meeting with the senior advisers, the Secretary followed to a considerable extent the memorandum Nitze and I had prepared for him. In the first place, he said, we must not confine our attention to cases on the agenda of the General Assembly; we must, for example, also have Egypt and Iran in mind. Before he had to decide on technical questions arising in the General Assembly, on which various offices in the Department send up to him divergent opinions, he would like everyone who had responsibility in these matters to think just where our interests are and where we are headed. Maybe the question is unanswerable; if so, we should know that this is the fact. But the kind of study he had in mind might bring out some guidelines. There are very many things to be borne in mind and the difficulty is to have all of these in the mind of one man at any one time. Thus one person may estimate the effect of a certain course of action upon an American election campaign, another may be analyzing its effect in Tunisia. If you reach a decision on principle and forget one of the important elements, you have to reconsider your decision. We must see where we stand in the whole struggle of the peoples inspired by the nationalist movement on the one hand (including in some cases the role of politicians who manipulate the movement) and, on the other hand, the situation of the Europeans who, in some cases, have been holding on too long. We need to know whether our allies are on the skids, and we need to know whether we can really get stability in the Middle East. A general, overall view is required, and at the same time it is necessary to assess the impingement of details by which the generalizations can be tested. We need to know whether the United Nations can actually help in any of these situations or can affect them in any way. If that is so and we are merely confronted with a mess, we ought to have that in mind.

Although the Secretary did not stress the point at that meeting, it was also true that we had to move fast since the General Assembly was to meet in less than a month. I resorted to a plan which was bureaucratically unconventional but democratically sound. I invited all those who, as the Secretary said, had responsibilities in these matters, to send me any drafts, papers, or memoranda they might have held in their desks, or might still be working on, or perhaps had sent to some colleague but had not circulated generally—no matter if they were uncorrected or had penciled inserts and corrections. The invitation was directed to junior as well as senior personnel. Of course I did not discourage the writing of new memoranda bearing on the points the Secretary raised, but I did insist that the time limit was very short.

I remember that there was a very good response but I returned to their authors the actual pieces of paper and I do not doubt that various memoranda were written but reconsidered or disapproved and not put into my hopper. I do have one memorandum which is important as indicating one way in which the problem was approached. It was written on September 20 by William Nunley, and by James Graham Parsons of the Office of European Regional Affairs, who focused on an analysis of the effect of our policies on NATO circles. They found that an anti-United States trend was already apparent in Europe. If the United States were to lend strong support to nationalist movements, that trend would grow stronger. Some of the antagonism to our policies was based on the belief that we were impractical idealists, while others charged us with the desire to attain a position of dominance in the economies of the colonial territories. Our policies would tend to hinder European unity, especially because of French reaction. If France gave up Indochina, it would be true that the French could devote more resources to NATO; but if the United States and the United Kingdom took over that burden in Southeast Asia, we could give less support in Europe. If we did not take over, we would be abandoning the stand we took when Korea was invaded by the Communists and we might lose important air bases. A shift in favor of more support to the nationalistic movements might seriously impair the attainment of our objectives in Europe, but from a long-range point of view we must support the nationalistic aspirations of the Arab-Asian group. The problem was to persuade both the Europeans and the Arab-Asians.

Another source of provender for our future policies was to be found in the numerous memoranda prepared by many offices suggesting what the Secretary should say in his address during the annual general debate in the General Assembly. A UNA view at first urged that the speech should be aimed at the Arab-Asian block and the right to independence should be emphasized. However, on October 1, Hickerson sent to the Secretary an outline of the whole address which had been drafted by Harding Bancroft from UNA and Louis Pollak from my office; it included but did not feature the colonial issues.

This attitude of compromise reflected the view set forth in a memorandum of September 26, largely drafted by me and given restricted circulation to certain key officers in the Department, with authority granted to geographical areas to distribute to chiefs of mission in their discretion. The memorandum recited that it was the result of an analysis of a very large number of detailed studies that had been prepared at the Secretary's request. Although the document had not been cleared and should not be interpreted as necessarily setting forth a firm U.S. position on particular questions of detail, it was believed that the general conclusion was correct and should be helpful to the Department in dealing with specific questions which might arise. In other words, it sought to set out guidelines, but the lines obviously did not have the strength of hempen hawsers and should not be relied on to moor the Ship of State if the tide turned.

The general conclusion, resulting from a study of all the papers prepared in various offices in the Department, was that no individual had been able to suggest actions which the United States or the United Nations could take at that time that would solve any one of the current issues involving our relations with the Arab-Asian group. No such action would terminate nationalist agitation in North Africa, end the apartheid policies of South Africa or the opposition to those policies, or put an end to Arab-Israeli antagonism. It would have to be borne in mind that policy decisions in these cases must be made with a view to alleviating difficulties, reducing frictions, and contributing to ultimate progress toward solutions, while avoiding actions which would have the opposite results. More broadly, it was suggested, the United States should try to follow a course of action which would maintain in the world the moral position of the United States as a counter to the Communist appeal. The actions which the United States might take in pursuing its general objectives were not confined to those in the United Nations, but the memorandum stated that it did not purport to elaborate specifics.

I had actually anticipated this memorandum in a top secret paper for the Secretary which I wrote on September 23, 1952, entitled "Preliminary Analysis of Considerations Affecting Decisions on the Arab-Asian Problems in the United Nations General Assembly." [7] The theme was that the United States needed a course of action which would maintain its moral position in the world as a counter to the Communist appeal. The lines were drawn in the conflict between nationalism and French "colonialism." Although the focus at the moment was on Tunisia and Morocco, decisions on our course of action in the General Assembly should be made against a wider background. The United States was interested in improving the position of France in North Africa so that this area would be a source of strength rather than a drain on French resources, and so that North Africa would be preserved as a stable area for basing Western operations in case of general war. (The possibility of such a war was constantly in our minds.) In regard to the Arab-Asian countries, our interests were similar and we hoped to promote a sympathetic attitude toward a Middle East

Defense Organization, toward base rights and oil concessions, and toward cooperation in the United Nations in cases like Korea.

We had, I wrote, a third interest which was to strengthen the United Nations. We would not want any nation to withdraw from the organization in anger at some measures taken by the United Nations against them. As for putting on the General Assembly's agenda items on Tunisia and Morocco, we would have to vote against France on the issue of competence, but this would not be a breaking point with France. Nor would the Arab-Asians expect us to join in any stiff condemnation of France. The actual situation in Tunisia and Morocco could not be improved except by France; no UN resolution could bring about such improvement, but perhaps our quiet steady pressure on the French might do so. Any strong UN resolution would encourage the extremists in Tunisia and Morocco. The United States had to be in a middle position, as it had been in the Palestine case.

In regard to South Africa, the United States should not put itself publicly in the untenable position of supporting or condoning their racial practices commonly known as "apartheid." The desire to maintain cordial relations with South Africa was not nearly as important as keeping French cooperation. However regrettable it would be, we must consider South African withdrawal from the United Nations as a calculated risk.

In summary, my memorandum stressed that we could not buy the favor of the Arab-Asian countries with aid programs; that we must maintain a moderate position in the General Assembly, urging parties to seek solutions; that it was not a violation of Article 2(7) for the United Nations to discuss these issues, but if the question of competence were referred to the International Court for an advisory opinion, the United States delegation should abstain.

When the General Assembly was in session, the Department, to clarify the American position, instructed our UN Mission in

New York that Tunisia was not within the exclusive domestic jurisdiction of France within the meaning of Article 2(7) of the Charter; therefore the question of what constitutes "intervention" within the meaning of that article did not arise.* The General Assembly was competent to discuss the issue and to adopt a resolution, but we reserved our position concerning the type of resolution which we might approve. Subsequently, the Mission was told that the Department did not know what tactics the French and British intended to use in the General Committee when the question of approving the item for the agenda came up. Neither was it known how they intended to deal with the Moroccan question. Did they intend to ask the International Court of Justice for an advisory opinion on the jurisdictional issue? No such tactic was used and on October 16, the Assembly, over the French objection but with the affirmative vote of the United States, decided to include the item on the agenda.

False rumors are part of the permanent backdrop of the diplomatic scene at the United Nations. Foreign Secretary Anthony Eden's anxiety was aroused by information given to him by René Massigli, the French ambassador in London, who said the United States had decided to vote in favor of inviting Tunisian or Moroccan representatives to come and state their views in Committee I of the General Assembly. This was false. He said the United States was in favor of appointing a Good Offices Committee to go to Tunisia. That notion had indeed been mentioned in a departmental memorandum earlier on, but it had not been approved and the position of the United States was that we would not favor any type of UN intervention in Tunisia.[8]

* United Nations Charter, Article 2(7): "Nothing contained in the present Charter shall authorize the United Nations to intervene in matters which are essentially within the domestic jurisdiction of any State or shall require the Members to submit such matters to settlement under the present Charter; but this principle shall not prejudice the application of enforcement measures under Chapter VII."

Foreign Minister Schuman made a full statement of French policy and aims in Tunisia on November 10 in his address to the plenary session of the General Assembly. He said that France intended "to guide the peoples for whom she had assumed responsibility toward freedom to govern themselves and toward the democratic administration of their own affairs." However, since France felt that discussion in the Assembly would only increase instability in Tunisia and Morocco and since France considered that the United Nations lacked competence to discuss this domestic French issue, the French delegation would not take part in the discussion of the item.

Early in December Committee I began its discussion of the Tunisian item. The French delegation absented itself but from an office on the thirty-fourth floor of the Secretariat building, Francis LaCoste followed the debates on a loud speaker and kept in touch with us by phone and messenger. We worked hard on drafting the statement which I would have to make in representing the United States. It seemed to me that the spirit of Woodrow Wilson could helpfully be invoked, and I began combing for a suitable quote, which I found in a little volume my friend Vail Motter had just edited, publishing for the first time a speech Wilson had delivered in 1890.[9] It was somewhat grandiloquent but I thought the occasion called for a little theater. Routinely we sent the draft to the Department and naturally expected changes, but I was somehow slightly annoyed to learn that the Department had submitted my draft also to the embassy in Paris for comment; perhaps I felt we were going to lean too far toward the French position. Actually the Department accepted some of the embassy's suggestions and rejected others. Dean Acheson was attending the UN meetings in New York and again there was one of those situations where "the Department" was telegraphing its views to the Secretary of State. In their "top secret" telegram of November 27, addressed to Acheson and me, they said that Bruce, Mathews, and officers of EUR had studied my draft in the light of the Paris em-

bassy's comments and all agreed that it should contain more
positive points. They suggested some items from Fisher's conciliatory opening speech in the Moroccan case at The Hague
Court, some points which were in a letter Acheson had written
Schuman, and some quotations from Schuman's speech of November 10 in the general debate. I had the advantage of having
the Secretary of State in New York with me and was able to
reply to Bruce, Mathews, and Perkins on November 28 that we
had also been developing changes in New York in consultation
with the Secretary, but on the whole thought the Department's
text was better. We inserted their substantive ideas and they
left in my flowers. However, we would omit any reference to
Morocco, since that would introduce a complication; the
French had rejected our suggestion that the two items should
be bracketed. I indicated our latest changes and noted particularly that the Secretary had approved the final text. The telegram was initialed by Acheson and David Popper, Paul Taylor
of UNA, who was on the delegation, and Richard Winslow as
Secretary-General of the Mission.

My speech as delivered in Committee I, included these
passages:

Our own memory of the American struggle for freedom stems
from an earlier historical date, but I assure our friends that it is still
fresh and vivid. All of us who are citizens of the United States are
steeped in the tradition of Jefferson and the Declaration of Independence. That tradition has been freshened throughout our history by the fervor and eloquence of a Lincoln, a Wilson, a Franklin
Roosevelt. Who would ask us at the same time to forget La Fayette
and Rochambeau? Who would deny that parallel to the current of
our national spirit has flowed the great liberal tradition of France,
of Montesquieu, and Montaigne? We know from painful experience
as Woodrow Wilson said that "The great stream of freedom, which
'broadens down from precedent to precedent' is not a clear moun-
tain current such as the fastidious man of chastened thought likes to
drink from: it is polluted with not a few of the coarse elements of
the gross world on its banks; it is heavy with the drainage of a very
material universe."

No action of the General Assembly would be wise if it impeded the flow of this stream of freedom which we believe should be navigated by the French and Tunisians together. . . .

We place our trust in the peoples and governments of France and Tunisia. It is they who must work out their destinies. Let us here in this General Assembly declare that the responsibility and the opportunity are theirs.

The French then set us back on our heels by suddenly releasing, without prior notice to us, a note they had written to the Bey of Tunis which we thought was definitely not helpful. Acheson telegraphed our embassy in Paris that he was shocked. The importance of the French keeping us informed as a precondition to our support was a point we had often stressed and which he had personally emphasized to Schuman.

It seems unnecessary to review the General Assembly debate, which followed its expected course. Sir Zafrullah Khan, as the representative of Pakistan, made the most comprehensive statement of the Arab-Asian view, the Soviet bloc charged us with aiding France in a joint aggressive imperialistic policy toward North Africa, and a number of the Latin Americans under the leadership of Ambassador Muñiz of Brazil supported our plea for moderation. On December 12, 1952, the Committee rejected an Arab-Asian draft resolution by 27 against, 24 in favor, and 7 abstentions. A moderate Latin American resolution, after rejecting an Indian amendment which would have deleted a statement of confidence in France's objectives, was adopted by a vote of 45 to 3 with 10 abstentions; the U.S. delegation campaigned ardently to secure this result. The encouraging climax came on December 17, 1952, when the plenary session approved the resolution by 44–3–8, the Arab-Asian states voting for adoption.

The Moroccan case, as already noted, was not cradled with the Tunisian item but was put on the agenda separately and was debated immediately after the Tunisian item was disposed of. The debates followed much the same course, and I made a statement which sounded the same notes, although pointing out that there were significant differences between the Moroccan and Tunisian situations. Again the moderate Latin Americans carried their resolution in the Committee and finally in the plenary on December 19 by a vote of 45–3–11.

Since I resigned from government office with the end of the Truman administration in January 1953, I was not actually *accoucheur* to Tunisia and Morocco, whose independent birthdays did not come until March 1956. What I have called baptism into the United Nations followed quite quickly; the Security Council recommended their admission to membership in July 1956 and the General Assembly completed the process on November 12 of that year. It was Premier Pierre Mendès-France who took the step of recognizing the independence of the two states. The intervening three years were full of prenatal troubles.

In December 1952, there were bloody riots in Casablanca, and the French used repressive measures. The pro-French Pasha of Marrakech, El Glaoui, led a revolt against the Sultan and in August 1953 named the Sultan's uncle as the imam or religious leader of Morocco. The French Resident General, who had not been able to induce the Sultan to agree to certain governmental changes which would have increased French influence, deposed the Sultan and replaced him with his uncle. The Arab-Asian bloc reacted strongly and appealed to the Security Council. The French representative, of course, denied their charges that the French had instigated the revolt and claimed they had acted to protect the Sultan and to establish peace in the country. Speaking for the United States, Ambassador Henry Cabot Lodge, Jr., told the Council on August 27 that, while the United States favored self-government in Morocco as elsewhere, the situation in Morocco was not a threat to the peace and there was thus no basis for action by the Security Council; on September 3, the Council voted 5–5–1 not to put the item on its agenda.

As before, the Arab-Asian group resorted to the General Assembly and the inclusion on the agenda of the Moroccan and Tunisian items this time was not opposed, although the French again absented themselves when the items were debated in committee and in the plenary. Ambassador Lodge felt that the new reforms which France announced for Morocco were encouraging and "cautioned against allowing the debate to take a course that might 'promote disorder or confusion in Morocco.'" As before, the Latin Americans supported a draft resolution more moderate than that of the Arab-Asian bloc, but India, Indonesia, and Burma carried amendments which deleted an expression of confidence in French progress in developing self-government, and which inserted an assertion of the right to "complete self-determination." Over the opposition of the United States, this amended resolution was carried in committee, but the United States and others of the pro-French states succeeded in killing the resolution in plenary session so that no new action on Morocco was taken at this eighth General Assembly.

In 1954, Premier Mendès-France himself explained to the General Assembly his new policies especially in Tunisia. There was the usual interplay between Arab-Asian drafts and Latin American amendments which the United States supported, but without success, in committee. In the plenary vote on December 17, the United States changed its stand and the relatively mild Arab-Asian resolution was carried by 55 to 0 with 4 abstentions. In the following year, 1955, after an outbreak of violence, the French, with the acquiescence of El Glaoui, restored Sultan Mohammed V to his throne, and the various groups in the General Assembly were able to agree on a resolution which expressed satisfaction and confident hopes for the future; it was carried in plenary on December 3 by a vote of 51–0–5.

As already stated, 1956 witnessed the actual birth of Morocco as an independent state. On March 2, 1956, France ended the protectorate and recognized Moroccan independence. Admission to the United Nations soon followed.

As for the Tunisian embryo, although it was not actually delivered from the protectorate by French recognition of independence until March 20, 1956, eighteen days after the Moroccan birth, progress was smoother. In 1953, however, the Arab-Asian group presented the usual type of resolution which was watered down by amendments and still failed to receive the necessary two-thirds vote required for passage in the plenary. Ambassador Lodge, for the United States, voted against the resolution, making the usual speech about our adherence to the ideal of self-government and our confidence in the progress of French negotiations with the Tunisian leaders. In July 1954, Premier Mendès-France, on a visit to Tunis, announced that Tunisia was to be granted full internal autonomy. Soon a new Tunisian government was formed and the French National Assembly approved the Premier's policies. The General Assembly was satisfied that progress was being made and an innocuous resolution was adopted 56–0–3. On June 3, 1955, Franco-Tunisian conventions were signed and Secretary Dulles in August expressed his satisfaction. The Arab-Asian group, by not proposing the inclusion of the Tunisian item on the further agendas of the General Assembly, showed that it, too, was content, and the independent state of Tunisia was duly born. Like Morocco, Tunisia was admitted to membership in the United Nations in 1956.

I am not competent to assess whether these colonial trials and tribulations had any long-range effect on Franco-American relations.[10] I rather doubt it, but it is true that there persists in French circles the belief that the Americans are trying to oust them from North Africa in order to obtain economic advantages; that may be so. In both France and the United States during the 1950s, parliamentary or congressional reactions were more emotional and irrational and subjective than were those of the officials in the executive departments of the governments. The Quai d'Orsay was sometimes supplanted by the generals, but this was not one of the times when in Washington the Pentagon supplanted the State Department. I can testify that relationships of personal friendship were not affected. It was true of both the English and the French that some of the old-line, long-experienced colonial administrators were inflexible and unconvertible. They could not contemplate laying down "the white man's burden." Perhaps the devoted enthusiasm of some of us Americans for the United Nations was almost as fanatical, but often others will resort to UN forums if we do not. Who takes the initiative often has the advantage.

I am satisfied in retrospect that the United States had the longer and truer vision in realizing that the colonial era was coming to an end and that a new day was dawning for formerly dependent peoples. The cause of those peoples had popular support in the United States and, as some of the State Department documents have shown, the realists saw the military disadvantage of having unfriendly countries in North Africa, in the Middle East, and in Asia. Just as de Gaulle saved France from further agony and disaster in Algeria, so I believe it can be said that the United States was largely instrumental in saving France from the quicksands of Morocco and Tunisia.

Unhappily we did not apply to ourselves the logic of the lessons we sought to teach others. Considerations deemed to be of strategic importance have dominated later policy. Concurrently, especially in the present administration, the United Nations has been treated contemptuously. Without attempting here adequate justification for my view, I hold the opinion that our general international posture at the time of the Korean war was greatly improved by our invocation of the United Nations and that conversely during the Vietnam war we have suffered from our unilateralism.

The sharpness of the difference of view between officers of the State Department responsible for different geographical areas, or substantive activities such as legal and United Nations affairs, emerges distinctly in the history of the Moroccan and Tunisian cases. It required great patience and skill for the Legal Adviser to handle the Moroccan case in the International Court of Justice when the interests of France were pressed from Paris and in Washington. In the geographical battle, the outcome of every study was the conclusion that the advancement of the interests of the United States required the balance of a tightrope walker. One side or the other might win a skirmish in the Department but the battle was usually a draw.

Popular opinion reflected in the press, as usual, tended to favor the underdog. Although, as in the Indonesian case, the United States may have invoked that opinion to counter the French insistence upon its importance in France, in the Moroccan case at least, those interested persons who manipulated public opinion had their impact on Congress which the Department often finds to be a formidable antagonist rather than a helpful colleague. Although considerations of strategic defense appear in many State Department papers, the cases in this chapter do not directly reveal, so far as my available sources indicate, the dominant participation of the Pentagon in deciding what course of action should be followed at any given moment.

Ambassador Jessup with U.S. Ambassador Muccio (right), President Syngman Rhee of the Republic of Korea, and Korean Foreign Minister Ben Limb (far right)

Debating the Indonesian question, June 1948: at the table, from the left, are Jacob Malik, USSR; V. Lawford, U.K.; Philip C. Jessup, U.S.; José Arce, Argentina; John D. L. Hood, Australia; and Eelco N. van Kleefens, Netherlands, who is addressing the Security Council

Arriving with Jack Ross (left) at the Palais de Chaillot for the first Paris meeting of the Security Council, September 1948

...nsidering the complications of Southeast Asian Affairs, March 1950, with Assistant Secretary of ...ate for Far Eastern Affairs W. Walton Butter-...orth (left) and Secretary of State Dean Acheson ...enter)

ACME PHOTÓ

With Emperor Bao Dai of Vietnam at the Imperial Palace, Hanoi, January 1950

COMMISSARIAT DE LA REPUBLIQUE POUR LE TONKIN ET LE NORD ANNAM, BUREAU PRESSE INFORMATION, SERVICE CINÉ PHOTO

With Prime Minister Nguyen Phan Long in Hanoi, January 1950

COMMISSARIAT DE LA REPUBLIQUE POUR LE TONKIN ET LE NORD ANNAM, BUREAU PRESSE INFORMATION, SERVICE CINÉ PHOTO

*With Ernest Bevin (center) and Hector McNeil (right) of the United Kingdom,
October 1949*

OFFICIAL UN PHOTO, DEPARTMENT OF PUBLIC INFORMATION

With Sir Alexander Cadogan of the United Kingdom, January 1949

OFFICIAL UN PHOTO, DEPARTMENT OF PUBLIC INFORMATION

With Ting-fu Tsiang, chairman of the Chinese
delegation, November 1949

With João Muñiz of Brazil (left) and Luis Padilla
Nervo of Mexico (right), December 1949

OFFICIAL UN PHOTO, DEPARTMENT OF PUBLIC INFORMATION

The Jessups arrive in Singapore, February
1950

CHUNG SHING JIT PAO PHOTO

Discussing the Palestine-Arab mediation with Count Folke Bernadotte (left) and Ralph Bunche, July 1948

Discussing disarmament with Senator Warren Austin (center) and Secretary of State Dean Acheson (right), November 1951

OFFICIAL UN PHOTOS, DEPARTMENT OF PUBLIC INFORMATION

Announcing the U.S. recognition of the state of Israel to the General Assembly, May 14, 1948

With Eleanor Roosevelt and Sir Zafrulla Khan, Pakistani Minister of Foreign Affairs, December 1952

*At the Khyber Pass, an unexpected delegation of tribesmen petition for indepen-
dence for Pushtoonistan, February 1950*

5

The Abortive Empire of Bao Dai

Having left Korea, as described in chapter 2, we made brief
stop-overs at Okinawa and Hong Kong and visited Taiwan and
Manila, before arriving at Saigon on January 24, 1950. Since
this begins my story of the "Birth of Vietnam," or "The Abortive Empire of Bao Dai," I must go back and fill in the special
nature of my visit to Vietnam, where the French were still in
control.

It is still a difficult time at which to write about Vietnam
since most of us are so emotionally disturbed by American involvement there that it is almost impossible to look even at the
background dispassionately. Events and policies which I shall
try to describe seem to me to have been skipped over too rapidly or else ignored in many of the accounts I have read. I can
quite agree that my own experience in Vietnam is unimportant. Most of those other accounts concentrate on the horror
that has been revealed to us, not only in the Pentagon Papers
but in such reports as those of the Mylai monstrosity. In an
overall view of history, I agree entirely that it is this odious
side of our tragic intrusion in Vietnam that is of such terrible
importance. The attitudes of 1948 and 1949 and 1950, on

which I shall concentrate, are less dramatic. No doubt there were mistakes in those days too, but I am dealing with another example of the birth of a nation. Perhaps the result was a miscarriage. I think our objective twenty-two years ago was a good objective; we never really attained it. In the case of Korea, although we failed to attain the unity of North and South, a republic was established and creditably endures today. The Korean war was ugly as all wars are ugly, but the Republic of Korea exists today with as much peace and stability as many older states in other parts of the world. Seoul can be contrasted with Belfast, for example. As this is being written, North and South Korea have begun friendly negotiations on ways to reunite the country. Unlike the Korean case, the United Nations played no role in the birth of Vietnam; perhaps that is one of the reasons why the new state did not mature.

The general background of the Indochinese story after World War II is familiar and I do not pretend to retell it. For the purposes of this personal narrative, which concentrates on one individual—Bao Dai—and on a brief period during which I was officially concerned with United States policy toward Vietnam, I find it necessary to refer in some detail to Bao Dai and the role he played in a complicated drama. But I cannot pretend to write a biography of "His Majesty." It is a fascinating, tragic drama in which Vietnamese characters are as numerous and more difficult to remember and their names to pronounce to oneself than the ninety-seven persons who figure in the *dramatis personae* in *Anna Karenina*. For the facts, I have relied—in addition to the State Department files to which I have access—largely on two writers, Philippe Devillers and Ellen Hammer.[1] By focusing attention on what are to the historian merely details, I risk a distortion of the whole; it may be that United States policy in 1948 to 1952 was based on a distorted interpretation.

Annam won its independence from China early in the fifteenth century. It produced a number of able rulers who, in ensuing centuries, struggled against French advances in the pattern of Western aggression against the small states of Asia. In 1884, France established a protectorate over Annam and Tonkin and thereby started a wave of insurrection. The young Emperor Ham Nghi, who was then fifteen years old, fled to the mountains but raised an army against the French invaders. The tides of opposition rose and fell until 1925, when another boy, aged twelve, became emperor; his dynastic name was Bao Dai.

Bao Dai was educated in France, returning to his "empire" and ascending the throne in the old imperial city of Hué in 1932 at the age of nineteen. But he was emperor in name only and had no reason to be attracted to the French in Indochina any more than had his predecessor, Emperor Ham Nghi. He appointed as his chief minister Ngo Dinh Diem, an able young mandarin of thirty-two, who was thwarted in all his efforts by the French and soon resigned; Diem was much sought after by principal Vietnamese factions in later years. In 1955 Diem would oust his old chief after a referendum in which Bao Dai was roundly defeated and Diem became Vietnam's first president.

When in 1945 the Japanese offered to "liberate" Vietnam, Bao Dai was quite ready to cooperate with them. Our American war psychology lingers at least subconsciously, and we think of the French as allies and therefore of Bao Dai as a "collaborator" in the pejorative sense of that term. But Franklin Roosevelt had little use for the French and, to the Vietnamese, the French were the white oppressors who had mistreated them for sixty years; the Japanese were fellow Asians and had not then done anything to offend the Vietnamese; Bao Dai was ready to cooperate with the Japanese Asian Co-Prosperity Sphere. On March 11, 1945, he issued an imperial proclamation which announced that, in view of the world situation and particularly the situation in Asia, the government of Vietnam publicly proclaimed that from that date the protectorate treaty with France was abolished and the country reclaimed its right to independence.

March 19, 1945, Bao Dai personally assumed the responsibilities of power, accepting the collective resignation of his ministers. The Emperor tried to persuade Ngo Dinh Diem to return as premier but when Diem refused, he designated Tran Trong Kim, an historian who was known for his nationalist opinions and who had fled to Bangkok and Singapore to escape the French. His government was composed mostly of young patriots, raised in the French tradition and culture, but ardently insistent on their independence. The Japanese demonstrated that they were not real liberators, although they did finally transfer control of Cochin China to Bao Dai just before the A-bomb dropped on Hiroshima.

Meanwhile Ho Chi Minh had been strengthening the power of the Viet Minh and, since he took a stand against the Japanese, was helped by the French and by the Americans through the OSS (Office of Strategic Services), which parachuted arms and supplies and radios and maintained a personal contact with Ho Chi Minh, who has been characterized as "one of the most remarkable leaders of the Asian liberation movement," a man opposed to violence and properly to be compared to Gandhi.[2]

In August 1945, Bao Dai merged his government with the Viet Minh under Ho, who had taken control of Hanoi and was supposed to have the support of the Western allies. Bao Dai himself appealed to President Truman, to King George V of England, to Chiang Kai-shek, and to General de Gaulle to preserve the independence of Vietnam after the Japanese surrender.[3] Under pressure from some of his entourage, Bao Dai abdicated on August 24 but sought to assure a legal transfer of authority by having representatives of the Viet Minh come to his palace at Hué, where he turned over to them the imperial seals and signed an act of abdication. Urging everyone to cooperate with the new Viet Minh government, Bao Dai, taking his old family name of Vinh Thuy, announced that after ruling for twenty years he was now a free citizen in an independent country:

"Vive l'independence de Viet-Nam
Vive notre Republique Democratique."

The United States Chief of Intelligence, OSS, for the China Theater, reported that during the week of September 10, he

had an interview with Bao Dai, former emperor of Annam, at which Ho Chi Minh, the president of the Provisional Government of Viet Nam, and Prince Souphanouvong, the brother of the king of Laos, were present. The interview was on a friendly unofficial basis, as a result of an invitation from Ho Chi Minh. . . .

Bao Dai, during the interview, stated that he had voluntarily abdicated, and was not coerced by the Provisional Government. He said that he would no longer see his people oppressed, and that, approving the nationalistic action of the Viet Minh, he therefore abdicated as an example to his people. He said that his great hope was that the people of Viet Nam could gain the independence they so ardently desire, and that he would rather live as a private citizen with a free people than rule a nation of slaves.[4]

Ho Chi Minh designated Bao Dai as Supreme Counselor of his government. Some say that Ho personally disapproved of Bao Dai's abdication, preferring a combination (which was in fact considered on August 22) of the monarchy plus a Viet Minh government which Ho believed would have enabled him quickly to secure international recognition. Robert Shaplen prints the text of a letter sent by Ho Chi Minh to his American contact, known as "Lieutenant John," shortly after the Japanese surrender. He wrote that the National Liberation Committee "begs U.S. authorities to inform United Nations the following. We were fighting Japs on the side of the United Nations. Now Japs surrendered. We beg United Nations to realize their solemn promise that all nationalities will be given democracy and independence. If United Nations forget their solemn promise and don't grant Indochina full independence, we will keep fighting until we get it." [5] (Ho seems to have been referring to the "United Nations" as the wartime coalition and the principles of the Atlantic Charter first adopted by Roosevelt and Churchill, and not to the international organization established at San Francisco in 1945.)

In the winter of 1946 it seems that Ho Chi Minh, as well as Bao Dai, were in Paris where Ho was negotiating with the French. The story is that Ho offered to change places with Bao, making Bao the head of the government while Ho became Supreme Counselor. Bao consulted his American adviser, Major Buckley of the OSS, who said that that was just the combination they had hoped for. But on the same day, Ho changed his mind and withdrew the offer.[6] Ho reached an agreement with the French on March 6 which was widely heralded as a French accommodation with Asian nationalism, but it lacked the essential substance. Nevertheless, this agreement, signed in Hanoi by Jean Sainteny for France and by Ho Chi Minh, recognized the Democratic Republic of Vietnam as "a free state with its own government, parliament, army and finances, forming part of the Indochinese Federation and the French Union." The question of uniting Tonkin, Annam, and Cochin China was to be determined by a referendum.[7]

The cooperation between Ho and Bao Dai continued, at least superficially. On March 18, 1946, Bao Dai, at Ho's request, flew to China in an American plane to appeal to the Americans and Nationalist Chinese to help keep the peace in Asia.[8] But Bao Dai then made Hong Kong his headquarters for three years, lending support to the report that he was just a playboy; he did stay aloof from politics, but was wooed by both Ho Chi Minh and the French. Both Ho and Bao were insisting on the unity and independence of Vietnam, but by September 1946, they were already at odds.

From December 1946, the French were practically at war with the Viet Minh. On May 22, 1947, Ambassador Jefferson Caffery in Paris cabled that Foreign Minister Georges Bidault assured him "that they did not contemplate any sort of a puppet government under Bao Dai." But on the previous day Consul Charles Reed in Saigon had said in a telegram that one of the two main contenders was the "National Union Front with Bao Dai—not personally popular but important only through former position." But Reed also thought that the French would not install a puppet regime and that there were rumors that Bao Dai and Ho Chi Minh were in communication. In August, however, Reed reported the French were "exhausting all means to get Bao Dai to return [from Hong Kong] and obviate their having to treat with Ho."

Part of the National Front was said to want Bao Dai and constitutional monarchy, but the other part wanted a repubic. At almost that moment, the National Front acted to get in touch with Bao Dai in Hong Kong so that he might direct the nationalist movement for independence and territorial unity. At the end of August, the French told Ambassador Caffery: "Strong sentiment has developed recently in favor of Bao Dai and practically everyone who is not pro-Communist is turning towards him, not that they think highly of Bao Dai, but because they are afraid of the Communists and he is the only man in sight we can build up to face Ho Chi Minh and his Communist gang." However, "the French are not enthusiastic about Bao Dai. When he was Emperor he took little or no interest in government affairs, preferring 'to play tennis and drive his car and stay a lot around the palace with his wife, to whom he is devoted.' " On October 28, 1947, Caffery reported that the French were likely to reach an agreement with Bao Dai and that this would result in "a considerable increase in the strength of Bao Dai's followers" and possibly would induce elements of the Viet Minh and perhaps Ho himself to reach an agreement with Bao Dai and the French.

In January 1948, Ho made a last attempt at cooperation with Bao; the attempt failed. In June 1948, Bao signed with the French the second of the so-called Baie d'Along agreements which he thought assured independence and unity, but his advisers said he had been taken in. After the first of these agreements, December 7, 1947, Bao had fled to France for four months; it was then he gained the sobriquet of "the night club emperor."

There ensued a prolonged period during which Bao negotiated with the French, as Ho had done, but his path and Ho's had finally diverged. At times, Bao negotiated stiffly with the French, and then vacillated. Back in Vietnam, groups were hopelessly split. "To many of his countrymen Bao Dai did not symbolize the cause of independence. It is not unusual in history, however, to find even puppet rulers transformed by the pressure of events into nationalist leaders—and this happened to Bao Dai." [9] In January 1948, two important Indochinese groups patched up their differences and pledged support to Bao Dai; these were the Cao Dai and the Hoa Hao. Pham Cong Toc, the Cao Dai pope, "openly aligned himself with the Bao Dai government in July 1949." The Cao Dai League claimed one to two million adherents.[10]

In the West, I think in London as well as in Washington, Bao Dai gradually became the symbol of Vietnamese nationalism, while Ho Chi Minh was identified not as a nationalist, but as a Communist. He was indeed a Communist, a confirmed Marxist, but undoubtedly a patriot. Once we ceased to need Ho Chi Minh's help against the Japanese, we allowed ourselves to think of him as in another enemy camp—the camp of the Communists. The British had a comparable experience training and equipping the guerrillas in the jungles of Malaysia to fight the Japanese and then after the war turning to a long bitter campaign to destroy them as Communists.[11] Just as the Dutch missed an opportunity, shortly after the surrender of the Japanese forces, to make a compromise but peaceful deal with the Indonesians, so the French, dominated in this matter by a colonialist tradition and by arrogant military men, went with sublime confidence down the road to disaster along which we allowed ourselves to be dragged.

After Bao Dai went from Hong Kong to France, he signed, on March 8, 1949, an agreement with President Vincent Auriol of France at the Elysée Palace in Paris, an agreement which promised much and withheld a good deal. The March 8 agreement did recognize the independence of Vietnam, Cambodia, and Laos within the French Union. In June 1949, Cochin China, which had been a separate colonial area, was merged with Annam and Tonkin in Vietnam, and Bao Dai became head of state. The March 8 agreement was formalized on June 14, 1949, by an exchange of letters in Saigon between the French High Commissioner and Bao Dai. Just as the French thereafter took every opportunity to ask us for help, we never missed a chance to urge them to ratify the March 8 agreement and to give real independence to Vietnam.

The posture of the United States toward Indochinese independence was made evident during the summer of 1948, after the signature of the Baie d'Along agreements and while the French politicians were delaying ratification. That same general outlook had prevailed in the State Department for some time. Acting on a memorandum of John Carter Vincent, Director of Far Eastern Affairs, dated December 3, 1946, Dean Acheson, then Under Secretary of State, told the French Ambassador we would like to help but would not mediate. He warned that the French could not conquer the country by military means; the British had been wise enough not to attempt such a course in Burma. In this same meeting he noted that if some other state brought the matter to the UN Security Council, as had been done in the Indonesian case, there would be a question whether Indochina was a purely internal French concern or a situation likely to disturb the peace of the world.[12]

In February 1947, the American embassy in Paris, and subsequently Secretary of State Marshall, said "there is no escape

from the fact that the trend of the times is to the effect that colonial empires in the XIX Century sense are rapidly becoming
things of the past," as shown by British experience in India
and Burma and the Dutch in Indonesia.[13]

On May 13, 1947, Secretary Marshall told the embassy to impress on the French that we had no solution of our own to suggest but we were "inescapably concerned with the situation in
Far East generally, upon which developments [in] Indochina
are likely to have a profound effect. . . . Vietnam cause [is]
proving rallying-cry for all anti Western forces and playing in
hands [of] Communists all areas." He hoped the French would
deal generously with the Vietnamese in finding a solution and
restoring peace. He urged that in finding a representative Vietnamese they would avoid setting up an "impotent puppet
Govt. along lines [of] Cochinchina regime." He feared that an
attempt to restore Bao Dai would imply that the "democracies
reduced [to] resort[ing to] monarchy as weapon against
Communism." [14] This last remark seemed not to take into account the fact that monarchical regimes were indigenous to the
area—in Thailand, Laos, Cambodia, and Vietnam—although
the republican pattern was beginning to emerge after the end
of the war. The monarchical aspect soon ceased to figure in the
State Department's thinking; the question was whether Bao
Dai could rally the support of the Vietnamese people.

On July 10, 1948, before events had progressed in Indochina, Woodruff Wallner, First Secretary of our embassy in
Paris, with the concurrence of Ambassador Jefferson Caffery,
suggested that the Department might authorize the embassy to
tell all levels of the officials of the Schuman government that
the United States was convinced that France must unequivo-
cally and promptly approve the principle of the independence
of the three states in Indochina within the French Union, or
lose Indochina. On July 14, the Department gave the authorization to apply persuasion and pressure as the embassy thought
likely to produce results. The United States was disposed to

support such a move by the French as a forward-looking step toward settlement in Indochina.

In August 1948, the same views were repeated. On October 1, 1948, Ambassador Caffery reported that some French officials appreciated the position of the United States but there was little hope of getting action by the French Assembly where the Socialists were committed to negotiating with Ho Chi Minh. The embassy had been told that Bao Dai was furious at the lack of progress and was consoling himself on the Riviera.

After the signature of the March 8 accord in the spring of 1949, the tone of the Department's instructions to the Paris embassy seem rather more cautious, but the effort still was to impress the French with the need to prove that they were not using Bao Dai only as a puppet. On June 29, 1949, the American Consul in Saigon was instructed to tell French High Commissioner Pignon that the United States considered the March 8 accord merely as a starting point beyond which the French would have to move. The Consul was told for his own information that India and Thailand both regarded the March 8 agreement as a cloak for continued French domination; they were probably correct.

By the summer of 1949, as Ambassador-at-Large, I was officially involved with American policy in Asia. On August 22, 1949, Charles S. Reed, Chief of Southeast Asian Affairs, sent me a memorandum summarizing conclusions of his division. He put first of all the need for pressing the French for larger concessions and full implementation of the March 8 agreement with Bao Dai. If we could get the French to move, we should then try to enlist the support for Bao Dai of other Asian countries such as India, Pakistan, Burma, Thailand, and the Philippines that were now holding back to see what the French would do. As a next step, we should be prepared to take the risk of recognizing the Bao Dai government and giving it economic aid and military supplies. Reed cautioned that these views had not been cleared with the Western European Division; one knew that they would tend toward supporting the French position. Reed ended on the note that we should use the United States Information Service to the utmost since we were fighting communist ideas and ideas were fought best with other ideas and not with guns.

This is frankly a personal narrative, and I must not linger too long attempting to summarize a complex bit of history. The first item I have from the archives recording my own expression of views on Vietnam is dated September 8, 1949. Of course these were the official views, but I found them entirely sound. On September 8, Henri Bonnet, the French ambassador in Washington, came to see me in the State Department. His theme was one to which we listened many times—the need of France for our support in France's struggle against communism in Asia. Bonnet said that Secretary Acheson had talked about nationalism in Southeast Asia as a counter to communism. With that he said he agreed, but the Communists were developing nationalism. All the more reason, I replied, that we should build up the non-Communist nationalists. I mentioned then, as I did often in later days, the importance of such gestures as the transferring of Indochinese affairs from the French Colonial Office to their Foreign Office.

In the following week, a battery of the experts from Far Eastern Affairs, headed by Walton Butterworth, had a conference with a group of British officials, including Dening of the Foreign Office, suggesting that it would be helpful if Foreign Secretary Ernest Bevin would urge Foreign Minister Robert Schuman to follow the policy lines the United States was advocating. The British stated that they had been urging Nehru to deal with Bao Dai instead of with Ho Chi Minh. This staff meeting with the British was just before Secretary Acheson met with Bevin and Schuman in Washington. Acheson and Bevin urged Schuman to move along with further concessions to Bao Dai. Schuman was told that as early as May 1949 we were discussing the opportunity for recognizing the government of Bao Dai but believed we could not move until the French ratified the March 8 accords, although we were considering *de facto* recognition which is, so to speak, a half-way stage. We hoped that some of the Asian states would take the lead in recognizing Bao Dai but as they delayed, we decided to move forward.

I was never a "Far Eastern expert" but for some twenty-five years I had been actively involved as an officer of the Institute of Pacific Relations, a remarkably fine organization which was judicially determined by a federal court to be an educational and not a propaganda organization, but was none the less effectively killed by the China Lobby and Senator Joseph McCarthy. When in 1949, as Ambassador-at-Large, I was given official responsibility for dealing with Far Eastern matters, I had a certain academic background, an acquaintance with many of the leaders of Asian countries, and a deep interest in the emergence of new nations from their colonial status, but I had never been in Asia. Before my Far Eastern trip in 1950, I had represented the United States in the UN Security Council in its attempts at another case of midwifery—the birth of Indonesia—which, I believe, does represent a United Nations achievement in which the United States should be proud to recall that it played a leading part. The case of Korea has also already been described.

As Ambassador-at-Large in 1949, I had the advantage of special advisers in addition to the regular officers of the State Department. As noted in chapter 2, to assist in our concentrated study of Asian affairs, Secretary Acheson had agreed to the appointment of two men who, while not Far Eastern specialists, were familiar with the area and its problems and who had the stature to be dispassionate and wise weighers of evidence. These two "consultants," as they were called, were Raymond Fosdick, who had become president of the Rockefeller Foundation after playing a major role in setting up the Secretariat of the League of Nations, and Everett Case, president of

Colgate University. I was also fortunate enough to have detailed to the office of Ambassador-at-Large at that time one of the ablest of the younger Foreign Service officers, Charles Yost.

Yost wrote for Fosdick, Case, and me two memoranda on November 1 and 7, 1949, in which he reviewed the situation in Southeast Asia. His memoranda do reveal our attitude toward Communist expansion and our conviction that Ho Chi Minh was a tool of Moscow, but they also underline the fact that, at that period, we did not contemplate any military involvement whatsoever in Southeast Asia.

Yost noted that, despite the success of the Round Table Conference at The Hague which signaled Dutch acceptance of the independence of Indonesia, and despite gradual improvement in the situation in Burma and Malaya, various components of the Southeast Asia region, and especially Indochina, remained weak and vulnerable. We had to face the possibility that Communist control of Indochina might be consolidated in a few months with psychological and political effects of crisis proportions in neighboring countries. The indigenous Chinese communities in the Southeast Asian countries would be stimulated and supplied with arms. The somewhat opportunistic and insecure regimes of the area, particularly in Burma and Thailand, might accommodate themselves to the "wave of the future" or be replaced through *coups d'état* by other regimes which would bow. These developments might well occur before our economic and technical aid or educational programs had time to take effect, and before we had strengthened the internal security forces of these countries.

He concluded that we could not accept the loss of Indochina without exploring every possible expedient to prevent it—but he did not suggest that armed intervention was one of the possible expedients. Yost suggested we consider turning over the responsibility for Southeast Asia to the British, French, and Dutch, but warned that if the situation was really critical we could not escape the consequences for the United States by claiming it was someone else's business.

He doubted that it would be possible to make a satisfactory deal with Ho Chi Minh; since we believed Ho was a Kremlin-inspired Communist, any assurance he might give us would be worthless. Like the Chinese, Ho would continue to follow the Kremlin line unless he was convinced it was to his advantage to stop doing so. Unless there were proofs to the contrary, we must assume Ho was and would remain a Moscow stooge. Therefore we must try every feasible step to prevent Ho from consolidating control of Indochina.

This would not be easy, but we must continue to press Robert Schuman of France to ratify and implement the March 8 agreement within weeks. After ratification we must take steps to support the international status of Bao Dai and thereby strengthen his regime in the country. We should offer needed economic aid, which the French could not supply.

If the Chinese Communists should aid Ho with troops or arms, the United States should bring the case to the United Nations and urge setting up a UN frontier commission. We should encourage French or international efforts to negotiate a truce between Bao Dai and Ho, but only if this could be done without leaving Ho in command of the situation. Even if these efforts were unsuccessful, Yost suggested, we must mobilize our "nonmilitary strength" now to show neighboring countries our real interest and be in a better position to help them if necessary.

Even countries such as India and Australia would support us only if we succeeded in our policies. If our policies did not succeed, we would have to reconsider our whole strategic position in Asia, in conjunction with the powers concerned and, if need be, pick out which areas must be held, as the northern frontier of Greece was being held. This last point about Greece referred to the Truman Doctrine for the protection of Greece and Turkey from Soviet attack or subversion. But a secret memorandum of November 25, 1949, by James L. O'Sullivan of Far Eastern Affairs, stated that a containment policy like the one adopted for Greece was impossible in Indochina, where the solution had to be an internal political one.

In his second memorandum on the subject, Yost pressed his points. He did not think we needed to become associated with Bao Dai unless he showed capacity to win a much larger segment of Annamese opinion. The trouble was that, in our distaste for French colonialism and for Bao as its "running dog," and our desire to be on the side of the angels in the Far East, we might accept Ho as an angel and be led by him down the garden path as he had led a majority of his countrymen. The evidence showed that Ho was the most dangerous and powerful agent of Soviet communism in Southeast Asia. There was danger that we might conclude that since he was powerful he was irresistible and we might try to comfort ourselves by thinking he might not be so bad after all.

Then followed the important statement, rather ahead of its time in American thinking, that if we believed the people in Indochina passionately desired communism, we might have to acquiesce, but this was not then the reality. The reality was that a Moscow-trained Communist, largely through the stupidity of the French and the absence of an acceptable alternative, had captured the nationalist movement in one of the key countries of the area. Finally, Yost recommended that we should not place all our bets on Bao Dai, but should explore with the French every possibility of finding an alternative to Ho that would be acceptable to the Indochinese.

These memoranda are summarized at length because they reveal informed opinion in the State Department at the time. Most likely Yost had seen drafts of the paper which became the key National Security Council study on Asia, known as NSC 48/2, approved by President Truman on December 30, 1949. The NSC paper said that "Particular attention should be given to the problem of French Indochina and action should be taken to bring home to the French the urgency of removing the barriers to the obtaining by Bao Dai . . . of the support of a substantial proportion of the Vietnamese." [15] But Yost's suggestion for resort to the UN Security Council in case of actual Chinese intervention was perhaps just a personal view inspired by the use of the Security Council in the Palestine and Indonesian cases. (Yost was much later to become United States ambassador to the United Nations.)

However, we warned the French as early as December 1946 that some other state might take the case to the United Nations as had been done with Indonesia. Possible recourse to the United Nations was discussed later as will be noted. The general stress was on the identity of Soviet imperialist expansion and communism, the complete lack of any thought of military intervention, and the search for solutions acceptable to the Indochinese; France was the stumbling block.

I followed this line of thought in a conversation with Ambassador Jean Chauvel, permanent representative of France to the United Nations, after a dinner at his apartment on November 10, 1949.

Chauvel was considered an expert on Indochina, and he told me that he was very close to Georges Bidault, who was twice Prime Minister and eight times Foreign Minister. When Chauvel was in the Foreign Office, Bidault had asked him to take over Indochina, but he had refused because he would have had the responsibility without power, since Indochina was not under the Foreign Office. He asked me to tell him the attitude of the United States toward the Indochina problem. I said I would give him my personal view, but that the Department's view was similar. This view was that it was very difficult for the United States or other countries to recognize or further support Bao Dai before France had ratified the March 8 agreement and taken other action indicating that they were treating him as an independent ruler. The transfer of Indochina affairs to the Foreign Office was one example of what needed to be done. I urged upon him our view that the experience of the Dutch and the British showed the folly of reluctant, slow yielding to emerging nationalism instead of voluntary cooperation in the achievement of independent statehood.

Chauvel neither agreed nor disagreed but said he would be getting in touch with Bidault. Just before I started on my trip to the Far East, Ambassador Bonnet told me in Washington that he hoped the United States and Great Britain would recognize Bao. Actually, the United States hesitated as a matter of policy and not due to any thought that we were not free to recognize Bao. On January 5, 1950, Deputy Legal Adviser Leonard Meeker informed the political officer in charge of Southeast Asian Affairs, that although the French still limited the powers of Vietnam, the United States was entitled to extend recognition if it wished and that Vietnam was already eligible for membership in the United Nations. The same conclusions applied to Laos and Cambodia. It is thus clear that when we did recognize Bao Dai, it was not merely a nervous reaction to Peking's and Moscow's recognition of Ho Chi Minh's Democratic Republic of Vietnam, although some accounts give this impression.

It is quite true that in the case of Bao Dai, the Department of State followed a recognition policy quite different from that which governed its attitude at that time toward recognition of the Chinese Communist government in Peking. While there have long existed certain criteria for the recognition of governments, which Secretary Acheson expounded to the Senate Committee on Foreign Relations in executive session in October 1949, the extension or withholding of recognition is a matter of policy and not of obligation under international law. I do not intend to include here an essay on this subject, which I have often described in my writings as a professor of international law. I got into some trouble in testifying to a Senate committee in 1951 that we had not even "considered" recognizing the Peking government; a hostile Senator retorted that it was the Department's business to "consider" all alternative lines of policy. I had to explain that I meant the reasons for not recognizing were so overwhelmingly conclusive at the time, we discarded the possibility of extending recognition and thus stopped giving it "serious consideration."

The fact is that the recognition policy of the United States has, throughout our history, fluctuated between widely different attitudes from the criteria of Thomas Jefferson which rested on the will of the people substantially declared, to Woodrow Wilson's unfortunate moralistic policy toward Mexico, on through Stimson's punitive nonrecognition policy which was supposed to act as a deterrent: the Stimson policy was applied to the bastard Manchukuo which I discuss in chapter 8. Around 1950, the domestic political turmoil surrounding the China "tangle" caused so much popular misunderstanding of the problem of recognition, that I suggested to the State Department's Historical Office that a complete historical-legal study be made and published. My files indicate they did draft such a study but for sundry reasons, both tactical and practical, it was not published.[16]

On October 12, 1949, I accompanied Secretary Acheson to an executive session of the Senate Foreign Relations Committee; Consultants Case and Fosdick also attended. Acheson was trying to give the Senators an understanding of our attitude toward Far Eastern problems and especially toward the French in Vietnam. He told the Committee: "If we put ourselves sympathetically on the side of nationalism, which is the dominant spiritual force in that area, we have put ourselves on the side of the thing which more than anything else can oppose communism. . . . We will get nowhere, I think, by supporting the French as a colonial power against Indo-China."

It was in that session that he explained the standard criteria for recognition. He told the Senators he had discussed the question of recognition with Bevin and Schuman but that the

United States was not intending to recognize. He did say: "If the Chinese, after thinking it all over, want to be Communists, that is their business. We do not think they will. . . . This Chinese government is really a tool of Russian Imperialism in China. That gives us our fundamental starting point."

Just before leaving Washington on December 14, 1949, I briefed a group of the members of the Foreign Affairs Committee of the House of Representatives about my trip. I was accompanied by Jack McFall, Assistant Secretary for Congressional Relations, and we talked with Congressmen Kee, Democrat of West Virginia, Eaton, Republican of New Jersey, and "Mike" Mansfield, Democrat of Montana. The Congressmen were chiefly interested in discussing relations with Communist China, but Mansfield did ask about the situation in Thailand and Indochina and I sketched the situation as we saw it. I explained that in addition to visiting various individual countries, there would be a meeting in Bangkok with the American chiefs of mission of all countries in the area, where the thinking in the State Department could be checked with the experience of the people in the field and their recommendations could be obtained. The State Department would be represented by Assistant Secretary of State Walton Butterworth and me.[17]

We arrived in Saigon January 24, 1950, but Emperor Bao Dai was not to be found in that capital city. With the stupid arrogance which unhappily has frequently characterized European colonial administrators—and, I am sorry to say, our own military in their dealing with less advanced peoples as in the Philippines and Vietnam—the French had taken the Norodom Palace in Saigon as their Government House and told Bao Dai he could occupy the much humbler No. 2 palace in the city. He declined and took up his residence in Hanoi, where I was to see him three days later. Meanwhile I would talk with the French officials and with Bao Dai's Prime Minister and Minister of Foreign Affairs, Nguyen Phan Long. Long, as Robert

Shaplen says, was a competent man and pro-American, but unsuccessful in winning over the *attentistes*—the fence-sitters.
The French forced Bao Dai to dismiss Long a few months later
because, Shaplen records, of his attempts to "foster a strong independent nationalist position." [18] The French High Commissioner told me Long was intelligent but knew nothing about
government or administration.

My talk with the Prime Minister dealt largely with economic
and governmental administrative matters but of course we
talked about the prospects for peace. He told me there were a
good many who were then working with the Viet Minh (now
called Viet Cong) but who were true nationalists and not Communists. When real power was transferred by the French to
Bao Dai, there would be a great rallying to his side, and resistance of the population would gradually cease. He told me, as I
was to be told again in Hanoi, that the French could not pacify
the country and he pleaded for arms for the Vietnamese. He
said there were some 40,000 men in the Vietnamese army but
only half of them were armed. There were also some 10,000 of
the Cao Dai sect which opposed the Viet Minh.

Naturally I got different opinions as I talked on January 25
and 26 with French High Commissioner Pignon and his civil-
ian and military colleagues. I had received at Saigon a long telegram from Assistant Secretary for the Far East Walton Butterworth, restating the Department's position as background for
my talk with Pignon. Butterworth said that Bao Dai had ex-
hibited qualities better than we had dared to expect but that
popular opposition had not been checked. The United States
was studying the question of recognition; the British were inclined to extend *de facto* recognition as Malcolm McDonald,
their High Commissioner for the Far East, had recommended.
India was opposed to Bao Dai but, aside from India and Pakistan, it was thought other Commonwealth countries would follow the British lead. As soon as the French ratified the March 8
accord, the State Department would recommend to the Presi-

dent the recognition of Bao Dai in such a way as to be most helpful to him. This statement of the British position was in line with a cable from the American embassy in London on November 9, 1949, which I had seen before leaving Washington.

Pignon was kind enough to explain to me his concept of Oriental psychology. The Oriental, he said, is not motivated by political theories or principles. Throughout history he has always regarded success as the manifestation of the will of God and not the result of any effort on the part of man. Failure is an indication of the wrath of the gods of chance. The life of the Oriental is regulated by "favorable" and "unfavorable" signs, since he is devoted to superstition and astrology. He is a gambler. Bao Dai, according to Pignon, was the typical Oriental. He did not, said Pignon, proceed on the basis of right or wrong, but on whether or not what he proposed to do would succeed. (If one accepts this diagnosis, one wonders whether any American politicians have Oriental blood!) Diplomatic Counselor du Gardier also stressed to me the Oriental gambling instinct.

Pignon said that the return of Bao Dai to Vietnam from France was one of the important events in 1949. (The French did not like his being in France pressing his country's cause with French officials.) But Pignon did not have a high opinion of Bao Dai's government. He did say there were very few Vietnamese qualified technically for government jobs although there were many "intellectuals." Bao Dai had only two really first-rate administrators, one of whom was Governor Tri, whom I would meet in Hanoi. He also admired Tran Van Huu but did not mention to me that Huu was a French citizen. (It was Huu who later succeeded Long as Prime Minister when the French forced Bao Dai to dismiss Long.)

Pignon asserted that he considered the principal task of the French was to build up Bao Dai, and recognition by the United States and Great Britain would be of enormous psychological value. He admitted that ratification of the March 8 accord was an important step to be taken before recognition could follow. He denied that Bao Dai was a French puppet. But while he agreed with me that other steps should follow, he said that any French announcement of an evolutionary policy, while having a good effect abroad, would have a bad effect in Indochina. The *attentistes* would claim that they had forced concessions and should continue their fence-sitting in order to get even more. He sidestepped my question about giving the best palace in Saigon to the Emperor; after all, Hanoi was the traditional capital, he said. (In a telegraphic instruction to the American embassy in Paris on March 29, 1950, the State Department said that it considered the transfer of the Saigon palace to Bao Dai with appropriate ceremonies was the most important single propaganda move that the French could make.) Pignon said it was important that public opinion in Vietnam not receive an impression that I left with a bad opinion of Bao Dai. Later the French were to feel that I was too exuberant in my tributes to the Emperor.

General Marcel Carpentier filled me in on the military situation. He said there were recurrent waves of terrorism and frankly stated that the then current wave was a direct result of my visit. He stressed the enormous sacrifices France was making. French forces in Indochina totaled about 150,000 men. More French officers were killed in a year in Indochina than France graduated annually from St. Cyr, the French West Point. Pignon added remarks which were in effect echoed in the United States in 1972; the French in Indochina are thousands of miles from their mother country and find it increasingly difficult to understand why the best of young Frenchmen are being killed at the rate of 1,000 a month for a cause they do not understand and for which they alone are bearing the burden.

General Carpentier said the Viet soldier was a good one but the problem was training officers. He said later he would resign before consenting to give arms directly to the Vietnamese. I found the French were unwilling to admit that Vietnamese could be trained as commissioned or even noncommissioned officers more rapidly than were Frenchmen in their own normal training system at home. The French apparently could not see that the Vietnamese could train their own people; they thought the product would not be good unless French soldiers and officers trained them. It was clear to me that they really did not trust the Vietnamese and were unwilling to turn over to them the arms and the military authority which the Vietnamese wanted to have and felt that they must have to establish peace in their country.

I found convincing a thorough memorandum which our able Consul General in Saigon, George Abbott, gave me on my arrival. In his analysis, reasons why Bao Dai was having such a hard time in winning more of his people to side with him openly, included these:

1. Lack of confidence in French good faith in living up to the March 8 agreement they made with Bao Dai.

2. Dissatisfaction with those agreements and desire for absolute independence.

3. Fear that political instability in France might result in a new French government which would either repudiate the March 8 accord as too liberal (that would be the Gaullists) or decide to deal with Ho Chi Minh (that would be if the Communist-Socialist front came to power).

4. The physical difficulty and danger of escaping from the clutches of Communist-controlled Viet Minh secret police and fear of Viet Minh reprisals in the villages. The arrival of the Chinese Communists at the frontier led to fear of Ho's victory.

5. Opposition to Bao Dai or members of his entourage, generally based on anti-monarchist feeling or belief that the Emperor represented reactionary right-wing elements.

With this background we left for Hanoi on January 26, 1950. The runway at Hanoi was too short for the U.S. Air Force plane which had flown us from Okinawa to Hong Kong and

Manila and on to Saigon, so we went in a French plane, a long flight over endless miles of jungle said to contain more tigers and elephants than any other place in the world. I suppose today some of it is defoliated and the animals dead or fled. Having looked down on those great forests in 1950 it is not hard for me to understand how hopeless it was for our air force to prevent the Viet Cong and North Vietnamese from coming south.

As we approached Hanoi we had a welcoming buzzing from small planes—I thought they came uncomfortably close. We landed, were greeted, and motored into the city of Hanoi escorted by armored cars, through lines of Vietnamese soldiers stationed every fifty feet on either side of the road, facing the bush with rifles readied. Viet Cong raids were not infrequent at Hanoi in those days.

The usual official demonstrations of "spontaneous" welcoming had been prepared. Little children waved American flags, and banners over the streets hailed the American Ambassador. We visited schools, workshops, an orphange, an art school, and a pottery shop. Security precautions were much in evidence.

On January 27 in the afternoon, accompanied by Consul General Abbott, then our ranking representative in Vietnam, and William Gibson, a Foreign Service officer who was my invaluable aid throughout the whole trip, I called on Emperor Bao Dai at the imperial palace. We were ushered up a broad carpeted staircase to the second floor and into a large sun-filled room furnished with comfortable sofas and chairs near the Emperor's desk. Bao Dai came forward and welcomed us as our escort disappeared; the Emperor had no one with him during our interview. We conversed in French.

My impression of Bao Dai was like that which Robert Shaplen records as told to him by an American diplomat who came to know the Emperor well. I quote it:

Bao Dai, above all, was an intelligent man. Intellectually, he could discuss the complex details of the various agreements and of the whole involved relationship with France as well as or better than anyone I knew. But he was a man who was crippled by his French upbringing. His manner was too impassive. He allowed himself to be sold by the French on an erroneous instead of a valid evolutionary concept, and this suited his own temperament. He was too congenial, and he was almost pathologically shy, which was one reason he always liked to wear dark glasses. [He was not wearing them when I met him.] He would go through depressive cycles and when he was depressed, he would dress himself in Vietnamese clothes instead of European ones, and would mince no words about the French. His policy, he said to me on one of those dour occasions, was one of *"grignotage,"* or "nibbling," and he was painfully aware of it. The French, of course, were never happy that we Americans had good relations with Bao Dai, and they told him so. Unfortunately, they also had some blackmail on him, about his relationship with gambling enterprises in Saigon and his love of the fleshpots. [19]

I read to the Emperor a message from Secretary of State Dean Acheson that had been planned and drafted in Washington before I started my Far Eastern trip. The message indicated the position already taken in the State Department and I quote part of it:

> The Secretary of State, Dean Acheson, has instructed me to express to Your Majesty the gratification of the United States Government at the assumption by Your Majesty of the powers transferred by the French Republic at the beginning of this year, and its confident best wishes for the future of the State of Vietnam with which it looks forward to establishing a closer relationship.

The State Department did not consider that the delivery of this message constituted "recognition," but official recognition did follow within ten days, as I shall indicate.

Bao Dai asked me to send his thanks to the Secretary, but we noted later that while the message was carried in the local press, there was no comment on this gesture. He referred to the recognition of the Ho Chi Minh government by the Chinese Communists and said this would be a boomerang to Ho's prestige in Vietnam since it would convince the fence-sitters—the *attentistes*—that Ho was affiliated with Peking and Moscow. He asked my impressions of the situation in Vietnam and I said we hoped good relations could continue to be maintained by Bao Dai with the French. He said France was a friend of Vietnam and he had no desire to break his country's ties with her.

The first task, he said, was to restore peace and for that he needed French help, although he said the French forces, even if increased, were not sufficient to pacify the country. The French would have to give the Vietnamese forces a free hand and the necessary arms. He talked about the March 8 agreement he had reached with President Auriol, the difficulties which had to be overcome, but the results of which he felt justified the concessions on both sides. He referred to Indochina as the "bastion of defense against communism in South East Asia."

I said that the U.S. government had three immediate interests in relation to Indochina: first, was our interest in seeing the realization of the independence and nationalist aspirations of the people; second, was our great interest in the political development of democratic ideals and practices in recently freed territories; and third, was our interest in good international relations.

Bao Dai assured me that under his jurisdiction, Indochina would follow principles of democratic procedure and noted that, although he was an hereditary monarch, he had been elected a deputy in their legislature in a free election. When elections were again possible they would be held and his own future would depend upon them.

He had an amazing detailed knowledge of economic statistics such as rice and rubber production and the volume and value of exports and imports. He spoke of relations with Laos and Cambodia and the right of Laos to have an outlet to the sea without the need to clear through Cambodia or Vietnam. In regard to his relations with France, he spoke always of the

"French Union" and did not, as I learned he had on other recent occasions, suggest that he wanted to break those ties.

In sending a telegraphic report of this meeting to Secretary
Acheson, I said I had a very favorable impression of the Emperor's sincerity and full understanding of economic and political problems, but not of great personal force or strength. The
chief problem was to win the fence-sitters; to this end French
ratification of the March 8 accords would help but more was
needed. The United States, I said, should extend recognition as
soon as possible since the Vietnamese attached much importance to that. When recognition was given, the message should
stress that it resulted from their own achievements, their actual
independence, and our sympathy with their national aspirations.

That evening the Emperor gave us a magnificent state ban-
quet. I quote a description of it from a letter my wife wrote to
her family at home:

[It was] all Vietnamese food and strong rice wine—the only concession to the French being Pommery champagne. The Emperor is
a very young, very smiling gentleman. His wife and children are living on the Riviera—it is too dangerous here for them, he told me.
He consoles himself with a beautiful singer who attended the dinner.
There were about 60 guests. The head table, which formed a T
at the end of a longer one, was covered with the three national flags
laid out in flower petals. After dinner we were entertained by native
singers, including the Emperor's lady, and an orchestra. The music,
I must confess, was not particularly impressive to these Western
ears, being a modernized and rather sentimental version of Chinese
nasality and whinings.

Before the dinner I had useful talks with British Consul
General Trevor Wilson, with two Catholic priests and also a
representative of the International Red Cross, who was having
very little success in attempts to locate and to help the French
prisoners of the Viet Minh. At 6 P.M. I had paid a courtesy call
on General Allesandri, French Commander in Tonkin and
Acting French Commissioner.

After dinner I had a private talk with Governor Nguyen Huu Tri, who was perhaps the best of Bao Dai's high officials —some were distinctly inferior types. As we reported to the State Department, Tri enjoyed the respect of both Vietnamese and French authorities—perhaps the only high-ranking official who did. He was a carry-over from the old Mandarin class of Vietnamese functionaries who had served during the French colonial period and even before that. He had no enemies, although some of the other officials in the Vietnam government criticized his conservatism.

In talking with me he stressed his view that the Viet Minh could be eliminated only by fully armed Vietnamese troops acting apart from the French—the same view which Prime Minister Long and Bao Dai had expressed. (There is nothing new in the idea—now called Vietnamization.) Tri cooperated with the French but was working for the day when they would withdraw. He told me that the Viet government in Tonkin under his administration was quite capable of running the village and provincial governments in the Red River Delta area. Many more villages would rally round them if they were assured of protection against raiding parties of both the Viet Minh and the French. He hoped I could use my influence to permit American arms to be furnished to him as head of the police and the military groups in his area and he would not admit that such arms would be traded to the Viet Minh or stolen, although he did admit there had been such cases in the past. He spoke with admiration of Bao Dai and with emotion of the poverty of his people.

The next day, January 28, we attended the inauguration of the Vietnamese Faculty of Letters in the National University of Vietnam in Hanoi. The French, in one of their rather rare wise gestures, had just turned the university over to the Vietnamese. Although there was much infiltration of Viet Minh (or Viet Cong, as we would say now) in Hanoi, Bao Dai walked through the crowds in the street and spoke in the small crowded auditorium which must have been a nightmare to his security guards—of which there were many, in plain clothes—since the balcony, full of students and others, reached down almost to the stage. He spoke well and was well received. I had to respond in rather conventional terms to the awarding of an honorary doctorate of letters which I prize even though I know it was awarded to the American official and not to me in my personal capacity.

It had nothing to do with my visit, but the pressure which the United States and Great Britain had constantly applied bore fruit when the French Assembly, on January 29, 1950, by a large majority approved the bill ratifying the March 8 agreements and establishing the three autonomous states in the French Union. On February 2, Secretary Acheson sent a memorandum to President Truman recommending that the United States recognize the three states. The President gave his approval the next day, and on February 4, American Consul General Abbott in Saigon was instructed to deliver a message to Bao Dai and to the kings of Laos and Cambodia, extending full diplomatic recognition. Bao Dai was addressed as "Your Imperial Majesty." Abbott was to mention that we would like to have full diplomatic exchange—he was still only a consul-general, not a minister or ambassador. The State Department understood that if the three states requested a full diplomatic exchange, the French would acquiesce.

The message did not quite have the flavor I had recommended, but the act was all-important. Great Britain extended recognition on the same day. Secretary Acheson's public statement on the question of recognition was on February 1; I would not now agree with his statement that the Kremlin's recognition of Ho proved that he was not a "nationalist," the sense being he was a Communist stooge. If that were true, it might be said that the recognition by the French, the British, and the American governments proved that Bao was not a "nationalist" but a French puppet. Acheson spoke of the French "transfer of sovereignty," the anticipation of early ratification, and the subsequent recognition by the United States.

I left Vietnam with the feeling that the policy of the United States was well grounded and on the right road. Moreover, my talks with Pignon and other French officials led me to believe that France approved our policy and hoped that we would give still more support to Bao Dai. I was to learn later that there were limits to what the French government would approve. At our Bangkok conference attended in mid-February by the American diplomatic representatives from the whole Asian and Pacific region, it was felt that after my return to Washington it would be helpful for the President or Secretary Acheson to issue a strong statement reasserting the United States interest in Southeast Asia and our determination to resist Communist aggression there. I suggested that such a statement might be made in a congressional resolution. But the conferees were not prepared to make any recommendation about the use of United States armed force in the area and it was the group's opinion that it would be undesirable for the Seventh Fleet to pay a visit.

At about the time of the adjournment of the Bangkok Conference, on February 22, 1950, a telegram from Ambassador David Bruce in Paris to the Department, set out the picture. Bruce and Charles Bohlen went to see Alexandre Parodi in the Foreign Office at the latter's request. Parodi wished to clarify what had been said in recent conversations in Paris and in Washington. The French were thinking of sounding out Mao Tse-tung on the question of recognizing the Communist regime in Peking; such a démarche might be helpful in learning Mao's attitude toward the situation in Indochina. The French position in Vietnam was very grave and France could not continue without military help from the United States in the form of supplies equal to those China was supplying to Ho. France could not bear the burden alone and might have to abandon Indochina with serious effects on the rest of Southeast Asia and even India.

Parodi stressed that France was putting up to the United States questions of the very highest policy. He referred to the

American suggestion that France should issue a statement that the March 8 accord was evolutionary and that more progress could be expected along the lines of independence for the Associated States; he repeated the usual line that such a declaration would be harmful. Bruce told Parodi the United States must have a clear idea of French intentions about remaining in Indochina since we would not pour in assistance if they were going to quit. The United States had helped Greece because of full confidence the Greek government would continue to fight. It is notable that the discussion was in terms of arms and money and public declarations of solidarity, but not at all in terms of the supplying of American manpower in Vietnam. Nonetheless, this was the lead into American involvement, always tied to the problem of supporting France as an important ally in Western Europe.

After the end of the Bangkok Conference, as planned, I continued the trip around the Asian states, visiting Singapore, Jakarta, Rangoon, Calcutta, New Delhi, Madras, Ceylon, Pakistan, and Afghanistan. We almost ended the trip at Madras when one of the two engines on our embassy's plane died on take-off, but our pilot showed almost incredible skill in gunning his other engine till we got up to 700 feet and then circled back to the airfield without touching the surrounding hills! I shall mention in a postscript to this chapter an incident in our visit to Afghanistan.

From place to place I had to have a press conference and at some of these I got into trouble. For example, at Rangoon on February 10, I said:

The reason the United States has recognized the government of Bao Dai and the governments in Cambodia and Laos is that we have concluded on the basis of our examination of the situation that those governments have been established as independent states.

I had not specified "independent within and as members of the French Union." Nobody inside France or outside knew precisely what the French Union was or was going to be.[20] The Dutch had had during the war a somewhat comparable vague formula for an association of the East and West Indies with the Netherlands. But the Dutch had moved forward to recognizing full independence for Indonesia. The British, of course, evolved a definite concept of the British Commonwealth. But the French were aroused by my failure to mention the French Union and I was instructed to make a clarification, which I did on March 13, 1950, in a press conference in Paris.

When I was received on March 14 by President Auriol, he thanked me for that statement in which I emphasized that the three Indochinese states were of course "independent in the French Union." But Auriol records in his memoirs that he did not like the Americans and British intruding in what he considered to be a domestic French matter, and he vigorously rejected the idea we had urged that he issue an "evolutionary" statement, indicating that the March 8 agreement was only a first step. He rejected also the idea that the affairs of the three associated states should be handled by the French Foreign Office rather than the Colonial Ministry. He wrote that it was true that the Indochinese states were no longer colonies nor were they foreigners, but they were "associates." [21]

My talks along the westbound way dealt with various matters, but the situation in Indochina was a standard feature. In Bangkok, while our conference was going on, Butterworth and I talked with the Thai officials. They rather confirmed the French diagnosis when they told me that they had to be sure Bao Dai would succeed before they backed him since otherwise they would be the victims of Viet Minh animosity. They were not sure the French would let them send representatives to talk with Bao Dai; we thought that would be very desirable, but we could not speak for the French.

On February 25 I talked with Nehru in New Delhi. He agreed that Ho was a Communist and spoke strongly against the Communists, but he thought Ho was supported by many nationalists, including Catholics, who were not Communists. He was at odds with the French because of their unwillingness to return the Indian enclave of Pondicherry to India. When I talked about independence for the small states of Asia and the need to protect them, he spoke rather derisively of our pretending that the Philippines were independent; he said we would treat any attack on them as an attack on ourselves. I replied that perhaps the situation was identical with his attitude toward the "independent" kingdom of Nepal? Nehru hesitated and then smilingly agreed.

Nehru's attitude toward Bao Dai had not changed since the previous October when he had talked with Secretary Acheson in Washington. Nehru had then described the weaknesses of Bao Dai and had correctly foreseen that the French would not make concessions adequate to enable him to win the support of his people. Acheson had replied that he saw no alternative to recognizing Bao Dai while trying to influence the French. Nehru argued then, as he did in talking with me, that while Ho was a Communist, he had the support of nationalist elements, and Nehru believed a combined "popular front" government in Vietnam need not follow the pattern of such combinations in Western Europe.[22]

In Singapore (where another of my news conferences seemed to upset the French), I talked with Malcolm McDonald, the U.K. Commissioner General for Southeast Asia. On March 18 he wrote to me in Washington saying that they were already seeing good results of my visit in encouraging the confidence of the democratically minded Asians that they could defend themselves against Communist invasion or infiltration; "We all owe you a debt" he wrote—"you" meaning the United States.

It was in Karachi that I first learned that Senator Joseph McCarthy had made me the target of one of his attacks on the State Department, saying that I was "soft" on communism. I telegraphed the State Department to tell the congressional committees that I would be glad to appear before them to re-

fute such charges but meanwhile I wound up my trip although
I cut short my visit in Paris and came home by plane instead of
by ship—the latter was still an available and restful alternative
way of crossing the Atlantic.[23]

In Paris, I had a series of conferences. The first, before I was
received by President Auriol, was on March 13 with Foreign
Minister Robert Schuman, whom I had come to know and to
admire at meetings of the Council of Foreign Ministers which I
attended with Dean Acheson. Ambassador David Bruce and
First Secretary Woodruff Wallner were with me and another
old friend, Alexandre Parodi, the legal adviser of the Quai
d'Orsay, was with Schuman.

Schuman asked me for my impressions of the situation in Indochina and I stressed that while there was a good chance for
success with Bao Dai, a lot of work would be necessary. I said it
was the general view that the Chinese would not attack Indochina but would use subversion, aid to Ho, and the like. I
thought the Chinese would take over Tibet. As I emphasized
the next day also with Pierre-Henri Teitgen, the Minister of
Information, the French needed to publicize their role and
their future intentions. I noted that in the neighboring states
of Siam and Indonesia, the leaders were quite ignorant about
the March 8 agreement; the French diplomats in those countries were taking too much for granted. Schuman asked Parodi
to note that point, but he said that Nehru was being fed by reports from the Indian Consul General in Saigon, who was hostile to France, partly because of Pondicherry and the other
French settlements in India. Schuman agreed that the Dutch
had given much more to the Indonesians than France had
given to the Indochinese, but argued that the latter had much
to learn and that it was necessary to move slowly.

On the other hand, I warned, they needed assurance about
French intentions—ten months delay in ratifying the March 8
accords had not helped. I suggested that symbolic acts such as
transferring Indochinese affairs from what was considered a

ministry for the colonies would help. Schuman said it had been decided to do this but it had not been decided where to place that responsibility. He asked me whether I thought it would be more satisfactory to create a separate ministry for the Associated States like the British Commonwealth Office, or to have a special undersecretariat in the Foreign Office. I replied that I thought the latter would have more significance, but Schuman said they must make a distinction between the Associated States and the protectorates of Tunisia and Morocco, which were under the Foreign Office. I spoke of the good effect of turning over the university at Hanoi to the Vietnamese and explained why I had to go to Hanoi to see Bao Dai because the French would not let him have the Norodom Palace in Saigon. Schuman said Bevin had made that same point and told Parodi, "Il faut absolument arranger ça."

I have already referred to my conversation with President Auriol on March 14 where he thanked me for having explained in a press conference in Paris that when I had spoken of the "independence" of the Associated States, I meant "in the French Union." Like Schuman, President Auriol stressed the impact on the North African states and on Madagascar of any further concession to Vietnam, Cambodia, and Laos.

France indeed had welcomed American and British recognition of Bao Dai and of Cambodia and Laos and could not deny that these states had been born, but they were not willing that Uncle Sam, M.D., should cut the umbilical cord which bound the Associated States to France.

We arrived at Idlewild Airport, New York, on March 15, 1950, and proceeded by train to Washington. Walton Butterworth and I held a "background" press conference on March 23 in which I noted that I had visited fourteen countries (counting Hong Kong and Okinawa as separate entities.) I described Bao Dai, whom I had heard spoken of as a playboy, a French puppet who wore sports jackets and loud ties; I found a very well informed statesman who was by no means a "yes man." He had gained more from the French by the March 8 accord than Ho Chi Minh had gained in his negotiations in 1945. Bao had driven a hard bargain and was holding up his end, with some able men in his cabinet.

On March 29, Butterworth and I went with Secretary Acheson to another executive session of the Senate Foreign Relations Committee to report on my Asian trip and the Bangkok Conference. I do not now agree with one of the views I reported to the Committee, namely that I and all the conferees in Bangkok believed in the "very critically strategic importance of the whole Southeastern Asia area," but that was the prevailing idea in the State Department in 1949.

I noted the difficulty which we faced in having to support friendly governments that were weak and inexperienced. "Many of them are brought up in an oriental tradition which is a tradition of a good deal of cruelty and suppression of the individual . . ." I did say that I thought Bao Dai was gaining in strength and that there was less tendency to consider him a mere puppet. I reported that the Vietnamese "know that we are putting pressure on the French; they know that we are backing an independent state and . . . there is a very large body of the nationalist movement in Indochina which is back of Bao Dai because they consider that that is their best road to independence." Dean Acheson explained to the Committee the difficulty of providing military equipment for both the French and the Vietnamese forces. "We want to be very careful in what we do for the Indo-Chinese," he said, "that we do not substitute for what the French are doing, but that we add to what the French are doing. We do not want to get into a position where the French say, 'You take over; we aren't able to go ahead on this.' We want the French to stay in there. . . . The Commonwealth have got to really carry their burdens in Burma, the French have got to carry theirs in Indochina, and we are willing to help, but not to substitute for them."

In the State Department there was considerable debate over

the best way to induce the French to move forward with a program that would help to strengthen Bao Dai. A draft telegram was circulated that would have instructed Ambassador Bruce to deliver a note to the French government calling on it to make a declaration of future intent along the lines which I had discussed in Saigon. William Gibson, who had accompanied me on the trip and who was now in the Far Eastern Division, and I both thought that, in the light of our talks with the French officials, especially in Paris, there was no use in pressing officially for such a public declaration to which they were so strongly opposed. In a memorandum of March 20, 1950, to Butterworth, I said I had no objection to maintaining pressure on the French, but Ambassador Bruce had told me how my statement about "independence" had been interpreted in Paris as an attempt by the United States to drive a wedge between France and the Associated States with the purpose of bringing about a complete separation. We could not draft for them the kind of declaration which we thought would be helpful; it was a question of persuasion, and we should merely give Ambassador Bruce guidance on the lines he should follow to keep our policies aligned.

Elim O'Shaughnessy of the Western European branch expressed similar views, saying we should not threaten that no aid would be given to Indochina until the French made a statement satisfactory to us. Gibson took a similar line.

The telegram, which was sent to the embassy in Paris on March 29, stated that it took into account views expressed by Butterworth and Jessup. The theme was that the United States was proceeding on the assumption that the French were trying to strengthen Bao Dai and the kings in Cambodia and Laos, but it was evident that this policy was not given credence by large segments of the American press, by the Scandinavian states (which refused to extend recognition), and by various other sections of public opinion in both East and West. The United States was engaged in steps to accelerate its economic and financial assistance to the Indochinese states. France should make some tangible moves, such as turning the Saigon palace over to Bao Dai. Bruce was instructed to make strong oral representations to the French Foreign Office, using as guidelines the following statements:

The United States government has expressed its gratification at ratification by French government of agreements with governments of Vietnam, Laos, and Cambodia. The real and continuing interest of the United States in strengthening and stabilization of anti-communist national regimes in Indochina is well known to the government of France as is the full confidence of the United States in the intentions of the French government to adopt measures requisite to providing these three states with strength, political and military, without which they will be unable to defeat Ho and his foreign communist allies.

The governments of France and the United States have long considered that recognition of the governments of the three states by Asian states was of prime importance in order that anti-communist Asian national movements [be seen] as genuine national movements and not creatures of Western imperialism. The United States has recently approached the Asian governments to impress this on them. Thai recognition of the Indochinese states came on February 28. Others say they are French puppets or they are not convinced of French intentions to transfer full sovereignty and independence to the three states. If France would officially say these are just first steps, they [other Asian states] would consider recognition even before next steps are taken. The Department was determined as a matter of general policy to emphasize the interdependence of France and Indochina as was successfully done with Indonesia and the Dutch. The United States agreed that independence was within the French Union, recognized what France has done and the problems it faces, but urges them to issue a public statement soonest.

In May 1950, Secretary Acheson was attending meetings in Europe. On May 8 "Chip" Bohlen and I went with him when he talked with Foreign Minister Schuman in Paris. Schuman referred as usual to the great sacrifices France was making not only for itself but for all the Western world. France needed U.S. military as well as moral support. It was necessary to continue to support Bao Dai, but within the framework of the March 8 accord; Schuman could not hold out much hope of any immediate expansion of that agreement. They were going to create a separate ministry for relations with the Associated States and they would remove all the existing restrictions on the diplomatic representation abroad of the Associated States. Progress would be made.

Secretary Acheson said that he was much pleased by Schuman's statement. He agreed on the importance of Indochina and that U.S. help must be through the French. Bao Dai's prestige was now at a standstill and would disintegrate further unless steps were taken. If Bao Dai gained support, the fence-sitters would rally to him; it was a question of weeks not months in which steps must be taken to strengthen him. The United States hoped to give military aid to the French but that depended on Congress. The United States would also give economic help.[24]

Since Schuman had urged that a joint statement be issued, the United States had prepared a draft for a bilateral statement since it had been learned that Foreign Secretary Bevin was opposed to a tripartite statement including Great Britain. Schuman said that he would study the draft and stated that he "was very grateful to Mr. Jessup for the objective effort he had made during his mission in Southeast Asia and for the help which he had thus given to the common cause."

At the tripartite talks which followed at Lancaster House in London on May 13, 1950, Schuman again stated his case, noting that both Britain and France had direct responsibilities in Southeast Asia. Bevin said that he did not want joint or individual declarations by governments on their attitude toward Southeast Asia, having in mind especially relations with Pakistan, India, and Ceylon. Schuman urged a joint declaration but when Acheson supported Bevin, Schuman yielded.

At Washington, in July, there were other British–U.S. talks, and it was agreed that both would assist France to the extent possible in case of a Chinese Communist attack, but it was thought probable that neither could provide armed forces. On August 17, Ambassador Bruce telegraphed from Paris that Prime Minister René Pleven said the only chance of success was to build strong native armies and that this was the only way to convince the three Associated States of French intentions, but France needed more dollar help to carry on. He knew that some American officials had discussed with Bao Dai the training of a native army; France would welcome this and would then be able to help more in Europe. It was indeed true that I had discussed this question with Bao Dai and Nguyen Phan Long, his Prime Minister (today this would be called "Vietnamization").

On August 18, 1950, I sent a memorandum on this subject to Dean Rusk, then Assistant Secretary of State for the Far East. Rusk had discussed the building of a native army with General Merrill, and the matter was also being studied in the Department's Policy Planning Staff. It was obvious, I thought, that there were only two ways in which the French could reduce their troop strength in Indochina: they must either eliminate Ho and the danger from the Chinese Communists, or they must substitute some other force. There was no chance that Ho would surrender, and the only substitute force would be an indigenous army since no foreign force could be substituted for the French.

A strong native army might be a danger to the French but if they could not count on Bao Dai and his military forces, they would have to make an even greater effort to defeat Ho and to police the "pacified" areas of Vietnam; that was an impossible burden. It was therefore necessary to keep a Vietnamese army on the side of the French and in this we could help. The task of the French army would then be to guard the northern frontier line leaving the task of fighting the guerrillas to the indigenous forces. (I should stress here that the possibility of an invasion by the Chinese Communist armies was in these times constantly considered a danger.)

Three days later, on August 21, George Kennan sent a memorandum to the Secretary reflecting the same point of view many of us had reached, but realistically reaching a more pessimistic climax. In his view, the French position in Indochina was hopeless, and we should tell them so. "We might suggest," he wrote, "that the most promising line of withdrawal, from the standpoint of their prestige, would be to make the problem one of some regional responsibility, in which the French exodus could be conveniently obscured." [25] But at that stage, no alibi would have satisfied Paris.

On September 1, 1950, we sent a long telegram from the Department to the legation in Saigon. We said that the Department had viewed with increasing concern the growing signs of political and military deterioration. A conference at Pau, France, began in June to arrange the interrelations of the three states and France but it was still continuing. (Actually it ended in November with some gains registered by the Vietnamese.) Mostly the same old elements were stressed, such as the need to make dramatic moves to stir public opinion, to convince people of the sincerity of French intentions to move forward with independence, to win the *attentistes,* and (a new element) to cause no further depletion of Western European military potential, even improving it by releasing French troops from Indochina. It was agreed that the formation of a national army was the best course, but it was realized that that would take time. The legation was told to discuss with the French and with Bao Dai this program:

1. At the earliest moment a declaration by President Auriol and Bao Dai that in keeping with the March 8 accord, the Vietnam national army, under command of the Emperor, would become a fact, and all indigenous troops in French Union forces would be incorporated into the new national army.

2. Pursuant to Article 3 of the March 8 accord, it would be declared that a state of national emergency existed and that His Majesty, as Commander in Chief, had therefore placed the national forces under the French High Command in face of the threat of foreign invasion.

3. Following the emergency, the national army would be released from service under the French command to assure internal order, etc. Meanwhile the training of officers and non-coms would proceed.

Further steps were contemplated as possibilities, but it was recognized that there were drawbacks and only the need for positive action inspired these suggestions. At the same time the Paris embassy was told it could tell the French that the question of providing 200 billion francs for a two-year period to establish the national army was receiving active consideration.

My available information is fragmentary, but Shaplen reports that Bao Dai told one of his friends that there was no use building a national army since it would desert to the Viet Minh; he said he could not inspire the troops with a will to fight.[26] At other times his view was just the opposite.

On October 14, the Counselor of the French Embassy in Washington sounded out William Lacy, of the Far Eastern Bureau, on the question whether it would be desirable for the French to bring the Indochinese situation before the United Nations. He implied that General Douglas MacArthur or the Department might be encouraged by the support of the United Nation in Korea to think that a similar development might take place in Indochina. Lacy was under the impression that the French contemplated going to the United Nations out of desperation, and he carefully hedged his comments as being purely personal. He said that he did not think there was any developed view in the Department on this question but that the decision lay with the French, not the American government. He pointed out that if there were to be a UN border observation team, it would naturally include Asians, whose views would not be the same as those of the Western powers. Ten days later in Saigon, the French officials told Donald Heath, the American minister, they doubted the value of a UN frontier commission unless there were a Chinese invasion.

I am afraid that the State Department, exasperated by Bao Dai's unwillingness or inability to assume vigorous leadership instead of flitting around the Riviera, cruising on the imperial yacht, or relaxing in the resort town of Dalat in Vietnam, began to assume too paternalistic a tone.

As Devillers says, in his detailed and very fair history of Vietnam, hunting at Ban Me Thuot, yachting at Nhatrang, seemed more attractive to Bao Dai than the hard work of a politician.[27] On October 18, the legation in Saigon was instructed to deliver a message to Bao Dai immediately after his return to Saigon; the presentation should be oral but the Minister should emphasize it represented the studied opinion of the Department after careful consideration. I do not now think that it told Bao Dai anything he did not already know.

The message said that a crisis was approaching in Vietnam to decide whether the country would be allowed to develop independently or be another Sino-Soviet dominated satellite which was much worse than a colonial status. The United States was increasing its aid to France and to the Associated States to help defend their territorial integrity. Leadership was crucial; minor differences with France must be set aside. The person of Bao Dai was symbolic; his absences and excursions were not helpful. He should visit all parts of his country and make speeches. [There spoke American grass-roots experience!] He should announce that the United States and France would support national armies and that he, Bao Dai, intended to be their commander in Chief.

The French officials in Saigon were advised of this démarche and at least agreed with the program indicated. On October 25, Minister Heath in Saigon was told that both State and Defense believed that immediate political and military advantage of the national army plan would be to integrate the various native contingents such as the Cao Dai, the Hoa Hao and the Catholics, and others in one army under the command of Bao Dai. Technical difficulties must be overcome. On the same date Heath was advised that Ambassador Bruce in Paris would press the French to accelerate the formation of the national armies. We would not suggest submitting the Indochinese question to the United Nations and if the French raised the point, they would be told it was up to them to decide.

On the same question of using the United Nations, the U.S. Mission to the United Nations in New York was informed on November 22 that the Department did not favor a UN observation commission in Indochina even though it might help us by giving proof of Chinese Communist aid to the Viet Minh. But the Asian states in the United Nations would insist that any UN commission should look into all questions in Indochina. If the issue were to be laid before the United Nations, it should be done by the French, but there was no use their doing it unless they were ready to make a declaration of intent to grant full independence eventually to Indochina. The Department felt that a UN debate on the role of France in Indochina would have "hazardous results." The Mission was instructed not to explore this question with either the French or the British delegations in the United Nations. I have no personal record of discussions of this UN issue, but it seems probable that our reluctance was due to the fear that all the members of the United Nations would learn, as we had learned, how laggard the French were in contrast, for example, to the Dutch in Indonesia.

At the end of January 1951, President Truman talked with French Prime Minister Pleven in Washington. It was agreed that national armies should be built up, and we promised increased military aid. If the Chinese Communists attacked, the United States would give all possible aid for the evacuation of French forces if necessary. It was noted that our ability to give aid was limited by other demands, such as those in Korea, but there was no suggestion of the use of American troops or planes in Vietnam.

On the day following that conference at the Summit, there was a more detailed discussion in the State Department with a group of French officials. Among the American participants were Dean Rusk, and Minister Donald Heath from Saigon. Rusk asked what was the French thinking on eventual withdrawal from Indochina. Alexandre Parodi, then Secretary-General of the French Foreign Office, said that there was very little likelihood of a negotiated peace; in any negotiation between the native forces, Ho would be "the lion" and the Associated States would be "the lamb." There was a suggestion of the "domino theory" when Parodi said they were concerned about the effect on the rest of South Asia if Indochina were forsaken. If there were to be a negotiation with Ho or the Chinese Communists or both, that would have to be part of a general settlement for the whole of the Far East. In reply to another question from Rusk, Parodi said general elections in Vietnam were very unlikely in the foreseeable future; Nehru, he said, had pressed the French on this point during a recent visit to Paris. Bao Dai himself was said to be opposed to holding elections at that time. The Americans stressed the old theme of the need for vigorous French propaganda; Parodi said the French recognized this but that they were not very talented as propagandists. Minister Heath said they had improved.

When John Foster Dulles, who had been put in charge of the arrangements for concluding a peace treaty with Japan, raised with the French in Paris on June 11, 1951, the question of the participation in the peace conference of the Associated States, the French were hesitant but their doubts were overcome and on September 6 the three states were formally invited to the peace conference. This was indeed a substantial gesture and was recognized as such in Indochina.

On December 20, 1951, Paris, London, and Saigon were informed that our intelligence sources indicated that massive

Chinese intervention in Indochina was to be expected within a few weeks. It was necessary to know the French plans: what proof of Chinese intervention would they require—would it be enough if they sent in technicians or would one await an actual invasion of Tonkin by the Chinese armies? Would the case be brought to the United Nations by the French Union or by the chiefs of the Associated States? What action would the United Nations be asked to take? If there were a veto in the Security Council, would the French take the case to the General Assembly? What support did they think they would get in the United Nations?

The anticipated Chinese invasion did not take place and the UN problems became moot, but when our embassy in Saigon at the end of January 1952 reported an interview with Bao Dai, the Department's reply on February 7 revealed an attitude of disillusionment. The telegram said that Bao Dai's analysis of the situation in Vietnam was mistaken—and not for the first time. It was hard to see how a man who had shown so little readiness to exercise the considerable authority which he actually had could do more if his authority was increased.

If it was proposed that he succeed General Jean de Lattre in command of all the forces, this would of course increase his prestige, which the Department had always favored; but it was becoming disillusioned. Bao Dai had now refused to accept the transfer of the Norodom Palace in Saigon (a very belated French gesture), but the Department thought this was due to his reluctance to leave Dalat and to take on heavier burdens. It was fantastic to assume that he could lead all the armies against a Chinese invasion; that would not be accepted by Cambodia or Laos or by the French or their North African troops. Bao Dai would have to prove he was ready to buckle down in his job before he was encouraged to increase his role.

Secretary Acheson was due to meet with Bevin and Schuman in Paris in May 1952; a long paper was prepared by John M. Allison in FE as a background for those talks. The theme of the paper was that U.S. objectives in Indochina could be achieved only through the French and therefore measures to induce the French to withdraw were undesirable. The three "Service Secretaries"—of Army, Navy, and Air (Pace, Kimball, and Gilpatrick)—suggested that we urge the French to give the three Associated States a guaranty of full independence in a reasonable time; that there be an international program, preferably under the United Nations, to end the civil war * and to protect the three states against communism, and that this be coupled with a French commitment to defend the area.

The Far Eastern Bureau's paper said that this would be a self-defeating program; it would have a disastrous effect on the French will to continue and, if known to the Vietnamese, their confidence would be undermined and they would swing over to Ho Chi Minh. It was said to be impossible to commit the French to defend Indochina and at the same time give them a chance to withdraw. The French must keep to their responsibilities in Indochina and know that the United States was backing them.

The three secretaries from the armed services said that the situation continued to deteriorate, but the State Department, backed by the National Security Council, had contributed to preserving the area from communism for nearly two and a half years. It was noted that the national armies had greatly improved and could take over more and more of the task. (Again foreshadows of "Vietnamization"!) Despite Chinese aid to the North, the French had preserved control of the urban centers and the rice-producing areas of Cochin China and Tonkin. The French had made great sacrifices but this was due to help from the United States. In spite of all this, the State Department agreed with the three Service Secretaries that the French should not stay indefinitely and that there should be a transi-

* In view of later controversy, it is interesting to note that in 1952, the Pentagon regarded the conflict as a *civil* war and not as an *invasion* from another state. This became a crucial point in the Johnson and Nixon administrations.

tion from colonialism to self-government. It was anticipated that the United States might have to give the French more financial help.

This memorandum, which was drafted in the Far Eastern Bureau by Lacy, Gibson, and Stolle and signed by Allison, was approved by the Western European branch. I had left for Paris with Dean Acheson, and it was not until after our departure that the memorandum was approved by Under Secretary David Bruce and by the Policy Planning Staff. On May 19 it was discussed with President Truman by Bruce, Secretary of Defense Robert Lovett, and General Omar Bradley. Bruce reported to Acheson that at this meeting it was agreed that in the talks with the British and French, the following points should be the focus of discussion: the United States was in favor of developing the national armies of the three Associated States and was prepared to furnish further assistance toward that end; we should inform the British and French that we were in favor of warning the Chinese Communists against further aggression in Southeast Asia and wanted to work out with our allies the details of the context, timing, and method of delivery of such a warning. Among other things, that meant we would agree to take part in tripartite military conversation which would undoubtedly be proposed by the others.

The principal business of the Secretary of State in Europe in May 1952 was to make progress in the settlement of the German question and, in the nature of my job as Ambassador-at-Large, I had shifted to European from Far Eastern questions, but on our return to Washington in June, Indochina was again to the fore. Much importance was attached to the visit of Jean Letourneau, Minister in charge of the Associated States. In a briefing paper for Acheson's discussions with him, it was stated that we were opposed to the idea of bringing Australian or other foreign troops into Indochina except after a Chinese aggression, and then preferably under UN auspices. This position was definitely a reflection of the Korean experience. We could agree with the French thesis that France was taking part in the free world's struggle against communism and that in Indochina it was not simply protecting French interests.

At the same time, Secretary Acheson had a detailed talk with British Ambassador Sir Oliver Franks after he had talked with General Omar Bradley, Assistant Secretary of State George Perkins, and me. The Secretary in his conversation talked very candidly, as he always felt free to do with Franks. He said that if the Chinese came into Indochina in force, we would have to do something about it—we could not remain passive. No move was pleasant to contemplate. We could not warn the Chinese without knowing what we would actually do. We could not have another Korea. We could not put ground forces into Indochina. But the Secretary then went further than foreshadowed in earlier statements: he said we could take air and naval action. The only way to dissuade the Chinese would be to strike them where it hurt and blockade their trade, but it was not our mission to destroy the Communist regime in China. The danger that the Soviets might intervene was fully realized. It was important for the United States and England to reach political decisions before calling in the military; when the military issue arose at Paris, the British and French were not ready to discuss it. Acheson told Franks we had talked with Letourneau about the possibility of our helping to evacuate the French forces if necessary.

So far as I know, there was no major evolution of U.S. policy toward Indochina before the end of the Truman administration. It was the echo of an old bell when the final communiqué issued after the Foreign Ministers of France and the United Kingdom met with Secretary of State Dulles in Washington in July 1953: the British and Americans welcomed the proposal of France to take steps "toward completing the sovereignty and independence of the three states in Indochina."

Then came Dien Bien Phu and the Geneva Conference of 1954 and the fall of the United States into the physical and moral mire from which, at this writing, one hopes we are emerging. The era of Emperor Bao Dai has faded into history. Was our attempt to have the French build up his regime a mistake?

Robert McClintock, who was Deputy Chief of Mission in Saigon and saw a good deal of Bao Dai, was not an admirer of "His Majesty." He reports—and I have no basis for controverting him although I have not seen his supporting evidence—that Bao Dai, before his last return to France around 1955, sold "the concession for the police forces of Saigon-Cholon to the gangster band, the Binh Xuyen. From this deal . . . the absentee Emperor actually stowed away some 49 million francs in his personal airplane when he departed Saigon for Cannes." [28]

We had a different picture of Bao Dai, whose portrait was on the cover of *Time* magazine on May 29, 1950. If the French had given him power, would he have belied the apothegm that "power corrupts" since, according to McClintock, Bao Dai was corrupted when politically impotent? Would the history of other Vietnamese politicians and heads of government show that such corruption was a rare phenomenon in Southeast Asia? Not as we read news dispatches from Saigon in the 1970s! According to Robert Shaplen, the French approved the control of the police by the Binh Xuyen.[29]

Cambodia and Laos have been members of the United Nations since 1955. Like the divided states of Korea and Germany, Vietnam has been denied membership but it is a state to which the International Court of Justice is open by virtue of a declaration filed November 12, 1952, under Article 22 of the Treaty of Peace with Japan, and this is at least some acknowledgement of the Republic of Vietnam's international status. Moreover, the Final Declaration of the Geneva Conference of 1954 binds France, the People's Republic of China, the Soviet Union, and the United Kingdom, "to respect the sovereignty, the independence, the unity and the territorial integrity of" the state of "Viet-Nam." [30]

It may be noted that "recognition," in the technical international law sense, is not granted by the United Nations. The first Secretary-General of the United Nations, Trygve Lie, in a memorandum of March 8, 1950 (probably written by his legal adviser, Abraham Feller), discussed the point in connection with the representation of China. He wrote that the trouble was that the "question of representation has been linked up with the question of recognition" which was "unfortunate from the practical standpoint and wrong from the standpoint of legal theory." He noted that some writers had suggested that there should be "collective recognition" through the United Nations instead of individual state action, but this idea had not been accepted and "the United Nations does not possess any authority to recognize either a new state or a new government of an existing state. . . ." He pointed out that, both in the League of Nations and in the United Nations, some members stated expressly that the admission of a state to membership did not mean that they recognized the new member as a state. This was sound doctrine in 1950 and it is sound today.[31]

The empire of which Bao Dai was emperor dates back over many centuries. The Republic of Vietnam is perhaps its continuation under another name. When the United States recognized that Republic, it addressed its ruler as "Your Imperial Majesty." The natal metaphor breaks down but when I speak of "the abortive empire of Bao Dai," I have in mind that revitalizing of the ancient state which, for a few years after 1948, I hoped would reunite an independent Indochina.

It is necessary to repeat that this is a personal narrative and does not purport to rewrite the history of Vietnam. Bao Dai was still Chief of State when the French were defeated at Dien Bien Phu in May 1954, and retained that title until October 1955, when Ngo Dinh Diem unseated him in the referendum which was an overwhelming repudiation of Bao Dai. Diem became Vietnam's first president and there was no more a "majesty" nor a question whether Vietnam could be labeled as an "empire."

If the United States had succeeded in forcing the French to
turn over Vietnam to Bao Dai as in effect the United States
forced the Netherlands to give full sovereignty to Indonesia,
perhaps Bao Dai would have attained for his "empire" as much
status as Prince Norodom Sihanouk attained for a time for his
kingdom of Cambodia, although he renounced the throne, or
King Savang Vathana and his Premier Prince Souvana Phouma
for the kingdom of Laos. But such status was no guaranty of
peace. Perhaps the United States would have avoided the tragic
blunder of trying to take over the military task which we told
the French was impossible of successful completion.

Robert Shaplen reports visiting the Queen Mother, Tu
Cung, in Hué, the old imperial city, in June 1972. Frail, but
still regal at the age of eighty-three, she said she still received
letters from her son Bao Dai in France, although she thought
"the government here has confiscated some of them. He tells
me that if the people of Vietnam want him to return to help
bring about peace and reconciliation, he will do so. In the
meantime, I will wait. . . ." In May she had told another
American newsman who asked if Bao Dai had plans to return
to Vietnam: "It is not a good time even if he wanted to. It de-
pends on the wishes of the people." [32]

According to a news story in July 1972:

> In one of his rare public statements, the deposed Indochinese Em-
> peror, Bao Dai, appealed in Paris to the Vietnamese people for na-
> tional reconciliation and reconstruction. "The time has come," he
> said, "to put an end to the fratricidal war and to recover at last
> peace and accord."
>
> Addressing himself also to President Ton Duc Thang of North
> Vietnam and President Nguyen Van Thieu of South Vietnam he
> said, "Like any other Vietnamese citizen, I hope with all my heart
> to see national reconciliation. Let us stretch our hands to each other
> for the survival of Vietnam." [33]

In February 1973, Bao Dai interrupted his exile in France
and arrived in Tokyo. A communiqué was issued on his behalf

saying that he intended to return to his country "whatever happens." He planned to establish there a "third force." Although he thought he would be to many Vietnamese a symbol of national unity, capable of reconciling the opposing factions, he wanted to return just as an ordinary citizen. Through T. M. Bui, secretary-general of his "political bureau," the former monarch declared that the Vietnamese people as a whole do not feel that they are bound by "this Yalta type agreement concluded between M. Kissinger and North Vietnam." He considered that the agreement concerning the cease-fire was insufficient because there must be either international guarantees or self-determination. The Vietnamese "silent majority," which could want a personality who could assure reconciliation and continuity, was represented, Bui said, by a "silent cabinet" consisting of a group of some 60 persons." [34]

It was only an emperor's dream. In July, the Hong Kong correspondent of *The Economist* reported that Bao Dai had left for France after a month's stay incognito in a Hong Kong hotel. Whether or not he had established contact with Saigon or Hanoi does not appear, but apparently he was not invited to visit either capital. "So," writes *The Economist*'s correspondent, "the ghost has gone back to limbo."

Postscript: —Pushtoonistan

It will be recalled that my visits to Korea and to Vietnam took place in the course of a general official trip to a large number of Asian countries, only two of which are described in this account. As we flew westward, stage by stage, we visited Pakistan and Afghanistan. In view of the recent events in what was in 1950 East Pakistan and what is now Bangladesh, it seems appropriate to mention briefly an event which at the time seemed more theatrical than politically important, but which is not irrelevant to press accounts in February and March 1972 about further threats to the unity of Pakistan.

The scene is the famous Northwest Frontier, the mention of which stirs one's memory of many of Kipling's *Barrack-Room Ballads*. We stopped at Peshawar, the eastern terminus of the ancient trade route for the caravans which still come and go with their camels to and from Kabul, the capital of Afghanistan. We left Peshawar before dawn and soon began climbing the thirty-odd miles of the new auto road over the Khyber Pass, whose walls bear marble and bronze plaques marking places where British regiments fought the tribesmen known as Pathans, Pahktoons, or Pushtoons, and whose martial traditions are said to date back at least to the time when Alexander the Great invaded India. The Pathans have never been conquered, or at least not subdued, have taken heavy toll of the British armies, and their nationalism is still easily raised to the boiling point. In March 1972, the press reported that President Zulfikar Ali Bhutto had reached an agreement with Khan Abdul Wali Khan, leader of the National Awami party representing many of the Pahktoon tribesmen in Pakistan's western frontier province, thus averting a possible bloody struggle or the separation from Pakistan of another slice of its territory.

The sun had risen on that February morning in 1950 when we reached the summit of the pass and stopped for a cup of tea at the last guardhouse on the Pakistani side of the frontier. Perhaps a hundred yards further west, the narrow road was cut through solid walls of rock. From this short defile we emerged into Afghanistan. The road broadened there but was filled with a great crowd of tribesmen, dressed in loose baggy clothing, turban-like headdress, with their long silver-inlaid rifles hung over their shoulders, bandoliers of cartridges and a knife or pistol in the belt—just as one pictured them in descriptions of a century ago. More tribesmen had climbed on to the rocks along either side of the road.

I had not been briefed about such a situation but we were with an attaché from the American embassy in Kabul who stopped the car and suggested I get out to greet the handsome, patriarchal chief as he advanced smilingly to greet us. At that moment a car drove up from behind the crowd on the Afghan side and a man in Western dress pushed through the crowd and asked in English if he could be of service as an interpreter. I accepted his offer of course, and learned later from our escort that he was an officer in the Afghan army whose arrival at the psychological moment had evidently been carefully planned in advance.

The chief produced a long parchment scroll and began to read, pausing for translations. I was informed that he and his retinue were the representatives of the Pushtoo nation and were seeking to establish the independent Pushtoonistan to which they were entitled. But, according to the scroll, they were prevented by the evil Pakistanis, who wanted to keep them in slavery and who sent punitive expeditions against them and their villages. They appealed to the great United States of America and to its Ambassador to help to free them and to enable them to gain their independence.

The chief wound up the scroll and handed it to me. I uttered some sympathetic but noncommittal remarks which were duly translated and seemed to be acceptable. I got back into our car, the crowd parted, and we drove on through waving, cheering, smiling ranks of Pushtoos.

Our visit to Kabul was brief and in just a few days' time we drove the rather terrifying road back again, with the gorgeous snow-crowned heights of the Hindu Kush towering to 25,000 feet on our left, and the caravans of camels claiming their right to the inside of the road so that our car skimmed the bare edges of the road far above the gorges below. We descended the Khyber Pass on the Pakistani side in the late afternoon and as we reached the plain, there was a much larger crowd of tribesmen, indistinguishable by us from the others in visage, clothing, and weapons. The chief of this group greeted me with another scroll and in excellent English read to me their account of the troublesome tribesmen up in the hills who caused so much difficulty for the great Pakistani people, the true friends of all the Pushtoos who lived happily and prosperously under the kindly government of Pakistan. I was not to believe a word I might have heard about any desire of the tribesmen to establish an independent Pushtoonistan. Again I made what seemed to be received as an appropriate response, accepted the scroll, and drove on back to Peshawar.

Pushtoonistan is still unborn. I was struck by the appropriateness of a remark of an Indian official quoted in the New York *Times* on January 24, 1972, apropos the new state of Bangladesh: "It's like a doctor helping a woman give birth and then helping care for the baby later. That's the way nations are born and nurtured, too; other bigger nations have got to act as the doctor."

In 1950, Uncle Sam had no intention of being the doctor to help in the birth of Pushtoonistan and since it is "tilted" in favor of Pakistan in 1972, it is not likely to espouse that role now.

6

The United Nations Delivers Libya and Somalia Eritrea Is Stillborn

If the role of the United Nations in the birth of the Republic of Korea is considered somewhat marginal, the part played by the Organization in the births of Libya and Somalia was direct and conclusive. The disposition of Eritrea can be described here only as a stillbirth.

After Montgomery defeated Rommel at El Alamein in 1942, the German and Italian forces were finally expelled from North Africa in the spring of 1943. That was the end of the Italian colonial empire in North Africa, which had comprised Libya, Italian Somaliland, and Eritrea. In the Italian peace treaty, Italy renounced "all right and title" to those territories, parts of which were of high strategic interest to the United States, to England, to France, and to the Soviet Union.

It seems astonishing that the four powers agreed to let the General Assembly of the newly born United Nations decide what was to become of those former colonies. It is true, as Adrian Pelt, the UN Commissioner for Libya points out,[1] that England, the United States, and France were united in their

opposition to the establishment of a Soviet sphere of influence
on the southern shore of the Mediterranean, and it is also true
that the Soviet Union shared with the three Allies a desire to
influence the outcome of the Italian elections of April 1948 in
order to determine the ideological and political orientation of
Italy in the postwar period.[2]

The resort to the United Nations for help in solving the dispute over the Italian colonies was not a last-minute act of de-
spair. When the Council of Foreign Ministers met in London
in September 1945 to begin discussing the peace treaties, the
United States had already decided to propose that these Italian
colonies should be administered under a UN trusteeship while
preparing for independence.[3] Perhaps this show of confidence
in the Organization was due to the fact that the Charter did
not even enter into force until October 24, 1945. Expectations
that there would be a happy cooperation with the Russians in
the promotion of world peace were already diminishing, but
the natal aura of the United Nations had not yet been dis-
persed.

Even if one takes the view, which I do not, that every American gesture of early confidence in the United Nations was due
to our feeling that we had a safe "mechanical majority," that
was by no means true of this issue in 1947, when the four powers finally agreed to leave the decision on the future of the Italian colonies to the General Assembly if they failed to agree
among themselves. Although our interests were parallel to the
British, the French feared that U.S. emphasis on preparation
for the independence of the Italian colonies might stir premature hopes in Algeria and in the neighboring French-con-
trolled protectorates of Tunisia and Morocco. The Arab states
had their own concerns, and pro-Italian feelings in Latin
America were another important factor to be reckoned with.
The postures of Italy itself were of prime importance.

Since there had not yet been any experience with the administration of a trusteeship under the UN Charter, it was easy

enough to agree in principle that the device could be accepted; the question was, who would be the trustee, the administering power?

In preparation for the U.S. delegation's departure for London in 1945 to attend the first session of the General Assembly of the United Nations, three somewhat junior officers of the State Department had prepared drafts of trusteeship agreements; they were Ralph Bunche, Lawrence Finkelstein, a specialist on the trusteeship system, and Thomas Power, who became the Principal Secretary of the UN Mission in Libya. They drafted on the assumption that Italy would be the trustee, but the delegation *en route* decided in favor of direct United Nations administration. Some five years later one of their drafts was used by the Philippine delegation in connection with the Italian trusteeship for Somaliland.[4]

The United States plan as submitted to the Council of Foreign Ministers (CFM) provided for the appointment by the Security Council of an administrator for each colony, who would be assisted by an advisory council. China supported the U.S. plan, Georges Bidault for France favored Italy as the trustee, Ernest Bevin wanted time to consider, and Vyacheslav Molotov quoted a Russian proverb which says "A child which has seven nurses does not get nursed at all." He informed his colleagues that the Soviet Union wished to be trustee for Tripolitania, one of the three sections of Libya. (The others were Cyrenaica and the Fezzan. After the defeat of the Italians, temporary administrations were set up by the British in Cyrenaica and Tripolitania while the French similarly administered the Fezzan.) Bevin then bluntly stated that Britain could never agree to the Soviet claim for an individual trusteeship over Tripolitania but could accept the U.S plan except for Eritrea and Somaliland.[5]

Negotiations continued, but no agreement was reached when the CFM met again in Paris in April 1946. They recessed and reassembled in June. Molotov suddenly rendered the others speechless by agreeing to one disputed point after another. On the Italian colonies, he said, he accepted a U.S. proposal to postpone a decision for a year, after which if no agreement was reached, the General Assembly would be asked to decide and the powers would agree in advance to accept that decision. Thus it was provided in Annex XI to the Italian peace treaty that if the four powers could not agree upon the disposal of the Italian colonies within one year from the coming into force of the treaty, "the matter shall be referred to the General Assembly of the United Nations for a recommendation, and the Four Powers agree to accept the recommendation and to take appropriate measures for giving effect to it." It was a neat formula, since it did not purport to change the powers of the General Assembly as laid down in the Charter, but nevertheless gave, in advance to an Assembly recommendation, binding authority.[6]

It was a remarkable tribute to the potentialities of the United Nations that it should be given such authority, but in April 1949, when the General Assembly took up the challenge, peppery Herbert Evatt of Australia, who was then President of the Assembly, complained to a member of the U.S. delegation that Australia, and other smaller powers who had played an important role in the war, had not been given a chance to present their views to the CFM. He suggested such states might be put on a UN commission to study the problem and report to the next Assembly. As was often the case, Evatt's view was uniquely his own.

It was correct for Professor Rivlin to write in 1950 that:

The assumption that the bitter struggle over the Colonies stemmed from covetous desires on the part of the Powers concerned to annex the colonial riches of a defeated State is quickly disproved by the facts. The truth is—there are no known riches in Libya, Eritrea and Italian Somaliland. . . . The value of the Italian Colonies lies mostly in the strategic significance of their geographical locations.[7]

But the New York Times *Encyclopedic Almanac 1970* could report:

Libya, the first country to have achieved independence through the United Nations, is challenging Saudi Arabia and Iran as the leading producers of oil in North Africa and the Middle East.

Even at the Potsdam Conference of 1945, Stalin had made clear that the Russian desire for a base on the North African shore was due to strategic considerations. British strategic interests in the area were obvious and the United States wished to strengthen its own position by establishing an air base on the Libyan coast near Tripoli.[8]

After the signature of the Italian peace treaty, the deputies of the foreign ministers continued to work on the disposal of the colonies but without success. During the discussions of the deputies, the United States Joint Chiefs of Staff had made it clear that the strategic interests of the United States, supporting British strategic policy, opposed any single or joint control by the Soviet Union of any of the colonies. The Libyan bases, in particular, must be under British control. These views were restated to Secretary of Defense James Forrestal in the spring of 1948 when it was noted that agreements for certain air facilities in Libya had already been concluded with the British. In August the Joint Chiefs were even more emphatic and asked for opportunity to review positions to be taken by the State Department. There was nothing new in all of this any more than there was surprise that Russia would like a Mediterranean port. The struggle for influence in the Middle East continues today as the Soviets support the Arabs and the United States, trying to ride two horses, also gives arms to Israel.[9]

During the summer of 1948, the United States policies on the disposition of the Italian colonies were being actively studied. The British desired further bilateral talks to be followed by tripartite sessions with the French included. Ambassador Lewis Douglas in London kept the Department posted on the trend of British official thinking. At the end of May Britain was reported to be willing to take on "the thankless task" of a trusteeship for Tripolitania, in part to counter the French desire to reinstate the Italians there; such a move, the British told Paris, would "create another Palestine" but London knew—so it was said—that only the United States could convince the French. At this stage the British did not think that the unity of Libya was indispensable—what was wanted in Tripolitania and in Cyrenaica was independence and for the latter area an American trusteeship would be acceptable as a second best to British.

On August 6, 1948, the State Department sent to our embassy in London instructions for the deputies in their meeting scheduled for August 9. The Department was anxious to settle any item that was possible, but realized that the "chance of agreement on all Italian colonies is slight and that some part of the problem at least will go to the GA." The U.S deputy was not to make any commitment about the attitude which the United States might take in the Assembly, since the situation in that UN organ might necessitate some change of position.

Substantively, the Department preferred an Italian trusteeship for Somaliland. Eritrea could be partitioned, with the Muslim portion plus Asmara and Massawa under British trusteeship, the rest being ceded to Ethiopia. The United States attached importance to the port of Massawa and the town of Asmara, linked to it by railroad, because our military had a strong interest in the radio facilities at Asmara. The State Department opposed Bevin's proposal that Ethiopia should administer a trusteeship for Eritrea. In regard to Libya, the instructions were in part tactical: the United States should let the French and the Soviets speak first and then should say that the United States always favored trusteeship to be followed by independence at the earliest possible date. The United States considered the British the most suitable trustees for Cyrenaica, but the situation in Tripolitania and the Fezzan was more complicated and must be considered later in the General Assembly. If necessary, the U.S deputy could propose postponing all decisions on Libya until the debates in the United Nations, but the British were to be assured we would support them in the General Assembly.

This instruction from the Department crossed a dispatch from Ambassador Douglas in London. Douglas reported on a conversation he had just had with Bevin, who told him that the cabinet had reached a decision on the Italian colonies. The British position coincided with that of the United States regarding Somaliland, but not on Eritrea. Bevin wanted to press ahead with a settlement on Cyrenaica so that they could start work on bases there; the British base in Egypt might be jeopardized if an Egyptian government was under Soviet influence (as it indeed was at a later date). The British thought they could get General Assembly approval for their trusteeship over Cyrenaica. Bevin took it for granted that at least some of the issues would go to the General Assembly since agreement among the four powers was unlikely.

On September 4, 1948, Andrei Vyshinsky suggested that the CFM should reconvene, which it did on September 13. The State Department had already informed our delegation in London that the presence of the Secretary of State and Foreign Ministers was not obligatory; they could be represented by deputies. However, at the meeting on September 13, Vyshinsky objected that it was not a real meeting of the CFM since Bevin and Marshall did not attend. But the meeting proceeded and Vyshinsky first proposed that all the colonies be returned to Italy, then switched to a UN trusteeship for all of them. Since the four could not agree on any plan, they sent a collective note to the Secretary-General of the United Nations on September 15, 1948, informing him that the disposition of the Italian colonies now rested with the General Assembly.

It was in 1948 that the General Assembly first met in Paris; the session opened in the Palais de Chaillot on September 21, just six days after the four-power note on the Italian colonies. I was then Deputy Chief of the U.S. Mission to the United Nations and one of our delegates to the Assembly along with Secretary of State Marshall, Mrs. Roosevelt, Warren Austin, John Foster Dulles, and Benjamin Cohen.

The decision to hold the session in Paris was allegedly due to the fear that, during the American presidential election campaign, issues raised in the United Nations might be picked up by candidates and by the New York press with unfortunate repercussions. As soon as Paris was suggested as an alternative meeting place, the Latin American delegates danced for joy and their votes swept away the objection to the extra costs involved for the Organization in making such a move.

The French hastily did some remodeling of the Palais de Chaillot, which had been built in 1937 in place of the old Trocadero. It faces the Eiffel Tower across the Seine, houses several museums, and contains a large theater which served as the auditorium for the General Assembly, with the stage acting as the rostrum where the President and Secretary-General sat. It was also on the stage that the Security Council assembled when it was meeting. The gallery accommodated visitors, and there my wife usually sat with the wife of General Andrew McNaughton of Canada.

One day when I was presenting to the Security Council the case of the United States in regard to the Berlin Blockade, my wife and Mrs. McNaughton were attentive listeners in the gallery; my wife was knitting as she often did. An usherette approached and said: "It is forbidden to knit, Madame; it is rude to the speaker." "But," retorted my wife, "the speaker is Ambassador Jessup, my husband, and at the United Nations in New York we are always allowed to knit." The usherette withdrew, consulted a supervisor and quickly returned. "If it is permitted in your country, Madame, you are to knit here also." My wife was tempted to say that knitting on important occasions was also a traditional activity of the women of Paris in the days of the Revolution.

Having been accustomed to temporary partitions in the old

factory used by the United Nations at Lake Success, we did not take it amiss in committee meetings to have the skeleton head of a dinosaur peer at us over a screen that fenced off the museum's permanent exhibits which could not be removed from the Palais.

As in the United States, so in Paris, it was generally assumed during the autumn of 1948 that Thomas Dewey would defeat President Truman and would at once announce that John Foster Dulles would be his Secretary of State. General Carlos Romulo of the Philippines even staged a dinner in Paris on election night in Dulles' honor; the guest of honor carried off with aplomb what might have been an embarrassment to his host.

During the session, I had responsibility primarily for dealing with the case of the Berlin Blockade in the Security Council, but was also charged with handling some parts of the Palestine and Indonesian items on the Assembly's agenda.[10] Despite some efforts of the Russians to debate the question of the Italian colonies at the Paris session when they knew France was not seeing eye-to-eye with Britain and the United States, the item was not reached in the midst of other problems before the adjournment on December 12, 1948; the item was accordingly postponed to the second part of the third session of the Assembly which convened in New York April 5, 1949. It was placed as the first item on the agenda of Committee I (Political and Security).

The postponement of the item suited the United States for several reasons; it gave time for further consultations both inside the government in Washington and with Britain and France. The problem of securing a favorable vote in the U.N. for any plan was always kept in mind.

The principal factor was the need to reach a common view inside the government. The delegation's Working Group on Italian Colonies under the chairmanship of Dean Rusk, who was then Director of UNA, had reached agreement at the end of September 1948 that the subject should not be debated until after the presidential elections in the United States; the British concurred. But the eventual role of the United Nations was still being discussed in the delegation. Rusk thought there might be more support in the General Assembly if it were proposed that the United Nations itself should be the administering authority for Cyrenaica. Since Secretary of State George Marshall was in Paris as head of the delegation, Acting Secretary Robert Lovett cabled him on November 9, 1948, the views of the Joint Chiefs of Staff concerning Eritrea. They said it would be inadvisable to remove radio facilities from Asmara since there was no other suitable location in the Middle East. But if the territory were ceded to Ethiopia it would be necessary to get assurance of freedom from political and technical interference. Secretary of Defense James Forrestal suggested trying to obtain from Ethiopia written guarantees (but not in a form which would have to be registered with the United Nations under Article 102 of the Charter!) [11] which would in effect amount to "a sort of military extra-territoriality."

A few days later Lovett sent a cable for Dean Rusk and Ernest Gross, then an alternate delegate to the Assembly, noting reasons why the State Department did not favor a U.S. trusteeship for Tripolitania. The reasons included the difficulty of obtaining congressional approval; the inadvisability of trying to establish American administration over Arab territory in the light of the then relations with the Arab states due to the situation in Palestine; the adverse reaction in Italy if the United States not only failed to support Italian trusteeship but sought this territory for itself. A multi-power trusteeship including the United States was also disapproved.

When the General Assembly met again in New York on April 5, 1949, I had ceased to be Deputy Chief of the U.S. Mission to the United Nations but was stationed in Washington as U.S. Ambassador-at-Large. I was still a member of the U.S. delegation to the General Assembly.

It was the standard practice to assign each topic on the

agenda to some particular member of the delegation, but the delegation met as a group almost every day and, at those meetings, all participated in discussions of the position which the United States should take on each item. As the session progressed, the delegation would have daily reports from all the liaison officers who were constantly talking with other delegates to feel the pulse of various groups on general problems and gradually on the text of draft resolutions or amendments to them. As this chapter progresses, I shall take the occasion to try to give a picture of this process, particularly complicated in the case of the Italian colonies, which were treated as a single item but which involved disparate elements for Libya, Eritrea, and Somaliland.

John Foster Dulles was assigned the task of handling the issue of the Italian colonies, and my connection with it at this session was incidental. For example, in March 1949, I had a conversation in New York with Ambassador Jean Chauvel of France on another matter, and he raised the problem of reconciling the French and American views on the Italian colonies. I had not kept current with the Franco-American talks on the subject so remained noncommittal, just expressing the hope that we could reach agreement so as to avoid quarreling in the General Assembly debates or forcing another postponement. During the session, I dealt with the final stages of the Indonesian case, some aspects of the perennial Arab-Israeli problem, and on the side carried on discussions with Soviet Ambassador Jacob Malik on the raising of the Berlin Blockade, in addition to becoming involved in the State Department with Far Eastern questions, including the preparation of the China White Paper, which was published in July 1949.

In the meeting of the U.S. delegation on April 2, I said that an interim solution of the future of the Italian colonies might very well have to be considered if it appeared that the ultimate objective of independence for Libya could not be obtained by action of the General Assembly at that session. The General Assembly did fail to reach agreement on any of the Italian colonies and the item was again adjourned, this time to the regular fourth session which met in New York in the fall of 1949.

The difficulties in the second part of the third session during the spring of 1949 are well summarized by Rivlin:

> Facts and judgments about the Colonies were presented to the Committee by the various speakers in the light of their own interests. Thus, the Ethiopians spoke of Italian "maladministration" and "stultification" while the Latin Americans lauded the colonization and civilizing achievements of Italy; Egypt spoke of Libyan readiness for immediate independence while other States pointed to the lack of preparedness of the Libyans for self-government; the USSR claimed that peace and security in the Near East required the ejection of Britain from the Italian Colonies and the establishment of direct United Nations administration over the Colonies, while the United States, Britain and others argued that peace in the area could not be attained through direct United Nations administration and that furthermore it required Britain's presence in Cyrenaica.[12]

The situation in the United Nations had been complicated by the fact that on the day of the first meeting of Subcommittee 15, May 10, 1949, the press carried the news that Italian Foreign Minister Carlo Sforza had stopped off in London on his way back to Rome from New York, and had concluded with the British Foreign Secretary the Bevin-Sforza agreement on the disposition of the Italian colonies. The agreement was intended to appeal to the large pro-Italian bloc in the General Assembly, while favoring British interests. As in earlier British proposals, Eritrea was to be partitioned between Ethiopia and the Sudan; Italy was to be the trustee for Italian Somaliland. The plan for Libya was complex. As a basic principle it was to be declared that Libya would become independent at the end of ten years if the General Assembly should then so decide. Great Britain would meanwhile have a trusteeship for Cyrenaica, France would similarly administer the Fezzan, while Italy would be given a trusteeship over Tripolitania in 1951, the territory remaining meanwhile under British administration.

The Arabs were violently critical; there were riots in Tripoli and in Somaliland. The Latin Americans were pleased and the United States joined Britain and France in support. Indeed the French support of Italy was very strong. Foreign Minister Robert Schuman told Dulles on April 12 that France could not agree to limiting Italy to a trusteeship for Somaliland; Italy should be given the same role in Tripolitania. His reasoning was familiar: if the Italian people were not satisfied, the existing government might fall and Italian entry into NATO and the European Union would be endangered. Dulles told Schuman we would agree to any arrangement for Tripolitania which the British thought would be compatible with law and order, but perhaps he went somewhat beyond the official United States position. On the other hand, Carl Berendsen, the New Zealand statesman, was vitriolic in private criticism of the Bevin-Sforza plan, which he called the most naked sort of power politics, an abandonment of all principle, and a sell-out of the people of the territories concerned.

The Subcommittee took the Bevin-Sforza plan as a basis for discussion and when their report reached the full Committee, slightly more than the necessary two-thirds voted for all parts of the resolution except that which provided for Italian trusteeship in Tripolitania. On that paragraph the vote was one short of the required two-thirds, because of the efforts of Ali-Nourridine Unayzi, an official of the secretariat of the Arab League, who persuaded the Haitian delegate, Emilio Saint-Lot, to abandon Haiti's French and Latin American ties and to vote against. In the town of Tripoli, a street was then named "Sharia Saint-Lot" in his honor.[13] Another member of the Haitian delegation told one of the U.S. advisers that Saint-Lot had told him that he had strict telephone instructions from President Estime of Haiti to follow the U.S. lead in voting. But Saint-Lot was a senator and the president was afraid of him, so Saint-Lot acted in accordance with his personal views, which were violently hostile to the other states of Latin America. Aus-

tralian Foreign Minister Evatt had told Dulles there were rumors that the Arab delegations had offered to support the
Latin Americans on the question of the Italian colonies, if the
Latin Americans would support the Arabs against Israel. If
there was such a scheme, it came to nothing.

In plenary session the proposed draft resolution, bereft of its
pro-Italian features, was defeated by a combination of Latin
American, Arab, Asian, and Soviet bloc states; there were only
14 votes for the resolution, 37 against, and 7 abstentions. Obviously, the United States did not have a "mechanical majority." Willy-nilly, the delegates voted overwhelmingly to postpone the whole question to the fourth session of the General
Assembly.

One of my assignments as a U.S. delegate to the fourth session of the General Assembly, was to deal with this still unre-
solved problem of the disposition of the Italian colonies. The
item was again put on the agenda of Committee I and the substantive aspects were then delegated to Subcommittee 17, on
which I represented the United States. The debates continued
for some six weeks.

My deputy for dealing with the issues of the Italian colonies
was Jack Ross who, on an overall basis, was Ambassador Austin's right-hand man. As expert advisers I had Tom Power,
who became the deputy to Pelt in Libya; Sam Kopper, one of
the State Department's experts on the Arab world; and John
Utter, who was abundantly knowledgeable and wise about the
Middle East and North Africa. Utter was such a good teacher
that he made me sound quite convincing when I referred, in
speeches in the General Assembly's committees, to the pastoral
people inhabiting the plateau region of Eritrea, separated by a
great escarpment from the lowlands along the sea coast.

Three days before the debates began on September 30, 1949,
Secretary Dean Acheson received the Indian delegate, Sir Benegal N. Rau, commonly known as "Sir B. N." Sir. B. N. was a ju-
rist of great capacity and learning who went on to serve as a

judge on the International Court of Justice until his death in
1953. He played a leading part in the drafting of the Constitution of India, preparing memoranda in which he compared the
constitutional provisions of the United states and many other
countries as a background for India's own basic law. He was
one of my most congenial colleagues in any meeting of the
United Nations. He told Secretary Acheson that in regard to
Eritrea, India was, mindful of its own experience, suspicious of
partition; moreover the conflict in the reports of the factual situation in Eritrea were troublesome. Acheson said that it would
not be a favor to anyone to have another small independent
state with a population of dissimilar traditions and mores—
that is, a mixture of Muslims and Christian Copts. In regard to
Somaliland, Rau said it did not matter who was designated
trustee. Acheson asked him to think whether India would
really want the Soviet Union to be trustee of that area—would
not that make a difference? Rau agreed but said he had been
thinking only of likely choices. Italy, he said, was the apparent,
but to many the unwelcome, candidate for trustee, and under
the circumstances, the terms of the trusteeship should be safeguarded. Acheson said he would study the point.

On October 6, 1949, just before Foreign Secretary Ernest
Bevin left New York, he met with Secretary Acheson and
Couve de Murville of the French delegation (not yet Foreign
Minister). Bevin was accompanied by his secretary, Roderick
Barclay, while Charles Yost and I were with Dean Acheson.

It was Bevin who raised the question of the Italian colonies.
He had heard of a new proposal by Latin American delegations that there should be a UN trusteeship for Eritrea with
British troops remaining there. Bevin said such a plan was absolutely unacceptable to the United Kingdom and if such a resolution passed the General Assembly, British troops would be
withdrawn at once. Eritrea would not be viable as a separate
unit and would become a heavy charge on the British. Bevin
had persuaded the Sudan to agree to accept the merger of west-

ern Eritrea which was the Muslim area, and Bevin thought that would be the best solution.

I said there was a strong combination of Latin American and Arab delegations which opposed that solution, and Couve de Murville said partition would not get a bare majority in the General Assembly. I said that the Latin-Arab bloc favored Eritrean independence—the Arabs because there would be a Moslem majority in such a state and the Latins because this was the solution currently favored by Italy. Bevin asked whether this plan would give Ethiopia an outlet to the sea, and I reported that there were some who advocated an outlet at Assab while others suggested merely giving the Ethiopians transit rights over Eritrea.

Couve asked if a collective trusteeship might be possible, but Bevin said that would be absolutely unacceptable because the Slavs could not be permanently excluded from such a trusteeship and also because such a plan would be unworkable due to constant bickering over which country would have the primacy in such an administration. Couve pointed out that there was a difference between a "collective" trusteeship and an "international" one administered by the United Nations; for Somaliland, the Latin Americans had in mind that if a sole trusteeship were not given to Italy, there should be a collective trusteeship of four or five powers including Italy, with an Italian staff which would actually administer the country.

Returning to the Eritrean question, I said that there might have to be a temporary solution. There seemed to be wide agreement that the Christian Copts of the plateau region should join with Ethiopia, but there was much disagreement about the future of the Muslim population of the coast and lowlands. I thought there was still a chance of agreeing on a solution, but it might be necessary to hold over the Eritrean question for another year. (This proved to be the outcome.)

Turning to Libya, Bevin sounded the usual British refrain —they should not be interfered with in Cyrenaica. Things were working out well there and full independence would be granted in a few years. (Actually the British in June had recognized the emir as the head of the Cyrenaican government and he had visited London. The British granted him extensive powers but announced that these steps in Cyrenaica would not prejudice the eventual question of Libyan unity.) Bevin said that Tripolitania presented difficulty because of the French position in Tunisia. Couve said that France did not object to independence for Tripolitania but that they did not want the Senussi there. Bevin agreed. In Cyrenaica, most of the population were of the fanatical Muslim sect of the Senussi and they had helped the British forces against the Italians in 1941. On January 8, 1942, Foreign Secretary Anthony Eden had told the House of Commons that His Majesty's Government was "determined that at the end of the war the Senusis [sic] in Cyrenaica will in no circumstances again fall under Italian domination." But this pledge did not involve Tripolitania, where both the British and French at times favored an Italian trusteeship.

I said I thought there was no serious difficulty on these points and that it would be possible to work out a loose federation agreeable to the peoples of both territories. Bevin said that he wanted to make a treaty with Cyrenaica and not have it blocked by Tripolitania or by the United Nations. He had no objection to a UN commission in Tripolitania but he was afraid that if there were such a commission in Cyrenaica it might interfere with British administration and the use of essential airfields. (The strategic considerations were always uppermost.) I agreed with Bevin but said that we had to find a solution acceptable to the General Assembly which, by agreement of the four powers, had the authority to decide on the disposition of the Italian colonies. I felt that there must be some form of UN commission, but its function could be strictly limited so that it would not interfere with the existing British administration. Couve noted that it was important that the United Nations should recognize the new government in Cyr-

enaica. Bevin laid very great stress on the importance of unin-
terrupted maintenance of communications, especially by air,
through Libya. He said that this was as important to the
United States, to France, and to Italy, as to the United Kingdom. The whole Western position on the south shore of the
Mediterranean was at stake, he declared, and the Arabs were
"broken reeds" who could not be relied on to resist the Soviets.
Bevin hoped that the General Assembly could settle the Libyan question but it would be better to leave it unsettled than
to interrupt the very vital communications.

It is so fashionable to identify the cold war with the United
States as the chief antagonist of the Soviet Union that one
sometimes forgets that this American preoccupation loomed large
also in the minds of statesmen from other countries. At times
the ministers or ambassadors of other countries would waive the
red flag at us, so to speak, in order to induce us to refrain from
taking some action that, so we were told, would greatly
strengthen the Communists. But in Ernest Bevin's case, as in
Dean Acheson's, the menace of communism, which he identified with Russian imperialist expansion, was real and constant.

When the fourth session of the General Assembly opened at
the United Nations, there was an important statement by the
Italian Foreign Minister, Count Sforza. When he was in exile
from Mussolini's Italy, Sforza came to New York where President Nicholas Murray Butler of Columbia University be-
friended him as a refugee scholar. Since I was then a professor
at Columbia, as well as a trustee of the Carnegie Endowment
for International Peace, of which Butler was also president, I
came to know Sforza during the war years. I could agree with
what Dean Acheson wrote of Sforza, that he "was a man of
character and ability. . . . It could be said of him, as it has
been said of Balliol men, that he had a consciousness of effort-
less superiority." At the preceding session of the General Assembly, Sforza was compelled by the state of Italian domestic
politics to insist that Italy should return to Tripolitania as

trustee, but during the spring and summer he indicated that the Italian position could be compromised. At the opening of the debate on October 1, 1949, he announced that Italy had withdrawn its request for a trusteeship over Tripolitania and Eritrea and favored their early independence. As for Somaliland, Sforza argued that Italian withdrawal would hinder the development of the country and that Italy should be entrusted with the task of continuing to prepare the territory for independence.

The actual draft of proposals on Libya which I submitted for the United States to the UN Committee on October 10 suggested:

1. At the end of three years Libya would be independent and during the interval the powers administering Cyrenaica, Tripolitania, and the Fezzan should coordinate their activities to that end.

2. Representatives of the inhabitants of the three areas should meet at least one year prior to the date of independence to decide what form of government they would want for the new state.

3. An advisory council would be composed of Egypt, France, Italy, the United Kingdom, and the United States, one representative from Cyrenaica, and one from Tripolitania, to advise the administering authorities on various subjects. The advisory council would be empowered to visit the territory but should have its headquarters elsewhere.[14]

Other governments submitted other proposals for Libya and on October 11, Committee I decided to set up Subcommittee 17, consisting of twenty-one members. In that Subcommittee on October 14, I stated that the United States could not support the idea of a single commissioner, but preferred an Indian proposal for a commissioner and a council; this general approach was approved. We were making it clear that we did not want to predetermine the form of independent Libya's government, whether unitary or federal, since that was up to the

Libyans to decide for themselves. We definitely opposed carving it up into separate states. Hector McNeil of the U.K. delegation suggested to me that the council should consist only of representatives of the inhabitants, but we thought this would give the commissioner considerable, and undesirable, power to meddle in internal administration.

The Latin American group let it be known that it would not agree to any solution for Libya unless Italy were given the trusteeship for Somaliland, and the Arab objection to the latter arrangement had softened. Subcommittee 17 rapidly agreed on meeting this condition as soon as the principle was established that Somalia would become independent after ten years.

Turning back to the Libyan issue, the problem in Subcommittee 17 was not the basic question of independence, which was readily accepted, but rather the arrangements for the period of transition. Once again it was Sir B. N. Rau of India who drafted the proposal finally adopted. Under his plan, a single independent Libyan state was to come into existence no later than January 1, 1952. The constitution of the new state, including its form of government, was to be determined by representatives of the three areas meeting and consulting together in a national assembly. The Subcommittee accepted his formula providing "That for the purpose of assisting the people of Libya in the formulation of the constitution and the establishment of an independent government, there shall be a United Nations commissioner in Libya appointed by the General Assembly and a council to aid and advise him." The council, as proposed by Sir B. N., was to be composed according to a clever description of categories: Egypt as a neighbor; the United Kingdom and France as administering powers; Italy for useful past experience; the United States for "precious economic aid"; and Pakistan as a state which had recently acquired independence. There would also be on the council representatives of the three areas—Cyrenaica, Tripolitania, and the Fezzan, plus (according to a Guatemalan amendment) one representative of the Libyan minorities. A Polish proposal to include the Soviet Union in the council was not adopted.

Importance has been attached by many newborn states to membership in the United Nations as a final baptismal initiation into the international society. For the United States, I accordingly proposed the inclusion in the Libyan resolution of a provision that Libya would be admitted to United Nations membership as soon as it was established as an independent state. By agreeing to add the words "in accordance with Article 4 of the Charter" (which lists the conditions for membership), this proposal was adopted unanimously. The Soviets joined in this unanimity although, probably because they sought to woo the Arab world, they denounced the whole Libyan plan as a bit of "prettified" imperialism.

I do not know why the problem of the Italian colonies seemed to be of such relatively slight interest to Dean Acheson. His *Present at the Creation* largely ignores the provisions of the Italian peace treaty and the strategic considerations which so obsessed the mind of Ernest Bevin when Libya and Cyrenaica were mentioned. One will not find the names of those former colonial areas in the excellent index to Acheson's book.

In the record of the conversation with Bevin which has just been summarized, the note-taker, who was the superbly capable Charles Yost, does not record that Acheson contributed anything to that discussion of the Italian colonies. Perhaps it was because the United States had no special interest of its own aside from its agreement with the British on the strategic importance of keeping Russia from getting a foothold in the Mediterranean or Middle Eastern area, a result to be supported by assurance of American air and communication rights as stressed by the Joint Chiefs of Staff.

Beyond this, "all" that was necessary was to maintain and strengthen our friendly relations with the pro-Italian Latin Americans; cultivate with the Arabs as much warmth as the chill of our Palestinian policies would permit; and satisfy the

desires of our NATO partners, France and Italy! The latter
had finally, on U.S. urgings, been invited to be an original signatory of the NATO treaty in March 1949, our reasons being
largely those already indicated, namely to counter the possibility of a strengthened Italian Communist party swinging the
country's policy to the East.

On October 24, 1949, I wrote a memorandum to Acheson to
keep him informed of the course of events in the United Nations and of the difficulties confronting us in our dealings with
our British friends, a subject which the British ambassador, Sir
Oliver Franks, had brought up in talks with the Secretary of
State. I pointed out that the difficulty lay within the British
ranks.

Just the day before I wrote my memorandum, Jack Ross of
the U.S. Mission and I had talked at length with three quite di-
verse Englishmen. Sir Alexander Cadogan, permanent representative to the United Nations, the ideal experienced British
diplomat, who traced his lineage to the first Earl Cadogan and
a succeeding line of distinguished men who had served the
British government in high offices since the seventeenth century. When awakened at 2 A.M. in London during the war by a
telephone call from Winston Churchill, who was famous as a
night owl, Cadogan could reply: "Oh, stop bothering me, Winston! I told you all I know on that subject two hours ago"—
and slammed down the receiver.

Sir Alex married Lady Theodosia Acheson, daughter of the
Earl and Countess of Gosford. At the United Nations, she was
always known as Lady Theo and she was a delicious *enfant terrible.* Just before Andrei Gromyko was replaced as the Soviet
permanent representative to the United Nations, Lady Theo,
sitting next to him at a farewell dinner given by Trygve Lie,
blandly inquired: "Why do you go back to Moscow, Mr. Gromyko? Why don't you stay over here like that poor Mr. Kravchenko?" (who had just defected in Canada and had written a

best seller entitled *I Chose Freedom*). Gromyko rarely smiled, and this occasion was no exception.

Although there were moments when Sir Alex Cadogan's diplomatic operations tempted me to mutter to myself "Perfidious Albion!" I always enjoyed working with him and profited from his experienced shrewdness. The editor of Cadogan's *Diaries* had reason to write: "Cadogan held a unique position at the U.N., derived from a blend of receptivity, debating skill, unmatched experience, knowledge of procedure and obvious desire to make the organisation work." [15]

Then there was Hector McNeil, a delightful joyous Scotsman who, on a personal basis, got on swimmingly with Ernest Bevin. Hector was then Minister of State and Lord Gladwyn records that he might, except for a sorry mischance, have become Foreign Secretary. When I was sitting for the United States in a UN Committee seat in the established alphabetical order near Hector McNeil for the United Kingdom and a brilliant Armenian, Aroutunian, for the USSR, I have watched McNeil, at the end of a vigorous speech (and he was a very good speaker), poke Aroutunian in the ribs and say "I gave you a good one that time!" to which his Soviet colleague would respond: "Wait till it's my turn!"

The third member of the British group I am describing was a reserved typical British civil servant, George Clutton from the Colonial Office. I have mentioned how Sir Oliver Franks told me of the jealousies between the Foreign Office and the Colonial Office.

In the conversation with Jack Ross and these three men, McNeil disagreed with the views of the Colonial Office represented by Clutton, and both of them disagreed with Foreign Secretary Bevin. Cadogan let them do the talking. According to McNeil, the U.K. delegation was confronted with a fundamental inconsistency, since Bevin insisted on cutting down expenses by withdrawing from the administration of Eritrea and So-

maliland, while saying that unless a completely satisfactory
solution for all the colonies were arrived at, decisions on all of
them should be postponed for another year. In regard to Eritrea, McNeil had sent a strong message to Bevin and told me
that he had no substantial disagreement with us on tactics but
was hampered by his instructions. On Libya, McNeil agreed
that U.S. proposals would not prevent Great Britain from
carrying out its basic plan for strategic arrangements with Cyrenaica.

In reporting on this conversation to Dean Acheson, I told
him that I felt that Bevin—and not for the only time—was either misinformed about, or misunderstood, the then current
proposals on Eritrea and Somaliland and did not appreciate
how closely we were collaborating with the British delegation in
the United Nations. (As will appear later, it seems likely that
Sir Oliver Franks conveyed the gist of this view to Bevin.) In
my opinion, my memorandum to Acheson continued, Bevin
was so obsessed with his idea about the strategic importance of
Cyrenaica he was incapable of taking a balanced view of the
whole problem of the disposition of the Italian colonies. I suspected that he favored a postponement by the General Assembly of the entire issue, after which he would have Cyrenaica
proclaim its full independence and make a treaty of alliance
with Great Britain. I recalled that in earlier talks in Paris,
Bevin had told Acheson there was an analogy to the reasons
why the British had established Trans-Jordan as a separate
state. Originally part of the Palestine mandate, the British established Jordan as a semi-independent emirate in 1923. In
1946 the mandate over Jordan was ended and the Jordanian
kingdom was proclaimed, two years before Britain abandoned
the rest of the mandate in Palestine. So in North Africa, Bevin
might announce that the United Kingdom could no longer
continue to carry the burden and would withdraw—an ultimatum which, as in the case of Palestine, would force the issue.

Sir Oliver Franks who, on instructions from Bevin, had complained to Acheson about the attitude of the U.S. delegation in the General Assembly, would not, I thought, have been familiar with these dissonances in the British ranks in New York. I said we would continue to try to work out adjustments, but at the moment I thought the prospects of winning through to a favorable vote were rather slim. Subsequently we had to reassure Bevin on several occasions. On October 17 we were instructed by the State Department to tell the U.K. delegation at the United Nations that the United States shared Bevin's views about the importance of strategic objectives in Cyrenaica and Tripolitania. On October 31, when the British were contemplating offering changes in the Libyan decisions which had already been unanimously reached in the United Nations, we were at great pains to reassure Bevin that we would continue to cooperate and see that the UN Commissioner in Libya did not frustrate British plans. I discussed the issue with members of the U.K. delegation and Clutton telegraphed London asking that his instructions be changed. On November 5, Hector McNeil showed me a telegram just received from the Foreign Office, but said he would ignore it in order to speak in favor of our position. Ten days later Bevin gave McNeill full discretion to speak in agreement with the United States.

The Libyan solution reported by Subcommittee 17 was approved by Committee I and in plenary session. It was on November 21, 1949, that the General Assembly accepted the draft resolution, which dealt also with Somaliland and Eritrea, by 48 to 1 with 9 abstentions. Before going back to describe the solution for Somaliland and the postponement of the Eritrean question, some details may be filled in, even though the three threads of the story make it complicated.

As Rivlin says, "the United Nations was to serve as mid-wife in the birth of independence" for Libya by January 1, 1952. Meanwhile, the UN Commissioner would serve, one cannot say as "nanny" since the child was not yet born, but in terms of nations or states, one has to stretch the metaphor here; perhaps one might say that Libya was put in the incubator for two and a half years. As part of the final agreement in the General Assembly, it was decided that the Commissioner should be selected by a committee of five persons—the President and two Vice-Presidents of the General Assembly, and the Chairmen of Committee I and of the Ad Hoc Political Committee. They unanimously recommended Adrian Pelt, a Hollander, who filled the unique office with great distinction. Rather surprisingly, the secret ballot on which he was elected showed considerable diversity;there were 8 abstentions, Pelt received 28 votes, while José Arce of Argentina had 20 and Sir Zafrullah Khan of Pakistan got 3.[16]

I have referred to Libya as being in an incubator for more than two years, but the even temperature and quiet which one associates with an incubator for babies was not characteristic of the Libyan diplomatic and political scene during that UN interval, despite the skill with which UN Commissioner Pelt discharged his duties.

The strategic considerations which played so prominent a part in the early discussions among the Big Four at the end of the war had lost none of their emphasis. The principal interest of the United States was in retaining use of the Wheelus Air Base but final commitments with the Libyans were sedulously postponed until after independence. There were, however, preliminary talks and assurances that the United States would pay liberally for the privilege of using the base. In June 1951, President Truman recommended to Congress the inclusion of $1.5 million in the mutual security program for 1952, which was said not to be a *quid pro quo* for base rights although, hopefully, it would create a favorable atmosphere, since at least part of that amount would be available for general purposes of the Libyan budget. It was always a problem to serve two balls at once; one to Congress stressing U.S. needs for security which funds could assure, and another to the recipient government

emphasizing how much we liked it and how eager we were to
be helpful.

The British still toyed with the idea of early recognition of
the independence of Cyrenaica and a treaty with the emir to secure British rights. Count Sforza was suspicious of British intentions which might prejudice the position of the Italian colony in Libya. He thought London gave undue weight to the
opinions of British officials in Libya who, having been accustomed to wartime austerity in England, were luxuriating in
well-staffed, well-lardered palaces which they were reluctant to
leave. At the same time, Ambassador James Dunn in Rome was
being instructed to warn the Italian government against whip-
ping up Italian nationalist sentiment over the Libyan question.
The emir was bitterly anti-Italian. In January 1951, Bevin with
his usual bluntness told Sforza, at a NATO meeting in Brussels, that Italy would have to help the British in their plans for
Libya if Italy wanted any help for Italian interests. Ambassador
Dunn reported that the Italians were hurt by this "unsubtle
pressure" and suspected Bevin of trying to blackmail them.

As usual, the State Department was trying to avoid
antagonizing any of the political groups in Libya. In June
1950, the local disagreements were so intense that the Department hoped the UN Advisory Council would move to Geneva
during the Ramadan season of Moslem fasting, thus providing
a cooling-off period. As Assistant Secretary of State George
McGhee told Pelt, the United States was opposed to any continuing UN control of Libya after the country became independent. He said that the majority of the members of the
United Nations by their vote had declared that Libya was capable of exercising its sovereignty and were now estopped from
contending that the United Nations must continue its control.
When told that they must meet Arab charges of a new type of
colonialism or imperialism, McGhee defended the British sub-
vention of Libya as being comparable to that in the case of Jor-

dan, which the Arabs did not criticize. The charges, he said, were part of the straight Communist line and must not deter the United States from its policy of trying to aid Libya to stand on its own feet after adopting an adequate constitution; the framing of the constitution, with the protection of a variety of rights and interests, was a major element in the whole undertaking.

Eventually, Libyan independence was proclaimed in December 1951, just ahead of the deadline set in the UN resolution which had provided the interim arrangements. But Libya then had to wait until 1955 for the final baptism of admission to membership in the United Nations, as promised in the amendment which I had introduced when the General Assembly approached the end of the debate in 1949. This delay was due to a long controversy with the Soviet Union about the admission of new UN members that resulted in Russian vetoes of all membership proposals until a compromise blanket agreement was concluded. Interestingly, Italy was caught in the same membership freeze and was admitted to UN membership at the same time as its former colony.

As for Somaliland, the solid support of the Latin American bloc for an Italian trusteeship, and their refusal to agree to any solution of the Libyan problem unless their precondition for Somaliland was met, practically assured the result. The United States had favored Italian trusteeship, and I had developed the reasons at some length in my speech to Committee I on September 30, 1949. Subcommittee 17 quickly concurred when it was agreed that independence should come to Somaliland after ten years of trusteeship. This point was nailed down, as Committee I debated the Subcommittee's report, by a Philippine amendment which made independence mandatory at that time, instead of leaving to the General Assembly an option to decide upon it. The ten years were to be measured from the date of the approval by the General Assembly of the terms of the trusteeship agreement, but the Trusteeship Council was to approve, and did approve in January 1950, the terms drawn up (with considerable difficulty) by a special committee and, according to the agreement, Italy then began to administer the territory "provisionally." The transfer from British to Italian administration took place officially March 31, 1950, and on April 5 a small fleet consisting of two passenger vessels and two freighters steamed out of Mogadishu harbor, carrying the last of the British troops and officials.

Thus the new state, to be known as Somalia, entered upon its elephantine period of gestation, with Italy administering under the watchful eyes of a UN committee. The territory was granted internal autonomy in 1956 and, uniting with the adjoining British Somaliland protectorate, became independent in July 1960 and a member of the United Nations on September 20 of the same year.

ERITREA

During 1950, the fate of Eritrea hung in the balance. As Dean Acheson told Sir B. N. Rau, on September 30, 1949, it did not make sense to give birth to a small nonviable state whose population was an uneasy mixture of Muslims and Christian Copts. Ethiopia was bent on annexing the territory; and this seemed a reasonable solution for the highland area of the Coptic population, but not for the lowlands where the Muslims predominated. The final settlement on Somaliland was held up for a long time pending an agreement between Ethiopia and Italy on the question of Eritrea, including its boundaries with Somaliland.

As Rivlin points out, it was "one of those ironic twists of diplomacy" that, at the third session of the General Assembly, agreement was almost reached on Eritrea but the postponement was forced by disagreement on Libya and Somaliland. At the fourth session, the Libyan and Somali cases were settled, but there was no agreement on Eritrea. The General Assembly therefore set up a commission composed of representatives of Burma, Guatemala, Norway, Pakistan, and South Africa to study and report on the wishes of the inhabitants and how their welfare could best be promoted. The commission was also enjoined to take into account the interests of peace and security in East Africa, and the rights and claims of Ethiopia, including its legitimate claim to have access to the sea.

The territory was still under military control of the British, but they were unable to prevent the outbreaks of violence in which many people were injured or killed; this was a disturbing backdrop for the tour by the commission, which included seven field trips before it withdrew to Geneva to prepare its report for the General Assembly. According to the resolution, the report was to be given to the Secretary-General by June 15, 1950, and was to be considered by the Interim Committee of the General Assembly which would report to the fifth regular session. Before filling in the diplomatic background of the decision, one may note that on December 2, 1950, the General Assembly voted 46–10–4 that Eritrea be constituted "an autonomous unit federated with Ethiopia under the sovereignty of the Ethiopian Crown."

The commission's report in June actually submitted three alternative solutions for Eritrea. One would make Eritrea a self-governing unit federated with Ethiopia. The second proposed a union of Eritrea with Ethiopia, except that the Western province would remain under British administration for a limited time. The third proposal was that there should be a direct UN trusteeship for ten years, after which Eritrea would be completely independent.

The United States opposed the trusteeship idea as merely postponing the issue and also because it would give the Soviet Union more influence in the region. Independence was also opposed for the same reasons which Acheson had put to Sr. B. N. Rau, namely that it would be a small state torn between the rival interests of the Muslims in the west and the Christian Copts in the highlands.

Among the factors which complicated the problem of reaching a decision about Eritrea were these: 1) Ethiopian hostility to Italy which had conquered her in 1936 when Mussolini defied the League of Nations; 2) Ethiopian desires for an outlet to the sea; 3) the unsettled boundary between Eritrea and Somaliland; 4) the concern of Muslim states such as Pakistan that the large Muslim population—actually a majority—should not be put under Ethiopian rule; 5) the fact that for India and the Arab states, "partition" was a "dirty word"; 6) Italian insistence that special protection should be provided for the Italian minority.

Although the United Kingdom had favored the union of the western (Muslim) province of Eritrea with Sudan, by June 1950 it had become apparent that there would be insufficient support for that solution; it could not secure the necessary votes in the General Assembly. Toward the end of May 1950, Acheson and Bevin, at a ministerial meeting in London, had agreed on taking a common line in the attempt to solidify some international agreement, including a reconciliation of the Italian-Ethiopian attitudes. At that point, the British were strongly opposed to assuming for the future the burden of administering the western province as under a trusteeship.

By the middle of June, the State Department was leaning toward federation of all of Eritrea with Ethiopia; that solution would perhaps be a compromise between the Ethiopian demand to annex the area and the proposals for a UN trusteeship. By July 31, the State Department could report that several Latin American states, led by Ambassador João Carlos Muñiz of Brazil, who was often our staunch friend and supporter in the UN, were confidentially working in support of the idea of federation. This Latin American support was important because of Italy's opposition to the federation plan. Italian Ambassador Alberto Tarchiani had already been asked in the State Department whether Italy had circularized its missions in Latin America to tell them that Italy no longer insisted on independence for Eritrea and that UN trusteeship was impractical. The Ambassador said that they could not do that since in Italy that initiative would be considered a surrender, but if two or three of Italy's friends made such a statement in the General Assembly, the Italian representative would respond favorably in the Interim Committee to such an approach.

In September 1950, Acheson, Bevin, and Sforza were all in New York for a NATO meeting as the General Assembly was opening. I discussed the Eritrean situation with Acheson on the evening of September 20 and word was sent to Bevin that we were hopeful of a settlement. Bevin was informed that a reported threat that Britain would withdraw from Eritrea (as they had done from Palestine in 1948) was unfortunate and might increase Italian intransigeance. Bevin sent back word that he would consider Acheson's views and there would be further talk with one of the U.S. delegation before Bevin saw Sforza.

On September 21, I gave Acheson a memorandum of points to raise in his pending discussion with Count Sforza. I suggested he point out to the Italian Foreign Minister that it was Italian opposition which had blocked agreement at the previous General Assembly session. Padilla Nervo of Mexico had just told me that this Italian attitude had weakened Italy's influence with the Latin American delegations. I stated in my memorandum that the participation of Italian representatives in discussions with the UN Commission on Eritrea and in the Interim Committee had given the impression that Italy would not oppose the compromise plan for federation, although admittedly Italy was not actually committed to such a course. The United States was fully aware of Italy's domestic political problems but felt that the need to settle the Eritrean question should take precedence over other considerations. The Secretary should ask Sforza, I suggested, for assurance that Italy would not oppose the attempts of the United States to secure acceptance of the proposed solution.

My suggestion that Acheson should play down the Italian domestic situation was not in accord with the views of the Western European branch of EUR as conveyed to the delegation by Hayden Raynor of that office. Raynor stressed Italy's domestic troubles: the Communists and Socialists were supporting claims for higher wages while the government faced a budgetary crisis. Meanwhile the United States was urging the Italian government to exert maximum efforts to produce the military items required by NATO defense plans. An unfavorable solution of the Eritrean problem might unite the forces of Italian nationalism with the Communists and Socialists and if this result came about as a result of strong pressure by the United States, there might be serious repercussions on other aspects of Italo-American relations. Raynor ended with the sound proposition that the United States should not antagonize either the Italians or the Ethiopians!

Assistant Secretary of State George McGhee, whose area of responsibility covered the Near East and Africa, quite naturally had another perspective. He telegraphed on September 16 from London where he was having a series of consultations, hoping that the Secretary would take a strong line with Sforza, since the Italians were playing up their domestic troubles in the hope of getting acceptance of a formula which would give Italy and Italians a more favorable position in Eritrea. These "real" Italian motives should be explained to the Latin American delegations at the United Nations.

Meanwhile, also on September 21, Bevin had seen Sforza and, as happened on some other occasions, seemed to be "pulling a fast one." Bevin had repeated to Sforza that Britain would withdraw from Eritrea "if necessary," but had also said that Britain might consider staying on as military and civil administrator of the territory for three years, which was one year longer than the current proposal in UN circles for an interim in which arrangements for federation would be perfected.

This ploy surprised Washington because of the news which had previously come from Ambassador Lewis Douglas in London. On August 25, Douglas reported that Bevin had been considering how much longer Britain would be willing to administer Eritrea. The Italians were suggesting a five-year period, and Bevin was personally willing to consider that span, since it might be needed for working out properly any federation proposal and promoting stability. But Bevin said that he would have great difficulty in getting cabinet approval of the five-year period because of the expense; could the United States help meet the expenses? Douglas doubted it.

Douglas had a further talk with Roger Allen of the Foreign Office, who told him that the United Kingdom still thought that partition was the best solution but would agree to support (but not to sponsor) a federation formula if it were acceptable to both Italy and Ethiopia. However, such support might require a cabinet decision, especially if British administration were to continue more than two years. Allen hoped, however, that for a two-year period, Bevin himself would make the decision, since the cabinet was not available during the then current parliamentary recess. If Bevin could not make that decision, the British representative might have to attach a reservation to the report of the Interim Committee.

The State Department replied to Douglas on August 29 that it was surprised at Bevin's apparent willingness to agree to a five-year period; most delegations favored a two-year period and there was no likelihood of the United States sharing the expense of a longer period. The Department wondered what Bevin had in mind; was he motivated by strategic requirements or by the general international situation?

Julius Holmes, the chargé in London, reported a further talk with Allen on August 31. Allen said the British delegation in New York had been instructed not to agree to an interval longer than two years without first consulting the Foreign Office. When asked why Bevin had considered a longer interval, Allen said it was because of the difficulty of implementing the federation formula; the United Kingdom would be in the position of having to create a federal entity between a semi-feudal state and an area which at the moment had no international status or local institutions. Bevin felt the need for assuring stability in order to keep out the Communists.

Following the Bevin-Sforza talk of September 21, I suggested to Dean Acheson on the following day, that during the intervals in the NATO talks which were being held in the Waldorf Astoria Hotel, he take five minutes to speak privately to Bevin about Eritrea. I proposed that he tell Bevin he was informed about the talk with Sforza, that he wondered why Bevin had not consulted him in advance about his new compromise proposals. Acheson could say that he feared Bevin's new proposals had wrecked the chance to get the Eritrean question settled, since Sforza would cling to this alternative which was wholly unacceptable to Ethiopia.

Charles Noyes, of the staff of the U.S. Mission to the United Nations, on September 25 expressed much the same point of view in a memorandum to Ambassador Austin. Noyes said that Bevin's suggestions had confused the situation and there was no use in Secretary Acheson's seeing Sforza while Bevin's proposals remained open. The Secretary should see Bevin and ask him to withdraw his proposals; Foreign Minister Aklilou of Ethiopia had already urged that course on Bevin, but if the Italians publicly accepted Bevin's ideas, he might be caught. If the Eritrean question were not settled at that session of the General Assembly, according to Noyes, the British might withdraw, leading to Ethiopia's annexation of Eritrea with considerable bloodshed; or the British might surrender the eastern province to Ethiopia and continue in temporary administration of the western province. These were possibilities of which Bevin had warned Sforza. While the Ethiopians might be content with either one of those actions, the United States would find the situation worrisome.

On September 27, Secretary Acheson talked with Bevin. Bevin said he had just made some "procedural" suggestions which he hoped would help in the solution of the problem. However, neither the Italians nor the Ethiopians nor the United States liked the suggestions, he was not wedded to them, and was willing to drop them. He complained that after all these years no progress was being made and the British were inclined to want to withdraw from Eritrea. Acheson replied that the United States was opposed to the British threat of withdrawal; it might boomerang and result in the Italians getting together enough votes to put through some solution which would not achieve a useful purpose. Acheson intended to put the matter forcefully to Sforza, urging him to acquiesce in the compromise federation plan which was generally acceptable, and trying to persuade Sforza that he should tell the Latin Americans that while Italy did not like the compromise, they would acquiesce. Bevin agreed to cooperate in getting favorable action on the existing compromise plan.

Bevin could at times be very stubborn but Acheson could be very persuasive; he has recorded the warmth of their friendship in his book entitled *Sketches From Life of Men I Have Known*. Indeed it was touching that just after the first of the year 1951, Bevin sent a telegram to Sir Oliver Franks saying that he had missed an opportunity to tell Mr. Acheson, at a recent meeting in Brussels, how much he appreciated the support which the U.K. delegation had received from the American delegation in New York during the session of the General Assembly and in the two preceding months, when they had all been wrestling with the Eritrean question. He wanted the State Department informed that his government was aware that the passage of the resolution which he regarded as reasonably satisfactory, must to a great extent be attributed to the work of the U.S. delegation, and Bevin would like the officials concerned to be informed of this message. It was indeed the *amende honorable*.

When Acheson talked to Sforza on September 27, 1950, he found the Italian Foreign Minister in an accommodating frame of mind. He told the Secretary of State that Italy was now ready to support the federation formula if a few suitable changes were made. Italy was willing to give written assurances to this effect. Sforza stressed the importance of agreement on such questions as the local police and taxation for the protection of the Italian citizens resident in Eritrea. He said Italy would not advocate the compromise plan for federation but would go along with it if the General Assembly adopted it. Acheson urged the importance of unity among the NATO allies. On the same day, Acheson talked with Foreign Minister Aklilou of Ethiopia and two days later he and Bevin had further talks with Aklilou, who urged Bevin to withdraw British forces and turn the territory over to Ethiopia. Bevin said he would reserve his position in case there should be a deadlock in the Assembly. These top-level interchanges were in 1950 and had been preceded by the usual routine negotiations in 1949 at the session of the General Assembly which prepared the way for the principal decisions and made them necessary.

At the United Nations, we had kept up the usual round of consultations with other delegations to appraise the chances of various proposals being adopted. On September 25, 1949, I dictated, late in the evening, the usual memoranda of conversations—this time with six delegates separately. The most important ones were with Sir Zafrullah Khan of Pakistan and Ambassador Santa Cruz of Chile. Zafrullah said the decision about Eritrea depended upon the will of the people. I asked if he favored a plebiscite for that purpose but he said he was not thinking of the people at the bottom—the opinion of the leaders was important. Santa Cruz, while reasserting the dominance of Italian influence among the Latin American delegations, said that if the United States would frankly tell them that we had strategic interests to be safeguarded, they would support us on that basis. On the question of acceding to Ethiopia's desire for access to the sea, his reaction was pure Chilean: that would be a dangerous precedent since it would be used by Bolivia to reinforce its constant clamor for the same type of outlet, which could only be through Chilean territory.

So far as our strategic interests were involved, the U.S. delegation was briefed on September 28 to the effect that we had made arrangements with the Emperor of Ethiopia about our defense requirements and, from that point of view, cession of Eritrea to Ethiopia would be useful, but if the General Assembly defeated the idea of cession, our interests could be protected if Ethiopia controlled the area in some other way. The delegation revealed a fluid attitude.

On September 29, 1949, accompanied by John Utter, I talked with Couve de Murville, who said the French were not in favor of putting the Eritreans under the "primitive rule" of the Ethiopians. But, while maintaining French support for Italy, he admitted that not all the Latin American delegations supported the Italian campaign to give Eritrea independence. On Libya, the French would agree to a united Libya, but wanted to minimize the repercussion on Tunisia. They did not object to the position of the Senussi in Cyrenaica but the influence of this fanatical Muslim sect should not be extended; they already observed bad effects of it in southern Algeria and Tchad. The French really preferred to split Libya into two or three separate independent states, while the United States favored leaving it to the Libyans to decide for themselves.

On October 5 we gave a dinner for a group of delegates from Asia and the Near East. U So Nyun of Burma explained why he and others in Southeast Asia opposed Italy as trustee for Somaliland. He said that the Somali people were strongly opposed and the Burmese knew how they felt. "It is just as though after driving out the Japanese from Burma you should come back and suggest that we be placed under a Japanese trusteeship. You might say that General MacArthur had made the Japanese more democratic, but we would know they were the same Japanese." The always resourceful Sir B. N. Rau then suggested that the United Nations could draft a constitution to govern the Italian trusteeship. I asked U So Nyun and Al Faqih of Saudi Arabia whether this would cast a different light on the acceptability of Italian trusteeship; they said it certainly would and under such conditions they would reconsider the issue.

On October 3, 1949, Ambassadors Freitas Valle and Muñiz of Brazil had invited me, Jack Ross, and John Dreier (a State Department specialist on Latin American affairs) to lunch. They told us the Latin American delegations had just caucused with these results: independence for Libya with a UN commission to help them work out their new government; Italian trusteeship for Somaliland; independence for Eritrea, or if that was not possible, then some temporary arrangement until the wishes of the people could be ascertained. But our hosts told us that not many of the delegations had firm instructions except to help the Italians as much as possible. I stressed the U.S. views on Eritrea—that it was not easy to learn the views of the inhabitants, that the territory was artificially composed, that "partition" carried the implication that there was already a unitary state, which was not the case. We also thought it legitimate that the Ethiopians should have access to the sea. The Brazilians said the Latin Americans had rather a poor opinion of the Ethiopians. After lunch we got another side light from Padilla Nervo of Mexico, who said he had urged the caucus to consult the United States and other delegations before reaching conclusions, but he had been turned down.

On October 8, the line-up was summarized for me by David Wainhouse, whom I have described as my "coach" on the Korea case. He estimated we could probably get a two-thirds vote on Libya and perhaps on Somalia. The general view was to postpone the decision on Eritrea until a UN commission could visit the area and report back. On Libya the view was nearly unanimous that there should be independence without intervening trusteeship. On Eritrea it would be necessary to find a compromise between our idea of cession to Ethiopia of all except the western (Muslim) province, and the other proposal for immediate independence. On Somaliland, we might support a Liberian proposal which would terminate the trusteeship and grant independence after ten years.

It might seem that we paid undue attention to the Latin American view, but that bloc cast 20 votes out of a possible 55, which gave them the power to prevent a two-thirds vote on any proposition they opposed, granting that they would have at least some outside supporters. On October 10, 1949, I gave a dinner for ten of the Latin American delegates, Assistant Secretary of State John Hickerson, Jack Ross, my deputy on the Italian colony problem, John Utter, and a few other of our advisers from the State Department. The guests put great emphasis on Italian trusteeship for Somaliland, and we replied that they could not get a two-thirds vote for that unless there were some agreement on Eritrea. They said our plan for cession of Eritrea to Ethiopia would not get a single Latin American vote, whereupon Padilla Nervo of Mexico suggested the device of a "personal union" of Eritrea with the crown of Ethiopia, leaving local autonomy to the Eritreans, but thus getting Ethiopian support for the Italians in Somaliland. His able presentation enlisted considerable support, and I said it took account of the principal needs, which were Coptic union with the Ethiopians, Ethiopian outlet to the sea, and the opportunity for later Eritrean independence or full union if the people should so decide.

One does not expect all governments to be wholly altruistic, and it was no surprise that Ambassador Adolfo Costa du Rels of Bolivia refrained from expressing any view on the proposed resolutions but indicated aside to me that a Bolivian emissary had gone to Washington to seek United States help for Bolivia.

After dinner he told one of our staff privately that Bolivia would not cooperate with us on the Italian colonies unless their emissary in Washington secured our cooperation with Bolivian needs.

Padilla Nervo's plan for a personal union between Ethiopia and Eritrea was picked up by the imaginative Sir B. N. Rau, who conceived a plan for a federal union with a right of secession for the western province. When he was challenged to write such a constitution, he actually produced an excellent draft overnight.

Throughout we were having further talks with the Italians, both at the United Nations and through our embassy in Rome. I had a long talk with Sforza at his hotel in New York on October 4, 1949. He made the usual Italian arguments about Eritrea and Ethiopia; he said Ethiopian officials were corrupt and incompetent, as was even the Emperor himself. He thought the issue would have to be postponed. I said I would report his views to Secretary Acheson but we hoped for a decision at this session. On October 20 Ambassador Tarchiani drew me aside after a meeting of the Subcommittee at the United Nations and showed me a telegram he had just received from Sforza; he translated it to me. U.S. Ambassador Dunn had talked to Sforza about the plan for personal union of Eritrea and Ethiopia; Sforza said that was too subtle for the Eritreans to understand. Sforza said Italy could not recede from its support of complete independence of Eritrea without risking the fall of the government in Rome. I replied (as I noted in a memorandum of the conversation, "with some heat") that this was an unfair way to present the issue. The United States was not asking Count Sforza to make a public declaration reversing their position but merely that the Italians relax their pressure on the Latin American delegates. I said that the United States had done a great deal for Italy since the war and had helped them with the problems of Libya and Somaliland but that Italy was giving us no cooperation in return. I warned that if Italy did not cooperate in finding an Eritrean solution, it might not even get its trusteeship in Somaliland. But our embassy in Rome advised us that Italy was eager to settle the Eritrean question because it was necessary in order to enable them to reestablish their economic and cultural ties in North Africa.

On the other hand, Assistant Secretary McGhee told Secretary Acheson on November 1, 1949, that he was still concerned. Despite Italian promises of support, they had persuaded the Turks to withdraw their co-sponsorship of the resolution and other similar approaches had been reported. Acheson said if these reports were correct, it was a clear breach of faith, and he was prepared to take it up personally with Foreign Minister Sforza. He directed that the Italians be pressed for the written assurance which Sforza had promised, and if this were not forthcoming he would send a personal message to Sforza. Apparently the pessimistic reports proved to be ill-founded.

Toward the end of October, 1949, the United States was advocating the plan for a personal union of Eritrea and Ethiopia and on October 21, in a talk with Hector McNeil and Clutton of the U.K. delegation, McNeil agreed, provided that the United Kingdom could transfer authority to Ethiopia within six months. McNeil thought a postponement was intolerable, but Clutton, of the Colonial Office, argued in favor of it. At the same time our scouts were indicating we might have to agree to the appointment of a UN commission to visit Eritrea and report back. Our position was acceptable to Ethiopia, and Foreign Minister Aklilou approached me in the delegates' lounge on October 29 to express gratitude for the support we were giving. I had gone to Washington to discuss the project with the State Department, and it had acquiesced in the general outlines of the plan.

Finally, Italy was the one which brought the British firmly to our side. On November 19, 1949, John Utter told me that Clutton had called him out of the Assembly session to give him very confidential information from London. The Italian ambassador in London had called at the Foreign Office and suggested it was time for the United Kingdom and Italy to make a secret agreement regarding the future of Tripolitania in order to assure a predominant position for Italy there. The Foreign Office categorically rejected the proposal and told the Ambassador that Italy would be ill-advised to initiate any discussions on the future of Libya while the debates were going on in the General Assembly. The United Kingdom would definitely not make any secret agreement with Italy on the subject, then or later. The British were incensed and thought their relations with Italy would now worsen.

Perhaps the recital of all these twistings and turnings in the General Assembly and in the principal capitals will have revealed that it was through considerable travail that the United Nations finally achieved its really notable triumph of delivering two new states into independent life. I have already given away the denouements, Libya "incubated" under the watchful eye of UN Commissioner Pelt, Somaliland entrusted for ten years to Italian trusteeship with a UN advisory committee, and after a year's field investigation by a UN committee, the final decision to federate Eritrea as an autonomous unit under the sovereignty of the Ethiopian crown. In the autumn of 1950, before that decision was finally reached, the Soviet Union proposed immediate independence for Eritrea and the plan had a little support, although the Italians would have liked to join in sponsoring it.

Under the final plan as adopted December 2, 1950, Italy got some guarantees for the Italian residents; Ethiopia got its access to the sea; the United States retained its radio station at Asmara. For two years the British continued their military administration, marred by riots and other disorders.

Nevertheless, the British troops were withdrawn on the date specified in the General Assembly resolution and ten years later, in November 1962, the Eritrean assembly voted to abol-

ish its federal status by uniting fully with Ethiopia as its four-
teenth province.

A guerrilla nationalist movement exists; according to some
press reports it is rather formidable. The success of Bangladesh
in attaining independence stimulated the Eritrean nationalists
but there is no neighboring equivalent of India to give military support. The Eritrean nationalist lobbyists in the delegates' lounge at the United Nations say, a trifle wearily, that
they are not secessionists, they merely want their independence.[17]

7

The Birth of Israel

There are several books about the birth of Israel—that is the actual title of one of the recent ones, by Herbert Feis, published in 1969. There also is a massive volume (750 pages) entitled *Genesis 1948* by Dan Kurzman.[1] The author tells us that he interviewed nearly 1,000 people and he lists many of them; I was not one of them.*

Nor does his list include the following persons whom he quotes or refers to frequently: Robert Lovett, Under Secretary of State at the time; Dean Rusk, who was Director of the Bureau of United Nations Affairs in 1948; or Samuel K. C. Kopper who was a United Nations specialist in the spring of 1948. Kopper is characterized (at p. 19) as among the "passionate Arabophiles with close oil company connections." Of Rusk, Kurzman writes: "Israelis who dealt with Rusk regard him as having opposed the creation of Jewish State with possibly more zeal than any other top State Department official." Lovett

---

* It is particularly regrettable that Kurzman, in a footnote on p. 84, should make the false statement that "In 1950 Alger Hiss was convicted of spying for the Soviet Union . . ." Alger Hiss was convicted of perjury in denying the accusations of Whittaker Chambers, which is entirely different from every point of view.

seems to be described (at p. 212) as questioning the loyalty of American Jews. On the basis of close acquaintance with all three of those gentlemen, I completely disagree with Kurzman's portrayals.

On many points I have no information of the type he was able to secure but, on some matters in which I was personally involved, I find inaccuracies in Kurzman's account. To a very large extent he uses direct discourse in reconstructing important conversations, which one may attribute to the fact that, as he says in his preface, he was "using the techniques of the novelist and biographer." This technique makes for good reading, but I am sure that many of the quotations are not taken from tapings at the time of the conversation, and personally I find it rare for people accurately to recall verbatim what was said by them and to them many years ago. But this book presents a most readable and revealing account from the Jewish viewpoint, relying on Jewish and what he considers pro-Jewish sources.

A still more recent book frankly and appropriately proclaims its point of view in its title: *And the Hills Shouted for Joy: The Day Israel Was Born.*[2] The authors, Bernard Postal and Henry W. Levy, acknowledge help from a long list of individuals and point out particularly that Clark Clifford, President Truman's political adviser, and special contact with the American Jewish community, opened his files to them. They have a bibliography of Supplementary Reading, but avoid using footnotes, as I have generally done when relying on documentary sources. The book goes back into the history of the Balfour Declaration and only some 70 of the 430 pages deal with matters described in this chapter. I shall need to call attention to some points on which their version of events differs from mine. (The authors are consistent—and inaccurate—throughout in ascribing to me the middle initial "K"!)

I do not pretend that I can add substantially to the history of the events leading up to the establishment of the state of Is-

rael on May 14, 1948, but I intend to review part of the story
from the point of view of the role of the United Nations and
the operations of United States representatives in that world
body.

In 1971 the American press flooded its readers with reports
and comments on the question of Chinese representation in the
United Nations. Much of the talk on the radio and in the press
used language which would make one feel that the issue was
one of admitting a new member to the Organization. That, of
course, was not the case, and the repeated references to the "expulsion" of the Republic of China on Taiwan muddied the
controversy. Even official representatives of the United States
discussed the case as a possible and naturally dangerous precedent for the expulsion of other members of the United Nations.
The issue actually was on a question of credentials and the
identification of the government of a state popularly called
"China." I must not digress too long in considering the China
story, but it has elements of importance to an understanding of
the beginnings of the state of Israel.

The question of recognition and eventually of admission to
membership in the United Nations was considered very important by the new state of Israel. In the case of Israel, we have
statements which are official, and others which only reflect official views. These statements are in the volume of the Carnegie
Endowment's series of National Studies on International Organization, prepared by a study group set up by the Hebrew University of Jerusalem and published under the title *Israel and
the United Nations* (1956). The Israeli study group says (at pp.
49–50): "The first consideration was that admission [to UN]
would constitute the final regularization of Israel's international status, not only in relation to the Arab states, but with
all the nations of the world." They quote the statement by Mr.
Sharett (as his name was Hebraicized from Shertok) to the
Knesseth on June 15, 1949: "By our admission to the United
Nations, the highest seal has been placed on our international

recognition, even though that recognition is not yet universal."
Actually between May 14, 1948, when Israel proclaimed its independence, and May 11, 1949, when it was admitted to UN
membership, Israel had been recognized by 54 states, of which
45 were members of the United Nations. I shall return to this
question of recognition, but want to lay this groundwork.

We must also have in mind some of the historical background and salient points need to be recalled.

In the first place there is the fact that Great Britain had
been given a mandate over Palestine at the end of World War
I. The mandate system was a device promoted by President
Woodrow Wilson at the Paris Peace Conference to avoid the
traditional European practice of dividing the spoils among the
victors in a war. It was agreed that the former German and
Turkish colonies would be placed under the guidance of various advanced countries who would act as trustees for the
League of Nations. This idea was spelled out in Article 22 of
the Covenant of the League of Nations as follows:

> To those colonies and territories which as a consequence of the
> late war have ceased to be under the sovereignty of the states which
> formerly governed them and which are inhabited by people not yet
> able to stand by themselves under the strenuous conditions of the
> modern world, there should be applied the principle that the well-
> being and development of such peoples form a sacred trust of
> civilisation. . . .

It was recognized that the mandates would "differ according
to the stage of the development of the people" and other factors. Former Turkish territories were said to be practically
ready for independence subject to a little guidance. One of
these territories was Palestine, and on July 24, 1922, the Council of the League of Nations confirmed a mandate to be exercised by "His Britannic Majesty" as had been agreed by the
principal allied powers.

The preamble of the Palestine mandate recited that the
principal allied powers had also agreed that the mandatory

(that is Great Britain) "should be responsible for putting into effect the declaration originally made on November 2, 1917, by the Government of his Britannic Majesty, and adopted by the said powers, in favor of the establishment in Palestine of a national home for the Jewish people, it being clearly understood that nothing should be done which might prejudice the civil and religious rights of existing non-Jewish communities in Palestine." [3] This was a reference to the famous Balfour Declaration, which Arthur James Balfour, as then Secretary of State for Foreign Affairs, communicated to Lord Rothschild in a letter of November 2, 1917, as "essentially a Cabinet decision" to declare sympathy with Jewish Zionist aspirations and favoring the establishment in Palestine of a national home for the Jewish people.

According to Feis there were not more than 50,000 Jews in Palestine at the end of World War I, which number increased to 160,000 by 1928 or 20 percent of the population, 70 percent then being Muslim and 10 percent Christian.

The British—and others—were to learn that it was no easy task to administer a mandate for the world organization. His Britannic Majesty agreed also to be mandatory for several other territories in various stages of development. Among others, His Britannic Majesty, "for and on behalf of the Government of the Union of South Africa," undertook to administer the mandate for South West Africa. As we shall note, Britain gave up the effort to solve the Palestinian problem and threw it into the lap of the United Nations. On the other hand, the Union of South Africa has adamantly refused and still refuses to yield to the demands of the United Nations General Assembly, and the Security Council—even when backed by an opinion of the International Court of Justice—that it relinquish its control of South West Africa, which, in United Nations circles, is now known as Namibia.

I would like to state my own views about the South West African situation, but they are set out in the 119 pages of my dissenting opinion in the *1966 Reports of the International Court of Justice*. Finally, the General Assembly declared the mandate terminated, and the Security Council declared that the continued presence of South Africa in Namibia is illegal. The International Court agreed and held that South Africa is "under obligation to withdraw its administration from the Territory of Namibia." The Court held that other members of the United Nations are obligated to recognize the illegality of South Africa's presence.[4]

But, Namibia has not been born as a state. The United Nations Council for Namibia asserts a protective and administrative role but is powerless in the face of South African occupation. If Great Britain had decided to continue its occupation of Palestine after May 14, 1948, Israel could not have been born on that date, although the Jewish military capabilities then were far greater than those of the Namibians now. As will appear, however, the situations were quite different, one from the other.

The over-use of a metaphor is always dangerous because the metaphor often becomes mixed, but it will be seen that the policy of the United States early in 1948 regarding a Palestine solution was not to abort the state of Israel but to prevent a premature birth. In retrospect, some doctors of history will say the diagnosis was wrong, and others will argue that the therapy was inappropriate. Only a Master of the Ifs of History could say whether the proposed treatment would have prevented some postnatal afflictions.

One could terminate the story of the birth of Israel with its declaration of independence on May 14, 1948, but I have pointed out the importance that the Israeli government itself attached to admission as a member of the United Nations, which occurred almost a year later. Despite recognition accorded by many states, Israel's statehood and position in the international community, as Foreign Minister Sharett himself told the Knesseth, was not perfected until admission to the United Nations.

The situation of Indonesia was somewhat similar. Although after a long struggle and intensive efforts by the United Nations, the Netherlands transferred sovereignty to Indonesia on December 27, 1949, it was not until September 28, 1950, that Indonesia was admitted as the sixtieth member of the United Nations. The birth of Indonesia was more directly the result of UN action; the birth of Israel came in the midst of UN activity on the Palestine question but can hardly be called the *result* of UN action. And as for Namibia, the efforts of the United Nations to bring about its birth into independence have so far failed.

I intend to deal with some of the events in that year between May 1948 and May 1949, bearing in mind that Israel first applied for membership as early as November 29, 1948. It was a year of travail, but I shall not try to apply more precisely my metaphor of nativity.

I shall not describe or even list all of the various plans, resolutions, and actions of the United Nations in its efforts to find an acceptable peaceful solution for the tragic situation in Palestine. Secretary of State Marshall, in addressing the plenary session of the General Assembly on September 17, 1947, said that the United States intended "to do everything in its power . . . to assist in finding a solution for this difficult problem which has stirred up such violent passions and which is now resulting in the shedding of blood and in great mental and moral anguish." [5] The violence, the killings, the personal tragedies, and the excesses of all parties concerned have been pictured with graphic force by Leon Uris in *Exodus*. I do not think Uris would claim that his book is an objective historical account but, just as many thought of the Spanish Civil War in the 1930s as pictured by Picasso in his famous *Guernica,* which he painted a few weeks after the event, so, in retrospect, one might say that the picture of the bloody and tragic struggle in Palestine which Uris drew in words *ten years* after the birth of Israel was the backdrop in the mind's eye of many a delegate to the United Nations Security Council and General Assembly as those organs wrestled with the problem of Palestine. But obviously there was no general agreement on who was to blame.

I need to begin with the resolution adopted by the General Assembly on November 29, 1947, by a vote of 33 to 13 with 10 abstentions. By this resolution, the United Nations approved the plan for partition with economic union which had been proposed by a UN committee as one alternative solution. In the General Assembly's Ad Hoc Committee on Palestine, this plan had been approved by a smaller vote, less than the two-thirds required, and later obtained, for passage in the plenary session.

The United States and the Soviet Union both voted in favor of this resolution on partition with economic union. Such agreement was unusual. Great Britain announced that it would not accept responsibility for enforcing or carrying out any plan which was not acceptable to both Arabs and Jews. The British representative told the Assembly's committee that their troops would be evacuated not later than August 1, 1948. It was agreed that the mandate would come to an end on that date, but it was contemplated that the proposed Arab and Jewish states would not come into existence until two months later. In the meantime, the United Nations would somehow be in charge and the General Assembly asked the Security Council "to take the necessary measures" for the implementation of the partition plan. Subsequently, the British announced that they would turn over Palestine to the United Nations on May 14.

The plan for partition was vigorously supported by the Jews and wholly rejected by the Arabs. How, then, was it to be enforced? At 11 P.M., on the night of February 23, 1948, the U.S. Mission to the United Nations received a telegram from the State Department reporting that President Truman had approved the draft of a statement that Ambassador Austin was to make in the Security Council the following day, that is February 24; Ambassador Austin and Dean Rusk, who was also then in New York, were to be informed. The telegram stated

that the President would make a public statement immediately afterward announcing that Austin had correctly stated
the United States position, which had been developed through
long and exhaustive study.

The position to be covered by Austin's speech was the one
that the Palestine Commission had posed to the Security Council, namely the provision by the Security Council of armed assistance, "which alone would enable the Commission to dis-
charge its responsibilities on the termination of the Mandate."
The *"Report by the President to the Congress on United
States Participation in the United Nations* for 1948,* quotes (at
p. 40) the following two paragraphs from Austin's speech of
February 24:

The Security Council is authorized to take forceful measures with
respect to Palestine to remove a threat to international peace. The
Charter of the United Nations does not empower the Security
Council to enforce a political settlement whether it is pursuant to a
recommendation of the General Assembly or of the Council itself.
What this means is this: The Council under the Charter can take
action to prevent aggression against Palestine from outside. The
Council by these same powers can take action to prevent a threat to
international peace and security from inside Palestine. But this action must be directed solely to the maintenance of international
peace. The Council's action, in other words, is directed to keeping
the peace and not to enforcing partition.

The Security Council, on the initiative of the United States,
called on the permanent members of the Council to consult,
and widespread consultations ensued.

Postal and Levy regard this statement by Ambassador Austin
as the "first indication of American vacillation" in its support
of the plan for partition. They also call it "the first shot in the
retreat from partition" (p. 311). They are evidently not aware
that President Truman had approved in advance the draft of

---

* These are the official annual reports on U.S. action in the United Nations;
it seems curious that Kurzman does not include them in his bibliography. Apparently Postal and Levy also failed to use this basic source.

Austin's statement. They say (at page 292) that Austin's statement about the lack of the Security Council's power "to enforce a political settlement" was an "almost incredible interpretation of the UN partition resolution." On the contrary, the
position taken in Austin's statement, and approved by President Truman, is impeccable from a legal point of view. Postal
and Levy go on to reveal a complete lack of understanding of
the legal nature of a resolution of the General Assembly of the
United Nations. The literature on the subject is now very extensive and there are differences of view as to the legal weight
to be attributed to various types of General Assembly resolutions, but I do not believe that the most ardent advocates of
the binding legal effect of such resolutions would attribute legislative force to the partition resolution. Like most General Assembly resolutions, it was merely a recommendation. As I have
explained in the preceding chapter on the Italian colonies, the
General Assembly was given by the Italian peace treaty a
unique power to decide on a series of political settlements. The
General Assembly had no such authority in connection with
the arrangements in Palestine.[6] The failure to appreciate these
legal points in connection with the powers of the Security
Council and of the General Assembly, inevitably lead to or
reinforce the theory that the United States position "vacillated"
or that the State Department was disloyal to President Truman. I shall come back to this issue.

According to Kurzman's account (pp. 85–86), the U.S. National Security Council had met on February 17, a week before
this speech of Austin's and despite early disagreement between
the State Department and the military, finally "all members
agreed that the United States should support the creation of a
United Nations trusteeship" since the United Nations neither
had, nor was permitted to use, military force to enforce partition. On February 23, just before the U.S. Mission in New
York was instructed about the speech Austin was to deliver, an
unidentified member of the staff of the Mission wrote a memo-

randum suggesting that the United States should try to get the
Security Council to put partition into effect, but if that were
not possible, then some form of trusteeship would be best.

On March 5, the State Department sent a long telegram to
the U.S. Mission in New York, giving instructions on the
course to follow. (At this time I was still working on the Interim Committee of the General Assembly; it was not until
April that I was assigned to deal with the Palestine question.)
The telegram seems to have contemplated that the Security
Council would not vote to enforce partition, but the United
States should not appear to be voting against partition. The
United States should urge the Security Council to act to avoid
a threat to the peace and should ask the Secretary-General to
convoke a Special Session of the General Assembly. It was assumed that the attitudes of Jews, Arabs, and British would be
irreconcilable and, if no solution was obtained through the
five-power consultations with the parties, the Security Council
should consider recommending to the special session that until
the people of Palestine were ready for self-government, they
should be placed under the United Nations trusteeship system.
As a further effort to postpone the crisis, the Security Council
should ask the United Kingdom to reconsider its decision to
quit on May 14. On March 14, Samuel Kopper talked with several leading Arab delegates about the best solution in Palestine. He reported that "trusteeship would be the least favorable
solution in Arab minds," but that they were against partition.

The subsequent development of the proposal for a temporary UN trusteeship is clouded in conflicting accounts.
Kurzman (p. 86) writes: "When, at a White House meeting in
early March, State Department and Pentagon officials stated
that a war in Palestine now had to be prevented at all costs,
Truman did agree that a trusteeship, among other 'solutions,'
was a possible alternative if partition ultimately could not be
made to work." Kurzman's account further relates that, a few
days later on his "private train," the President was shown by a

State Department official "a first draft of a speech we may make at the United Nations." Truman is said to have given it a casual glance, noted that it mentioned the possibility of trusteeship as a temporary solution, and said it looked all right but not "intending his comment as any formal approval of a final draft." Actually, it was not usual to ask the President to approve speeches to be made at the United Nations once the general line of policy had been cleared with him.

Presumably the speech in question was the one which Ambassador Austin delivered in the Security Council on March 19, 1948. According to the synopsis in the *Report by the President to the Congress* (at p. 41), Austin

pointed out that the Palestine Commission, the Mandatory Power, the Jewish Agency, and the Arab Higher Committee had indicated that the partition plan could not be implemented by peaceful means under present conditions and that, if the mandate should be terminated prior to a peaceful solution of the problem, large-scale fighting between the two communities could be expected.

In the light of these facts, the United States Representative informally proposed that a temporary trusteeship for Palestine should be established under the Trusteeship Council of the United Nations, to maintain the peace and to afford the Jews and Arabs of Palestine further opportunity to reach an agreement regarding the future government of that country. Such a United Nations trusteeship would be without prejudice to the character of the eventual political settlement.

He further advocated the calling of a Special Session of the General Assembly, and that the Security Council should act to bring about a cease-fire and halt incursions into the area. "As a corollary of these proposals the United States suggested that the Security Council instruct the Palestine Commission to suspend its efforts to implement the proposed partition plan."

Against the background described above, I find it impossible to credit the further account by Kurzman (pp. 98–99) that President Truman was completely surprised and upset when on the morning of March 20 he read in his newspaper about

Austin's speech. Postal and Levy have the same version, also based on Clark Clifford's accounts. In his *Memoirs,* Truman does not suggest anything of the kind.[7] He records his conviction that Dr. Weizmann, whom he had assured of support for partition, understood the situation, but he asked Judge Rosenman to call on Weizmann to reassure him. On March 25, the President issued a public statement, in which he said that while the United States "vigorously supported the plan for partition with economic union, it had become clear that the partition plan could not be carried out at this time by peaceful means. We could not undertake to impose this solution on the People of Palestine by the use of American troops, either on Charter grounds or as a matter of national policy." That was why a temporary trusteeship had been proposed.

Truman further writes in his *Memoirs* "The suggestion that the mandate be continued as a trusteeship under the UN was not a bad idea at the time." On March 26, Secretary Marshall and Under Secretary Lovett met with Moshe Shertok and Eiliahu Epstein of the Jewish Agency, who "displayed considerable doubt that trusteeship would help the situation." Shertok said it was "wholly unacceptable to the Jewish Agency" and "intolerable" if Britain were the trustee. But he made a strong plea for putting Jerusalem under an international trusteeship to keep it from falling into the hands of the Arabs.

Eleanor Roosevelt's attitude toward all these events was important. Her international prestige was enormous, she was still an effective voice in Democratic politics in the United States, she was an ardent champion of the Jewish people, whose suffering under the Nazis weighed on her mind and spirit. She and I were congenial and fully cooperative colleagues on delegations to several meetings of the General Assembly. Joseph Lash gives a vivid picture of her strong feelings about the solution of the problem of Palestine and about the United Nations, to which she was also devoted.[8] Mrs. Roosevelt was not at first in favor of the partition plan but was swayed back and forth as arguments pro and con were presented to her by various people. She would pass on points of view to her husband and, after his death, to President Truman. She was much pleased when the British decided to refer the problem of Palestine to the United Nations, but was impatient with the delays involved in the appointment of the Special Committee on Palestine (UNSCOP) to report to the regular session of the General Assembly in September 1947. But when UNSCOP's majority reported in favor of the plan for partition with economic union, she strongly supported that proposal. When the partition plan was approved by the General Assembly, she felt keenly that the prestige of the United Nations depended on its effective implementation. From Lash's account, it would seem that Mrs. Roosevelt underestimated the difficulties of placing in Palestine an adequate military force; the actual issue of enforcing a political solution on the Arabs was quite different from the later use of a UN force to police an agreed armistice or cease-fire. The subsequent willingness of the administration in Washington to contribute to a UN force to support a trusteeship was based on the assumption that both sides would acquiesce in that plan. When it was found they did not agree, the plan was abandoned, as will be seen.

I do not accept the theory that the decision to urge a United Nations trusteeship to take effect when the British quit on May 14 and to avoid a holocaust was the result of a plot of U.S. officials who were anti-Semitic. It is no doubt true that Secretary of Defense Forrestal was afraid of endangering the vital supplies of oil from the Arab countries. He may have been mistaken, but defense was his business, and his concern was not reprehensible any more than it was reprehensible for those American officials who sought to secure the type of solution which favored the program of the Zionists; both were sincere.

Trygve Lie, Secretary-General of the United Nations, in his memoirs considered that Austin's speech was a repudiation of partition and that the "American turnabout on partition has never been explained." [9] He says "the American reversal was a blow to the United Nations." He called on Ambassador Austin and proposed that as a protest against the instructions under which Austin made the speech, and to point to the danger in which the UN had been placed, he and Trygve Lie should both resign. Austin did not look at the matter in that light, told Lie he would not resign, and urged Lie not to resign either. I had no official connection with the Palestine question at that date and do not recall having known about Lie's attitude at the time, but in retrospect I do not see any justification for it. Partition clearly could not have been carried out, and the suggestion for a UN trusteeship was the strongest kind of evidence of confidence in the Organization's capacity to deal with the thorny Palestine problem. But Eleanor Roosevelt shared the view of Secretary-General Lie and wrote President Truman and Secretary of State Marshall offering her resignation from the U.S. delegation to the UN. Truman's reply affirming his belief in the United Nations "moved her deeply," even if it did not convince her. But she did not resign.

The special session of the General Assembly met on April 16, 1948. Ambassador Austin, Francis Sayre, and I were appointed U.S. delegates, with Dean Rusk and John Ross as alternates.

The physical arrangements, that is to say, the geography or the logistics of the situation, was one of our problems in 1948. Nowadays, a representative of the United States steps out of our handsome new building on the corner of 45th Street and United Nations Plaza and walks across the street to the UN building where the Security Council and other councils meet and where the General Assembly holds its plenary session in that great auditorium and its committees meet in a variety of adequate chambers. In 1948, the U.S. Mission to the United Nations had offices at 2 Park Avenue, at the corner of 33d Street in Manhattan. The Committees of the General Assembly and the Security Council met at Lake Success, about an hour's drive out on Long Island. The United Nations had set up temporary partitions to make rooms out of the old Sperry Gyroscope plant there. But plenary sessions of the General Assembly were held at Flushing Meadows, in a building left over from the World's Fair of 1939. The access roads were not improved as they were for the last World's Fair, held on the same spot in 1964. When we came to the final debates on Palestine in May, as will appear, we had to count the hours and even the minutes before the critical moment was reached, so that travel time between Lake Success and Flushing Meadows was a prime factor.

We had a round-up of the views of the Latin American and the Canadian delegates at a buffet supper which Ambassador Austin gave on April 27 at his apartment in the Waldorf Towers—for many years the equivalent of an embassy-residence for the United States ambassador to the United Nations. All of the Latin American delegates except those from Haiti and Costa Rica, came, as did General Andrew McNaughton, the permanent representative of Canada. On the side of the United States, in addition to Ambassador Austin, were four members of his staff—Jack Ross, Charles Noyes, Gordon Knox, and I. After supper, Padilla Nervo of Mexico bluntly asked for an answer to the question uppermost in the minds of all present, namely, what did the United States have in mind about supplying forces to uphold a trusteeship in Palestine? Ambassador Austin replied that the problem could be solved by a truce or by economic aid, and he stressed the latter. He said that if the United States bore the whole burden of enforcing a trusteeship, we would be accused of reverting to the big stick of imperialism. We were, however, prepared to do our proper proportionate share of whatever was to be done by way of implementing trusteeship. He did not actually touch the question of the use of armed forces.

The Guatemalan delegate, Garcia Granados, who was the "prime exponent of partition" and champion of the Jewish point of view, reiterated, as he frequently did, his views with which all present were familiar. He said that he knew the full extent of the problem as a result of his intensive firsthand study. "Force" he said, "is absolutely necessary to impose either partition or trusteeship." He stated that the 100,000 troops which the British had in Palestine were insufficient; 150,000 would be needed. He asked whether public opinion in the different countries which might furnish troops would overlook the inevitable death of their sons. How far, indeed, was the United States prepared to go?

The Cuban delegate, Ambassador Guillermo Belt, said that the partition resolution "had been an improper one." He thought that this "obvious mistake" should be corrected and he would vote for trusteeship. Alfonso Lopez, former President of Colombia and at the time President of the UN Security Council, was undecided but said that it was necessary to avoid falling into the trap which Soviet Russia had set. Dr. José Arce, the distinguished Argentine surgeon and, at the time, President of the UN General Assembly, said that he looked at the question with impartiality but he was in favor of trusteeship. I made a few comments and Garcia Granados repeated his point of view. The party broke up as President Lopez left, but there were a few parting remarks by individuals. Ambassador Quijano of Panama said we could count on his vote. For Nicaragua, Ambassador Rodriguez Somosa left us with a clear impression that he thought trusteeship was the best solution. As we reviewed the situation after the guests left, we reached the conclusion that many delegates would be waiting to see if the Jews and Arabs would agree to a truce or if the United States would come out with a clear commitment to furnish most of the required armed forces. On this last point, we in the delegation had no clear instructions from Washington.

As we got into the special session, it was decided during the first week of May to appoint two subcommittees for Committee I of the General Assembly which was dealing with the Palestine question. Subcommittee 10 dealt with the special question of a regime for Jerusalem while Subcommittee 9 considered proposals for dealing with the whole of Palestine.

On May 4, Charles Fahy, then representing the Jewish Agency, gave to Acting Secretary of State Lovett a memorandum arguing that the United States should not oppose the proclamation of a Jewish state but should accept its proclamation when that came. On the same day from New York I telegraphed Dean Rusk in the State Department noting the danger that the Soviet Union, and possibly others, might recognize a Jewish or a Palestinian state if established. On the following day I wrote a memorandum to my chief, Ambassador Austin, analyzing possible positions of the United States after the end of the mandate, and the legal implications of any action by the United States recognizing either a Jewish or a Palestinian state. I urged that clear instructions should be given by the Department to the Mission in New York. As will be noted, such clear instructions were not received. On May 7 I drafted a resolution providing for trusteeship with the United Nations as the administering authority. On the next day, we of the U.S. delegation in New York decided to ask the Department's authorization to support the text of the trusteeship plan which Austin telegraphed to Washington.

On May 8 also, a memorandum was drafted in the State Department's Legal Adviser's office but did not receive clearance higher up. The memorandum reached the conclusion that on May 15 the United Nations Palestine Commission "becomes the legal government of Palestine under the partition plan." It seemed to be assumed that the United States probably should not recognize the existence of any new state in Palestine during the special session unless the Security Council should repeal its resolution of April 17 which the United States had promoted, but after the close of the special session, the United States would be free to recognize either a Jewish or an Arab state if established. On May 15, the memorandum concluded, the two communities would be entitled to proclaim states and organize their governments in the areas they occupied.

On May 9, Dean Rusk, then Director of UNA, phoned from Washington to me and to John Ross, an alternate representative to the special session, reporting that Moshe Shertok (later, Sharett) of the Jewish Agency did not think that the Jews were likely to proclaim their state right away but would start out only by establishing their provisional government. Meanwhile other delegations were urging us to go ahead with plans for a trusteeship; I personally thought that was the best course.

On May 11, John Ross and I had a further telephone talk with Dean Rusk, who was still in Washington. Rusk said that we had started with the plan for a trusteeship on the assumption that the parties would have agreed to a truce, but we had neither a truce nor the agreement of either party to a trusteeship. According to Rusk, "the President never did decide we had to impose a trusteeship against the wishes of either community." The problem was to determine the responsibility of the United Nations on May 15 when the mandate had come to an end. The General Assembly should back up the effort of the Security Council to get a truce. The transcript of our conversation continues thus (with explanatory matter added by me in brackets):

Rusk: "Phil, I think what is likely to come out from down here, particularly across the way [i.e., in the White House], is the idea that something has happened in fact over there [i.e., in Palestine]. It is not according to plan but nevertheless there is a community in existence over there running its own affairs [i.e., the Jewish community]. Now that community apparently is going to get an open shot at establishing itself. We have told them that if they get in trouble, don't come to us for help in a military sense. Nevertheless, I don't think the boss [i.e., President Truman] will ever put himself in a position of opposing that effort when it might be that the U.S. opposition would be the only thing that would prevent it from succeeding."

He ended by telling us, in negotiation with Jews and Arabs, to urge that the Trusteeship Council should undertake the international administration of the city of Jerusalem. I reported that we thought we could get a two-thirds vote in favor of trusteeship. Rusk warned that the United Kingdom would like to trap us into an arrangement where we would have to take on the responsibility of government which the United Nations might not be able to handle. We did not take this interpretation of the President's attitude to mean that the United States would actively promote the establishment of a Jewish state while the special session was still wrestling with the problem of finding an overall solution of the problems in Palestine.

It became clear, however, that contrary to our earlier estimates, we could not get the necessary majority vote for a UN trusteeship. Accordingly, on May 12, the Department informed us that the President had cleared the text of the resolution which would call for the appointment of a mediator. We were told to support such a resolution if introduced by another delegation but were authorized to introduce it ourselves if the negotiating situation at Lake Success indicated that course would be best. Nothing was said about recognition of the state of Israel if it were proclaimed.

The Jewish representatives were opposed to our proposal because they still backed the partition plan, which was the only one that provided for a Jewish state. The Soviet bloc supported them in their opposition, perhaps not averse to the thought that when the British withdrew, at 6 P.M. on May 14, if the UN did not take their place, there might be an opportunity for the Soviets to assert a Russian role. The tactics of the opposition to the U.S. proposal were to drag out the debate in Committee I so that no resolution could be reported for action by the plenary session before 6 P.M. Whether or not the Russians knew at the time of the intention of the Jews to proclaim the independence of Israel at 6 P.M., I do not know. It was the time when the crisis over the Berlin Blockade was coming to a head, and

Feis believes that suspicion of Soviet intentions was a strong factor in Washingtn thinking about Palestine.[10]

It was decided that I should make a major speech in Committee I on May 13, the day before the mandate was to expire. I talked to Robert McClintock in the Department on the phone that morning to ask how much leeway we had in accepting changes in the resolution we were proposing. Acting Secretary Lovett was consulted and instructed us to keep in close touch with the Department and not to accept any amendment which would change the sense of our resolution. We were to vote "No" on any amendment which would seek further to reduce the effect of the Security Council's resolution of November 29 which called for a truce. Lovett confirmed this position with President Truman, and while I was en route to Lake Success, this message came by telephone to the Mission. We actually did have a small booth with our own phone at Lake Success and we used it often to keep in touch with the Department, but the communications were not "secure." Later in the day McClintock showed Lovett the text of the statement we had drafted for me to make in Committee I; Lovett said it was too long and repetitious. By 5 P.M. we had clearance on a revised draft.

In my speech I said that our trusteeship proposal had commended itself to many members, but that neither the Jews nor the Arabs had agreed to it. "It was clear," I continued, "that, in the absence of agreement between the parties, armed forces would be essential to any trusteeship plan. The United States had offered to contribute a share of the required forces and had approached certain other governments which it felt might have a similar interest . . . but these governments were not in a position to participate. . . . In the view of the United States delegation, the United Nations had no power under the Charter, to impose a political decision against the will of the people concerned." However, we did believe that the Security Council, acting under Chapter VII of the Charter, had the power to keep the peace. I concluded that, in the light of the developments, the United States now proposed, instead of a trusteeship, a plan which had been recommended by Subcommittee 9, for the appointment of a mediator.

It was after 10 o'clock on the night of May 13, but we were aware that we faced a filibuster. Gromyko, speaking for the Soviet Union, said they wished to discuss the new proposal on the following day. The Committee, he said, could not be guided by the desire of certain delegations to adopt a decision by a certain hour the next day. "Perhaps the people of Palestine would be grateful to the General Assembly when the British retired from Palestine at 6 P.M. the next day." The chairman said that it was not possible to vote that evening, and he adjourned the Committee at 10:35 P.M.

The Rules of Procedure of the General Assembly had a provision for meeting a filibuster—something which many senators would have liked to achieve in the Senate in Washington. According to the rule:

A representative may at any time move the closure of the debate on the item under discussion, whether or not any other representative has signified his wish to speak. Permission to speak on the closure of the debate shall be accorded only to two speakers opposing the closure, after which the motion shall be immediately put to the vote.

The rule does provide that the president (chairman) of the Committee may limit the time to be allowed to speakers under this rule, but skilled filibusterers can open a long discussion on such a presidential ruling, arguing that the time set is too short, raising a point of order, etc. If a time limit is not set, the two opposing speakers may talk for hours. It was accordingly necessary to manage the procedural details as we met on May 14.

The chairman of the Committee was T. F. Tsiang, the very able permanent representative of China to the United Nations. He was a colleague with whom we had very friendly relations

—there was no question about Peking in those days. It was necessary that he should be aware of the plans.

A member of the U.S. staff first had a casual conversation with Ambassador Guillermo Belt of Cuba, who was cooperating with us. He agreed to make a very brief statement moving closure. Then, unobtrusively, the tactics were explained to Prince Wan, the distinguished head of the delegation of Thailand. He agreed to be one of the speakers against closure and would speak only for two or three minutes. Next, Nasrollah Entezam of Iran, a skilled parliamentarian, agreed to be the second speaker against closure. Chairman Tsiang was quietly advised that Prince Wan and Entezam would ask to be recognized as soon as Belt moved closure.

The plan worked like the famous baseball double play of Tinker to Evers to Chance. Ambassador Belt said the debate had gone on for four weeks; people were still making long speeches which would change no one's vote and the mandate was coming to an end. He moved the closure of the debate.

The chairman recognized Prince Wan, who said that his delegation wanted to speak and it would be better to limit the time for speeches than to close the debate. He said his delegation would vote against closure.

The chairman then gave the floor to Entezam, who agreed that a decision must be reached before 6 P.M., but said that the question was so important that no delegation should be prevented from expressing its opinion. He agreed with Prince Wan and suggested that all speeches should be limited to ten minutes. I think it was Entezam, rather than Francis Sayre as mentioned by Postal and Levy, who suggested that the Committee stay in session while delegates sent out for sandwiches to munch in the committee room.

The chairman, reading the rule which I have quoted, announced that he would put to the vote the motion for closure. It was carried by 23 to 15 with 10 abstentions. We were quite

sure that would be the result if we surmounted the procedural
hurdle; most of the delegations were tired of the filibustering
repetitive speeches and actually wanted the General Assembly
to act before 6 P.M.

There was a further delaying tactic. The Yugoslav delegate,
Mr. Vilfan, invoked Article 142 of the Rules of Procedure,
which calls for a budget estimate on any expenses which a resolution might involve. The Secretary-General stated that he had
available funds which he was authorized to use for this purpose
($2 millions—how Waldheim would like to be in that position
today!). Our substantive resolution was then put to the vote
and carried, 35–6–10.

I then moved that Committee I proceed at once to consider
the report of Subcommittee 10 on the status of Jerusalem. This
proposal was supported by Parodi of France and by Garcia
Granados of Guatemala. The latter, who with Professor
Enrique Fabregat of Uruguay, was a prime supporter of the
Jewish case, pointed out that after the termination of the mandate at 6 P.M. that evening, the United Nations would have no
right to establish any kind of authority in Palestine. If the report of Subcommittee 10 was not adopted by the General Assembly by 6 P.M., "there would exist no possibility in international law to make any special arrangement for Jerusalem."
The chairman then opened a general debate on the report of
Subcommittee 10.

The debate dragged along. Rabbi Abba Silver of the Jewish
Agency for Palestine took the floor. He announced that at 10
o'clock that morning a Jewish state had been proclaimed in
Palestine, the hour having been advanced out of respect for the
Jewish Sabbath. (The United States delegation was to learn
later that President Truman had been informed that the Jewish Act of Independence would become effective at one minute
after six o'clock, Washington time, but when Rabbi Silver
made his announcement we on the delegation at Lake Success
had no information on the matter.) Rabbi Silver read part of

the statement proclaiming the establishment of a Jewish state in Palestine to be called Israel.

It was then after 3 o'clock and the debate continued. I moved that the report of Subcommittee 10 be transmitted to the General Assembly without being voted on in Committee I. This motion being adopted by 15 votes to 0 with 26 abstentions, the chairman declared the work of the Committee finished, and the meeting rose at 3:45 P.M.

We rushed to our waiting cars and sped to Flushing Meadows, where the plenary meeting of the General Assembly began at 4:40. José Arce, President of the Assembly, announced that speakers would be limited to five minutes each, since the question of the future government of Palestine had been fully discussed in Committee I and its subcommittees. Tsarapkin of the USSR, on a point of order, objected to the ruling, appealing from the decision of the chair. President Arce put the issue to the vote, and he was upheld by 35 to 11 with 3 abstentions.

The debate opened on the Report of Subcommittee 10 on which Committee I had made no recommendation. There were some amendments, and the President of the Assembly noted that the resolution would require a two-thirds majority, or 36 votes, in order to be adopted. The resolution failed, having received only 20 votes in favor, 15 against and 19 abstentions. The General Assembly moved on to consider the resolution based on the report of Subcommittee 9 which the United States had fathered and which had been adopted in Committee I. It was after 6 P.M. and we had failed to secure any administrative arrangement for Jerusalem, but our resolution calling for the appointment of a mediator might still be useful.

At this point Ambassador Francis Sayre and I were the only members of the U.S. delegation in attendance, although we had a group of our advisers. Ambassador Warren Austin, the head of the delegation, had gone back to Manhattan, as I shall explain later. John C. Ross had been circulating among the other

delegations and came to us in some excitement to say there was
a rumor that the United States had recognized the new state of
Israel. We laughed it off—how could that happen without the
U.S. delegation being informed? Ross resumed his contacts and
the representative of Colombia formally asked the U.S. delegation if it was in a position to confirm the information given to
the press regarding the recognition of the government of the
Jewish state by the United States. Mr. Sayre was the senior
member of the delegation, and we felt that something had to
be said. In some embarrassment, he went to the rostrum and
said that "for the time being" he had no official information on
the subject. Ross, in considerable agitation, came back and said
he had been told that the fact of our recognition had been on
the press ticker. (My wife, who was sitting in the reserved visitors' seats off to the side, told me later that you could see the
rumor flowing over the delegates, like wind across a field of
wheat.) I turned to Betty Gough, documents officer of the delegation, who had never failed to produce a document when it
was called for. I told her she had to bring me a copy of that
ticker tape, and fast!

The debate continued. Mr. Katz-Suchy of Poland welcomed
the establishment of the Jewish state and thought the Arab
population of Palestine would follow suit. He said that the *de
facto* recognition of the Jewish state by the United States
showed that it agreed with him that the resolution they had
put through Committee I three hours before was already obso-
lete. Ambassador Belt of Cuba, who had helped us in the debates in Committee I, said he "was surprised to hear the
United States representative say that he had no information regarding his government's recognition of the new Jewish state.
It appeared that the representatives of the USSR and Poland
were better informed on events in Washington; it was pointless
now to vote on the resolution." (A little later, Porter
McKeever of our delegation had actually to restrain Ambassador Belt from returning to the platform where he intended to

announce that Cuba would withdraw from the United Nations rather than continue in an organization where a leading state like the United States was guilty of such duplicity.)

The Arab delegates turned to the attack. Faris Bey El-Khouri of Syria stated that he "at last understood why the United States representative had urged that priority should be given to discussion of the report of Subcommittee 10. The real intention of the United States had been to await the termination of the mandate before putting that resolution to the vote, so that the United States government could recognize the Jewish state as a *de facto* authority."

As he was speaking, Betty Gough returned with a crumpled piece of yellow paper in her hand. She told me that Secretary-General Trygve Lie's office was empty and she found this in his wastebasket. I went to the rostrum and said that the U.S. delegation had not wished to make any statement on the matter to which several delegates had referred until it had the full text of the statement issued by the President of the United States. I proceeded to read it, smoothing out the paper as best I could:

> This government has been informed that a Jewish state has been proclaimed in Palestine and recognition has been requested by the provisional government thereof. The United States recognizes the *de facto* authority of the new state of Israel. . . .
>
> The desire of the United States to obtain a truce in Palestine will in no way be lessened by the proclamation of a Jewish state. We hope that the new Jewish state will join with the Security Council Truce Commission in redoubled efforts to bring an end to the fighting, which has been, throughout the United Nations consideration of Palestine, a principal objective of this government.

I added that the appointment of a mediator was still desirable and the United States therefore still favored the passage of the resolution.

I took my seat and listened to the continued denunciations from delegates with whom our personal relations had always been of the best. Mahmoud Bey Fawzi of Egypt "thought that in view of the circumstances it would be a mockery unworthy of the General Assembly and of the United Nations as a whole to continue discussion of the proposal. The whole of the procedure followed had been a farce, and the fifty-eight nations that were the victims had been unaware of what was taking place behind the scenes. Such action was a blow not only to the United Nations but to international relations as a whole. The members of the Assembly were not mere individuals, they represented all mankind with its hopes and ideals and had to bear heavy responsibilities. All that had been betrayed."

El-Khouri of Syria again spoke, arguing that the recognition of the Jewish state "was to do exactly what the Security Council wished to avoid" in its effort to keep the peace. (Indeed the State Department had instructed the U.S. Mission on April 12 that in discussions with the British, French, Canadian, and other delegations, our proposals for a Security Council resolution included an "agreement to suspend all activity of a military *or political nature* pending consideration of the Palestine problem by the Special Session" of the General Assembly [emphasis added].)

Ambassador Charles Malik of Lebanon, professor of philosophy at the American University of Beirut, pointed out that "the present special session had been convened at the request of the United States through the Security Council, and that for four weeks the United States delegation had been assuring the parties that the only aim was to bring about peace and reconciliation. That was the meaning of the statement made hardly twenty-two hours earlier by the United States representative. [He was referring to a statement which I had made.] . . . . The step taken by the United States could hardly be interpreted as an action calculated to promote the objective conditions necessary for a reconciliation . . . . The United States had many interests in the Middle East, including intellectual, cultural, and spiritual ones. Those spiritual interests, which were of a more subtle, more important, and more lasting kind, would be deeply affected by the decision taken by the United States."

The vote came at about 8:30 P.M. and the resolution calling for the appointment of a mediator was adopted by 31 votes to 7 with 16 abstentions. (On May 20, 1948, Count Folke Bernadotte was appointed UN Mediator in Palestine.)

I did not linger to talk to any of the other delegates in the General Assembly, but hurried to my car and back to Manhattan. In that kind of situation it is possible to resign, but it is not possible to defend oneself publicly from such charges of trickery and deceit. I believe that somehow the word did get around that I personally was also taken by surprise, but the record of the United States was sullied.

Donald Blaisdell of the U.S. Mission learned about the recognition from Lionel Gelber of the Jewish Agency, who showed him, in the corridor at Flushing Meadows, a transcription of the White House press release about 6:15 on Friday evening, May 14; Blaisdell assumed we on the delegation had an official text. A telegram from Mr. Epstein, agent of the provisional government of Israel, dated May 14, notifying Secretary Marshall that they had proclaimed their independent republic and requesting recognition, was received at the Mission in New York together with the President's statement of recognition on May 16, two days later. It was on this same day that Secretary-General Trygve Lie notified Secretary Marshall and Ambassador Austin that they had received notice from Egypt that Egyptian armed forces had been sent into Palestine. The Security Council met, and the United States introduced a resolution calling for a cease-fire.

The situation in which we found ourselves in the United Nations was explained at some length in a telegram which Jack Ross and I drafted and which Ambassador Austin sent to Secretary Marshall on May 19. The telegram suggested that the Department would wish to have our appraisal of the situation as a basis for future instructions to the Mission in New York. We said that it was our best estimate that the recognition of the provisional government of Israel last Friday evening had deeply undermined the confidence of other delegations in our integrity and the Department should keep that fact in mind. A large number of delegations believed that recognition constituted a reversal of United States policy for truce plus trusteeship as urged in the special session and, in later stages, our compromise plan for truce plus mediation. In our previous efforts to secure a truce, both in the Security Council and in formal negotiations, the U.S. delegation had heavily emphasized that there should be no action of a political character that would alter the *status quo* or prejudice the rights, the claims, or the positions of Arabs or Jews. This position of ours was generally understood to apply primarily to the establishment of the Jewish state.

We had strongly backed the truce resolution in the Security Council in accordance with the instruction which we received, and which we understood had the highest clearance. We had persuaded other delegations of the correctness of our position and induced them to come forward and carry a large share of the burden of the argument. They thus became publicly identified with our position. It was true that the Jews had not accepted the truce, but they disregarded the admonitions of the Security Council, violated the spirit of the effort to get a truce, and prevented the formal conclusion of the truce. The feeling among other delegations was that by granting recognition, the United States not only condoned but endorsed these violations, thus striking a heavy blow at the prospect of concluding any truce and an equally heavy blow at the prestige and effectiveness of the Security Council and of the United Nations in general. Our immediate act of recognition was itself regarded as a violation of the Security Council's truce resolution, with the result that there was a lack of confidence in the integrity of United States intentions and disbelief of further statements of future intentions and policies. Other delegations now wanted to avoid being committed to any United States position since it might be reversed without notice.

An important contribution to these attitudes was the failure of the United States to inform or consult others before the announcement of the final step. We had developed at the United Nations very close and most friendly relations with a large number of delegations of other countries which wanted to support our foreign policies, not only in the United Nations but generally. We had kept each other informed, working out mutually acceptable points of substance, of tactics, and of strategy. Our sudden move without notice or consultation deeply offended many of our close collaborators. With two or three exceptions, our closest and most consistent supporters among other delegations, while expressing friendly personal feelings, were manifestly mistrustful of continuing cooperation on basic questions of policy or strategy or even of tactics. Naturally, we said in the telegram, the Arab delegations were particularly bitter but the reaction of others, such as Canada, China, and a number of the Latin Americans, was not based on a question of merits but was due to a feeling, which they frankly expressed, that they had been double-crossed.

The result of all this, in our opinion, was that if we pressed to a vote the resolution we had introduced in the Security Council, calling for action under Chapter VII of the Charter, the resolution would not get more than three or four affirmative votes. Many delegates thought it unrealistic to have the Security Council decide under Article 39 of the Charter that there had been a breach of the peace unless it were assured that sanctions would be applied if necessary; they were completely mistrustful of our readiness to participate in sanctions.

We concluded our telegram by saying that in the long run, the identity of broad interests between the United States and various other governments would tend to outweigh the current reactions but it would take time to dissipate the mistrust and suspicion with which others regarded us. The United States must therefore be careful not to advance major proposals on political issues, especially in the Security Council, without careful canvassing of other delegations. In many cases, our objectives might best be obtained through supporting the proposals of others. In general we should be responsive to indications on the part of other delegations of fear of Russian expansion and their underlying identity of interest with us.

No copies of this telegram were distributed to other members of the Mission in New York. I do not know what distribution it received in the State Department, but it is most unlikely that President Truman ever saw it. I do not suppose he ever knew the shock to his loyal representatives at the United Nations when the news of the recognition burst over our heads without warning. Postal and Levy correctly report how Sayre and I were completely taken by surprise.

Mrs. Roosevelt was "stirred . . . to new indignation" by the procedure which the United States had followed, since she felt it demeaned the United Nations. She wrote on May 16 to Secretary of State Marshall:

The way in which the recognition of Palestine [sic] came about has created complete consternation in the United Nations. . . . Much as I wanted the Palestine State recognized, I would not have wanted it done without the knowledge of our representatives in the United Nations who had been fighting for our changed position. I would have felt that they had to know the reason and I would also have felt that there had to be a very clear understanding beforehand with such nations as we expected would follow our lead.

Several of the representatives of other governments have been to talk to me since, and have stated quite frankly that they do not see how they could ever follow the United States' lead because the United States changed so often without any consultation.

Marshall replied: "We were aware here of the unfortunate effect on our situation with the United Nations, which is much to be regretted. . . . More than this, I am not free to say." [11]

In his *Memoirs,* President Truman explains in considerable

detail how he decided to grant immediate recognition to the state of Israel.[12] He says that he favored the partition plan and thought it would have worked, but his basic policy was in accord with the Balfour declaration—to establish in Palestine a Jewish homeland. He had no particular formula or timetable in mind, but thought the result should be achieved by peaceful means. He says that the "Jewish pressure on the White House did not diminish in the days following the partition vote in the UN." That vote, I remind, was November 29, 1947. Truman writes that he did not agree with "the extreme Zionists" and finally gave orders that no more of them were to be admitted to see him. Then his former partner in the haberdashery business back in Missouri in the old days, Eddie Jacobson, came and appealed to him to see the man who later became the first President of Israel—Dr. Chaim Weizmann. The President saw Weizmann on March 18, 1948, and had a long talk in which he explained his general view and policy. It was the day after this meeting that Ambassador Austin announced in the Security Council the U.S. plan for a temporary trusteeship for Palestine. The President approved this plan only as a temporary postponement of partition and records that it was no change in his basic policy. As already mentioned, he sent a message to this effect to Dr. Weizmann through Judge Samuel Rosenman, one of his close advisers.

President Truman writes that he was also under pressure from those who leaned toward the Arab cause. Secretary Forrestal kept warning him that if we antagonized the Arabs we would endanger our access to the vital oil supplies of the Middle East. Truman thought that the Department of State's specialists on the Middle East were unfriendly to the idea of a Jewish state and that some were anti-Semitic. But I would suggest that a conviction on the part of some of the officials that we should maintain friendly relations with the Arabs was no proof of anti-Semitism, nor, as some have suggested, that those officials were subservient to the oil companies.

The President writes that "on May 14 I was informed that

the Provisional Government of Israel was planning to proclaim
a Jewish state at midnight that day, Palestine time, which was
when the British mandate came to an end." That would be 6
P.M. Washington time. The President records that he told a
member of his staff to tell the State Department that he would
recognize the new state at once and that they should notify Ambassador Austin at the United Nations. It was about 5:45 P.M.,
Dean Rusk recalls, when he received a telephone call from one
of President Truman's principal assistants (it may have been
Clark Clifford), telling him that the State of Israel would be
declared at 6:00 P.M. and that the President wished him to inform our Delegation at the United Nations that he would
grant immediate recognition. Rusk protested that this cut
across what our delegation had been trying to accomplish in
the General Assembly under instructions and pointed out that
we already had a large majority for our proposals. The voice
from the White House said he had stated what the President
wished Rusk to do. Rusk immediately called on the telephone
and Ambassador Austin was summoned from the floor of the
Assembly to take the call.[13] Austin did not return to his seat
but went directly to his car and back to Manhattan.

According to one account the President was asked by Secretary of State Marshall to delay at least briefly, but he refused.*
Truman writes: "Exactly eleven minutes after Israel had been
proclaimed a state, Charlie Ross, my press secretary, handed
the press the announcement of the *de facto* recognition by the
United States of the provisional government of Israel." That
was the announcement which Betty Gough fished out of the
wastepaper basket for me.

President Truman adds in his *Memoirs:* "I was told that to
some of the career men of the State Department this announcement came as a surprise. It should not have been if these men
had faithfully supported my policy."

* However, Kurzman's account of events on May 11 and May 12 (at pp. 215 ff
and 251 ff) is not in accord with my information.

General Marshall doubted the wisdom of setting up the state of Israel at that time because he thought the Jews could not stand up militarily against Arab attacks and he favored trusteeship as a way to protect the Jewish community by a United Nations shield. I doubt if any participants thought that the recognition of Israel would bring peace to Palestine, but if they did, they entirely misjudged the Arabs, as the tragic history of a quarter century has now demonstrated.

All memories are fallible, including mine, and most memoirs are poor guides to history—including this memoir of mine. I admire Harry Truman and am confident he will go down in history as a great President, but his account of the recognition of Israel calls for some qualification.

I have quoted what he wrote about some career men in the State Department being surprised by his announcement of the recognition of the new state when he says "It should not have been (a surprise) if these men had faithfully supported my policy." I was not a career man—I was temporarily serving as our deputy representative at the United Nations and had been given the responsibility of managing the debate and explaining the view of the United States. Everything I said and did was under instructions from the State Department—that is, from Secretary of State Marshall or Acting Secretary Lovett. Neither I nor my advisers at the United Nations in New York had ever been told that it was the President's policy to recognize the state of Israel the moment it was proclaimed. Our official information in the delegation had been to the contrary. Secretary Marshall himself did not know it until May 14. And President Truman evidently was not aware that all of the friendly delegations who were working with us to bring about a peaceful solution of the Palestine crisis were taken completely by surprise. Diplomacy by surprise is a dangerous practice. It may be useful from the point of view of domestic politics, but it can be ruinous to our relations with other countries. Even on the domestic front, surprises like this create perpetual difficulties between the White House and the Foreign Relations Committee of the Senate. The newspapers are full of this conflict. It is the element of secrecy and surprise which was highlighted by the case of the Pentagon Papers.

Of course ambassadors are expendable but, in my opinion, the role of the State Department in managing foreign policy is not expendable. The White House sometimes thinks it is. Philip Bonsal, a retired Foreign Service officer with a long record of distinguished service, who was U.S. ambassador to Cuba in 1960, after Castro took over, tells in his recent book (*Cuba, Castro and the United States*) how President Eisenhower's Secretary of the Treasury, Robert Anderson, summoned representatives of the oil companies and told them it would be in accord with our government's policy to refuse to refine Soviet crude oil in their Cuban refineries, and if they acted jointly with other companies they would not be prosecuted under the anti-trust laws. Anderson did this without informing the State Department officials who were handling Cuban affairs, and against the advice of Ambassador Bonsal. As Bonsal had predicted, this action threw the Cubans into the hands of the Russians, who supplied the technicians and operated the refineries in Cuba without any decrease in their supplies.

In the winter of 1972 we knew that Japan, our strongest and staunchest ally in the Far East, was astounded, taken aback, and shocked by President Nixon's sudden announcement that he would visit Peking, a move of great political significance of which they had been given not a single word of warning in advance. The damage was not repaired by President Nixon's tour of the summits, another practice which is also full of danger, as George Ball has pointed out.[14]

I was also devoted to Ambassador Austin—a fine Vermont gentleman and sincere public servant. I never was told by him whether he had in fact received the news of the planned announcement for recognition much in advance and, if so, why he did not tell his deputies. He may have been almost in a state of shock—I could well understand that. And so far as I can ascertain, there was no authority given him to warn any of the other friendly representatives before the White House announcement was given to the press. It was too late to prevent the damage done to our standing with our friends. Kurzman (at p. 254) after stating that Austin was called from his seat in the Assembly and took a telephone call from Washington by which he was informed of the recognition of Israel, "walked slowly to his seat in the General Assembly. He conferred briefly with members of his delegation who happened to be present. Then wiping his face with a handkerchief, he strode out, got into his limousine, and ordered the chauffeur to take him to his hotel." As one of "his delegation who happened to be present," I can repeat that Ambassador Austin did not return to his seat or confer with us. Neither is it correct, as Kurzman says (at p. 255), that I telephoned Washington before making the statement from the rostrum which I have described and which he mentions. Postal and Levy are also incorrect in stating (at p. 274) that Lionel Gelber, a Canadian working with Rabbi Abba Silver for the Jewish Agency, "immediately went over to the U.S. delegation to advise Jessup of the Truman action" when the Jewish representatives got the news from Washington.

President Truman stresses that the keynote of his policy for Palestine was to bring about a peaceful adjustment of the conflict between the Arabs and the Jews. On May 14, 1948, when some of his political advisers, particularly Clark Clifford, were urging upon him the recognition of Israel, he acted without keeping in mind that the United States could make a contribution to a peaceful settlement only by trying to influence *both* sides—the Arab side and the Jewish side. President Truman had been advised that we were not in a position to intervene militarily in Palestine, although he was prepared to join others in furnishing a small contingent to support trusteeship if that plan had been adopted.

Our relations with the Russians are always a prominent feature of discussions of our Middle Eastern policy, but in 1948 it was the Russians who were backing and supplying arms to the Jewish forces. Truman had blocked the Soviets in Iran and on March 12, 1947, had announced the Truman Doctrine to support "free people" and specifically Greece and Turkey. No one was urging a further confrontation with Russia in Palestine. Curiously enough, it was in the Palestine case that the Soviet Union and the United States stood together to support the partition plan—a most unusual concurrence on a matter of political importance. But President Truman feared that the Soviet Union would be the first to recognize Israel and thus strengthen Russian influence. I was among a number of sources who informed Washington that Jewish representatives were saying that the Soviet Union planned to be the first to recognize the new state of Israel. T. F. Tsiang, the head of the Chinese delegation, had told a member of the U.S. delegation on May 13 that he expected Russia to recognize a Jewish state but thought the Arabs would recognize a Palestinian state. We had mentioned, in our long telegram of May 19, that fear of Russian expansion might be a reunifying factor. On May 11, Ross reported that conversation with the British and Canadians had revealed that they both felt something had to be done in Palestine to head off Russian penetration of the area. It must be recalled that this was a time of cold war tension in the relations between the Soviet Union and the Western Allies, when the Russian blockade was tightening around Berlin.

Ambassador to the United Nations Charles Yost, who unfortunately was replaced in 1970 in the midst of negotiations on the Arab-Israeli dispute, discussed the "Soviet military presence" in the Middle East in an article in the New York *Times* in December 1971. He pointed out that the United States had had a "substantial military presence" in that area for many years, "originally for the purpose of protecting two NATO allies, Greece and Turkey, who provided us with the necessary bases." The Soviets were eager to establish themselves there and turned to the Arabs for like facilities in exchange for military supplies. The Arabs, Yost pointed out, do not like any foreign presence but won't deny facilities to the Soviets as long as the conflict with Israel continues. Therefore, Yost concludes: "The only effective way to get the Soviets out of the Mideast, or at least reduce their presence, is to settle that conflict. The only way to settle the conflict is by painful concessions by both sides. . . . The existence of Israel is not at stake. The argument is about its boundaries. The question is whether or not its security will be better assured by the acquisition of substantial new territory or by peace agreements signed by the Arab states and guaranteed by the big powers."

The question of Israel's boundaries has, of course, been an issue all through the years. I shall mention one incident that occurred in the General Assembly in 1947 because it is illustrative of some of the pressures.* The UN Special Committee on Palestine, known as UNSCOP, had defined the boundaries of the proposed Jewish state and of the proposed Arab state under the plan of partition. Under their plan, the Negev, the great desert area to the south of Palestine, which now has been irrigated and reclaimed by Israel in recent years, was included in the UNSCOP's plan for the Jewish state. But in the course of the debates, efforts were made to reduce as far as possible the number of Arabs who would be left in the Jewish state and, as part of that plan, the U.S. delegation reported to the State Department that the population of the Negev at that time was predominantly Arab and that the area had an important relation to Arab routes of communication, and it therefore asked for authority to propose that the Negev be included in the Arab state. Acting Secretary Lovett, on November 19, 1947, instructed Ambassador Herschel Johnson at the United Nations that the facts regarding the Negev warranted its inclusion in the Arab state: "Accordingly you should not (repeat not) yield

* I was not officially involved at that time.

to demand of JA" (the Jewish Agency). But when the UN Committee did not agree, except for a narrow strip of the Negev along the Egyptian frontier, the U.S. delegation was authorized, as Johnson advocated, to bow to the will of the majority. Since the whole partition plan was later rejected and the boundaries remained unsettled, it is not surprising that in December 1948, the Security Council had to order a cease-fire when there was heavy fighting in the Negev.

The question of Israel's boundaries was raised also in connection with that state's admission to membership in the United Nations which was of course opposed by the Arab states. In arguing in the Security Council in favor of the admission of Israel, I had to answer the Arab arguments, one of which was that since the boundaries of Israel were undetermined, Israel was not a state. I pointed out that when the United States attained its independence, its Western frontier was practically unknown and certainly undetermined, and it was years later before our northern boundary with Canada was settled. (I may recall that questions about recognition are an essential part of every course on international law and I had been teaching such courses for twenty-five years, so the State Department let me frame my own arguments on this matter, but I relied also on my colleague in the Mission, James N. Hyde, an international lawyer by inheritance and in his own right.)

Another Arab argument was that the United States had not recognized the state of Israel "as a *de jure* authority," but only as "a *de facto* authority." I may quote my reply to that argument:

. . . Perhaps some confusion arises between recognition of the state of Israel and recognition of the provisional government of Israel. So far as recognition of the state is concerned . . . the recognition accorded by the United States government to the state of Israel was immediate and full recognition. There was no qualification. It was not conditional; it was not *de facto* recognition; it was full recognition of the state. So far as the provisional government of Israel is concerned, the United States did extend *de facto* recognition to that provisional government of Israel.

Postal and Levy consider that it was "ironic" that I should make this statement since, as they write, on May 14 "Jessup was pushing the UN to adopt *his* formula for some form of interim Palestine regime under a UN commission." I italicize "his" because this possessive pronoun reveals the authors' total lack of comprehension of the task and obligation of the representative of the United States in expounding the views of his government which have been conveyed to him in the form of instructions from the Secretary of State or his deputy. I like to think that my description here of what occurred shows that my exposition in the Security Council of the recognition problem was not "ironic" and that the trusteeship formula was not something I created. It is unfortunately this misconception of the role of a loyal diplomatic representative which has built up much of the legend about the State Dpartment's disloyalty to the President.

The United States extended *de jure* recognition to the government of Israel as of January 31, 1949, when a permanent government was elected.

There was a rather offensive article by Joseph Kraft in the *New York Times Sunday Magazine* for November 7, 1971, entitled "Those Arabists in the State Department." He begins with the quotation from Truman's *Memoirs* about the Department's Near East specialists being "unfriendly to the idea of a Jewish state." Then Kraft quotes William Phillips, whom he erroneously describes as "an American diplomat prominent in the Palestine affair," as saying: "I am not proud of the way our government handled its responsibility, nor do I like to dwell on the shameful manner in which Washington attempted to secure the Jewish vote." He quotes Parker Hart, who was Assistant Secretary of State and now heads the Middle East Institute, as saying: "The area experts, to a man, were scandalized

by what happened in 1948. We had made a tremendous effort
to lay the ground for good relations with the Arabs, and all of a
sudden, when we were in good position, all of our hopes were
dashed." Kraft names men to whom, he says, Truman and subsequent presidents have given a "watching brief on Israeli-Arab
affairs." They are said to have all had "good lines into the Jewish community."

Perhaps this explains one other incident in the course of the
debates on Palestine in the UN General Assembly. In 1952, I
was appointed an alternate delegate to the General Assembly
and was assigned to deal again with the question of Palestine as
well as the Tunisian item. During one of the Palestinian debates in which I was stating the position of the United States
on a pending resolution (the position having been prescribed
for the delegation by instructions from the State Department),
we got a message to go to the telephone to take an urgent call
from the Department. Louis Pollak, one of the able assistants it
was my good fortune to have, was sitting behind me and I
asked him to take the call, which was on the public phone in
the delegates' lounge. David Popper, then in the UNA Bureau,
was on the phone. Pollak was told to instruct Jessup immediately that he was to support the Israeli position. Which position? asked Pollak. Popper said that he had made it quite clear
that Jessup was to support "the Israeli position" and this instruction came from "the highest levels." Pollak protested that
if he meant the point for which the Israeli delegate had been
arguing, a shift to approval of that point would be a reversal of
what Jessup had just been saying in accordance with his instructions. He was told to carry out the new instructions which,
it was repeated (emphatically but with what Pollak sensed was
regret at the last-minute intervention from above), came from
"the highest levels." Pollak returned and gave me the message;
he recalls that my verbal acrobatics of reconciliation of two in-
consistent positions were not too obvious.*

* Professor Louis H. Pollak (former Dean of the Yale Law School), to the author.

It is a commonplace of American politics that politicians cater to various interest groups (be they blacks or Jews or Catholics or Italians or Irish or whatever) just as long as they vote. In one presidential campaign some years ago, a prominent Republican told the British ambassador in Washington he mustn't bother about campaign speeches which were anti-British; it was necessary to "twist the lion's tail," he said, in order to get the Irish vote, but once the Republicans were in power, relations with England would be of the best!

Tyler Dennett, in his life of John Hay, entitles his chapter 32, "Politics and Diplomacy." In that chapter he tells in detail the story of President Theodore Roosevelt's effort to cultivate the Jewish vote in 1903. According to Hay's biographer, Roosevelt was "playing the demagogue on an international scale for the sake of winning a presidential nomination. It is a pity that . . . Hay should have lent his cleverness to the support of any more similar gestures."

As "Scotty" Reston pointed out early in February 1972, when Secretary Rogers assailed Senator Muskie for speaking out against President Nixon's peace proposal, the Secretary of State ought to keep out of campaign politics. General Marshall and his successor, Dean Acheson, followed that course of political abstention.

I have no doubt that domestic political considerations and pressure from Jewish groups influenced the decision to recognize the state of Israel so abruptly in 1948. But not everyone who was shocked by that sudden announcement was anti-Semitic, nor are all the Americans who come back today from visiting Israel with enthusiastic reports of the remarkable agricultural and industrial developments there, anti-Arab.

I entirely agree with the following passages from the Postal and Levy book:

There is no denying the point made by, among others, Rabbi Leon I. Feuer of the Collingwood Avenue Temple of Toledo, Ohio, a close Silver associate and partisan, that American recognition of Israel's independence by President Truman was not a sentimental gesture, either to his onetime haberdashery partner, Eddie Jacobson, or to a blind old man, Dr. Weizmann.

Writing in November 1967, in the *American Jewish Archives* (Vol. XIX, No. 2), Dr. Feuer said: "Those kinds of political gestures simply do not take place. There was no miracle stemming from the coincidence that a man from Missouri named Truman happened to be President and his erstwhile partner and friend, Jacobson, happened to be a Zionist. What occurred was more prosaic but far more in line with the political realities. Truman was a candidate for President. He knew that the election of 1948 would be, as it was, uncomfortably close. He suspected that the Jewish vote in the populous states would be crucial. He knew all about, and as a politician respected, even if he was often visibly annoyed by, the pressure of the tremendously effective and nationwide organization which Silver had created. He had an opportunity, by recognizing Israel, to make a grab for these votes, State Department or not. He saw his main chance and he took it." (p. 282)

It seems to me also that the following summary from their book is also fair and probably accurate:

The full story of Truman's decision to recognize Israel so quickly is still locked away in classified documents in Washington and Jerusalem. In piecing together the known facts, four main elements emerge. The first was the President's disappointment with the failure of the United States delegation to the United Nations General Assembly to win acceptance of the American proposals for a temporary UN trusteeship, a truce, or any other solution that would have precluded the immediate establishment of the Jewish State. A second was the swift march of events in Palestine, particularly the Jewish military successes, which made it clear that nothing done at Lake Success could alter the partition of the Holy Land. Since the British had refused Washington's last-minute appeal to postpone the termination of the Mandate, Truman felt it essential to fill the legal vacuum by prompt extension of *de facto* recognition. A third factor was the big city Democratic party leaders who insisted that it was imperative in a presidential election year to pacify Jewish voters and their supporters who were turning against the Truman Administration because of its previous reversal on partition, a view that was effectively being promulgated by American Zionists under the leadership of Rabbi Silver. A fourth consideration was worry lest the Soviet Union beat the United States to the punch by becoming the first Great Power to recognize Israel. (pp. 300–1)

Anyone can speculate whether a peaceful solution could have been found for Palestine in 1948 if the United Nations could have gained more time to work out a solution. At the moment, the U.S. government, including President Truman, thought that it would be possible. I am sure that no knowledgeable official in Washington, or in the U.S. Mission in New York, thought that the abrupt recognition of the state of Israel would contribute to a peaceful settlement. The violent fighting which followed was no surprise.

Many of us who were laborers in the diplomatic vineyard understood that it was our assigned job to reap a harvest of peaceful agreements between Arabs and Jews. Others concentrated on making sure that the state of Israel would immediately ripen on the vine. From my own familiarity with President Truman, I have no doubt that he would at the time have referred—as his daughter Margaret reports in her affectionate biography—to the "striped pants conspirators" in the State Department who "opposed" his policy toward Israel. I would wager that a choice collection of unprintable adjectives would have prefaced the description when he talked, for example, to Clark Clifford. But if the President had really believed that there was the kind of insubordination which legend has been building up, he would have rooted out the "conspirators" as quickly as he ousted the alcoholic appointee whose fate I described in the introductory chapter.

A special dispatch from Tel Aviv to the New York *Times,* December 26, 1972, quoted Eliahu Elath, "Israel's first envoy in Washington," as praising Truman for his support of Israel but also alleging that "Mr. Truman had overruled the State Department and personally instructed the American Delegation to the United Nations to vote for the establishment of Israel ." It is natural and entirely appropriate that Harry Truman should be a hero in Israel, but it is unnecessary—and unfortunate—that his reputation should be bolstered by inaccurate historical detail.

In the appraisal we made in our telegram of May 19, 1948, which has been paraphrased at length, we had doubted whether we could get support in the Security Council for a strong resolution, since our "friends" would have no confidence that we would follow up with sanctions, but a week later the Department asked us in New York to make the best possible estimate of possible votes in the Security Council for sanctions. If the Arab delegations said they would refuse to accept a cease-fire order, the Mission must consult the Department again. In the light of the President's recognition of Israel, the Department noted that an Arab agreement to respect a cease-fire on condition that Israel be considered nonexistent would be interpreted by Washington as an outright refusal of a cease-fire. As for the Jewish attitude toward a cease-fire, Charles Fahy, as attorney for the Jewish Agency, had discussed the matter on the telephone with Dean Rusk in Washington. Rusk asked him whether the Jewish government would comply if the Security Council ordered a standstill and cease-fire. Fahy said he would consult; he phoned back later in the day to say that Israel would accept and comply immediately.

I was finally instructed to introduce in the Security Council a resolution which ordered both sides, under threat of sanctions pursuant to Chapter VII of the Charter, to observe a truce as from July 18. The Council adopted the resolution on July 15; both Israel and the Arab League bowed to the Security Council's order.

Although the Arabs opposed the partition plan with economic union, a plan which included a special regime for Jerusalem and the other holy places, it is my own view that some Arab elements would have acquiesced if the plan had been pushed by the United Nations, and a Palestinian state would have been set up alongside the state of Israel. I must agree, however, that some United Nations force would have had to be present to help keep the peace and that there was no chance of getting agreement on such a force. The United States boggled at the idea that Russia might have a place in the Middle East; now they are in, in spite of our efforts to keep them out, and largely because of our diplomatic blunders.

Under the rather vapid resolution which the General Assembly did adopt in May 1948, Count Bernadotte was appointed mediator. He proposed an elaborate plan which would have changed the allocation of territories as contained in the original partition plan, and the changes would have favored the Arabs. I never heard it suggested or saw any evidence that Count Bernadotte's proposals were inspired by anti-Semitism. The United States, through Secretary of State Marshall, at the Paris meeting of the General Assembly in the autumn of 1948, stated that Bernadotte's plan was "fair and sound." But Bernadotte had already been murdered by Jewish terrorists and the state of Israel later paid compensation to the United Nations for his death. The revulsion against the act of assassination was universal—just as much in the Jewish communities as among the Arabs and in the whole United Nations world.

President Truman had planned, following talks with Secretary Marshall, to keep the Palestine question out of the 1948 presidential campaign. But his opponent, Governor Thomas E. Dewey, accused him of going back on the Democratic platform. This led Truman to issue a statement, without telling Secretary Marshall, that the Bernadotte plan was merely a basis for new negotiations. Four days later, on October 28, he came out openly for Israel and against the Bernadotte plan.

This was the autumn when the UN General Assembly met in Paris. The Security Council also met there. Both of them had to deal with the situation in Palestine where Ralph Bunche, as acting mediator, was working hard for a solution. The Israeli armies had launched a general offensive against Egyptian forces in the Negev on October 14, 1948. The Security Council reaffirmed previous orders and called for with-

drawal of forces. There was partial compliance. I made a statement under instructions on November 20 that the boundaries
for Israel, set forth in the partition plan, could not be reduced
without the consent of Israel. Then followed an important sentence: "If Israel desires additions, it would be necessary for Israel to offer an appropriate exchange through negotiations."
The United States subsequently failed to back up that authorized position. Actually, the United States changed its postion
because the great Zionist leader, Dr. Chaim Weizmann, persuaded President Truman that the Jews could make the Negev
desert bloom like a rose, as indeed they have. Fighting broke
out again in December and, just before adjourning the Paris
meetings, the Security Council on December 29 ordered a
cease-fire with which, early in 1949, the parties complied.

Meanwhile the General Assembly had established a conciliation commission for Palestine and during 1949 the situation
seemed to promise hope of peaceful settlement. As I have mentioned, Israel was admitted to UN membership. This action
was recommended by the Security Council on March 4, 1949,
and the General Assembly, on May 11, concurred, taking note
of Israel's declarations and explanations concerning implementation of prior resolutions.*

I have used the metaphor of "the birth of nations," but nations may come of age as soon as they are born. The history of
the state of Israel since the times to which I have been referring is part of another story.

Few question the dangers to mankind of the population explosion among individuals. Some attention has been paid to
the problems created by the birth of many micro-states who, almost for the asking, are admitted to membership in the United

---

*On June 19, 1949, Andrew Cordier, *chef de cabinet* to Trygve Lie, told
"Tom" Power of the U.S. delegation, that Lie's personal idea was that Jessup
should be appointed UN representative to produce a solution of the entire Palestine problem for the fifth General Assembly to avoid the stalemate which he
anticipated. Jessup, said the Secretary-General, should be the "Bunche" of the
second phase of the Palestine problem.

Nations. While fostering that type of proliferating membership, we treat as yet unborn the two Germanys,* the two Koreas, the two Vietnams, and now many speak of the prospering state of Taiwan as if it were deceased as soon as its representatives lost their seats in the United Nations. While this is being written, Bangladesh is being widely recognized, while Rhodesia is not even admitted to the diplomatic maternity ward.

* This is written in June 1973.

8

"Manchukuo" — an Illegitimate Child

In the annals of royal history, bastardy was no disqualification for recognized monarchical eminence; it is sufficient to mention William the Conqueror, who was also called "William the Bastard." Robert Burton, in the *Anatomy of Melancholy,* goes so far as to declare that "Almost in every kingdom the most ancient families have been at first princes' bastards." Perhaps that is a melancholy thought. In international law, legitimacy is less important than success. In Korea, in Indonesia, in Morocco and Tunis, in Libya and Somalia, and in Israel, one may say there was a combination of legitimacy and of success since those states originated in the wills of the peoples who formed their populations, and after their births they were accepted into the international community personified in the United Nations—except for the Republic of Korea which still lacks only that final baptism. Although the more recent story of Bangladesh is not included here, one may classify its birth with those of the states just mentioned, despite the fact that it was Indian support which gave that Bengali revolt its triumph. But what of entities created by outside power that assumes the right of divine creativity? Even such, if they succeed in obtaining the recognition of established states, may achieve a permanent place in the family of nations. If they do not thus succeed, they remain mere puppets. It seems not inappropriate to end this book with the tale of the birth of a puppet.

The prime example of puppetry is "Manchukuo," the regime fashioned by Japan in Manchuria in 1932 in defiance of the League of Nations, of the United States, and of all the precepts of international law. Manchukuo did "exist" until reclaimed by China after the end of World War II. I shall return to some of the antecedents but note here that Japan was crushing China militarily, forced some Chinese to cooperate, and arranged for them to announce, on February 18, 1932, that a new Manchurian state had proclaimed its independence under the name of "Manchukuo." On March 9, Henry Pu-Yi, former deposed boy Manchu emperor, who had been living under Japanese care, was inaugurated as Regent of Manchukuo. As Nathaniel Peffer described Manchukuo:

> It was, of course, a fraudulent affair. Even Japanese officials in . . . the capital . . . could hardly suppress smiles when referring to the "government" of Manchukuo. There was a government structure with duly appointed officials, all Chinese, behind each of whom stood a Japanese adviser. The Chinese official was informed of his decisions after they were already being put into effect. The poor little emperor issued edicts that he saw for the first time when the Japanese handed them to him. He was indeed a pathetic little figure still in his twenties.[1]

The "emperor" invited recognition by the governments of the world and obviously had no trouble persuading Japan. Salvador, which was annoyed with the U.S. attitude toward the recognition of its own government, to spite the United States, recognized the Japanese puppet. As part of the diplomatic maneuvering leading up to the outbreak of World War II, Italy, Germany and Hungary recognized it in 1938 and 1939. The Soviet Union made, with Japanese delegates purporting to represent the puppet regime, a deal for the sale of the Chinese Eastern Railway in 1935, and the agreement was initialed in Tokyo with Japan guaranteeing Manchukuo's performance of its obligations. As will be seen, the rest of the world, resisting Japanese expansion, abided by the nonrecognition policy.

I have leapt ahead of the story to characterize the bastardy of Manchukuo but now return to a complicated background. It is a bit of history which takes one back before the birth of the United Nations into the days of the League of Nations, from which the United States, in its anti-Wilsonian isolationism, stood aloof but which it found it could not ignore. It will help to understand the situation if we digress into an exposition of the early relations, or the absence thereof, between Washington and Geneva. We shall be dealing with what I may call the multiple birth of the whole League of Nations, the idealogic progenitor of the United Nations. Then we may trace the origins of that illegitimate child, Manchukuo, and the efforts of the United States, partly through the League, to establish its illegitimation.

The birth certificate of the League of Nations is the Covenant incorporated in the Treaty of Versailles that established the peace at the end of World War I. The Treaty came into force January 10, 1920, which may be called the birthday of the first permanent international organization designed to eliminate war.

President Woodrow Wilson was the prime advocate of the League of Nations and was responsible—by which I mean deserves the credit—for its existence. The United States Senate was largely responsible, i.e., deserves the blame, for the American rejection of membership in the League.*

Despite American aloofness, the League of Nations existed in Geneva. It was probably true at first that the State Department had not decided how to deal with the League. In such a

---

* Wilson's unreasonable obstinacy during his illness indeed contributed to the rejection of American membership, which might have been obtained with some reservations.

situation the general diplomatic rule is to do nothing. I doubt whether there was in the State Department any deliberate attempt to injure the League. The shift to a rather pleasant cooperative attitude, at least on technical matters, was actually fairly rapid as such matters go. But senatorial opposition remained, and Warren G. Harding was certainly not the President to assert the executive prerogative in foreign affairs, nor was Calvin Coolidge who, according to Elihu Root, did not have an international hair in his head.

In his first message to Congress on April 12, 1921, President Harding stated that "in the existing League of Nations, world-governing with its superpowers, this Republic will have no part." Necessarily, Secretary of State Hughes and the State Department took this theme as a general guide. No one knew as yet to what extent the other governments of the world would do the world's business through the League. But within a year's time, the State Department found that there were new methods of diplomacy. Many of the statesmen who counted were meeting regularly at Geneva and were discussing and deciding there questions in which we had a keen interest. For some time we tried to carry on parallel discussions with individual governments in every continent but our method was less efficient and we were missing out. We did arrange and conduct the Washington Conference on Limitation of Armaments in 1921–1922 without foundering on snags but other issues could not thus be disposed of. Sir Eric Drummond, the Secretary-General of the League, naturally sought to obtain the cooperation of the United States to the greatest possible degree; Secretary of State Hughes just as naturally maintained a large degree of aloof reserve. It was unfortunate and disadvantageous, but it was not surprising after the American rejection of the League Covenant and Harding's election.

When Joseph C. Grew arrived in Berne as Minister to Switzerland in 1921, he was directed in his first instruction to obtain all League of Nations printed material affecting directly or indirectly the interests of the United States and its citizens.

So hypnotized was the Administration by the irreconcilables in the Senate, however, that Grew's contact with the League had to be practically on the level of espionage. His instruction was confidential. He was to send documents under cover of a confidential dispatch for the eyes only of the Secretary and Under Secretary. In fact, so secretive was his mission that Grew felt obliged to conceal from the State Department's own Bureau of Accounts the fact that he hired extra clerks to handle League materials.[2]

Some fifteen years later, a Department officer seeking League documents was finally informed by a little old lady in the Division of Communications and Records: "Oh yes, we've been getting those documents for years, but since they come in single copy I'm always careful to put them straight into the files without sending them to anyone."

Grew's principal contacts with the League were two Americans on the Secretariat, Huntington Gilchrist and Arthur Sweetser. Grew had known Gilchrist at the Paris Peace Conference and it was Gilchrist who procured League documents for him. "Grew would meet Sweetser either in the privacy of Princess Ella Radziwill's apartment, which he called his 'League of Nations Office,' or for walks along the Quai Mont Blanc where Sweetser 'crammed' him full of the latest League news." But Grew visited Geneva infrequently and briefly and even felt he was taking a risk when he extended Sweetser's passport!

It seems to be widely assumed that the State Department in the 1920s under Secretary Hughes made a point of being discourteous to the League, or of ignoring it as an adult may ignore a child. The chief count in the indictment is that communications from the League were left unanswered for six months or more and then were answered brusquely. The charge, if true, would be significant only if the League were singled out for this rude treatment. If one peruses the diplomatic correspondence in *Foreign Relations of the United States* from 1921 through 1924, one frequently is struck by the curt and chilly tone of communications to various and sundry governments. Perhaps it was not abnormally so and it is a mistake to let an image of Mr. Hughes's cold austerity explain the phrasing of all the notes; in the normal course, few would actually have been composed by the Secretary himself, although they went out over his signature. In some of the notes to Sir Eric Drummond, the Secretary-General of the League, one can find some of the most honeyed phrases of diplomacy, while some communications to the friendly British government are as curt as the form book permits. In both relationships, delays in handling correspondence were commonplace. Nor were American citizens immune from departmental delays. The Department at this time was solicitously watching out for the interests of American oil companies, but a letter of May 12, 1921, from the Sinclair Oil Corporation was "lost" in the Department files and no answer was sent until September, when a copy was brought to the Department by a representative of the company. A letter from Thomas W. Lamont of J. P. Morgan and Company, written in Lamont's capacity as Chairman of the International Committee of Bankers on Mexico, was "lost" in the State Department in 1921.

January 16, 1922, the Italian government invited the United States to attend an economic and financial conference scheduled to meet at Genoa on March 8. This conference was arranged by the Allied governments and not by the League. On February 26, the United States had not replied but received word from the Italian government that the meeting had been postponed. On March 8, Hughes answered that the conference appeared to be chiefly political; "This Government cannot be unmindful of the clear conviction of the American people, while desirous, as has been abundantly demonstrated, suitably to assist in the recovery of the economic life of Europe, that they should not unnecessarily become involved in European political questions." The invitation was accordingly declined but our ambassador in Rome was authorized to go to Genoa as an observer "to keep your Government informed, as far as possible, of what transpires."

Hughes's early attitude toward the League was made clear in

an informal and confidential conversation with French Ambassador Jules Jusserand and former Premier René Viviani at the State Department on March 30, 1921. Viviani suggested that if the American objections to the League related only to Article X (which contained a guaranty of the territorial integrity of all the members) they could easily be met. In Viviani's "personal opinion, Article X was perfectly valueless and unimportant." "Secretary Hughes replied that the Peace Conference had departed from the original idea of the League of Nations by making it not only an instrument for conference and conciliation, . . . but also by charging it with certain definite duties in connection with the enforcement of the terms of the Treaty." He said that "the opposition of the American people to the League had grown after seeing it in operation," and mentioned as an example, the action of the League Council in disturbing mandates "not only without the consent, but over the formal protest of the United States."[3] Nevertheless, as time went on, Hughes and his successors found that the interests of the United States required it to deal with the League, even if it did so through devious and inefficient channels.

In regard to disarmament, the United States captured the initiative by convening a conference in Washington in 1921. The motivation was to give some demonstration of devotion to the principle of international cooperation in the cause of peace which had been advocated by the thirty-one prominent Republicans who had signed an appeal to pro-League Republican voters to support Harding for the presidency. It was the same Republican attitude which in 1928 blossomed into the conclusion of the Pact of Paris—the Kellogg-Briand Pact for the Renunciation of War as an Instrument of National Policy. Senator William Borah, archfoe of the League of Nations, in 1920 introduced in the Senate a resolution urging the President to invite Great Britain and Japan to a conference for limiting naval armament. The resolution passed the Senate by a vote of 74 to 0 and the House by 332 votes to 4 in the early summer of 1921. Hughes insisted on including France and Italy in the invitations. The American proposal coincided with a British inquiry about U.S. participation in a conference with Japan and China to discuss the problems of the Far East. The British yielded the initiative when Hughes broadened the agenda of the Washington Conference to include both limitation of naval armaments and Far Eastern questions; [4] this enlarged agenda gave Britain the opportunity to sound out the American attitude toward the pending renewal of the Anglo-Japanese treaty of 1902.

This account is not concerned with the results of the Washington Conference or of the abortive tripartite naval conference in Geneva in 1927 or the London naval conference of 1930, except to note that Secretary of State Stimson participated in the last of these meetings and thus had a firsthand introduction to some of the European problems, particularly the Franco-Italian rivalry. It was also at London that he formed his favorable impression of the Japanese "liberals" like Baron Kijuro Shidehara; within two years Stimson was obliged to wage a campaign for nonrecognition of the bastard Manchukuo.

Full cooperation with the League on disarmament and other matters would have been generally advantageous, but it was a period of tentative advances. Lord Robert Cecil, a most enthusiastic and effective British supporter of the League, wrote rather too optimistically to Chief Justice William Howard Taft, in November 1922. Lord Robert thought that "at the present moment the United States was entering into the phase of executive cooperation with the League of Nations." He anticipated the eventual extension of this cooperation and added "just a word of most profound gratification that this happy solution has now been achieved."

In February 1924, American Minister Joseph Grew in Switzerland was authorized to attend a meeting of the League's Temporary Mixed Commission, which was then studying the traffic in arms. While he was attending these meetings and taking an active part in them, the Secretary of State cabled him on

February 7, 1924: "It has been stated in four reports that you have indicated that this Government's basic objection was to the proposal to vest administrative control in the League of Nations. This is incorrect." He said administration by the League would cause difficulties for the United States but that this administrative problem should not be allowed to block the elaboration of a satisfactory convention.[5]

All in all, one cannot say in retrospect that the record of American relations with the League from 1921 on is admirable. Reviewing the record at the end of 1929, Elihu Root asked:

Has there ever been an exhibition by America of friendship [for the League] or sympathy with its work? . . . It came to be a common thing that we should read in the newspapers and hear in speech and conversation expressions of expectation that the League would fail, and evident pleasure when it seemed that it might fail.[6]

Raymond Fosdick, who had been selected by Sir Eric Drummond in 1919 as one of two Under Secretaries-General, and who remained after his resignation in 1920 perhaps the leading American advocate of the League, blasted the policies of Secretary Hughes in a letter to the New York *Times* on October 19, 1924, in which he wrote:

It is all very well for Mr. Hughes to say that we are not a member of the League of Nations, and that he has no authority to act as if we were. The point is whether in spite of our non-membership . . . we have to treat the League with cavalier contempt just to prove that we do not belong to it. Do expediency and party loyalty justify a Secretary of State in playing hide-and-seek with an agency which is working for the world's peace? [7]

Moreover, the United States suffered from its own policy as much as did the League. Time and again we found ourselves ill-informed and at a distinct disadvantage because on matters with which we were much concerned we had to obtain our information belatedly and by devious routes. We were similarly ill-served in regard to Russian affairs during the long period of nonrecognition from 1918 until 1933.

It may be well to note here in passing that it is a mistake to think of the United States as isolated from Europe and the rest of the overseas world during the Harding and Coolidge administrations. As will be made apparent, we were in the thick of it, our fingers deep in some of the most political pies of the European and Asian powers. For all of those issues there were officers in the State Department whose particular responsibility it was to watch relations with and of each of the countries involved. But unlike the period after 1945, there was no senior official whose business it was to specialize on the international organization itself and our relations to it. Moreover, for our relations with various foreign powers we had our resident embassies and legations who reported and interpreted regularly. During the 1920s we had no comparable permanent representative reporting on the League of Nations from Geneva; our Minister to Switzerland was in Berne and our other representatives were *ad hoc*. We got most of our information from Arthur Sweetser of the League Secretariat. Hugh Gibson, at the legation in Berne, referred to Geneva as "Sweetserland."

Nevertheless, in 1924 and 1925, the staff of the American consulate in Geneva was supplemented by two junior officers who were sent with the express mission of picking up any useful scraps of information. Their arrival with fresh instructions was revolutionary for the Consul, William Haskell, who had been instructed to keep clear of the League. Haskell took this instruction seriously and stayed at the consulate on the Rue Petitot across the Rhone from the seat of the League. The new arrivals were Pinkney (commonly known as "Kippy") Tuck and Stanley Woodward. They were encouraged to establish social relations with people at the League and began reporting directly to the Department. Both of them from time to time attended meetings such as those on the opium traffic but only with the rather ignominious title of "unofficial observer," which meant that they were not allowed to speak at the meetings.[8]

It was not until the 1930s that the Assistant Chief of the

Western European Office in the Department, Prentiss Gilbert, was sent to Geneva with the rank of Consul and with the task of keeping track of League affairs for Secretary of State Stimson. The announcement of his appointment was called by the opposition press in the United States a "Wilsonian delusion" and a "sample of nit-wit diplomacy," but there was no dissent in the Senate.[9]

Apparently it was at about that time that the Department set up a separate "League of Nations Desk," comparable to the "desks" for various countries which were the smallest units within the geographical "divisions." The League Desk, camouflaged for political safety as dealing with European organizations, had been handled by Gilbert as a subdivision of the Western Europe branch; it was later manned by Noel Field, a man of considerable eccentric brilliance, who had passed the Foreign Service examinations in 1926 and whom Gilbert had rescued from some humble role in the library of the Department. Field's future mysterious career was not anticipated in 1930.[10] On January 22, 1932, Field drafted a memorandum which the Office of Western European Affairs sent to Under Secretary William R. Castle, weighing the relative advantages of having Wilson or Gilbert observe a session of the League Council. It was noted that Wilson would soon be coming from Berne to Geneva to attend a meeting of the Disarmament Conference; the nuance seems to have been that while Wilson should be regarded as the principal representative available in Switzerland, Gilbert had done "excellent reporting" and could be counted on to continue to do so as the Council met.

THE SPAWNING OF MANCHUKUO:
THE FAR EASTERN CRISIS
OF 1931–1932

When Henry L. Stimson came to Washington as Secretary of State in late March 1929, "there still hung over America the

fog of isolationism that had been created when the warm idealism of Wilson crashed against the cold nationalism of Brandegee and Lodge." [11] As Stimson acknowledged, he was new to
the general field of foreign policy, but he was destined to be
the central figure in the evolution of our contacts with the
League. His first Under Secretary was Joseph P. Cotton, an
outstanding lawyer and delightful individual, intolerant of protocol, who was recommended by Felix Frankfurter and whose
relations with Stimson were of closest friendship. Stimson
could depend absolutely on Cotton, and rightfully so, although
Cotton also was inexperienced in foreign policy. When Cotton
died suddenly in 1931, he was replaced by William R. Castle,
who was President Hoover's choice for the position. Castle had
the experience in foreign affairs but lacked the personality to
become one to whom Stimson felt close or in whom he placed
full confidence. Stimson's own additional choices were persons
close to him but without broad international experience. Allen
Klots was a brilliant junior partner in Stimson's New York law
office. Harvey Bundy was a Boston lawyer with interests in financial matters. James Grafton Rogers came close to filling Cotton's place at Stimson's side, but again was not an international
specialist. Perhaps the most skillful of his selected aides was
Herbert Feis, who stayed on also in the next administration to
serve as the Department's Economic Adviser. But both Harvey
Bundy and Feis were chosen after men closer to Stimson had
declined appointments.

McGeorge Bundy gives a clear picture of the differences of
temperament and outlook which kept Stimson and Hoover
from forming a completely sympathetic team like that which
existed between Root and Roosevelt or Acheson and Truman.
Stimson was always loyal, and when necessary subordinate, but
the two men were not *simpatico*.

It is pertinent to refer even so briefly to these interpersonal
relationships when examining the handling of the Far Eastern
crisis of 1931–1932 which resulted from Japan's sudden mili-

tary aggression in Manchuria. Although Stimson had been in London for the 1930 naval conference, and again in 1931, he had no real personal intimacy with the European leaders of the League of Nations who were the "friends" with whom he had to seek to find a coordinated policy. Stimson did not have the intellectual agility of Root or Acheson or Dulles that enabled them to shift rapidly from one problem to another as a Secretary of State must do and, in the Far Eastern crisis, he tried to do much that he should have left to his staff.

In the midst of the Far Eastern crisis, on October 17, 1931, Stanley Hornbeck, the brilliant Chief of the Far Eastern Bureau in the State Department, wrote Secretary Stimson a personal letter which has a distinctly fatherly tone, warning the Secretary that he had been working under great pressure and cautioning against hasty decisions.

By way of conserving your energies and safeguarding yourself against being pushed too fast either by the disputants or by the League, may I suggest that you impose upon your staff more of the responsibility and accountability for initiative and execution in relations to this matter. And, may I suggest that, as (a) we are probably going to be in action for weeks and months to come on this "case," and (b) there may at any time come new periods of special stress, you give thought to (1) the conservation of the energy of your shock troops and (2) the establishing and maintenance of "reserves."

In the end, Stimson's failure to persuade President Hoover to accept his rather strong verbal militancy in dealing with Japan was frustrating. Stimson had the reputation of being a man with drive, eager to push to a decision without too much cautious preplanning, but he hesitated to grasp firmly the League of Nations nettle. Writing about the Far Eastern crisis in 1936, however, Stimson concluded:

. . . to the League Covenant, although a proponent, we are not a party. Nevertheless that League today remains the medium by which the great majority of the governments of the world seek to limit and prevent a general war and our relations to it in such a matter are therefore of vital concern both to it and to us. The development of effective methods of cooperation between it and us is an underlying international problem of the most urgent importance in the world today. It pressed upon us in regard to Manchuria in 1931; it pressed upon us in regard to Ethiopia in 1935; it has not yet been adequately solved.[12]

It never was solved until the United Nations had succeeded the League.

However, as noted, in June 1930, Prentiss Gilbert was appointed Consul in Geneva, and was given new and larger quarters and able assistants. Gilbert himself was a man of remarkable talents, and three of those who served under him in Geneva became top-rank ambassadors—James Riddleberger, "Tommy" Thompson, and Jacob Beam. But Gilbert had only consular rank and was undercut by Hugh Wilson, the U.S. Minister in Berne, who was jealous of Gilbert's independence and skill. Arthur Sweetser, the ranking American citizen in the Secretariat of the League, and the principal contact between Geneva and Washington until Gilbert arrived, did not ignore or seek to supplant Gilbert as did Hugh Wilson. Wilson's published memoirs are well indexed, but the names of Gilbert and Sweetser are not included nor is the name of Stanley Hornbeck, the influential Chief of FE during the Manchurian crisis when Wilson purported to be an important figure dealing with that crisis in Geneva.

Prentiss Gilbert, who was to become our closest and most effective contact with the League at Geneva, stood out from among his fellow officials in Washington and in Geneva because of his unusual background which included: teen-age soldiering in the Philippines, where he nearly died of tropical diseases which left him with a permanent lameness; beachcombing; and puckish humor.[13] In the State Department in 1924 I knew him as a kindred spirit with Harry Dwight, who had accepted the post of Librarian of the Department, who had keys made to a locked door in that library and found a large collection of erotica left by one of his predecessors, who rummaged in the vast cellars where he discovered hitherto unknown historic documents and mementos, who, as author, described the monuments which adorn(?) the parks in our Capital in an article entitled "The Horrors of Washington," who published excellent books of short stories, and who became curator of the Frick Collection in New York.

What a refreshing pair they made among the old-line bureaucrats! At Geneva, that cradle of rumors, Gilbert invented a "rumor testing machine." The temporary League Assembly building was very long and narrow. Gilbert would station the members of his staff at fixed intervals along the corridor with synchronized watches. Then he would come in at one end and start a rumor. The staff would report the time and form in which they heard it. As Gilbert expected, the results were usually startling.[14] In his excellent reporting to the Department, he could separate rumors from actualities or appraise the probabilities that the rumor was founded in fact.

September 19, 1931, brought the news that the Japanese army had occupied Mukden and other cities in South Manchuria. Two days later, China, which had just been elected a member of the Council of the League, appealed to the Council to act under Article XI of the Covenant to prevent further developments endangering international peace and to restore the *status quo ante*.

The United States and Japan were parties to two treaties which Japan was flouting. One was the Nine Power Treaty concluded at the Washington Conference of 1921 to "respect the sovereignty, the independence, and the territorial and administrative integrity of China." The other was the much-touted Kellogg-Briand Treaty for the Renunciation of War as an Instrument of National Policy, concluded in 1928. The problem was seen by Stimson to be to protect American interests in the Far East without acting under the Covenant conjointly with the members of the League of Nations and without pushing Japan to extremes. Stimson had consulted with the major powers in 1929 and had secured an invocation of the Kellogg pact when China and Russia seemed to be on the brink of hostilities. More than forty signatories joined in those representations but Japan held aloof, and the Soviet Union snubbed the United States which had refused to grant it recognition.

In the State Department in 1931, the Bureau of Far Eastern Affairs was strongly manned, but in the first weeks of the Manchurian crisis, Stimson ran the show.[15] Stimson believed that he knew "the Oriental mind" and he trusted the Japanese moderates. He wanted "to let the Japanese know we are watching them and at the same time to do it in a way which will help Shidehara [the Japanese Foreign Minister], who is on the right side, and not play into the hands of any Nationalist agitators."[16] Under Secretary Castle shared Stimson's approach, but Hornbeck's leanings were toward China, and at first he tried to persuade Stimson and Castle to denounce Japan. His first memorandum to Stimson on September 20, however, was moderate. He began:

I regret to have to report that in my opinion the action of the Japanese military forces in Manchuria constitutes a violation of the Kellogg Pact, . . .

But it was Hornbeck's feeling

that we should not, as on our initiative, invoke or refer to the Kellogg Pact . . . That question, whether the Kellogg Pact has or has not been violated, is one which might, it seems to me, very well be brought to the World Court. China and Japan are both parties to the World Court arrangements. If the course followed by the Japanese Government in the handling of the situation . . . proves unsatisfactory to the Chinese (or to the world) the case might well, it seems to me, be carried by the Chinese Government to the Court.

Hornbeck did not seem to be aware that the World Court had no compulsory jurisdiction and that Japan could not be hailed into Court without its consent; China had indeed deposited a declaration accepting the Court's jurisdiction but Japan had not. China might have urged the Council of the League to request the Court to give an advisory opinion on the question but this apparently was not what Hornbeck—or, one may add, the Council—had in mind.

Nelson Johnson, U.S. Minister in Peking, had no doubts about the violation of the Treaty. He cabled on September 22, 1931, that Japan had clearly violated the Kellogg Pact which "was a solemn undertaking on the part of the nations of the West and those nations now stand at the bar of the nations of the East to answer for their sincerity." Johnson thought that "the powers signatory to the Kellogg Treaty owe it to themselves and to the world to pronounce themselves in regard to this Japanese act of aggression."

On September 22 also, Hornbeck's assistant, Ransford Miller, noting that both the League and the Chinese government had inquired about the applicability of the treaties to which the United States was a party, thought that we should indicate that the spirit "if not the terms" of both the Nine Power Treaty and the Kellogg Pact had been violated and that the United States should act "as far as possible, in harmony with the League of Nations."

On Sunday, September 20, Stimson sent Hornbeck to call on the Japanese ambassador in Washington and on the following Tuesday Stimson himself talked at length with the ambassador, who expressed his own surprise and consternation at the events in Manchuria. The Secretary of State read to him a memorandum which had been preprepared indicating our friendship for Japan, our concern at the recent developments which created a situation

of concern, morally, legally, and politically to a considerable number of nations. It is not exclusively a matter of concern to Japan and China. It brings into question at once the meaning of certain provisions of agreements, such as the Nine Powers [sic] Treaty . . . and the Kellogg-Briand Pact.

Prentiss Gilbert was reporting all the details by telegrams from Geneva. On September 23 he cabled that

the Chinese representative has stated privately that China did not desire to invoke the Kellogg Pact because for technical reasons China did not wish by inference to admit the existence of a "state of war" which the provisions of the Kellogg Pact is understood to envisage.

Hornbeck reported to Castle and Stimson that this position was easy to understand because a "war" would be ended only by a peace treaty, the terms of which would be dictated by the stronger power. Stimson accepted this position and concluded that when the United States acted under the Kellogg Pact, it should not invoke the first article which contains the renunciation of war, but only the second article which states the obligation to settle all disputes by peaceful means.[17]

On September 22 the President of the League Council sent identical telegrams to China and Japan appealing for a peaceful settlement and the withdrawal of troops. The United States backed this up with similar messages but asked only that they refrain from hostilities, not that they withdraw their troops, but that they observe treaty obligations. The Chinese Foreign Office expressed surprise that the United States did not mention the Nine Power Treaty or the Kellogg Pact. On September 30, the Council adopted a resolution which committed the Japanese to a troop withdrawal.

Meanwhile, Stimson received a telephone call from Norman Davis in Geneva. Davis was a Wilsonian internationalist who played an important part, especially in disarmament matters, during the 1920s and 1930s. Davis told Stimson the United States now had a prime opportunity to cooperate with the League in maintaining or restoring international peace. He urged Stimson to have an American representative sit with the

Council; Stimson said this was impossible when the League was acting under the Covenant, but if the League could not cope with the Manchurian crisis, the United States might join other powers in invoking the Kellogg Pact or the Nine Power Treaty.[18]

In the first week of October the news from the Far East was highly disturbing. The Japanese military were not being deterred by admonitions or appeals, although the creation of "Manchukuo" was still to come. Hornbeck was writing daily memoranda to Secretary Stimson warning that the League might try to throw the whole problem into the lap of the United States. He believed some affirmative step was necessary and suggested that it could be proposed to the governments of Japan and China that they negotiate in the presence of observers from the states parties to the Nine Power Treaty. But "Such a suggestion, if made, should emanate from and appear to have originated in the Council of the League." This suited Stimson's book and on October 10, the day after he had made a full report to the Cabinet, he had a long talk with President Hoover, "whose mind up to that time had been so preoccupied with the financial crisis at home that necessarily he had been able to give but little thought to Manchuria." Now at last, Stimson records, Hoover "plunged vigorously and sympathetically into my problem" and approved the idea of a joint session with the League but centered on the Kellogg Pact.[19]

Then ensued a series of trans-Atlantic telephone conversations which are not lacking in comic elements but which do reveal the personalities of Stimson and Prentiss Gilbert and the difficulties of communicating without misunderstanding. At a later phase during 1932 and 1933, Stimson negotiated by telephone with Sir John Simon, British Foreign Secretary, and the misunderstandings were serious. According to Morison, one reason for the misunderstandings was

static on the telephone, for another the Secretary of State was never at his clearest in oral exchanges, especially in oral exchanges by wire, and for still another each man brought to the conversations somewhat different intentions blurred around the edges by somewhat similar hopes.[20]

Hugh Wilson, Minister to Switzerland, recorded that Sir John Simon used to tell him what had been said in these conversations but the State Department did not tell Wilson its side of the story and Wilson did not report what Sir John told him. Wilson, the career diplomat, thought that

the telephone between two responsible statesmen is a method of communication which is fraught with danger. Few men in the world are able to think rapidly enough or accurately enough in matters involving war and peace to take the immediate decisions that a telephone conversation calls for. Messages of this importance should be carefully drafted, experts in both Foreign Offices should go over them thoroughly.[21]

Stanley Hornbeck and Prentiss Gilbert were close friends and it is probable that Hornbeck drafted the telegram which was sent to Gilbert on the evening of October 20:

Department appreciates the pressure under which you and your staff are laboring, but suggests that in telephoning to the Secretary you confine the calls and the subject matter to most urgent matters only, avoid matters which can await treatment by exchange of cables, and make your statements as concise as possible. You will realize that it is desirable in connection with most questions of policy to allow more time for consideration than is possible in the course of the give-and-take of a telephone conversation and that the Secretary does not desire to have to make comments or commitments with regard to such matters on the basis of and during their oral communication to him.[22]

In the telephone conversation of October 12, Under Secretary Castle sat in with Stimson and occasionally put in a word. The conversation did not begin auspiciously. Gilbert in Geneva asked whether the Secretary clearly understood the information he had sent about Secretary-General Drummond's views on the application of the Kellogg Pact. Stimson could not remember any such message although the Department had asked Gilbert to ascertain Drummond's views and Gilbert had replied fully on October 11. Gilbert said Drummond doubted the applicability of the Kellogg Pact and said that its invocation would bring in new issues. Stimson told him he had telegraphed his policy of cooperation with the League; the United States was not itself invoking the Pact lest it cross wires with the League. Then came the historic decision: "You are authorized if invited to join in the meeting with the Council to discuss the whole matter of the application of the Kellogg Pact." The United States would not act alone "certainly at present; if any action is taken on the Kellogg Pact it should be taken by all or the great majority of the signatories in the way in which it was invoked two years ago." Stimson told Gilbert that since the principal powers signatory to the Pact would be meeting in the Council, Gilbert could discuss those matters with them there. But "We do not want you to discuss questions which are peculiar to the League, such as questions of sanctions."

Prentiss Gilbert was a positive character and was quite ready to argue with his chief. Stimson has described himself when he was Governor General of the Philippines as "an Oriental Potentate . . . all I have to do is express a wish and it is taken as the law of the Medes and Persians." Gilbert had seen military service in the Philippines as a young man but not under Colonel Stimson; in Geneva he was loyal to his chief but evidently felt that the Secretary did not fully appreciate the workings of the minds of the principal characters in the League. Indeed Stimson, although constantly insisting that the League must act independently, at times was impatient at its failure to agree with every point he made.

As the telephone conversation of October 12 continued, Stimson refused to authorize Gilbert to let Drummond pass on to the members of the Council the information which the United States was getting from its representatives in the Far East, which Gilbert had been authorized to give to Drummond

in confidence, and which was considered more informative
than that available in Geneva from any other source. As Gilbert argued about the procedure in the Council, Stimson said:

You are trying to unite the powers not on the treaties but on us. I
am very much disappointed. I feel that Drummond is afraid of the
Kellogg Pact. I do not share in this.

Gilbert: I am giving you Drummond's views.

Stimson: I think he is wrong. I think it is time for the Kellogg
Pact to come in but it must be brought in at the meeting of the
League and not by us coming in from outside.

Gilbert: If the big show is not put on now, they feel the situation
will get out of hand and the Japanese will think they have America
coming in with them.

Stimson: I think the big show should be the Kellogg Pact. I
think Drummond's timidity on that is likely to wreck the whole
thing. . . .

Gilbert: I am only expressing to you what is represented to me
here.

Stimson: Express my views with equal clearness to them.

Reverting to the question of Gilbert's sitting with the Council, Stimson told him to let him know at once when he was invited since he could not give out the information in Washington
until he knew the invitation had been issued. Gilbert asked for
"full instructions how to act" when the time came. Stimson said
the telephone conversation constituted his instructions: "You
are to participate in the discussion so far as it relates to the
Kellogg Pact and not the rest."

Parenthetically, it may be remarked that I do not know to
what extent trans-Atlantic telephone messages in 1931 were "secure." In regard to the coded messages telegraphed from the
State Department, Hornbeck warned more than once that he
was quite sure the Japanese had broken the code and knew just
what we were confidentially telling our representatives in the
Far East and in Geneva.

The Council of the League reconvened on October 13 under
the presidency of Aristide Briand, the co-author with Secretary

Kellogg of the Kellogg-Briand Pact. Briefed by Gilbert, Briand on October 16 sent to Stimson a carefully phrased message which emphasized Article 2 of the Pact, concerning peaceful settlement, and avoided mention of Article 1, which would have raised the issue whether China and Japan were at war. He said he spoke for his colleagues in inviting the United States to be associated with their efforts by sending a representative to sit at the Council table to discuss how the Pact could best be applied. Stimson in his book *The Far Eastern Crisis* prints the invitation *in toto* and says that on October 16 he authorized Gilbert to sit at the Council table; he does not mention the telephone conversation of October 12 or many other communications.

Meanwhile further phone talks and telegrams went back and forth between Gilbert and Stimson. On October 13, before the Briand invitation was received, Gilbert pressed the Secretary for the text of the statement he was to make when he took his seat. Stimson wondered if there would be time to draft and send it, but this was done. On October 13, Stimson in a Cabinet meeting was handed a telegram from Gilbert, saying he had made some changes to meet developments in Geneva. Stimson was upset and telephoned Gilbert he was worried; he hoped Gilbert had kept the essentials of the statement sent to him. Gilbert telegraphed his new text. Whosever text it was, Stimson refers to it in his book as having been expressed "in felicitous language."

On October 17, the members of the Council other than China and Japan decided to call the attention of those two governments to their obligations under Article 2 of the Pact. The French government undertook to notify the other signatories, including the United States. Stimson telegraphed this satisfactory development to President Hoover, who was then aboard a warship at Hampton Roads.

At this point Stimson's published account diverges from the official records printed in *Foreign Relations of the United*

States. Stimson does not mention the fact that Gilbert continued to attend a few secret meetings with Briand, British Foreign Secretary Lord Reading, and others.

According to the records, on October 19, Stimson told Gilbert on the telephone to withdraw from the secret meetings and to leak to the press the information that he had done so. In considerable alarm, Lord Reading phoned Stimson the same day saying that Gilbert's withdrawal at that moment might be "disastrous"; Briand might fall as Foreign Minister. Stimson replied that he was pressed by American public opinion but he yielded to Reading's request and telegraphed Gilbert he could attend one more secret meeting and then sit in the public session until after an expected Japanese statement and Gilbert's reply to that, after which he should move to the observer's seat where he and others who were not at the Council table customarily sat. Gilbert phoned Stimson again on October 20, explaining the feeling in Geneva about his withdrawing. Stimson, exasperated, confided to his diary:

. . . there came a telephone call from Geneva from Gilbert, bringing up again this infernal question of his seat at the table. Briand seemed to think that if we moved his seat from the table it would upset the whole stability of Europe, and then Gilbert read me a terribly long message from Briand on the subject . . . finally I decided that so long as Gilbert kept out of secret meetings . . . I would let him go on sitting at the damned table. He is, however, to keep his mouth shut.[23]

Stimson subsequently gave him permission, if Briand considered it best, to state that he had been called to Washington for "consultation." But Stimson said on the phone: "I am very busy. I am getting ready for the Laval visit" (the French Premier). It was then that the Department sent the telegram already quoted warning Gilbert not to telephone the Secretary unless absolutely necessary. On October 21, Stimson canceled the authorization to come to Washington. Gilbert reported on the Japanese statement and his reply, and on October 24 the

Secretary of State "directed" him to retire from his "temporary seat at the table of the Council"—a needless direction since the session was over.

It was earlier on this day, October 24, 1931, that the League Council voted 13 to 1 for another resolution which called upon the Japanese to withdraw their troops by November 16 when the Council was to meet again in Paris; it was Japan which cast the negative vote. Hornbeck and Stimson thought this time requirement was not wise, but Hornbeck told the Secretary that Briand and Reading were highly skilled in the arts of diplomacy and even if they were not very familiar with the Far East and the situation in Manchuria, they would handle the problem adroitly.

Stimson clearly found the situation at the end of October irritating. The moderate Japanese statesmen on whom he relied were not in control, the Japanese military were not being responsive to the world's moral reprobation on which he had relied, and the League had deviated from some of the proposals which he had favored. Stimson records that he told his Cabinet colleagues on November 17, 1931, that he foresaw that Japan would set up a puppet government under its control in Manchuria.[24] Three months later, February 18, 1932, "Manchukuo" was proclaimed.

I have no evidence that Stimson was dissatisfied with the way in which Gilbert had carried out his assignment but when the Council met in Paris on November 16, Stimson had decided that the United States should be

represented in our cooperation with the League at this meeting by the most prominent and experienced public man of whose services we could avail ourselves at this moment—our London ambassador, Charles G. Dawes, the former Vice-President of the United States. His instructions were similar to those given to Mr. Gilbert in October, except that it was left entirely to his discretion as to whether and when he should attend in person the actual meetings of the Council. In view of his prominence as a public man, I counted on his having easy opportunities for informal discussions with the representatives of other countries and at the same time I believed that his personality and reputation would do much to assure the people in this country of the importance of his work as well as the discretion with which he would carry it on. In both respects my anticipations were fulfilled.[25]

Gilbert already had the personal contacts but not the prestige at home. Dawes recounts that when he was attending the annual Lord Mayor's dinner at Guildhall and actually during the Prime Minister's speech, a note was handed to him saying that the Secretary of State wished to speak with him on the telephone on an urgent matter.[26] He does not say whether he waited until the speech was finished but the gist of the telephone conversation was repeated on November 10 in a confidential telegram. As the telegram was first drafted by Hornbeck, it stated "You will not sit as a member of the Council of the League . . ." but this was altered to read "It is not anticipated that you will find it necessary to attend the meetings of the Council. . . ." Stimson told Dawes: "I do not, repeat not, desire that the American Government be put in the position of instigator or initiator of League action; nor do I desire that we shall either push or lead in reference to this whole matter." Dawes should leave it to Briand to lead. In their first telephone talk, Stimson had said he had a "real he-man's job" for Dawes but definitely said he did not want him to go to the Council table since "a lot of people" in America had been scared by the ceremony and formality which attended Gilbert's appearance. Dawes agreed to "lay low." [27]

On the same day Hornbeck sent a memorandum to Under Secretary Castle recommending that Gilbert should be sent to Paris,

as a sort of "technical adviser" to Dawes. He has both the knowledge and the "feel" of what has transpired and would be able to give information with greater celerity and accuracy than would be possible for anyone else. Also, if he is left out of the matter entirely, it will mean that we unnecessarily subject our Consul at Geneva to a lot of loss of "face." (The implication would be that we are dissatisfied with his functioning up to date.)

Gilbert had been telegraphing almost daily from Geneva the course of the behind-the-scenes negotiations there. But Hornbeck's recommendation was not approved by Stimson. Castle replied that Dawes would decide whether he needed Gilbert but that in any case Gilbert ought not to go until after the first Council meeting. As in the earlier period of the 1920s, Arthur Sweetser, the leading American on the League Secretariat, served as the contact between Dawes and Drummond, as Dawes stayed in his suite in the Ritz Hotel in Paris. It was like those early days when Sweetser crammed Minister Grew full of League of Nations news in the apartment of Princess Radziwill. But Dawes was a very different type and Sweester long remembered his first interview at the Ritz when Dawes spat on the carpet and damned the League in unprintable language.

Dawes communicated directly and indirectly with the principal figures in Paris for the Council meeting. He stayed in Paris four weeks and records that his telegraphic exchanges with Washington during that period aggregated over 100,000 words, in addition to numerous telephone conversations with President Hoover and Secretary Stimson. Dawes described in his telephone talks with Stimson how all the principal characters came to his hotel room—not quite all, since Briand sent Massigli, but Drummond came and Sze for China and Matsudaira for Japan, and others. Dawes did not want to leave his room because he was telephoned so frequently.

In talking by telephone with Stimson on December 7, the Secretary of State (evidently thinking of their constant preoccupation with American isolationist criticism of dealing with the League) said "there is absolutely no criticism against you of doing too much. The only criticism that has been made at all has been by very zealous advocates of the League that you have been too much of a hermit. . . ." Dawes was to feel perfectly free to go around and talk to members of the Council. But Dawes replied: "If I run around making a spectacle of myself, I won't do any good. I think I had just better go along and do only what is proper to do instead of going to see people and making a show of it. The people watch me all the time."

"I am one hundred percent satisfied," replied Stimson, "but I wanted you to know that in case it becomes necessary in your opinion to fly around a little more, do not hesitate to do it." Neither Stimson nor Dawes correctly estimated the positions of Briand or Sir John Simon of England, as Gilbert would have done.

On December 10, 1931, the Council of the League, with the assent of the Japanese representative, passed the resolution for the creation of the Lytton Commission of investigation on which they had all been consulting, and Dawes reported the fact to Stimson on the phone. Amid a welter of misunderstandings and contradictions, Dawes did an about-face and told Sweetser he would appear at the Council's table and make a statement. Dawes's automobile was waiting at the door of the Ritz with its motor running when Stimson got through to Dawes on the telephone forbidding his to make such an appearance. When Sweetser, moments later, told Dawes on the phone that all was ready, Dawes replied, "Get off that phone, you son of a bitch, and tell them I'm not coming."

Stimson made a statement in Washington describing the nature of our cooperation as signatory to the Kellogg Pact and to the Nine Power Treaty. The United States consented to the service of General Frank McCoy of the American Army on the Lytton Commission (provided for in the resolution) to go to Manchuria and to keep the Council informed of developments there.

The day after the League decided to set up its Lytton Commission of inquiry, the Japanese cabinet was driven from office and Stimson's last hopes, which had been centered on Baron Shidehara, were shattered. As Dorothy Borg writes, in this second phase of the crisis "Secretary of State Stimson was to seize the initiative which he had so far insisted belonged to the League." [28] But when the League Council reconvened in January 1932, there was inconclusive discussion in the Department on the question whether Wilson or Gilbert should observe and report; no active role was contemplated for any U.S. representative except General McCoy.

With a political-obstetrical prescience, Secretary Stimson had forecast the birth of a Japanese puppet in Manchuria. With President Hoover's agreement (and perhaps in response to Hoover's suggestion) [29] Stimson on January 7, 1932, delivered to the Japanese ambassador in Washington a note that in diplomatic and legal language warned the Japanese that the United States would not admit the legality of any situation created in China in violation of the rights of the United States under various treaties. Thus was Manchukuo bastardized before its birth by what has come to be known as the Stimson nonrecognition doctrine.

The British government did not choose to endorse the diagnosis or the warning. As the London *Times* wrote editorially on January 11: "the American Government may have been moved by the fear that the Japanese authorities would set up a virtually independent administration in Manchuria which would favor Japanese interests. . . . It is clear that the (British) Foreign Office does not share these apprehensions."

Perhaps the British, with their closer ties to Japan, thought that they might be able to deal advantageously even with an illegitimate puppet.

Possibly encouraged by the lack of unanimity among the Western powers, the dominant Japanese military brought about the unity which Stimson could not evoke. The Japanese attack on Shanghai with its heavy bombardment and the shelling of Nanking, coupled with the heroic and unexpected defense put up by the Chinese forces, turned the tide. On March 7, 1932, the British proposed to the Assembly of the League of

Nations the adoption of a resolution closely paralleling the Stimson note of January 7; it was "incumbent upon the Members of the League of Nations not to recognize any situation, treaty or agreement which may be brought about by means contrary to the Covenant of the League of Nations or to the Pact of Paris." The resolution was passed unanimously in the Assembly on January 11, China and Japan not voting.

Japanese military measures had succeeded in conquering Manchuria but its further military excursions against China had not lived up to Tokyo's expectations. It was then that they delivered their puppet Manchukuo on February 18, 1932, with the boy-"emperor" Pu-yi rising rapidly from its cradle to its throne. The four states (in addition to Japan) that recognized Manchukuo, namely El Salvador, Germany, Italy, and Hungary, had all withdrawn from membership in the League, but it is unlikely that the Assembly's resolution of January 11, 1932, would have restrained them if they had still remained members of the League.

If Japan and its European allies had won World War II, international politics being what they are, Manchukuo would have been legitimated. But since the need for its artificial personality would have evaporated, Manchuria as a whole might have been incorporated into the Japanese empire just as Korea had been annexed. Puppets are very likely to be the victims of infanticide.[30]

Epilogue

Writing, like painting, is, or ought to be, an art form. If a reader of this book tells me in mournful numbers that I seem to aspire to be, as it were, a Jackson Pollock dribbling blobs of recollection across the pages of history, I would have to confess that I am not very fond of Jackson Pollock's canvases. But I might remark that while one cannot take and reuse a blob of paint from a canvas, one can recycle an incident, an anecdote, a quotation, from a printed page.

Notes

1. INTRODUCTORY

1. Dean Acheson, "Philip C. Jessup, Diplomatist," Introduction to *Transnational Law in a Changing Society: Essays in Honor of Philip C. Jessup*, Wolfgang G. Friedmann, Lewis Henkin, and Oliver Lissitzyn, eds. (New York, Columbia University Press, 1972).

2. I confess I was not familiar with "prosopography" until I read Arthur Schlesinger, Jr. in "The Historian as Participant", *Daedalus* (Spring 1971), pp. 339 and 345. And I hope I do not commit the sin described by G. M. Young when he said that "the greater part of what passes for diplomatic history is little more than the record of what one clerk said to another clerk" (quoted from Gordon A. Craig, "PoliticalHistory," *ibid.*, pp. 323 and 327).

3. The functioning of delegations in the UN General Assembly has been well described especially in chapter 6 of Richard F. Pederson, "Diplomacy in the United Nations," unpublished manuscript prepared for the Center for International Studies, Massachusetts Institute of Technology (1960); James N. Hyde, "United States Participation in the United Nations," 10 *International Organization* 22 (1956). See also Donald G. Bishop, *The Administration of United States Foreign Policy through the United Nations* (Dobbs Ferry, N.Y., Oceana, 1967). The comparable experience of the Netherlands delegations has been described by Peter R. Baehr, *The Role of a National Delegation in the General Assembly*, Carnegie Endowment for International Peace Occasional Paper No. 9 (December 1970).

4. *Observations on the United Nations,* Report of Senators Bourke B. Hickenlooper and Mike Mansfield, Members of the United States Delegation to the Thirteenth General Assembly of the United Nations (Washington, D.C., Government Printing Office, 1959), p. 7.

5. Francis O. Wilcox, *Congress, the Executive and Foreign Policy* (New York, Harper, 1971), p. 60.

6. *Diplomacy in the '70's,* being the Macomber Report, Dept. of State Publication No. 8551, pp. 11–12.

7. Richard E. Neustadt, *Alliance Politics* (New York, Columbia University Press, 1970), pp. ix–x.

8. Gaddis Smith, *Dean Acheson,* (New York, Cooper Square, 1972), p. 187.

9. *Khrushchev Remembers* (Boston, Little Brown, 1970), pp. 498–99.

10. See Dean Acheson, "The Eclipse of the State Department," *Foreign Affairs* (July 1971), pp. 593–606, and Charles Yost in *The New York Times,* Op. Ed. page, May 30, 1971.

11. Charles Bohlen, *The Transformation of American Foreign Policy* (New York, Norton, 1969), p. 44.

12. Dean Acheson, *Present at the Creation* (New York, Norton, 1969), p. 84.

13. Harold Macmillan, *Riding the Storm 1956–1959* (New York, Harper and Row, 1971), p. 178.

14. However, if a speech is to influence foreign countries, it must be translatable. I have noted that President Roosevelt's impressive listing of the "Four Freedoms" lost in translation the effectiveness of the original concept and presentation because in practically no other language is it possible to speak about "freedom of" and "freedom from"; see Jessup, "Random Elements in the Formulation and Execution of Foreign Policy," 95 *Proceedings of the American Philosophical Society* (1951), pp. 93 and 96.

15. Gaddis Smith, p. 402.

16. John P. Leacacos, *Fires in the In-Basket* (New York, World, 1968), p. 149.

2. MIDWIFE TO KOREA

1. Kennan's account is in George Kennan, *Memoirs 1925–1950* (London, Hutchinson, 1967), ch. 15.

2. The quotation is from Wolfgang G. Friedmann, Lewis Henkin, and Oliver Lissitzyn, eds., *Transnational Law in a Changing Society: Essays in Honor of Philip C. Jessup* (New York, Columbia University Press, 1972), p. 8. Acheson's testimony will, of course, be considered by the "revisionists" (and by others as well) to be prejudiced. Personally, and on the basis

of comments by various scholars, I am satisfied that the volume is an honest one. Theodore Draper has written of it: "But at least the documents themselves were made available, and from a scholarly point of view, they were pure gain, even if they left something to be desired in the way of completeness." (*New York Times Magazine,* Feb. 4, 1973, pp. 10, 46.) The latter remark expresses our own feelings, but we had the choice between early publication or waiting an indeterminate time to break down the barriers thrown up between us in the State Department and the files of the Pentagon and of the White House during the Roosevelt administration.

3. It was also in line with concurrent studies in the National Security Council which were advocated by Secretary of Defense Louis Johnson on June 10, 1949; see p. 218 of the *Pentagon Papers* Committee Print, Book 8. In the chaotic compilation of those papers in 12 volumes for the House Committee on Armed Services, (1971), see the NSC references in II. A. 1, p. A-46 and II. B. 1, p. B-5, all in Book 1.

4. "Nomination of Philip C. Jessup," *Hearings before a Subcommittee of the Committee on Foreign Relations,* U.S. Senate, 82d Cong., 1st Sess., September–October 1951, p. 603.

5. *United States-Vietnam Relations 1945–1967,* Study Prepared by the Department of Defense, Committee Print, Book 8 of 12. The arrangement of documents in this volume makes it difficult to cite specific pages. The best guide is the list on pp. i–xxvi, which are inserted after p. 272.

6. The brilliant exception is Professor Leland Goodrich's book entitled *Korea* (New York, Council on Foreign Relations, 1956).

7. Goodrich, *Korea,* p. 59.

8. We subsequently visited the Philippines, Taiwan, Vietnam, Indonesia, Thailand, Burma, Ceylon, India, Pakistan, and Afghanistan, but of these, this book describes in detail only Vietnam, Indonesia, and a few incidents on the western leg of our return journey.

9. Goodrich, *Korea,* p. 49.

3. INDONESIA IS BORN

The Indonesian case in its United Nations setting has been described *inter alia,* in William Henderson, *The Indonesian Question 1946–1949* (New York, Woodrow Wilson Foundation, 1954); Rosalyn Higgins, *United Nations Peacekeeping, 1946–1967, Documents and Commentary,* Vol. II, issued under the auspices of the Royal Institute of International Affairs by Oxford University Press (London, 1970); and Alastair Taylor, *Indonesian Independence and the United Nations* (Ithaca, Cornell University Press, 1960). See also Evelyn Colbert, "The Road Not Taken—

Decolonization and Independence in Indonesia and Indochina," 51 *Foreign Affairs* (1937), 608

1. In January 1969, the second chamber of the Dutch parliament approved a proposal that the government should be asked for a report on allegations made in television programs of the Socialist Broadcasting Corporation VARA, that Dutch troops had committed atrocities during the "police actions" in Indonesia in 1947 and 1948. The subject received considerable attention in the Dutch press, and in February 1969 the government appointed a cabinet committee to supervise the collection of data on the subject. The Prime Minister submitted a report to Parliament in June, describing as "horrifying and revolting" the crimes committed by a relatively small number of individual Dutch soldiers in Indonesia, but noted that many of the offenders had been tried in military courts and punished. The press reports, as read in the summer of 1971, bear a marked resemblance to recent discussion in the United States about allegations of atrocities committed by American forces in Vietnam.

2. See Dirk Stikker, *Men of Responsibility: A Memoir* (New York, Harper and Row, 1966), Part Two, ch. 1. Actually, Under Secretary Lovett had told Ambassador van Kleffens that a visit from Stikker would suggest to the Indonesian Republic American collusion with the Dutch, but that if Stikker wished to come, they would be glad to see him. Presumably the Ambassador phrased this statement diplomatically in reporting to his Foreign Minister.

3. Congressional opinion was not comparably aroused in favor of the Indochinese nationalists when support for France was in question.

4. There are striking parallels to the impact and invocation in diplomatic negotiations of the dangers of aroused public opinion in connection with the Cyprus troubles in 1957. See for example, Stephen G. Xydis, *Cyprus, Conflict and Conciliation, 1954–1958* (Athens, Ohio State University Press, 1967), p. 353.

4. PRENATAL PAINS OF MOROCCO AND TUNISIA

1. Henry Dwight Sedgwick, *Lafayette* (New York, Bobbs-Merrill, 1928), ch. II.

2. Dean Acheson, *Present at the Creation* (New York, Norton, 1969), pp. 561 and 579.

3. *Ibid.*, pp. 648–49.

4. This account of the domestic judicial proceedings has been drawn from the records of the case in the District Court in Washington, which were most helpfully made available to me by Herbert N. Haller, Assistant Clerk for Public Services. Adrian Fisher and Edward H. Hickey helped me to identify the source.

5. When I was a Judge on the International Court of Justice, we had to consider the conditions under which a case could be discontinued. The case was that of *The Barcelona Traction Co.* and the applicable article of the Rules is No. 69, para. 2. I think Pollak's statement which I used, was sound. See *I.C.J. Reports 1964,* pp. 6, 20.

6. *I.C.J. Reports 1952,* pp. 176, 185.

7. My classification of this memorandum can be cited as an example of the evils of the system which has been so widely debated in connection with and subsequent to the affair of the Pentagon Papers. I may have overclassified the paper but in any event it needed only temporary privacy and could perfectly well have been declassified (without needing to be published) in a few months time. But we had no routine for declassification!

8. Although it is outside the Truman administration and thus beyond the chronological scope of this account, it is fair to recall that in certain situations, the attitude of the United States infuriated our English cousins. "Rab" Butler, who was Lord Privy Seal in Eden's cabinet in 1955 and later, in 1963, Foreign Secretary, gives a devastating account of the actions of the American administration at the time of the Anglo-French support of the Israeli attack on Egypt in 1956. Butler concludes: "The simple desire of Mr. Eisenhower to be re-elected on a peace platform and the maddening twists and turns of Mr. Dulles's legalistic mind were less important than the fears of the United States that any forcible action against Egypt would incite the Arab world to regard or even call in Russia as their ally." See *The Art of the Possible—The Memoirs of Lord Butler K.G. C.H.* (London, Hamish Hamilton, 1971), p. 190. In my view, all three of the attacking states—Israel, England, and France—deserve condemnation, but I sympathize with Butler's exasperation as Washington twisted and turned.

9. *Leaders of Men by Woodrow Wilson,* T. H. Vail Motter, ed., (Princeton, Princeton University Press, 1952).

10. Relations between the United States and France in the Middle East are discussed in "Intérets et Politique de la France et des Etats-Unis au Moyen-Orient et en Afrique du Nord," *Politique Etrangère* (revue publiée tous les deux mois par le Centre d'Etudes de Politique Etrangère), Numero spécial (36e année) No. 5–6, 1971.

5. THE ABORTIVE EMPIRE OF BAO DAI

1. Philippe Devillers, *Historie du Vietnam de 1940 à 1952* (Paris, Editions du Seuil, 1952); Ellen J. Hammer, *Vietnam Yesterday and Today* (New York, Holt, Rinehart, and Winston, 1966) and, more in detail, the same author's *The Struggle for Indochina 1940–1955* (Stanford, Stanford

University Press, 1966). I have also found valuable Robert McClintock, *The Meaning of Limited War* (Boston, Houghton Mifflin, 1967), ch. 9, and Robert Shaplen, *The Lost Revolution: The United States in Vietnam, 1946–1966,* rev. ed. (New York, Harper and Row, 1966). I have also examined Book I of the twelve volumes of the Pentagon Papers as printed for the House Committee on Armed Services. Volume VI of *Foreign Relations of the United States, 1947* (Washington, D.C., U.S. Dept. of State, 1972), has now been published and quotations for the events of 1947, unless otherwise indicated, are from that volume. This period is also treated by Evelyn Colbert, "The Road Not Taken: Decolonization and Independence in Indonesia and Indochina," 51 *Foreign Affairs* (1973), 608.

2. Devillers, p. 183. The relations between officers of the United States and Ho Chi Minh have been described in "Causes, Origins, and Lessons of the Vietnam War," *Hearings Before the Committee on Foreign Relations,* U.S. Senate, 92d Cong., 2d Sess., May 9, 10, and 11, 1972.

3. In early 1946, Ho addressed letters to President Truman, and the governments of China, Russia, and Britain asking for support of Annamese independence; he invoked the Philippines as a model. Pentagon Papers, p. A-29. There were no replies, at least not from Washington.

4. "Causes, Origins, and Lessons of the Vietnam War," *Hearings,* p. 304.

5. Shaplen, p. 30; Pentagon Papers, p. C-59.

6. Based on Devillers, p. 216.

7. Hammer, *The Struggle for Indochina,* p. 153; Pentagon Papers, p. A-25.

8. Pentagon Papers, p. C-83, have a copy of a letter written from Hanoi on October 22, 1945, to Chiang Kai-Shek and signed with Chinese style names of "Hu Chih-Ming and Yuan Yung-Jui (former Emperor Pao Ta)." They requested an interview with the 'Gimo.

9. Hammer, *Vietnam Yesterday and Today,* p. 140.

10. Pentagon Papers, p. B-59.

11. The picture is graphically painted by F. Spencer Chapman in *The Jungle is Neutral* (New York, Norton, 1949).

12. Pentagon Papers, pp. 43–44, and U.S. Dept. of State, *Foreign Relations of the United States, 1946* (Washington, D.C., 1972), VIII, 75.

13. Pentagon Papers, pp. C-44 and A-45.

14. *Foreign Relations of the United States, 1947,* p. 97.

15. Pentagon Papers, Bantam Books ed. 1971, p. 9.

16. There is a balanced account of the Chinese recognition issue in a Staff Study by Robert M. Blum prepared for the use of the Committee on Foreign Relations, United States Senate, Committee Print entitled "The United States and Communist China in 1949 and 1950: The Question of Rapprochement and Recognition," January 1973, Govt. Printing Office

Stock Number 5270-01689. I appreciate especially Mr. Blum's remark in footnote 9 when quoting the source of an alleged remark of mine; "This, at least, is what was recalled when it was fashionable to damn Philip Jessup." The alleged remark of mine apparently originated with Harold Stassen, whose false statement that I had advocated the recognition of the Peking government at a certain meeting in the White House involved us in considerable trouble to establish by an accumulation of documentary evidence that, on the date and at the time identified by Stassen, I was conferring with Dwight D. Eisenhower in his New York office at Columbia University, of which he was then President. When I was making preparations for my Far Eastern trip, a suggestion was made that I might meet secretly with representatives of the Chinese Communists in Hong Kong; I am tempted to say we didn't even "consider" such a scheme but Charles Yost did write a memorandum warning against it.

17. This account of Vietnam does not include the story of the Bangkok Conference which was held in February 1950.

18. Shaplen, p. 67.

19. *Ibid.*, p. 64.

20. When the delegates to the Constituent Assembly discussed the shape of the new French Union in Paris in the summer of 1946, the Vietnamese put forward a plan which "called for an annual conference of the various governments. Each member of the Union would be represented in the others by a delegate with diplomatic functions accredited to the Ministry of Foreign Affairs. There would be a court for the Union modeled on the International Court of Justice, with the right of appeal to the International Court" (Hammer, *The Struggle for Indochina*, p. 171, note). This type of use of the International Court of Justice as a court of appeal has, unhappily, never been achieved in any region or grouping of states.

21. Vincent Auriol, *Mon Septenat 1947–1954* (Paris, Gallimard, 1940), p. 246.

22. Nehru's conversation with Acheson is recounted in David Halberstam, *The Best and the Brightest* (New York, Random House, 1972), p. 334.

23. The McCarthy persecutions are now as dead and discredited as the Spanish Inquisition but, if one wishes to read the story, it is accurately told by Fred J. Cook, *The Nightmare Decade* (New York, Random House, 1971).

24. For the aid program, see Samuel P. Hayes, *The Beginning of American Aid to Southeast Asia: The Griffin Mission of 1950* (Lexington, Mass., Heath Lexington, 1971). Mr. Hayes was Deputy Chief of the Griffin Mission.

25. George Kennan, *Memoirs*, Vol II: *1950–1963* (Boston, Little Brown, 1972), p. 59. Kennan's memorandum to the Secretary of State on August 21, 1950, reflected the point of view which had been pressed on the

French in Washington and in Paris for a considerable period of time. I do not know whether Kennan then had in mind the Pacific Pact which General Carlos Romulo of the Philippines was promoting and which I discussed with him and others from time to time in the period 1949–1952. I told Romulo, just after I returned from my Far Eastern trip, that I found no enthusiasm for a regional arrangement in Southeast Asia, but he thought most of the governments would send delegates to a meeting he was organizing. Romulo told me he was authorized by President Quirino of the Philippines to offer Nehru the presidency of the proposed Pacific Union but he thought Nehru was unaware of the dangers of communism. In January 1951, John Foster Dulles wrote detailed comments on a proposed draft of the Pacific Pact; this may have led to his organization of SEATO when he became Secretary of State.

26. Shaplen, pp. 78–79.

27. Devillers, p. 458.

28. McClintock, p. 160.

29. Robert Shaplen, "The Cult of Diem," *The New York Times Magazine,* May 14, 1972, pp. 16, 46.

30. See Marjorie Whiteman, *Digest of International Law,* State Dept. Pub. 7553 (Washington, D.C., 1963), Vol. 2, p. 238. The United States did not sign the Geneva Final Declaration.

31. *Cf.* Rosalyn Higgins, *The Development of International Law Through the Political Organs of the United Nations* (Oxford, Oxford University Press, 1963), pp. 146 ff.

32. Robert Shaplen, "Letter from Vietnam, June 15, 1972," *The New Yorker Magazine,* June 24, 1972, p. 78. Sydney H. Schanberg's despatch in the New York *Times,* May 16, 1972.

33. "Notes on People," the New York *Times,* July 12, 1972.

34. The reports from Tokyo are taken from *Le Monde,* Feb. 14, 1973, and the *Neue Zürcher Zeitung,* Feb. 14 and 21, 1973.

6. THE UNITED NATIONS DELIVERS LIBYA AND SOMALIA—ERITREA IS STILLBORN

1. Adrian Pelt, *Libyan Independence and the United Nations: A Case of Planned Decolonization* (New Haven, Yale University Press 1970), p. 33. This valuable book may be consulted for details and bibliographies.

2. I have relied extensively on Benjamin Rivlin, *The United Nations and the Italian Colonies* (New York, Carnegie Endowment for International Peace, 1950), *cf.* here p. 18. This important pamphlet is also a good guide to the pertinent United Nations and other official documents.

3. James F. Byrnes, *Speaking Frankly* (New York, Harper, 1947), p. 92. As Secretary of State from 1945 to 1947, Byrnes was in charge of the negotiations of the peace treaties.

4. Dr. Finkelstein to the author. Finkelstein is author of *Somaliland Under Italian Administration: A Case Study in United Nations Trusteeship* (New York, Woodrow Wilson Foundation, 1955).

5. Byrnes describes the negotiations at pages 96 ff.

6. In his separate opinion in the *Namibia* case, Judge Hardy Dillard noted this source of power for the General Assembly, *I.C.J. Reports 1971*, pp. 3, 162. *Cf.* the problem of the powers of the Security Council in regard to Trieste, also covered by the Italian Peace Treaty: Higgins, "The Advisory Opinion on Namibia," *Int. & Comp. Law Q.* (April 1972), p. 270.

7. Rivlin, pp. 1–2.

8. Pelt, p. 61 and sources in footnote 40.

9. See John C. Campbell and Helen Caruso, *The West and the Middle East* (New York, Council on Foreign Relations, 1972).

10. My account of "The Berlin Blockade and the Use of the United Nations" is in *Foreign Affairs* (October 1971), p. 163. The ensuing negotiations with Ambassador Malik for lifting the blockade are in my article "Park Avenue Diplomacy—Ending the Berlin Blockade," *Political Science Quarterly*, LXXXVII (1972), 377. The Indonesian case has been described already in chapter 3 of this book and the Palestinian problem is covered in chapter 7.

11. Article 102 of the Charter reads in its paragraph 1: "Every treaty and every international agreement entered into by any Member of the United Nations after the present Charter comes into force shall as soon as possible be registered with the Secretariat and publish ed by it."

12. Rivlin, p. 32.

13. Pelt, p. 84.

14. Text in UN, GAOR, 4th Session (1949), Committee I, *Annexes* to SR agenda item 19 (A/C.1./497, 10 October, 1949), pp. 23–24. Supporting generally the British views already expressed by Hector McNeil, I had expounded the United States position in the opening debate on September 30 but without submitting any draft resolution until October 10. On September 19, Secretary Acheson had rejected the views of Hayden Raynor of EUR who favored specifying five years as the period within which Libya was to attain independence; Acheson decided the United States should not approve a longer interval than three or four years.

15. *The Diaries of Sir Alexander Cadogan, 1938–1945*, edited by David Dilks (New York, Putnam, 1972), "Epilogue (1945–1968)," p. 789.

16. Ralph Bunche, who had already achieved outstanding success as UN Acting Mediator in Palestine, indicated to a member of the U.S. delegation that he would have been willing to accept an appointment as Commissioner for Libya unless any part of the solutions for the Italian colonies was repugnant to him. He was opposed to Italian trusteeship for Somaliland, since he felt sure it would lead to bloodshed. When Ambassador Muñiz of Brazil asked Bunche if he would serve as Libyan Commis-

sioner, Bunche replied he was a servant of the United Nations and would do whatever Secretary-General Trygve Lie wanted him to do.

17. See the article by Eric Pace in the New York *Times*, Dec. 15, 1971.

7. THE BIRTH OF ISRAEL

1. Dan Kurzman, *Genesis 1948* (New York, World, 1970).

2. Bernard Postal and Henry W. Levy, *And the Hills Shouted for Joy: The Day Israel Was Born* (New York, McKay, 1973).

3. See H. Duncan Hall, *Mandates, Dependencies and Trusteeship* (Washington, D.C., Carnegie Endowment for International Peace, 1948), p. 296.

4. See *I.C.J. Reports 1971*, pp. 54 and 58.

5. *The United States and the United Nations*, Report by the President to the Congress for the Year 1947, p. 48.

6. As a judge of the International Court of Justice, I participated in the Court's Advisory Opinion on "Certain Expenses of the United Nations," *I.C.J. Reports 1962*, p. 151; the Court had to consider the juridical character and legal effect of certain resolutions of the General Assembly. In my dissenting opinion in the "South West Africa Cases," *I.C.J. Reports 1966*, pp. 429 ff., I discussed the importance of General Assembly resolutions in settling international standards. This is hardly the place for an extended bibliography on the subject.

7. Harry S Truman, *Memoirs*, 2 vols. (New York, Doubleday, 1955–1956), II, 161 ff.

8. Joseph P. Lash, *Eleanor: The Years Alone* (New York, Norton, 1972), especially chapter V, "The United Nations and a Jewish Homeland."

9. Trygve Lie, *In the Cause of Peace* (New York, Macmillan, 1954), p. 169.

10. Herbert Feis, *The Birth of Israel* (New York, Norton, 1969), p. 50.

11. Lash, p. 133.

12. Truman, Vol. II, ch. 12.

13. Letter from Dean Rusk to the author.

14. George W. Ball, "Nixon's Appointment in Peking—Is This Trip Necessary?", *New York Times Magazine*, February 13, 1972, p. 11.

8. "MANCHUKUO"—
AN ILLEGITIMATE CHILD

In general, the sources relied on in this chapter are the National Archives, from which material was skillfully culled for me by Mrs. Bonnie Wilson, and the series *Foreign Relations of the United States*. I am deeply indebted to Professor Gary B. Ostrower, who made available to me the manuscript of his thorough scholarly study, *Collective Insecurity: The United States and the League of Nations During the Early Thirties.* His bibliography runs from p. 370 to p. 394.

1. Nathaniel Peffer, *The Far East* (Ann Arbor, University of Michigan Press, 1958), p. 360.

2. These items on Grew are taken from Waldo H. Heinrichs, Jr., *American Ambassador: Joseph C. Grew and the Development of the United States Diplomatic Tradition* (Boston, Little, Brown, 1966), pp. 52 ff.

3. U.S. Department of State, *Foreign Relations of the United States 1921,* I, 966.

4. On the Washington Conference on the Limitation of Armaments, see generally Philip C. Jessup, *Elihu Root,* 2 vols. (New York, Dodd, 1938), Vol. II, ch. 47. No attempt is made here even to outline the far Eastern policy of the United States.

5. Hughes defended his policy and argued that we had not been rude to the League. See extracts from his Baltimore speech of October 23, 1924, at p. 458, in Charles Cheney Hyde, *Charles Evans Hughes: Secretary of State,* Vol. X of Samuel Flagg Bemis, ed., *American Secretaries of State and Their Diplomacy,* 10 vols. (New York, Knopf, 1929).

6. See Denna Frank Fleming, *The United States and World Organization, 1920–1933* (New York, Columbia University Press, 1938), p. 276.

7. As quoted in Raymond B. Fosdick, *Chronicle of a Generation: An Autobiography* (New York, Harper, 1958), p. 223.

8. Letter from Stanley Woodward to the author, December 21, 1971.

9. Elting E. Morison, *Turmoil and Tradition—A Study of the Life and Times of Henry L. Stimson* (Boston, Houghton Mifflin, 1960), p. 381.

10. Field's career is traced in Flora Lewis, *The Red Pawn: The Story of Noel Field* (New York, Doubleday, 1965).

11. H. L. Stimson and McGeorge Bundy, *On Active Service in Peace and War* (New York, Harper's, 1948), p. 159.

12. Henry L. Stimson, *The Far Eastern Crisis: Recollections and Observations* (New York, Council on Foreign Relations, 1936).

13. His biography has been written for the first time by Professor J. B. Donnelly with the aid of Gilbert's friends and family and with sympathetic appreciation.

14. I am grateful to my friend Ambassador Theodore C. Achilles, who manned the League of Nations Desk in the Department from 1935 to 1939 for this and other items about Prentiss Gilbert and early U.S. connections with the League.

15. Here and in subsequent pages I rely on an essay by James C. Thomson, Jr., "America and East Asia in the Thirties: Stanley Hornbeck at the Department of State." I am indebted to Professor Thomson for a copy of the essay which is published as "The Role of the Department of

State," in Dorothy Borg and Shumpei Okamoto, eds., *Pearl Harbor as History: Japanese-American Relations, 1931–1941* (New York, Columbia University Press, 1973).

16. Quoted from Morison, p. 314.

17. Stimson, p. 61.

18. Based on Dorothy Borg, *The United States and the Far Eastern Crisis of 1933–1938* (Cambridge, Harvard University Press, 1964), p. 3, citing *Foreign Relations of the United States 1931*, pp. 43–47.

19. Stimson, p. 60.

20. Morison, p. 391.

21. Hugh Wilson, *Diplomat Between Wars* (New York, Longmans, 1941), pp. 277–278. Cf. Borg, *The United States and the Far Eastern Crisis of 1933–1938*, p. 564, note 31.

22. U.S. Department of State, *Foreign Relations, 1931*, p. 276.

23. Robert H. Ferrell, *American Diplomacy in the Great Depression: Hoover-Stimson Foreign Policy 1929–1933* (New Haven, Yale University Press, 1957), pp. 142–43.

24. Stimson, p. 193.

25. *Ibid.* p. 75: The United States at the time had no ambassador in Paris.

26. Charles G. Dawes, *Journal as Ambassador to Great Britain* (New York, Macmillan, 1939), p. 410.

27. On the Dawes mission I have relied especially on J. B. Donnelly, "An Empty Chair in Paris: Dawes, Sweetser, and the Manchurian Crisis, 1931," *Studies in the Arts and Sciences*, Topic: 19 (Washington, Pa., Washington and Jefferson College, Spring 1970), pp. 37 ff.

28. Borg, *The United States and the Far Eastern Crisis of 1931–1938*, p. 7.

29. A letter to President Hoover of October 12, 1931 from Congressman Kent E. Keller of Illinois advocated a declaration of non-recognition akin to that ultimately issued by Stimson. The letter was referred to the State Department but was brought to the attention of the President. (National Archives File No. 793.94/2138). William Starr Myers, *The Foreign Policies of Herbert Hoover* (New York, Scribner, 1940), asserts and offers evidence to prove that Hoover originated the policy of non-recognition; see pp. 163 ff.

30. It is hardly necessary to stress the fact that this chapter does not purport to be a history of the period or the area; an effective summary may be read in Dorothy Borg, *The United States and the Far Eastern Crisis of 1931–1938*, pp. 519 ff.

Index

Abbott, George, 176, 177, 182
Acheson, Dean G., 2, 11, 12, 43, 60, 201, 297, 316, 337n.1, 338nn.10,12, 340n.2; at Bretton Woods Conference, 1944, 15; and Chinese question, 23-30, 170-72, 202, 238n.2; and the colonies of Allies, 87, 97-99, 171; and communism, 16, 164, 172, 202, 228 (*see also* Communism and communists); and Indonesian question, 87; and Italian colonies, 224-25, 231, 234, 239-47, 251-52, 345n.14 (*see also* Eritrea; Libya; Somalia); and Korean question, 10, 40; legal and analytical skills of, 10, 11, 117-19, 137-38; and Moroccan question, 100-7, 111, 114, 117-20, 128-32, 141-47; and NATO, 2, 89, 100, 106, 110, 118, 139; on recognition, 170-71; speeches of, 16, 140; and Tunisian question, 108-20, 137-47; and UN, 10, 87; at UNRRA Conference, 1943, 14; and Vietnam, 161, 164-65, 178, 180, 182-83, 186-87, 189, 191-92, 199-202
Achilles, Theodore C., 347n.14
Adams, John Quincy, 7, 16
Afghanistan, 113, 184, 207-10, 339n.8

Aklilou, Foreign Minister of Ethiopia, 245, 247, 252
Alaska, 99
Al Faqih, 249
Algeciras, Act of, 121, 128, 133
Algeria, 95, 150, 212
Allen, Roger, 244-45
Allen, Ward, 135
Allesandri, General, 180
Allison, John M., 135, 199-200, 201
American Trade Association of Morocco, 121, 123
Anderson, Robert, 290
Angola, 1, 94
Annam, 154-55, 158, 161
ANZUS Treaty, 26
Arab-Asian Bloc, 95, 96, 108, 109, 111, 112, 116, 120, 132, 136, 137, 140-42, 146, 147-48, 149, 224, 230, 231
Arab League, 107, 223, 300
Arce, José, 33, 236, 271, 279
Argentina, 33, 79, 271
Aroutunian, Amasasp A., 233
Asian nationalism, 158
Asmara, 216, 220
Assab, 226
Assam, 19

Atlantic Charter, 158
Auriol, Vincent, 161, 179, 185, 188, 194, 343*n*.21
Austin, Warren, viii, 11, 33, 59, 64, 83, 90, 106, 218, 224, 245, 262-64, 266-69, 270, 272, 279, 283, 287, 288, 290-91
Australia, 18, 26, 31, 34, 39, 44, 45, 47, 48, 49, 52, 53, 68, 73, 79, 81, 84, 89, 90, 214
Awami party, 208
Azzam Pasha, 107-8

Bacon, Ruth, 135
Baehr, Peter R., 337*n*.3
Baie d'Along agreements, 159, 161
Balfour, Arthur James, 259
Balfour Declaration, 256, 259, 287
Ball, George W., 290, 346*n*.14
Bancroft, Harding, 62, 63, 79, 140
Bangkok Conference 1950, 172, 183, 185, 189, 343*n*.17
Bangladesh, 207, 209, 254, 303, 305
Bao Dai, 152-206, *passim;* ascends throne 1932, 155; cooperates with Japanese, 155; and Ho Chi Minh, 156-60, 167-68, 170, 178, 189, 193; in Hong Kong, 158, 206; negotiations with French, 158-61, 163, 167, 169, 172, 174, 176, 179, 182, 187, 190-94, 197-99; March 8 agreement of 1949, 161, 163, 169, 175, 176, 182, 184, 187, 189; Norodom Palace issue, 172, 175, 188, 191, 199; personal qualities of, 50, 158, 159, 160, 174, 176, 177-82, 195, 196, 203, 205-6; succeeded by Diem, 204; U.S. support for, 158, 162-65, 167-70, 173-75, 178-80, 182-83, 185-86, 188, 190, 192-93, 194; unsuccessful attempt to recover influence in Vietnam, 205-6; *see also* Vietnam
Barclay, Roderick, 225
Barco, James, 58-59
Baruch, Herman B., 59-60, 63
Batavia, *see* Jakarta
Battle, Lucius, 101
Beam, Jacob, 318
Belgium, 33, 47, 67, 73, 79, 81, 82
Belt, Guillermo, 271, 277, 280

Berendsen, Carl, 223
Berlin Blockade, 86, 218, 219, 221, 274, 292, 345*n*.10
Bernadotte, Folke, 283, 301
Bernhard, Prince, 88
Bevin, Ernest, 27, 28, 62, 63, 80, 171, 192, 199, 213, 216, 217, 222-23, 225-28, 231, 233-35, 237, 241, 242-47
Bevin-Sforza Agreement, 222-23, 245
Bey of Tunis, 135, 146
Bhutto, Zulfikar Ali, 208
Bidault, George, 158, 169-70, 213
Binh, Xuyen, 203
Bishop, Donald G., 337*n*.3
Blaisdell, Donald, 283
Blom, Nico, 61
Blum, Robert, 342*n*.16
Board of Economic Warfare, 14
Bohlen, Charles E., 12, 17, 24, 62, 83, 112, 135, 191, 338*n*.11
Bokhari, Ahmed, 113
Bolivia, 248, 250
Bonbright, James, 102, 105, 129-30, 136-37
Bonnet, Henri, 101-5, 108, 113, 116, 126, 129, 130-31, 164, 170
Bonsal, Philip, 105, 290
Borah, William, 311
Borg, Dorothy, 332, 348*nn*.15, 18, 21, 28, 30
Bourguiba, Habib, 107, 126
Bradley, Omar, 10, 201-2
Brandegee, Frank B., 316
Brazil, 35, 133, 137, 146, 241, 249, 345*n*.16
Bretton Woods Conference, 14, 17
Brewster, Owen, 89
Briand, Aristide, 326-32
Bruce, David: as ambassador to France, 104, 106, 183-84, 187, 190-91, 193, 197; as Under-Secretary of State, 97-98, 108, 111, 112, 113, 116, 126, 128-30, 136-37, 144-45, 201
Bryce, James, 6
Buckley, Major (O.S.S.), 158
Bui, T. M., 206
Bunche, Ralph, 29, 213, 301, 345*n*.16
Bundy, Harvey, 316

Bundy, McGeorge, 12, 316
Burma, 27, 137, 148, 161, 163, 166, 189, 240, 248, 339n.8
Burton, Robert, 305
Butler, Lord ("Rab"), 341n.8
Butler, Nicholas Murray, 228
Butterworth, Walton, 24, 28, 51, 56, 61, 62, 66, 70, 71, 72, 82, 83, 85, 164, 172, 173, 185, 188-90
Byrnes, James F., 344n.3, 345n.5
Byroade, Henry, 111, 135, 136

Cadogan, Alexander, 33, 35, 84, 232-33, 345n.15
Cadogan, Theo, 232
Caffery, Jefferson, 62, 158, 159, 162-63
Cairo Conference and Declaration, 1943, 30, 36
Cambodia, 162, 170, 179, 184, 190, 203, 205; see also Vietnam
Campbell, John C., 345n.9
Canada, 26, 31, 33, 34, 35, 39, 79, 84, 85, 86, 95, 106, 270
Cao Dai, 160, 173, 197
Cargo, William I., 135
Carpentier, Marcel, 175
Caruso, Helen, 345n.9
Case, Everett, 27, 165-66, 171
Castle, William R., 315, 316, 320, 322, 324, 330-31
Cecil, Robert, 312
Central Intelligence Agency, 12
Ceylon, 70, 192, 339n.8
C.F.M., see Council of Foreign Ministers
Chapman, F. Spencer, 342n.11
Chauvel, Jean, 169-70, 221
Chiang Kai-shek, 156, 342n.8
Chile, 247
China, 20-21, 23-30, 31, 44, 73, 79, 81, 84, 85, 86, 167, 169, 170-72, 176, 178, 183, 186-87, 194, 196, 197-99, 201-2, 203, 213, 257, 276, 306, 312, 319, 320, 322, 327, 331, 333-34, 342n.16; see also Manchukuo; Taiwan
China Lobby, 21, 24, 165
China White Paper, 15, 24, 25, 26, 27, 30, 221

Chinese Eastern Railway, 306-7
Churchill, Winston, 20, 158, 232
CIA, 12
Clifford, Clark, 256, 267, 288, 291, 299
Clutton, George, 233, 235, 252
Cochin China, 156, 158, 162, 200
Cochran, Merle, 47, 55-56, 57, 58, 59, 60-61, 63, 65-66, 67-68, 82, 85, 88, 89, 90
Cohen, Benjamin, 218
Colbert, Evelyn, 339, 342n.1
Cold war, 19-23, 43, 50, 228, 292
Colombia, 73, 79, 81, 271
Colonial issue, 20, 27, 43, 56, 75, 87, 91, 93, 94, 96-99, 105, 112, 113, 114, 115, 135, 141, 149, 150, 162, 165, 168, 171, 258
Communism and communists, 129, 139, 182; and Arab states, 115, 141; Chinese, 167, 169, 172, 176, 178, 186-87, 194, 197-99, 201-2; containment policy for, 22-23, 29-30, 50, 77, 164, 166, 168, 188 (see also Kennan, George); in Indonesia, 50, 53, 58-59, 61-64, 67, 75, 78; Italian, 228, 232, 238, 243; McCarthy exploits fear of, 21-23, 165, 186; Soviet Russian, 11, 21-22, 29-30, 41, 87, 172, 217, 228, 238, 243, 245; in Vietnam, 50, 75, 159-62, 164, 166-68, 172, 183, 185-86, 191, 198-200
Containment policy, see Communism and communists; Kennan, George
Cook, Fred J., 343n.23
Coolidge, Calvin, 308, 314
Copts, 225-26, 239, 240-41, 250
Cordier, Andrew, 32-33, 302
Costa du Rels, Adolfo, 250
Costa Rica, 270
Cotton, Joseph P., 316
Council of Foreign Ministers, 18, 212, 213-16, 217
Couve de Murville, Maurice, 225-28, 248
Craig, Gordon A., 337n.2
Critchley, Thomas, 53-54, 56-58
Cuba, 84, 85, 86, 271, 277, 280, 290
Cuban missile crisis, 11
Cung, Tu, 205

Cyprus, 340n.4
Cyrenaica, emir of, 237
Cyrenaica, see Libya

Davies, John Paton, 24-25, 26, 27, 28, 39
Davis, Norman, 322
Dawes, Charles G., 329-32, 348n.27
de Beus, J. G., 91
de Gaulle, Charles, 20, 95, 96, 150, 156
de Lattre, Jean, 199
de Margerie, Roland J., 105
Dening, William, 77, 164
Dennett, Tyler, 297
Department of State, see State Department
de Rose, Francois, 85
Desai, Manilal, 77
Devillers, Philippe, 154, 196, 341n.1, 342n.2
Dewey, Thomas E., 218, 301
Diem, Ngo Dinh, 155-56, 204
Dien Bien Phu, 202, 204
Dillard, Hardy, 345n.6
Disarmament: General Conference on, 312; London Conference on, 1930, 312, 317; Washington Conference on, 308, 311-12
Donnelly, J. B., 347n.13, 348n.27
Douglas, Lewis, 215-17, 244
Draper, Theodore, 339n.2
Dreier, John, 249
Drummond, Eric, 308, 310, 313, 324-26, 331
du Bois, Coert, 47, 53-54, 55, 56-58, 85
du Gardier (French representative in Hanoi), 174
Dulles, John Foster, 16, 69, 149, 198, 202, 218, 219, 221, 223, 224, 317, 341n.8, 344n.25
Dunn, James, 117, 137, 237, 251
Dwight, Harry, 318-19

Eaton, Charles A., 172
Economic Cooperation Administration (ECA), 66, 127
Eden, Anthony, 98, 143, 227, 341n.8

Egypt, 85, 86, 100, 101, 106, 113, 133, 135, 138, 217, 222, 229, 230, 282, 341n.8
Eisenhower, Dwight D., 17, 50, 341n.8, 343n.16
El Alamein, 211
Elath, Eliahu, 299
El-Khouri, Faris Bey, 281, 282
El Salvador, 31, 306, 334
Elting, Howard, 100
Entezam, Nasrollah, 34, 277
Epstein, Eliahu, 267, 283
Eritrea, 211-54 passim, 211-28, 229, 233, 239-40, 248, 253-54
Estime, President of Haiti, 223
Ethiopia, 216, 222, 226, 239-41, 244, 245, 247, 248, 250-53, 318
European Recovery Program, 74; see also Marshall Plan
European Union, 223
Evatt, Herbert, 68, 214, 224

Fabregat, Enrique, 278
Fahy, Charles, 272, 300
FAO, 13
Fawzi, Mahmoud Bey, 86, 282
FEA, 14
Feis, Herbert, 255, 259, 275, 316, 346n.10
Feller, Abraham, 204
Ferrell, Robert H., 348n.23
Feuer, Leon I., 297-98
Fezzan, see Libya
Field, Noel, 315, 347n.10
Finkelstein, Lawrence, 213, 345n.4
Fisher, Adrian, 125, 127-29, 131-33, 145, 340n.4
Fleming, Denna Frank, 347n.6
Flushing Meadows, see Lake Success
Food and Agricultural Organization, 13
Foreign Economic Administration, 14
Formosa, see Taiwan
Forrestal, James Vincent, 215, 220, 268, 287
Fosdick, Raymond B., 27, 165-66, 171, 313, 347n.7
France, 20, 28, 31, 76, 79, 81, 82, 93, 94-95, 211, 219, 221, 223, 225-29, 248,

278, 341nn.8, 10; *see also* 93-151
passim
Frankfurter, Felix, 316
Franks, Sir Oliver, 80, 97-99, 103, 202, 232, 234, 246
French colonies in North Africa, *see* Morocco; Tunisia
French spoliation claims, 96
French Union, 158, 161, 184-85, 188, 194, 343n.20; *see also* Vietnam
Friedmann, Wolfgang G., 337n.1, 338n.2

Gelber, Lionel, 283, 291
Geneva Conference of 1954, 202
Genoa Economic Conference, 310
George V, King, 156
George, Walter, 122
Gerig, Benjamin, 135
Germany, 94, 117, 203, 303, 306, 334
Gibraltar, 94
Gibson, Hugh, 314
Gibson, William, 177, 190, 201
Gilbert, Prentiss, 315, 318-19, 322, 323, 324-32, 333, 347nn.13, 14
Gilchrist, Huntington, 309
Gilpatrick, Roswald, 200
Glaoui, El, 147, 148
Goodrich, Leland, 39, 42, 339n.6
Gough, Betty, 280, 281, 288
Graham, Frank P., 47, 48, 49, 51-53
Granados, Jorge Garcia, 270-71, 278
Great Britain, *see* United Kingdom
Greece, 20, 23, 80, 167-68
Green, Theodore Francis, 4
Grew, Joseph C., 308-9, 312, 331
Griffin mission, 343n.24
Gromyko, Andrei, 33, 232, 276
Gros, André, 126, 128, 129, 132
Gross, Ernest, 107, 110-11, 121, 122, 220
Guatemala, 240, 270, 278
Guernica, 261
Guinea (Bissau), 1, 94

Hackworth, Green, 133
Haiti, 223
Halberstam, David, 343n.22
Hall, H. Duncan, 346n.3
Haller, Herbert N., 340n.4

Hammer, Ellen, 154, 341n.1
Ham Nghi, Emperor, 155
Hanoi, 156, 158, 172, 173, 175, 176-82, 188, 206
Harding, Warren G., 308, 311, 314
Harriman, Averell, 89
Hart, Parker, 295
Haskell, William, 314
Hatta, Mohammed, 44, 52, 54, 58-59, 61, 66, 67-70, 71, 88
Hawaii, 99
Hay, John, 297
Hayes, Samuel P., 343n.24
Heath, Donald, 196-98
Heinrichs, Waldo H., Jr., 347n.2
Helb, H. A., 62, 72, 80
Henderson, William, 339
Henkin, Lewis, 337n.1, 338n.2
Hickenlooper, Bourke B., 4, 124, 338n.4
Hickenlooper Amendment, 124-25, 127
Hickerson, John, 51, 61, 67, 71, 85, 97, 108-10, 116, 117, 135, 250
Hickey, Edward H., 124, 340n.4
Higgins, Rosalyn, 339, 344n.31, 345n.6
Hiroshima, 156
Hiss, Alger, 255
Hoa Hao, 160, 197
Ho Chi Minh, 50, 156, 157, 158, 159, 160, 163, 164, 167, 168, 170, 176, 178, 183, 185, 187, 189, 193, 200, 342n.2
Holms, Julius, 244
Hong Kong, 153, 158, 159, 161, 206
Hoo, Victor, 33
Hood, J. D. L., 84
Hoover, Herbert, 12, 316-17, 323, 327, 331, 333, 348n.29
Hopkins, Harry, 12
Hornbeck, Stanley, 317, 318, 320-24, 326, 329, 330-31, 347n.15
Hoskins, Harold B., 115
House, Edward M., 12
Hsia, Ching-Lin, 77
Hué, Vietnam, 155, 156, 205
Hughes, Charles Evans, 12, 308-13, 347n.5
Hulley, Benjamin, 67
Hungary, 306, 334
Huu, Tran van, 174

Hyde, Charles Cheyney, 347*n*.5
Hyde, James Nevins, 66, 68, 70, 72, 294, 337*n*.3
Hydera bad, 19, 113

Ignatieff, George, 34
India, 20, 31, 33, 44, 45, 84, 87, 90, 133, 137, 148, 163, 173, 186-87, 192, 224-25, 230, 339*n*.8
Indochina: State Dept. policy statement, 1948, 30, 42, 75, 94; *see also* Vietnam
Indonesia, 2, 20, 26, 43-92 *passim*, 113, 165, 261; Japanese occupation and surrender, 44; Linggadjati Agreement, 44, 45, 83, 84; police action: first Dutch, 45, 340*n*.1, second Dutch, 66, 70-71, 73, 81, 340*n*.1; proposals of du Bois-Critchley, 53-54, 56-58; proposals of Cochran-Scott, 59-61; Renville agreement, 48-49, 52, 53, 58-59, 70, 81, 83, 84; Round Table Conference, 90-91, 166; Stikker: in Holland, 56, 63, 66, 68, 70, 74, 87-89, in Indonesia, 64, 65, in Washington, 60-61, 340*n*.2; UN Consular Commission in, 46, 82; UN Good Offices Commission in, 46, 47, 48-49, 52-59, 62, 64, 66, 68-69, 70-74, 80-81, 84, 89; UN Security Council debates, 45-47, 52-55, 57, 64-82, 83-90; *see also* Graham, Frank; Hyde, James N.; Palar, Lambertus N.; Scott, Joseph; United Nations; van Kleffens, Eelco; van Roijen, Jan Herman
Institute of Pacific Relations, 165
Interim Committee (UN), *see* Little Assembly
International Bank for Reconstruction and Development, 14-15, 17
International Court of Justice, 19, 45, 80, 85, 103, 120-34, 143, 151, 203, 225, 259-60, 341*n*.5, 343*n*.20, 345*n*.6, 346*nn*.4, 6
International Monetary Fund, 14, 18, 129
Iran, 20, 34, 43, 98, 104, 135, 138, 277, 292

Iroquois Indians, 19
Israel, 2, 69, 82, 255-305 *passim*; British mandate for Palestine, 258-60; parliamentary problems and maneuvers in UN, 276-79; *see also* Jerusalem; Kurzman, Dan; Postal, Bernard and Levy, Henry N.; United Nations
——*plans for solving problem:* partition with economic union, 246, 262-65, 268, 271, 294, 300; trusteeship, 264-75; truce and a mediator, 274-79, 301
——*recognition of*, 294, 295; effect in UN, 280-86, 300; role of U.S. delegation, 274, 280, 281-86; Truman's reasons for, 286-92, 297
Italian colonies, *see* Eritrea, Libya, Somalia; *see also* Italian Peace Treaty
Italian Peace Treaty, 134, 215, 211-17, 222-23, 225, 249, 253, 264, 345*n*6
Italy, 94, 232, 243, 251, 306, 334; *see also* Sforza; Italian Peace Treaty

Jacobson, Eddie, 287, 297
Jakarta (Batavia), 46, 51, 53, 55, 56, 57, 62, 88, 89
Japan, 26, 30, 44, 94, 306-7, 311-12, 317, 319-23, 326-29, 331, 332-34
Japanese Asian Co-Prosperity Sphere, 44, 155-56
Jebb, Sir Gladwyn, 97, 135, 233
Jefferson, Thomas, 7, 145, 171
Jerusalem, 257, 272, 274, 278, 279, 300
Jewish Agency, 266, 267, 273, 278, 283, 294, 300
Jogjakarta, 64, 71, 88
Johnson, Herschel, 293-94
Johnson, Louis, 339*n*.3
Johnson, Nelson, 321
Joint Chiefs of Staff, 10, 11, 215, 220, 231
Jordan, 234, 237-38
Josephus, Flavius, 3
Juin, Alphonse, 126
Juliana, Queen, 88, 89
Jusserand, Jules, 311

Kabul, 207-9
Katz-Suchy, Juliusz, 280
Kee, John, 172
Kelchner, Warren, 14, 15
Keller, Kent E., 348n.29
Kellogg, Frank B., 326
Kellogg-Briand Pact, 311, 319-27, 332, 334
Kennan, George, 8, 17, 22-23, 24-25, 27, 28, 194, 338n.1, 343n.25
Keynes, John Maynard, 15
Khan, Abdul Wali Kahn, 208
Khrushchev, Nikita, 11, 338n.9
Khyber Pass, 207, 209
Kim, Tran Trong, 156
Kimball, Dan A., 200
Kirk, Alan, 67-68
Kissinger, Henry, 12, 29, 206
Klots, Allen, 316
Knesseth, 257, 260
Knight, Ridgeway, 112-13, 117
Knox, Gordon, 34, 270
Knox, Philander, 5
Kopper, Samuel K. C., 224, 255, 265
Korea, 2, 10, 19-42, 80, 150, 154, 195, 197, 203, 211, 303, 305, 334
Kraft, Joseph, 295-96
Kravchenko, Victor, 232
Kurzman, Dan, 255-56, 263n., 264, 265, 266, 288, 291

Lacoste, Francis, 144
Lacy, William, 51, 195, 201
La Fayette, Marquis de, 95, 96, 145
Lake Success and Flushing Meadows, 9, 41, 78, 82, 219, 269-70
Lamont, Thomas W., 310
Laos, 161, 162, 170, 179, 182, 184, 188, 190, 199, 203, 205; see also Vietnam
Lash, Joseph, 267-68, 346n.8
Latin American Bloc, 112, 146-48, 218, 224, 226, 230, 231, 241, 248, 250-51
Laval, Pierre, 328
Laws, Bolitha James, 124
Leacacos, John, 17, 338n.16
League of Nations, 14, 94, 104, 258, 305-34 passim, 306, 307-9, 312-14, 316, 317-19, 321, 322-34

Lebanon, 39, 282
Lehman, Herbert H., 13-14
Lend-Lease, 14
Letourneau, Jean, 117, 201-2
Levy, Henry W., 256, 263-64, 267, 277, 286, 291, 295, 297
Lewis, Flora, 347n.10
Libya, 2, 211-27, 220-31, 235-36, 238, 345n.16
Lie, Trygve, 107, 204, 232, 268-69, 281, 283, 302, 346n.9
Limb, Ben, 40-41
Lincoln, Abraham, 145
Linggadjati Agreement, 44-45, 83, 84; see also Indonesia
Lippmann, Walter, 22
Lissitzyn, Oliver, 337n.1, 338n.2
Little Assembly (Interim Committee), 31-39, 50, 240, 242, 244, 265
Lodge, Henry Cabot, Jr., 122, 147-49, 316
Long, Nguyen Phan, 172-73, 174, 181, 193
Lopez, Alfonso, 271
Lovett, Robert, 9, 17, 51, 56-57, 61, 63, 66-67, 68, 73-74, 80, 201, 220, 255, 267, 272, 275, 289, 293, 340n.2
Lovink, A. H. J., 70, 87
Lytton Commission, 332

MacArthur, Douglas, 39, 44, 195, 249
McBride, Robert, 110, 129-30, 131
McCarran, Patrick Henry, 23
McCarthy, Joseph, 21, 23, 165, 186, 343n.23
McClintock, Robert, 68, 71-72, 80, 203, 275, 342n.1
McCoy, Frank, 332-33
McDonald, Malcolm, 28, 173, 186
McFall, Jack, 172
McGhee, George, 28, 29, 103-4, 123, 126, 128, 237, 243, 252
McKeever, Porter, 280
Macmillan, Harold, 16, 338n.13
McNaughton, Andrew, 84, 86, 270
McNaughton, Mrs., 218
McNeil, Hector, 230, 233-35, 252, 345n.14

Macomber Report, 338n.6
Madison, James, 7
Makin, N. J. O., 73-74
Malaya, 75, 166
Malik, Charles, 282
Malik, Jacob, 69, 79, 221, 345n.10
Manchukuo, 2, 3, 171, 306-7, 315-34
Manchuria, 306, 318, 319, 320-21, 323, 329, 333
Mandate system, 258
Manila, 153
Mansfield, Michael, 4, 172, 338n.4
Mao Tse-tung, 183
March 8 agreement 1949, 161, 163, 169, 175-76, 179, 182, 187, 192, 194-95
Marshall, George C., 10, 49, 51, 60-61, 62-63, 161, 162, 218, 220, 261, 267, 269, 283, 286, 288-89, 297, 301
Marshall Plan, 17, 21, 23, 61, 89
Masigli, René, 143, 331
Massawa, 216
Mathews, H. Freeman, 12, 105, 112, 135, 144, 145
Matsudaira, Tsuneo, 331
Meeker, Leonard, 170
Mendès-France, Pierre, 148-49
Menon, Parakat, 33, 34-35, 37
Merrill, Frank D., 193
Mexico, 33, 242, 250, 270
Middle East Command, 135
Miller, Edward, 135
Miller, Ransford, 321
Mogadishu, 239
Mohammad V, Sultan of Morocco, 126, 148
Mohammedans, see Moslems
Molotov, Vyacheslaz M., 213
Monnet, Jean, 111
Monroe, James, 7
Monroe Doctrine, 16
Montaigne, Michel de, 145
Montesquieu, Charles Louis, 145
Montgomery, Bernard, 211
Morgenthau, Henry, 15, 17-18
Morison, Elting E., 323, 347n.9
Morocco, 2, 20, 93-151 passim, 95-107, 114, 121-35, 137, 140-48, 212
Morrison, Herbert, 100

Moscow, see Soviet Union
Moslems, 114-15, 216, 225, 226-27, 237, 239, 241, 248, 250, 259
Motter, Vail, 144, 341n.9
Moyers, Bill D., 17
Mozambique, 1, 94
Muccio, John, 40
Mukden, 319
Muniz, Joao Carlos, 35, 137, 146, 241, 249, 345n.16
Muskie, Edmund S., 297
Muslims, see Moslems
Muso, 61-62
Myers, William Starr, 348n.29
Mylai, 153, 340n.1

Namibia, see South West Africa
Nanking, 333
National Security Council, 12, 26, 30, 168, 200, 339n.3
National Union Front, 159
National University of Vietnam, Hanoi, 181-82
NATO, 2, 21, 23, 26, 89, 100-1, 103, 110, 139, 223, 232, 237, 242-43, 247
Negev, 69, 82, 293-94, 301-2
Nehru, Jawaharlal, 26, 86, 87, 164, 185, 187, 198, 343n.22, 344n.25
Nehru, R. K., 62
Neo-Destour political party, 107, 135
Nepal, 186
Nervo, Padilla, 33-34, 242, 249, 250-51, 270
Netherlands, 43-92 passim
Neustadt, Richard, 7, 338n.7
New Zealand, 26, 39, 223
Nicaragua, 271
Nine Power Treaty, 319-23, 332
Nisot, Joseph, 33
Nitze, Paul, 112, 116, 135, 137
Nixon, Richard M., 6, 10, 290, 297
Nolting, Frederick, 51, 56, 67
Norodom Palace, Saigon, 172, 175, 188, 191, 199
North Atlantic Treaty Organization, see NATO
Norway, 84, 85, 86, 240

Noyes, Charles, 55, 86, 245, 270
Nunley, William, 139

OAS (Organization of American States), 5
Office of Foreign Relief and Rehabilitation Operations (OFRRO), 13-14
Office of Strategic Services, 156, 157, 158
Ogburn, Charlton, 48, 57-58
Okamoto, Shumpei, 348n.15
Okinawa, 31, 153
Ordonneau, Pierre, 34
Organization of American States, 5
O'Shaughnessy, Elim, 190
OSS (Office of Strategic Services), 156, 157, 158
Ostrower, Gary B., 347n.
O'Sullivan, James L., 168

Pace, Eric, 346n.17
Pace, Frank, 200
Pacific Pact, 344n.25
Pact of Paris, see Kellogg-Briand Pact
Pakistan, 36, 113, 146, 163, 173, 184, 192, 207-10, 230, 240, 241, 247, 339n.8
Palais de Chaillot, 69, 217-19
Palar, Lambertus N., 52, 63, 66, 68, 87, 91
Palestine, see Israel; United Nations
Panama, 271
Parliamentary diplomacy, 3
Parodi, Alexandre, 86-87, 183-84, 187, 198, 278
Parsons, James Graham, 139
Pasvolsky, Leo, 13
Pathans, see Pushtoonistan
Pearson, Lester, 35
Pederson, Richard F., 337n.3
Peffer, Nathaniel, 306, 347n.1
Pelt, Adrian, 211, 224, 236, 237, 253, 344n.1
Pentagon Papers, 30, 153, 290, 339n.3, 341n.7, 342n.1
Perkins, George, 28, 104, 112, 117, 120, 130-31, 135, 136, 145, 202
Permanent Court of International Justice, 104, 320-21

Pershing, John J., 96
Peshawar, 207
Pham Cong Toc, 160
Philippines, 25-26, 31, 61, 107, 163, 186, 213, 339n.8, 342n.3, 344n.25
Phillips, William, 5, 295
Phouma, Prince Souvana, 205
Picasso, Pablo, 261
Pignon, Léon, 163, 173-75, 183
Pinay, Antoine, 117
Pleven, René, 117, 120, 193, 197
Plitt, Edward, 107
Point IV Aid Program, 97
Poland, 43, 280
Policy Planning Staff (State Dept.), 8, 22, 24, 112, 116-17, 135, 201
Pollak, Louis, 131, 140, 296, 341n.5
Pollock, Jackson, 335
Pondicherry, 186, 187
Popper, David, 117, 145, 296
Portugal, 1
Postal, Bernard, 256, 263-64, 267, 277, 286, 291, 295, 297
Potsdam Conference, 1945, 30, 215
Power, Thomas, 213, 224, 302
Protectorates, 93, 95, 121, 123, 128, 133, 134, 149, 155, 188, 212, 239
Protitch, Dragon, 63
Puerto Rico, 118
Pushtoonistan, 113, 207-10
Pu-Yi, Emperor Henry, 306, 334

Queuille, Henri, 117
Quijaro, Ambassador, 271
Quirino, president of Philippines, 25, 344n.25

Radziwill, Princess Ella, 309, 331
Ramadan, 237
Rau, Benegal N. ("B.N."), 224-25, 230, 240, 249, 251
Rau, Benegal Rama, 82, 84, 87
Raynor, Hayden, 64, 243, 345n.14
Reading, Lord, 328, 329
Reber, Samuel, 56
Recognition of states and governments, 1, 44, 121, 134, 149, 163, 165, 170-74, 178, 180, 182, 183, 184-85, 188, 190-91,

Recognition (*Continued*)
204, 237, 258, 272, 274, 280-81, 283-84, 286-91, 294, 295, 297-98, 300, 306, 307, 320, 333, 334, 342-43n.16
Reed, Charles S., 28-29, 57-58, 62, 159, 163-64
Renville Agreement, 48-49, 52, 53, 58-59, 70, 81, 83, 84
Reston, James, 297
Rhee, Syngman, 40
Rhodesia, 94, 303
Riddleberger, James, 318
Rivlin, Benjamin, 214, 222, 235, 239, 344n.2
Roberts, Frank, 62
Rochambeau, Jean Baptiste, 145
Rodes, Robert Emmet, 121, 122, 123
Rogers, James Grafton, 316
Rogers, William P., 297
Rommel, Erwin, 211
Romulo, Carlos, 107, 219, 344n.25
Roosevelt, Eleanor, 11, 108, 218, 267-69, 286
Roosevelt, Franklin Delano, 11, 12-13, 16, 20, 94, 145, 155, 158, 268, 338n.14
Roosevelt, Theodore, 297, 316
Root, Elihu, 42, 308, 313, 316-17, 347n.4
Rosenman, Samuel, 267, 287
Ross, Charlie, 288
Ross, John C., 59, 224, 232, 233, 249, 250, 269, 270, 273, 279-80, 283, 292
Rothschild, Lord, 259
Round Table Conference (The Hague), 90-91, 166
Rusk, Dean, 22, 24, 28, 40, 49, 51, 56, 57, 58, 62-63, 75, 83, 85, 89, 193, 198, 219-20, 255, 262, 269, 272, 273, 288, 300, 346n.13
Russia, *see* Soviet Union

Sainteny, Jean, 158
Saint-Lot, Emilio, 223
Saltonstall, Leverett, 122
Sanders, William, 66
Sandifer, Durward, 34
Santa Cruz, Hernán, 247
Sarper, Selim, 36

Saudi Arabia, 249
Sayre, Francis, 269, 277, 279-80, 286
Schanberg, Sydney H., 344n.32
Schlesinger, Arthur, Jr., 337n.2
Schuman, Robert, 27, 28, 63, 100, 101, 102, 105, 117, 130, 136, 144, 145, 146, 162, 164, 167, 171, 187-88, 191-92, 199, 223
Scott, Joseph, 48, 55, 56, 59, 60, 70, 72, 79, 86
SEATO, 344n.25
Sedgwick, Henry Dwight, 340n.1
Senussi, 227, 248
Seoul, National University, 40
Seven Years' War, 95
Sforza, Carlo, 222, 228-29, 237, 242-43, 245-47, 251, 252
Shanghai, 333
Shaplen, Robert, 157, 173, 177, 195, 203, 205, 342n.1, 344nn.29, 32
Sharett, (Shertok), Moshe, 107, 257, 260, 267, 273
Shidehara, Kijuro, 312, 320, 332
Shotwell, James T., 13
Sihanouk, Prince Norodom, 205
Silver, Abba, 278, 291, 297-98
Simon, John, 323, 324, 332
Sjahrir, Soetan, 44
Smith, Gaddis, 10, 16, 338n.8
Somalia (Somaliland), 2, 211-224, 229-30, 233, 236, 238-9
Somosa, Rodriguez, 271
Souphanouvong, Prince, 157
South Africa, 94, 105, 141, 142, 240, 259-60
South-East Asia Treaty Organization, 344n.25
South West Africa, 259-61, 345n.6, 346n.6
Soviet Union, 11, 19-23, 25-26, 30-31, 33, 34, 41, 43, 52, 69, 70, 79, 81, 83, 91, 94, 102, 105, 146, 170, 172, 211, 212-13, 215-17, 219, 222, 225, 228, 231, 238, 253, 262, 274, 276, 292-93, 301, 306-7, 313, 320; *see also* Cold War; Communism
Spaak, Paul Henri, 63, 67-68, 88
Spain, 94, 125

Stalin, Joseph, 215
Stassen, Harold, 343n.16
State Department: organization of, 3-8, 10-13, 22, 122, 196
St. Cyr, 175
Steere, Lloyd, 66, 70
Stikker, Dirk, 56, 60-61, 63, 64-65, 66, 68, 70, 74, 87, 88, 89, 340n.2
Stimson, Henry L., 10, 171, 312, 315-17, 319-33
Stolle, Charles Clarkson, 201
Stone, Lawrence, 3
Sudan, 100, 113
Suharto, 88
Sukarno, 44, 71, 81, 85, 88, 90
Sultan of Morocco, Mohammed V, 126, 148
Sumitro, Djojohadikusumo, 74
Sweeney, Joseph, 128, 129
Sweetser, Arthur, 309, 314, 318, 331-32, 348n.27
Syria, 31, 73, 79, 81, 104, 281, 282
Sze, Alfred, 331

Taft, William Howard, 312
Taiwan, 102, 153, 257, 303, 339n.8
Tarchiani, Alberto, 241, 251
Tate, Jack, 132
Taylor, Alastair, 339
Taylor, Paul, 145
Teitgen, Pierre-Henri, 187
Thailand, 26, 162, 163, 166, 172, 191, 277, 339n.8
Thang, Ton Duc, 205
Thieu, Nguyen Van, 205
Thompson, Llewellyn, E., 318
Thomson, James C., Jr., 347n.15
Thorpe, Williard L., 123
Tibet, 187
Tonkin, 155, 158, 161, 180, 181
Treaty of Paris, 1783, 1
Tri, Nguyen Huu, 174, 181
Trieste, 345n.6
Tripolitania, see Libya
Truman, Harry S., 2, 8-11, 17, 24, 40, 73, 119, 156, 168, 182, 183, 197, 219, 236, 256, 262-66, 268, 269, 273, 275, 278, 286-92, 295-99, 301, 302, 316, 342n.3, 346n.7
Truman, Margaret, 299
Truman Doctrine, 16, 20, 23, 167, 293
Trusteeship, see United Nations, Charter Provisions
Tsarpkin, delegate to UN, 279
Tsiang, T. F., 36, 276-77, 292
Tuck, Pinkney, 314
Tunisia, 2, 20, 95-99, 100-20, 135-49, 212, 248
Turkey, 20, 23, 36, 168
Tyree, David, 48

Ukraine, 31, 43, 81
Unayzi, Ali-Neurridine, 223
Union of Soviet Socialist Republics, see Soviet Union
United Kingdom, 20, 29, 30, 35, 43, 44, 45, 62-3, 73, 76, 77, 80-81, 82, 84, 85, 86, 94, 97-99, 135, 139, 143, 173, 185, 192, 202, 203, 211-13, 215-17, 219, 222-23, 225-29, 230, 232-39, 241, 242-47, 252, 258-59, 262, 268, 297, 311-12, 341n.8
United Nations, 8, 9-10, 13, 15-16, 20, 27, 42, 47, 92, 110, 117, 142, 150, 154, 158, 167-69, 197, 211-12, 214, 234, 254, 262, 307; membership in, 1, 92, 147, 149, 231, 238, 257-58, 260-61, 294, 302-3; national blocs in, 95, 108-9, 112, 116, 120, 136-37, 140-41, 146-49, 224, 226, 238; procedural devices and problems in, 4, 7-10, 33-37, 41, 63, 73, 84-87, 102, 105, 106, 116, 136, 137, 212, 219, 269-86, 337n.3; recognition not a function of, 204; resolutions of General Assembly, effect of, 264, 346n.6; sanctions by, 45, 76-78, 80, 300; see also International Court of Justice; Italian Peace Treaty; Little Assembly; Vietnam
——Charter provisions applicable: Art. 2(7) on domestic questions, 45, 74-79, 80, 85, 142-44; Chapter VI, 45; Chapter VII, 45, 71, 78, 275, 285, 300; trusteeship, 94, 212-13, 216-17, 220,

United Nations (Continued)
222-23, 225-26, 249, 253, 264-70, 272-76, 284, 287, 289, 291, 298; Art. 102, 220
——Commissions of: Eritrea, 240, 242, 249; Indonesia: 43, 84, 90, Consular Commission, 46, 82, Good Offices Commission (GOC), 46-89; Korea, Temporary Commission, 31-39, 41; Libya, 211, 227, 229-30, 235, 236, 249, 253, 345n.16; Palestine: 69, 262-63, 268, 272, 302, mediator for, 276-83, 301, 345n.16; Tunisia, 114, 143; Vietnam, 167, 169
United Nations Relief and Rehabilitation Administration (UNRRA), 13-14
United Nations Special Committee on Palestine (UNSCOP), see United Nations, Commissions of
United Nations Trusteeship System, see United Nations
Uris, Leon, 261
Uruguay, 278
U So Nyun, 248-49
USSR, see Soviet Union
Utter, John, 117, 224, 248, 250, 252

Valle, Cyrode Freitas, 249
Vandenberg, Arthur H., 103
van Kleffens, Eelco, 49, 53, 54, 56-57, 63, 72, 74, 340n.2
Van Laethem, Gabriel, 130-31
van Langenhove, Fernand, 73
van Mook, J., 48, 54
van Roijen, Jan Herman, 64-65, 66, 79, 82, 85, 88, 91
van Vredenburgh, 48
Vathana, King Savang, 205
Vergennes, Comte de, 95
Versailles, Treaty of, 307
Viet Minh (Viet Cong), 156, 157, 158, 173, 176, 177, 180-81, 197
Vietnam, 152-206 passim; Annam, 154-55, 158, 161; Vincent Auriol and, 161, 179, 184, 185; Baie d'Along agreements, 159, 161; Xuyen Binh, 203; Cambodia and, 75, 161, 162, 170, 179, 182, 188, 190, 199, 203, 205; Cao Dai, 160, 173, 197; Cochin China, 156, 158, 161, 162, 200; Ngo Dinh Diem, 155-56, 204; Dien Bien Phu, 202, 204; in French Union, 158, 161, 184-85, 188, 194, 343n.20; Geneva Conference, 1954, 202, 203; Nghi Ham, 155; Hanoi, 156, 158, 172, 173, 175, 176-82, 188, 206; historical background, 154; Hoa Hao, 160, 197; Hué, 155, 156, 205; Tran Van Huu, 174; Japan and, 155; Japanese Peace Conference and, 198, 203; Tran Trong Kim, 156; Laos and, 75, 161, 162, 170, 179, 182, 188, 190, 199, 203, 205; Nguyen Phan Long, 172-73, 174, 193: March 8 agreement, 1949, 161, 167, 175, 179, 187, 189, 194-95; Mylai, 153, 340n.1; Norodom Palace, 172, 175, 188, 191, 199; OSS contacts in, 156, 157, 158; Nguyen Van Thieu, 205; Ton Duc Thang, 205; Tonkin, 158, 161, 181, 200; Nguyen Huu Tri, 181; United Nations and, 8, 150, 154, 167, 169, 195-96, 197, 199, 201, 203-4, 303, 343n.20; U.S. French relations and, 2, 20, 161-204; "Vietnamization," 181, 193, 197; Viet Minh (Viet Cong), 156-57, 158, 173, 176, 177, 197; Vinh Thuy, 157; see also Acheson, Dean; Bao Dai; Communism; Ho Chi Minh; Yost, Charles
Vietnamization, 181, 193, 197
Vilfan, Joze, 278
Vincent, John Carter, 161
Vinh Thuy, 157
Viviani, René, 311
Vyshinsky, Andrei, 43, 217

Wainhouse, David, 37, 100-1, 249
Waldheim, Kurt, 278
Wallner, Woodruff, 117, 162, 187
Wan, Prince, 277
Wang Shih-Chieh, 63
Webb, James E., 24, 122
Weizmann, Chaim, 267, 287, 297, 302
Wheelus Air Base, 236

White, Harry Dexter, 15
Whiteman, Marjorie, 344*n*.30
White Paper, *see* China White Paper
Wilcox, Francis, 5, 338*n*.5
Wilson, Bonnie, 346
Wilson, Hugh, 315, 318, 324, 333, 348*n*.21
Wilson, Trevor, 180
Wilson, Woodrow, 20, 94, 144, 145, 171, 258, 307, 316
Winslow, Richard, 145
Woodward, Stanley, 314, 347*n*.8
World Court, *see* International Court of Justice; Permanent Court of International Justice

Xydis, Stephen G., 340*n*.4

Yalta Conference, 12
Yost, Charles, vii, 12, 28, 166, 167, 168, 225, 231, 292-93, 338*n*.10, 343*n*.16
Young, G. M., 337*n*.2

Zafrullah Kahn, Muhammad, 146, 236, 247
Zionists, 259, 268, 287, 298, 302